The Origins of Intelligence in Children

The origins of intelligence in children

JEAN PIAGET, the noted Swiss child psychologist, was edu-
cated at Neuchâtel, Zurich, and the University of Paris. He
has been professor of child psychology and history of scientific thought at the University of Geneva since 1929, and
director of the International Bureau of Education and of the
Institut J. J. Rousseau. Among his other books are *The Language and Thought of the Child, Judgment with Reasoning in
the Child, The Child's Conception of the World, The Child's
Conception of Physical Causality, The Moral Judgment of the
Child, The Reconstruction of Reality in the Child, The Growth
of Logical Thinking from Childhood to Adolescence,* and
The Child's Conception of Geometry.

IN THE NORTON LIBRARY

BY JEAN PIAGET

Play, Dreams and Imitation in Childhood
The Origins of Intelligence in Children
The Child's Conception of Number
Genetic Epistemology

BY JEAN PIAGET AND BARBEL INHELDER

The Child's Conception of Space
The Early Growth of Logic in the Child

THE ORIGINS
OF INTELLIGENCE
IN CHILDREN

JEAN PIAGET

Translated by
MARGARET COOK

The Norton Library
W · W · NORTON & COMPANY · INC ·
NEW YORK

SBN 393 00202 0

W. W. Norton & Company, Inc. is also the publisher of
the works of Erik H. Erikson, Otto Fenichel, Karen Horney and
Harry Stack Sullivan, and the principal works of Sigmund Freud.

PRINTED IN THE UNITED STATES OF AMERICA
8 9 0

CONTENTS

Conclusions

"SENSORIMOTOR" OR "PRACTICAL" INTELLIGENCE AND THE THEORIES OF INTELLIGENCE

FOREWORD TO THE SECOND EDITION

This work, a second edition of which has very kindly been requested, was followed by *La Construction du réel chez l'enfant* and was to have been completed by a study of the genesis of imitation in the child. The latter piece of research, whose publication we have postponed because it is so closely connected with the analysis of play and representational symbolism, appeared in 1945, inserted in a third work, *La formation du symbole chez l'enfant*. Together these three works form one entity dedicated to the beginnings of intelligence, that is to say, to the various manifestations of sensorimotor intelligence and to the most elementary forms of expression.

The theses developed in this volume, which concern in particular the formation of the sensorimotor schemata and the mechanism of mental assimilation, have given rise to much discussion which pleases us and prompts us to thank both our opponents and our sympathizers for their kind interest in our work. It is impossible to name here all the authors on whose observations we would like to comment, but we should single out for mention the remarkable studies made by H. Wallon and P. Guillaume.

In his fine work *De l'acte à la pensée*, H. Wallon did us the honor of discussing our work at length; we have already commented on this in *La formation du symbole chez l'enfant*. Wallon's main idea is the distinction which he makes between the realm of the sensorimotor (characterized by the "understanding of situations") and that of expression (verbal intelligence). His remarkable study on *Les origines de la pensée chez l'enfant*, published since, places the origins of thought at the age of four, as if nothing essential transpired between the attainments of the sensorimotor intelligence and the beginnings of conceptual expression. It is apparent how antithetical to everything we maintain in this book this radical thesis is, and we can answer it today by invoking two kinds of arguments.

In the first place, meticulous study of a definite area, that of development of spatial perceptions, has led us with B. Inhelder to discover an even greater correlation than there seemed to be between the sensorimotor and the perceptual. Doubtless nothing is directly transmitted from one of these planes to the other, and all that the sensorimotor intelligence has constructed must first be reconstructed by the growing perceptual intelligence before this overruns the boundaries of that which constitutes its substructure. But the function of this substructure is no less apparent. It is because the baby begins by constructing, in coördinating his actions, schemata such as those of the unchanging object, the fitting in of two or three dimensions, rotations, transpositions, and superpositions that he finally succeeds in organizing his "mental space" and, between preverbal intelligence and the beginnings of Euclidean spatial intuition, a series of "topological" intuitions are intercalated as manifested in drawing, stereognosis, the construction and assembling of objects, etc.; that is to say, in the areas of transition between the sensorimotor and the perceptual.

In the second place, it is primarily preverbal sensorimotor activity that is responsible for the construction of a series of perceptual schemata the importance of which in the subsequent structuring of thought cannot, without oversimplification, be denied. Thus the perceptual constants of form and size are connected with the sensorimotor construction of the permanent object: For how could the four-year-old child think without having reference to objects having form and invariable dimensions, and how would he adapt his belief without a long preliminary development by the sensorimotor?

Probably the sensorimotor schemata are not concepts, and the functional relationship which we stress in this book does not exclude the structural opposition of these extremes, despite the continuity of the transitions. But, without preliminary schemata, nascent thought would be reduced to mere verbalism, which would make one suspicious of many of the acts mentioned by Wallon in his latest work. But it is precisely on the concrete plane of action that infancy makes its intelligence most manifest until the age of seven or eight, when coördinated actions are converted into operations, admitting of the logical construction of verbal thought and its application to a coherent structure.

In short, Wallon's thesis disregards the progressive construction of performance and that is why it goes to extremes in stressing the verbal at the expense of the sensorimotor whereas the sensorimotor substructure is necessary to the conceptual for the formation of the operational schemata which are destined to function finally in a formal manner and thus to make language consistent with thought.

As far as P. Guillaume's[1] very interesting study is concerned, it, on the other hand, agrees in the main with our conclusions, except in one essential point. In accordance with his interpretations influenced by "the theory of form," P. Guillaume presents a fundamental distinction between the perceptual mechanisms and the intellectual processes which explains the second in terms of the first (the reverse of Wallon). This controversy is too lengthy to consider in detail in a preface. Let us limit ourselves to answering that the systematic study of the child's perceptions, in which we have since collaborated with Lambertier[2] has, on the contrary, led us to doubt the permanence of perceptual constants in which P. Guillaume believes (the invariability of size, etc.) and to introduce a distinction between instantaneous perceptions which are always passive and a "perceptual activity" connecting them with each other in space and time, according to certain remarkable laws (in particular a mobility and reversibility increasing with age). This perceptual activity, which the theory of form partially disregards, is but one manifestation of the sensorimotor activities of which preverbal intelligence is the expression. In the development of the sensorimotor schema in the first year of life, there is undoubtedly a close interaction between perception and intelligence in their most elementary states.

[1] P. Guillaume, L'intelligence sensori-motrice d'après J. Piaget, *Journal de psychologie*, April–June 1940–41 (years XXXVII–XXXVIII, pp. 264–280).

[2] See Recherches sur le développement des perceptions (I–VIII), *Archives de psychologie*, 1942–1947.

INTRODUCTION*

The Biological Problem of Intelligence

The question of the relationships between mind and biological organization is one which inevitably arises at the beginning of a study of the origins of intelligence. True, a discussion of that sort cannot lead to any really definite conclusion at this time, but, rather than to submit to the implications of one of the various possible solutions to this problem, it is better to make a clear choice in order to separate the hypotheses which form the point of departure for our inquiry.

Verbal or cogitative intelligence is based on practical or sensorimotor intelligence which in turn depends on acquired and recombined habits and associations. These presuppose, furthermore, the system of reflexes whose connection with the organism's anatomical and morphological structure is apparent. A certain continuity exists, therefore, between intelligence and the purely biological processes of morphogenesis and adaptation to the environment. What does this mean?

It is obvious, in the first place, that certain hereditary factors condition intellectual development. But that can be interpreted in two ways so different in their biological meaning that confusing the one with the other is probably what has obfuscated the classic controversy over innate ideas and epistemological *a priorism.*

The hereditary factors of the first group are structural and are connected with the constitution of our nervous system and of our sensory organs. Thus we perceive certain physical radia-

---

* Another translation of this chapter was published in *Organization and Pathology of Thought,* by David Rapaport (New York: Columbia University Press, 1951). The footnote commentary to that translation provides an introduction to Piaget's thinking, and may serve as an introduction to the investigations and thinking contained in this volume.

tions, but not all of them, and matter only of a certain size, etc. Now these known structural factors influence the building up of our most fundamental concepts. For instance, our intuition of space is certainly conditioned by them, even if, by means of thought, we succeed in working out transintuitive and purely deductive types of space.

These characteristics of the first type, while supplying the intelligence with useful structures, are thus essentially limiting, in contradistinction to the factors of the second group. Our perceptions are but what they are, amidst all those which could possibly be conceived. Euclidean space which is linked to our organs is only one of the kinds of space which are adapted to physical experience. In contrast, the deductive and organizing activity of the mind is unlimited and leads, in the realm of space, precisely to generalizations which surpass intuition. To the extent that this activity of the mind is hereditary, it is so in quite a different sense from the former group. In this second type it is probably a question of a hereditary transmission of the function itself and not of the transmission of a certain structure. It is in this second sense that H. Poincaré was able to consider the spatial concept of "group" as being *a priori* because of its connection with the very activity of intelligence.

We find the same distinction with regard to the inheritance of intelligence. On the one hand, we find a question of structure: The "specific heredity" of mankind and of its particular "offspring" admits of certain levels of intelligence superior to that of monkeys, etc. But, on the other hand, the functional activity of reason (the *ipse intellectus* which does not come from experience) is obviously connected with the "general heredity" of the living organism itself. Just as the organism would not know how to adapt itself to environmental variations if it were not already organized, so also intelligence would not be able to apprehend any external data without certain functions of coherence (of which the ultimate expression is the principle of noncontradiction), and functions making relationships, etc., which are common to all intellectual organization.

Now this second type of hereditary psychological reality is of primary importance for the development of intelligence. If there truly in fact exists a functional nucleus of the intellectual organization which comes from the biological organization in its most general aspect, it is apparent that this invariant will orient the whole of the successive structures which the mind will then work out in its contact with reality. It will thus play the role that philosophers assigned to the *a priori;* that is to say, it will impose on the structures certain necessary and irreducible conditions. Only the mistake has sometimes been made of regarding the *a priori* as consisting in structures existing ready-made from the beginning of development, whereas if the functional invariant of thought is at work in the most primitive stages, it is only little by little that it impresses itself on consciousness due to the elaboration of structures which are increasingly adapted to the function itself. This *a priori* only appears in the form of essential structures at the end of the evolution of concepts and not at their beginning: Although it is hereditary, this *a priori* is thus the very opposite of what were formerly called "innate ideas."

The structures of the first type are more reminiscent of classic innate ideas and it has been possible to revive the theory of innateness with regard to space and the "well-structured" perceptions of Gestalt psychology. But, in contrast to the functional invariants, these structures have nothing essential from the point of view of the mind: They are only internal data, limited and delimiting, and external experience and, above all, intellectual activity will unremittingly transcend them. If they are in a sense innate, they are not *a priori* in the epistemological sense of the term.

Let us analyze first the functional invariants, and then (in §3) we shall discuss the question raised by the existence of special hereditary structures (those of the first type).

§1. THE FUNCTIONAL INVARIANTS OF INTELLIGENCE AND BIOLOGICAL ORGANIZATION.—Intelligence is an adaptation. In order to grasp its relation to life in general it is therefore necessary to state precisely the relations that exist between the organism and the environment. Life is a continuous creation of increasingly complex forms and a progressive balancing of these forms with the environment. To say that intelligence is a particular instance of biological adaptation is thus to suppose that it is essentially an organization and that its function is to structure the universe just as the organism structures its immediate environment. In order to describe the functional mechanism of thought in true biological terms it will suffice to determine the invariants common to all structuring of which life is capable. What we must translate into terms of adaptation are not the particular goals pursued by the practical intelligence in its beginnings (these goals will subsequently enlarge to include all knowledge), but it is the fundamental relationship peculiar to consciousness itself: the relationship of thought to things. The organism adapts itself by materially constructing new forms to fit them into those of the universe, whereas intelligence extends this creation by ·constructing mentally structures which can be applied to those of the environment. In one sense and at the beginning of mental evolution, intellectual adaptation is thus more restricted than biological adaptation, but in extending the latter, the former goes infinitely beyond it. If, from the biological point of view, intelligence is a particular instance of organic activity and if things perceived or known are a limited part of the environment to which the organism tends to adapt, a reversal of these relationships subsequently takes place. But this is in no way incompatible with the search for functional invariants.

In fact there exists, in mental development, elements which are variable and others which are invariant. Thence stem the misunderstandings resulting from psychological terminology some of which lead to attributing higher qualities to the lower stages and others which lead to the annihilation of stages and operations. It is therefore fitting simultaneously to avoid both the preformism of intellectualistic psychology and the hypothesis of mental heterogeneities. The solution to this difficulty is precisely to be found in the distinction between variable structures and invariant functions. Just as the main functions of the living being are identical in all organisms but correspond to organs which are very different in different groups, so also between the child and the adult a continuous creation of varied structures may be observed although the main functions of thought remain constant.

These invariant operations exist within the framework of

the two most general biological functions: *organization* and *adaptation*. Let us begin with the latter, for if everyone recognizes that everything in intellectual development consists of adaptation, the vagueness of this concept can only be deplored.

Certain biologists define *adaptation* simply as preservation and survival, that is to say, the equilibrium between the organism and the environment. But then the concept loses all interest because it becomes confused with that of life itself. There are degrees of survival, and adaptation involves the greatest and the least. It is therefore necessary to distinguish between the state of adaptation and the process of adaptation. In the state, nothing is clear. In following the process, things are cleared up. There is adaptation when the organism is transformed by the environment and when this variation results in an increase in the interchanges between the environment and itself which are favorable to its preservation.

Let us try to be precise and state this in a formal way. The organism is a cycle of physicochemical and kinetic processes which, in constant relation to the environment, are engendered by each other. Let a, b, c, etc., be the elements of this organized totality and x, y, z, etc., the corresponding elements of the surrounding environment. The schema of organization is therefore the following:

$$(1)\ a + x \longrightarrow b;$$
$$(2)\ b + y \longrightarrow c;$$
$$(3)\ c + z \longrightarrow a, \text{etc.}$$

The processes (1), (2), etc., may consist either of chemical reactions (when the organism ingests substances x which it will transform into substance b comprising part of its structure), or of any physical transformations whatsoever, or finally, in particular, of sensorimotor behavior (when a cycle of bodily movements a combined with external movements x result in b which itself enters the cycle of organization). The relationship which unites the organized elements a, b, c, etc., with the environmental elements x, y, z, etc., is therefore a relationship of *assimilation*, that is to say, the functioning of the organism does not destroy it but conserves the cycle of organization and coördinates the given data of the environment in such a way as to incorporate them in that cycle. Let us therefore suppose that, in the environment, a variation is produced which transforms x into x'. Either the organism does not adapt and the cycle ruptures, or else adaptation takes place, which means that the organized cycle has been modified by closing up on itself:

(1) $a + x' \longrightarrow b'$;
(2) $b' + y \longrightarrow c$;
(3) $c + z \longrightarrow a$.

If we call this result of the pressures exerted by the environment *accommodation* (transformation of b into b'), we can accordingly say that *adaptation is an equilibrium between assimilation and accommodation.*

This definition applies to intelligence as well. Intelligence is *assimilation* to the extent that it incorporates all the given data of experience within its framework. Whether it is a question of thought which, due to judgment, brings the new into the known and thus reduces the universe to its own terms or whether it is a question of sensorimotor intelligence which also structures things perceived by bringing them into its schemata, in every case intellectual adaptation involves an element of assimilation, that is to say, of structuring through incorporation of external reality into forms due to the subject's activity. Whatever the differences in nature may be which separate organic life (which materially elaborates forms and assimilates to them the substances and energies of the environment) from practical or sensorimotor intelligence (which organizes acts and assimilates to the schemata of motor behavior the various situations offered by the environment) and separate them also from reflective or gnostic intelligence (which is satisfied with thinking of forms or constructing them internally in order to assimilate to them the contents of experience)—all of these adapt by assimilating objects to the subject.

There can be no doubt either, that mental life is also *accommodation* to the environment. Assimilation can never be pure because by incorporating new elements into its earlier schemata the intelligence constantly modifies the latter in order to adjust them to new elements. Conversely, things are never known by themselves, since this work of accommodation is only possible as a function of the inverse process of assimilation. We shall thus see how the very concept of the object is far from being innate and necessitates a construction which is simultaneously assimilatory and accommodating.

In short, intellectual adaptation, like every other kind, consists of putting an assimilatory mechanism and a complementary accommodation into progressive equilibrium. The mind can only be adapted to a reality if perfect accommodation exists, that is to say, if nothing, in that reality, intervenes to modify the subject's schemata. But, inversely, adaptation does not exist if the new reality has imposed motor or mental attitudes contrary to those which were adopted on contact with other earlier given data: adaptation only exists if there is coherence, hence assimilation. Of course, on the motor level, coherence presents quite a different structure than on the reflective or organic level, and every systematization is possible. But always and everywhere adaptation is only accomplished when it results in a stable system, that is to say, when there is equilibrium between accommodation and assimilation.

This leads us to the function of *organization*. From the biological point of view, organization is inseparable from adaptation: They are two complementary processes of a single mechanism, the first being the internal aspect of the cycle of which adaptation constitutes the external aspect. With regard to intelligence, in its reflective as well as in its practical form, this dual phenomenon of functional totality and interdependence between organization and adaptation is again found. Concerning the relationships between the parts and the whole which determine the organization, it is sufficiently well known that every intellectual operation is always related to all the others and that its own elements are controlled by the same law. Every schema is thus coördinated with all the other schemata and itself constitutes a totality with differentiated parts. Every act of intelligence presupposes a system of mutual implications and interconnected meanings. The relationships between this organization and adaptation are consequently the same as on the organic level.

The principal "categories" which intelligence uses to adapt to the external world—space and time, causality and substance, classification and number, etc.—each of these corresponds to an aspect of reality, just as each organ of the body is related to a special quality of the environment but, besides their adaptation to things, they are involved in each other to such a degree that it is impossible to isolate them logically. The "accord of thought with things" and the "accord of thought with itself" express this dual functional invariant of adaptation and organization. These two aspects of thought are indissociable: It is by adapting to things that thought organizes itself and it is by organizing itself that it structures things.

§2. FUNCTIONAL INVARIANTS AND THE CATEGORIES OF REASON.—The problem now is to ascertain how these functional invariants will determine the categories of reason, in other words, the main forms of intellectual activity which are found at all stages of mental development and whose first structural crystallizations in the sensorimotor intelligence we shall now try to describe.

It is not a matter of reducing the higher to the lower. The history of science shows that every attempt at deduction to establish continuity between one discipline and another results not in a reduction of the higher to the lower but in creating a reciprocal relationship between the two terms which does not at all destroy the originality of the higher term. So it is that the functional relations which can exist between intellect and biological organization can in no way diminish the value of reason but on the contrary lead to extending the concept of vital adaptation. It is self-evident that if the categories of reason are in a sense preformed in biological functioning, they are not contained in it either in the form of conscious or even unconscious structures. If biological adaptation is a sort of material understanding of the environments, a series of later structures would be necessary in order that conscious and gnostic image may emerge from this purely active mechanism. As we have already said, it is therefore at the end and not at the point of departure of intellectual evolution that one must expect to encounter rational concepts really expressing functioning as such, in contrast to the initial structures which remain on the surface of the organism and of the environment and only express the superficial relationships of these two terms to each other. But in order to facilitate analysis of the lower stages which we shall attempt in this work it can be shown how the biological invariants just mentioned, once they have been reflected upon and elaborated by consciousness during the great stages of mental development, give rise to a sort of functional *a priori* of reason.

Here, it seems to us, is the picture thus obtained:

Biological Functions	Intellectual Functions	Categories
Organization	Regulating function ...	A. Totality x Relationship (reciprocity)
		B. Ideal (goal) x Value (means)
Adaptation ...	Assimilation...Implicative function	A. Quality x Class
		B. Quantitative rapport[1] x number
	Accommodation...Explicative function	A. Object x Space
		B. Causality x Time

The categories related to the function of organization constitute what Hoeffding calls the "fundamental" or regulative

---

[1] In this diagram we distinguish between "relationships" in the most general sense of the word and "quantitative rapport" which corresponds to what is called, on the level of thought, the "logic of relationships." The relations which the latter envisages in contradistinction to the logic of classes are always quantitative, regardless of whether they interpret "more" or "less" as comparisons (for example, "more or less dark," etc.), or whether they simply imply ideas of category or of series (for example, family relationships such as "brother of" etc.), which presuppose quantity. On the contrary, the relationships on a par with the idea of totality surpass the quantitative and only imply a general relativity in the widest sense of the term (reciprocity between the elements of a totality).

"categories," that is to say, they combine with all the others and are found again in every psychic operation. It seems to us that these categories can be defined, from the static point of view, by the concepts of *totality* and *relationship* and, from the dynamic point of view, by those of *ideal* and *value*.

The concept of *totality* expresses the interdependence inherent in every organization, intelligent as well as biological. Even though behavior patterns and consciousness seem to arise in the most uncoördinated manner in the first weeks of existence, they extend a physiological organization which antedates them and they crystallize from the outset into systems whose coherence becomes clarified little by little. For example, what is the concept of "displacement groups," which is essential to the formation of space, if not the idea of organized totality making itself manifest in movements? So also are the schemata belonging to sensorimotor intelligence controlled from the very beginning by the law of totality, within themselves and in their interrelationships. So too, every causal relation transforms an incoherent datum into an organized environment, etc.

The correlative of the idea of totality is, as Hoeffding has shown, the idea of *relationship*. Relationship is also a fundamental category, inasmuch as it is immanent in all psychic activity and combines with all the other concepts. This is because every totality is a system of relationships just as every relationship is a segment of totality. In this capacity the relationship manifests itself from the advent of the purely physiological activities and is again found at all levels. The most elementary perceptions (aş shown by Köhler with regard to the color perception of chickens) are simultaneously related to each other and structured into organized totalities. It is useless to emphasize analogous facts that one finds on the level of reflective thought.

The categories of *ideal* and of *value* express the same function, but in its dynamic aspect. We shall call "ideal" every system of values which constitutes a whole, hence every final goal of actions; and we shall call "values" the particular values related to this whole or the means making it possible to attain this goal. The relations of ideal and value are therefore the same as those of totality and relation. These ideals or value of every category are only totalities in process of formation, value only being the expression of desirability at all levels. Desirability is the indication of a rupture in equilibrium or of an uncompleted totality to whose formation some element is lacking and which tends toward this element in order to realize its equilibrium. The relations between ideal and value are therefore of the same category as those of totality and of relations which is self-evident, since the ideal is only the as yet incomplete form of equilibrium between real totalities and values are none other than the relations of means to ends subordinated to this system. Finality is thus to be conceived not as a special category, but as the subjective translation of a process of putting into equilibrium which itself does not imply finality but simply the general distinction between real equilibria and the idea equilibrium. A good example is that of the nórms of coherence and unity of logical thought which translate this perpetual effort of intellectual totalities toward equilibrium, and which therefore define the ideal equilibrium never attained by intelligence and regulate the particular values of judgment. This is why we call the operations relating to totality and to values "regulative function," in contradistinction to the explicative and implicative functions.[2]

How are we to consider the categories connected with adaptation, that is to say, with assimilation and accommodation? Among the categories of thought there are some, as Hoeffding says, which are more "real" (those which, besides the activity of reason, imply a *hic* and a *nunc* inherent in experience such as causality, substance or object, space and time, each of which operates an indissoluble synthesis of "datum" and deduction) and some which are more "formal" (those which, without being less adapted, can nevertheless give rise to an unlimited deductive elaboration, such as logical and mathematical relations). Hence it is the former which express more the centrifugal process of explication and accommodation and the latter which make pos-

2 In *The Language and Thought of the Child,* London, Routledge, 1932, p. 236, we called "mixed function" this synthesis of implication and explication which at the present time we connect with the idea of organization. But this amounts to the same thing since the latter presupposes a synthesis of assimilation and accommodation.

sible the assimilation of things to intellectual organization and the construction of implications.

The implicative function comprises two functional invariants which are found again at all stages, the one corresponding to the synthesis of *qualities,* that is to say, *classes* (concepts or schemata), the other to that of *quantitative relations* or *numbers.* Ever since the formation of the sensorimotor schemata the elementary instruments of intelligence reveal their mutual dependence. With regard to the explicative function, it concerns the ensemble of operations which makes it possible to deduce reality, in other words to confer a certain permanence upon it while supplying the reason for its transformations. From this point of view two complementary aspects can be distinguished in every explication, one relating to the elaboration of *objects,* the other relating to *causality;* the former is simultaneously the product of the latter and conditions its development. Whence the circle object x *space* and causality x *time* in which the interdependence of functions is complicated by a reciprocal relation of matter to form.

We see the extent to which the functional categories of knowledge constitute a real whole which is modeled on the system of the functions of intelligence. This correlation becomes still more clear on analysis of the interrelations of organization and adaptation, on the one hand, and assimilation and accommodation, on the other.

As we have seen, organization is the internal aspect of adaptation, when the interdependence of already adapted elements and not the adaptational process in action is under consideration. Moreover, adaptation is only organization grappling with the actions of the environment. Now this mutual dependence is found again, on the level of intelligence, not only in the interaction of rational activity (organization) and of experience (adaptation) which the whole history of scientific thought reveals are inseparable but also in the correlation of the functional categories: Any objective or causal spatial-temporal structure is only possible with logical-mathematical deduction, these two kinds of reality thus forming mutually interconnected systems of totalities and relations. With regard to the circle of accommoda-

THE BIOLOGICAL PROBLEM OF INTELLIGENCE

tion and assimilation—that is to say, of explication and implication—the question raised by Hume concerning causality illustrates it clearly. How can the concept of cause be simultaneously rational and experimental? If one puts causality in a purely formal category reality escapes it (as E. Meyerson has admirably shown) and if one reduces it to the level of a simple empirical sequence, necessity vanishes. Whence the Kantian solution taken up by Brunschvicg according to which it is an "analogy of experience," an irreducible interaction between the relation of implication and the spatial-temporal known data. The same can be said of the other "real" categories: They all presuppose implication although constituting accommodations to external known data. Inversely, classes and numbers could not be constructed without connection with the spatial-temporal series inherent in objects and their causal relations.

Finally, it remains for us to note that, if every organ of a living body is organized, so also every element of an intellectual organization also constitutes an organization. Consequently the functional categories of intelligence, while developing along the major lines of the essential mechanisms of organization, assimilation and accommodation, themselves comprise aspects corresponding to those three functions, the more so since the latter are certainly vicarious and so constantly change in point of application. The manner in which the functions which thus characterize the chief categories of the mind create their own organs and crystallize into structures is another question which we shall not take up in this introduction since this whole work is devoted to study of the beginnings of this construction. To prepare for this analysis it is simply fitting to say a few more words about the hereditary structures which make this mental structuring possible.

§3. HEREDITARY STRUCTURES AND THEORIES OF ADAPTATION.—Two kinds of hereditary realities exist, as we have seen, which affect the development of human reason: the functional invariants connected with the general heredity of the living substance, and certain structural organs or qualities, connected with man's particular heredity and serving as elementary instruments for intellectual adaptation. It is therefore fitting to examine how the hereditary structures prepare the latter and how biological theories of adaptation are able to cast light on the theory of intelligence.

The reflexes and the very morphology of the organs with which they are connected constitute a sort of anticipatory knowledge of the external environment, an unconscious and entirely material knowledge but essential to the later development of real knowledge. How is such an adaptation of hereditary structures possible?

This biological problem is insoluble at present, but a brief summary of the discussions to which it has given and still gives rise seems useful to us, for the different solutions supplied are parallel to the various theories of intelligence and can thus illuminate the latter by setting off the generality of their mechanism. Five principal points of view exist concerning adaptation and each one corresponds, *mutatis mutandis*, to one of the interpretations of intelligence as such. Of course this does not mean that if a certain author chooses one of the five characteristic doctrines that can be discerned in biology he is forced by this to adopt the corresponding attitude in psychology; but whatever the possible combinations with regard to the opinions of the writers themselves may be, "common mechanisms" undeniably exist between biological and psychological explanations of general and intellectual adaptation.

The first solution is that of Lamarckism according to which the organism is fashioned from the outside by the environment which, by its constraints, trains the formation of individual habits or accommodations which, becoming hereditarily fixed, fashion the organs. There corresponds to this biological hypothesis of the primacy of habit *associationism* in psychology according to which knowledge also results from acquired habits without there being any internal activity which would constitute intelligence as such to condition those acquisitions.

Vitalism, on the other hand, interprets adaptation by attributing to the living being a special power to construct useful organs. So also *intellectualism* explains intelligence by itself by endowing it with an innate faculty for knowing and by considering its activity as a primary fact whence everything on the psychic plane derives.

With regard to *preformism,* the structures have a purely endogenous origin, virtual variations being made up-to-date simply by contact with the environment which thus only plays a role of "detector." It is through the same sort of reasoning that various epistemological and psychological doctrines that can be labeled *apriorism* consider mental structures as being anterior to experience which simply gives them the opportunity to manifest themselves without explaining them in any respect. Whether structures are considered to be psychologically innate, as they are thought to be by the classic proponents of innate ideas, or merely as logically eternal, "subsisting" in an intelligible world in which reason participates, is of little importance. They are preformed in the subject and not elaborated by him as a function of his experience. The most parallel excesses in this respect were committed in biology and in logic. Just as a hypothesis was made of a preformation of all the "genes" which were made manifest in the course of evolution—including genes injurious to the species—so also Russell came to allege that all the ideas germinating in our brains have existed for all eternity, including false ideas!

A separate place could be set aside for the biological doctrine of "emergent evolution," according to which structures appear as irreducible syntheses succeeding each other in a sort of continuous creation, parallel to the theory of "shapes" or "Gestalt" in psychology. But actually only a more dynamic apriorism of intention is involved which, in its particular explanations, only amounts to apriorism properly so called to the extent that it is not frankly directed toward the fifth solution.

The fourth point of view which we shall call *mutationalism* is held by biologists who, without believing in preformation, also believe that structures appear in a purely endogenous way but then consider them as arising by chance from internal transformations and adapting to the environment due to a selection after the event. Now, if one transposes this method of interpretation to the level of nonhereditary adaptations one finds it is parallel to the schema of "trials and errors" belonging to *pragmatism* or to *conventionalism:* according to this schema, the adjustment of behavior patterns is also explained by selection after the event of behavior arising by chance in relation to the external environment. For example, according to conventionalism Euclidean space with three dimensions seems to us more "true" than the other kinds of space because of the structure of our organs of perception, and is simply more "convenient" because it permits a better adjustment of those organs to the known data of the external world.

Finally, according to a fifth solution, the organism and the environment form an indissoluble entity, that is to say, beside chance mutations there are adaptional variations simultaneously involving a structuring of the organism and an action of the environment, the two being inseparable from each other. From the point of view of awareness, that means that the subject's activity is related to the constitution of the object, just as the latter involves the former. This is the affirmation of an irreducible interdependence between experience and reasoning. Biological *relativity* is thus extended into the doctrine of the interdependence of subject and object, of assimilation of the object by the subject and of the accommodation of the latter to the former.

The parallel between the theories of adaptation and those of intelligence having been outlined, study of the development of the latter will of course determine the choice it is fitting to make between those different possible hypotheses. However, in order to prepare for this choice and primarily in order to expand our concept of adaptation—given the continuity of the biological processes and the analogy of the solutions that an attempt has been made to supply on the different planes on which this problem is encountered—we have analyzed on the plane of the hereditary morphology of the organism a case of "kinetogenesis" suitable for illustrating the different solutions we have just catalogued.[3]

3 For details, see our two articles: Les races lacustres de la 'Limnaea stagnalis' and Recherches sur les rapports de l'adaptation héréditaire avec le milieu, *Bulletin biologique de la France et de la Belgique,* LXII, 1929, pp. 424–455; and 2. Adaptation de la Limnaea stagnalis aux milieux lacustres de la Suisse romande, *Revue Suisse de Zoologie,* XXXVI, pp. 263–531.

There is found in almost all European and Asian marshes an aquatic mollusc, the *Limnaea stagnalis* (L.) which is typically elongated in shape. Now in the great lakes of Switzerland, Sweden, etc., this species is of a lacustrine variety, shortened and globular, whose form can easily be explained by the animal's motor accommodation, during growth, to the waves and movement of the water. After having verified this explanation experimentally, we succeeded in proving, by means of many breedings in the aquarium, that this shortened variety whose geological history can be followed from the paleolithic age to our own, became hereditary and perfectly stable (those genotypes obey in particular the laws of Mendelian segregation) in the places most exposed to the winds in the lakes of Neuchâtel and Geneva.

Thus it appears at first glance as though the Lamarckian solution fits such a case: The habits of contraction acquired under the influence of waves would have ended by transmitting themselves hereditarily in a morphologico-reflex ensemble constituting a new race. In other words, the phenotype would be imperceptibly transformed into a genotype by the lasting action of the environment. Unfortunately, in the case of the Limnaea as in all others, the laboratory experiment (breeding in an agitator producing an experimental contraction) does not show a trace of the hereditary transmission of acquired characteristics. Moreover the lakes of medium size do not have all the shortened varieties. If there is an influence of the environment in the constitution of hereditary contraction this influence is subjected to thresholds (of intensity, duration, etc.) and the organism, far from suffering it passively, reacts actively by an adaptation which transcends simple imposed habits.

Regarding the second solution, vitalism would not be able to explain the particulars of any adaptation. Why does the unconscious intelligence of the species, if it exists, not intervene everywhere it could be useful? Why did contraction take centuries to appear after the post glacial stocking of the lakes and why does it not yet exist in all the lakes?

The same objections apply to the solution of the problem in accordance with the theory of preformation.

On the other hand, the fourth solution appears to be impregnable to attack. According to the theory of mutation the hereditary shortened structures would be due to chance endogenous variations (that is to say, with no relation to the environment nor with the phenotypic individual adaptations) and it would only be after the event that these forms, better preadapted than the others to the rough zones of the lakes, would multiply in the very places from which the elongated shapes would be excluded by natural selection. Chance and selection after the event would thus account for adaptation without any mysterious action of the environment on hereditary transmission, whereas the adaptation of non-hereditary individual variations would remain connected with the environmental action. But, in the case of our Limnaea, two strong objections to such an interpretation can be made. In the first place, if the elongated forms of the species could not endure as such in the parts of the lakes where the water is roughest, on the other hand the shortened genotypes can live in all the environments in which the species is represented, and we have introduced some to a new climate years ago, in a stagnant pond in the Swiss Plateau. If it were, therefore, a question of chance mutations, those genotypes should be scattered everywhere; but, in fact, they only appeared in lacustrine environments and moreover in those most exposed to the wind, precisely where the individual or phenotypic adaptation to the waves is most evident! In the second place, selection after the event is, in the case of the Limnaea, useless and impossible, for the elongated forms can themselves give rise to shortened variations which are not or not yet hereditary. One cannot therefore speak of chance mutations or of selection after the event to explain such adaptation.

Therefore only a fifth and last solution remains: This is to admit the possibility of hereditary adaptations simultaneously presupposing an action of the environment and a reaction of the organism other than the simple fixation of habits. As early as the morphologico-reflex level there exist interactions between the environment and the organism which are such that the latter, without passively enduring the constraint of the former, nor limiting itself on contact with it to manifesting already preformed structures, reacts by an active differentiation of reflexes (in the particular case by a development of the reflexes of pedal adherence and of contraction) and by a correlative morphogenesis. In other words, the hereditary fixation of phenotypes or individual adaptations is not due to the simple repetition of habits which gave rise to them but to a mechanism *sui generis* which, through recurrence or anticipation, leads to the same result on the morphologico-reflex level.

Concerning the problem of intelligence, the lessons furnished by such an example seem to us to be the following. From its beginnings, due to the hereditary adaptations of the organism, intelligence finds itself entangled in a network of relations between the organism and the environment. Intelligence does not therefore appear as a power of reflection independent of the particular position which the organism occupies in the universe but is linked, from the very outset, by biological apriorities. It is not at all an independent absolute, but is a relationship among others, between the organism and things. If intelligence thus extends an organic adaptation which is anterior to it, the progress of reason doubtless consists in an increasingly advanced acquisition of awareness of the organizing activity inherent in life itself, and the primitive stages of psychological development only constitute the most superficial acquisitions of awareness of this work of organization. *A fortiori* the morphologico-reflex structures manifested by the living body, and the biological assimilation which is at the point of departure of the elementary forms of psychic assimilation would be nothing other than the most external and material outline of the adaptation whose profound nature the higher forms of intellectual activity would express increasingly well. One can therefore believe that intellectual activity, departing from a relation of interdependence between organism and environment, or lack of differentiation between subject and object, progresses simultaneously in the conquest of things and reflection on itself, these two processes of inverse direction being correlative. From this point of view, physiological and anatomical organization gradually appears to consciousness as being external to it and intelligent activity is revealed for that reason as being the very essence of the existence of our subjects. Whence the reversal which is at work in perspectives as mental development progresses and which explains why the power of reason, while extending the most central biological mechanisms, ends by surpassing them at the same time in complementary externalization and internalization.

PART I

Elementary Sensorimotor Adaptations

Intelligence does not by any means appear at once derived from mental development, like a higher mechanism, and radically distinct from those which have preceded it. Intelligence presents, on the contrary, a remarkable continuity with the acquired or even inborn processes on which it depends and at the same times makes use of. Thus, it is appropriate, before analyzing intelligence as such, to find out how the formation of habits and even the exercise of the reflex prepare its appearance. This is what we are going to do in the first part, dedicating one chapter to the reflex and to the psychological questions that it raises, and a second chapter to the various acquired associations or elementary habits.

CHAPTER ONE

THE FIRST STAGE:

The Use of Reflexes

If, in order to analyze the first mental acts, we refer to hereditary organic reactions, we must study them not for their own sake but merely so that we may describe *in toto* the way in which they affect the individual's behavior. We should begin, therefore, by trying to differentiate between the psychological problem of the reflexes and the strictly biological problem.

Behavior observable during the first weeks of life is very complicated, biologically speaking. At first there are very different types of reflexes involving the medulla, the bulb, the optic commissures, the ectoderm itself; moreover, from reflex to instinct is only a difference of degree. Next to the reflexes of the central nervous system are those of the autonomic nervous system and all the reactions due to "protopathic" sensibility. There is, above all, the whole group of postural reflexes whose importance for the beginnings of the evolution of the mind has been demonstrated by H. Wallon. It is hard to envisage the organization of the foregoing mechanisms without giving the endocrine processes their just due as indicated by so many learned or spontaneous reactions. Physiological psychology is confronted at the present time by a host of problems which consist of determining the effects on the individual's behavior of each of these separate mechanisms. H. Wallon analyzes one of the most important of these questions in his excellent book on the disturbed child (*l'Enfant turbulent*): "Is there an emotional stage, or a stage of postural and extrapyramidal reactions prior to the sensorimotor or cortical stage?" Nothing better reveals the complexity of ele-

23

mentary behavior and the need to differentiate between the successive stages of concurrent physiological systems than Wallon's scholarly study of their genesis in which a wealth of pathologic material always substantiates his analysis.

Notwithstanding the fascinating conclusions thus reached, it seems to us difficult at the present time to go beyond a general description when it comes to grasping the continuity between the earliest behavior of the nursling and the future intellectual behavior. That is why, although in complete sympathy with Wallon's attempt to identify psychic mechanisms with those of life itself, we believe we should limit ourselves to emphasizing functional identity, from the point of view of simple external behavior.

In this respect the problem which arises in connection with reactions in the first weeks is only this: How do the sensorimotor, postural, and other reactions, inherent in the hereditary equipment of the newborn child, prepare him to adapt himself to his external environment and to acquire subsequent behavior distinguished by the progressive use of experience?

The psychological problem begins to pose itself as soon as the reflexes, postures, etc., are considered no longer in connection with the internal mechanism of the living organism, but rather in their relationships to the external environment as it is subjected to the individual's activity. Let us examine, from this point of view, the various fundamental reactions in the first weeks: sucking and grasping reflexes, crying and vocalization,[1] movements and positions of the arms, the head or the trunk, etc.

What is striking about this is that such activities from the start of their most primitive functioning, each in itself and some in relation to others, give rise to a systematization which exceeds their automatization. Almost since birth, therefore, there is "behavior" in the sense of the individual's total reaction and not only a setting in motion of particular or local automatizations only interrelated from within. In other words, the sequential manifestations of a reflex such as sucking are not comparable to the periodic starting up of a motor used intermittently, but constitute

[1] We shall return to the subject of prehension, vision and vocalization in the course of Chapter II.

an historical development so that each episode depends on preceding episodes and conditions those that follow in a truly organic evolution. In fact, whatever the intensive mechanism of this historical process may be, one can follow the changes from the outside and describe things as though each particular reaction determined the others without intermediates. This comprises total reaction, that is to say, the beginning of psychology.

§1. SUCKING REFLEXES.—Let us take as an example the sucking reflexes or the instinctive act of sucking; these reflexes are complicated, involving a large number of afferent fibers of the trigeminal and the glossopharyngeal nerves as well as the efferent fibers of the facial, the hypoglossal and the masseteric nerves, all of which have as a center the bulb of the spinal cord. First here are some facts:

Observation 1.—From birth sucking-like movements may be observed: impulsive movement and protrusion of the lips accompanied by displacements of the tongue, while the arms engage in unruly and more or less rhythmical gestures and the head moves laterally, etc.

As soon as the hands rub the lips the sucking reflex is released. The child sucks his fingers for a moment but of course does not know either how to keep them in his mouth or pursue them with his lips. Lucienne and Laurent, a quarter of an hour and a half hour after birth, respectively, had already sucked their hand like this: Lucienne, whose hand had been immobilized due to its position, sucked her fingers for more than ten minutes.

A few hours after birth, first nippleful of collostrum. It is known how greatly children differ from each other with respect to adaptation to this first meal. For some children like Lucienne and Laurent, contact of the lips and probably the tongue with the nipple suffices to produce sucking and swallowing. Other children, such as Jacqueline, have slower coördination: the child lets go of the breast every moment without taking it back again by himself or applying himself to it as vigorously when the nipple is replaced in his mouth. There are some children, finally, who need real forcing: holding their head, forcibly putting the nipple between the lips and in contact with the tongue, etc.

Observation 2.—The day after birth Laurent seized the nipple with his lips without having to have it held in his mouth. He immediately seeks the breast when it escapes him as the result of some movement.

During the second day also Laurent again begins to make sucking-like movements between meals while thus repeating the impulsive movements of the first day: His lips open and close as if to receive a real nippleful, but without having an object. This behavior subsequently became more frequent and we shall not take it up again.

The same day the beginning of a sort of reflex searching may be observed in Laurent, which will develop on the following days and which probably constitutes the functional equivalent of the gropings characteristic of the later stages (acquisition of habits and empirical intelligence). Laurent is lying on his back with his mouth open, his lips and tongue moving slightly in imitation of the mechanism of sucking, and his head moving from left to right and back again, as though seeking an object. These gestures are either silent or interrupted by grunts with an expression of impatience and of hunger.

Observation 3.—The third day Laurent makes new progress in his adjustment to the breast. All he needs in order to grope with open mouth toward final success is to have touched the breast or the surrounding teguments with his lips. But he hunts on the wrong side as well as on the right side, that is to say, the side where contact has been made.

Observation 4.—Laurent at 0;0 (9) is lying in bed and seeks to suck, moving his head to the left and to the right. Several times he rubs his lips with his hand which he immediately sucks. He knocks against a quilt and a wool coverlet; each time he sucks the object only to relinquish it after a moment and begins to cry again. When he sucks his hand he does not turn away from it as he seems to do with the woolens, but the hand itself escapes him through lack of coördination; he then immediately begins to hunt again.

Observation 5.—As soon as his cheek comes in contact with the breast, Laurent at 0;0 (12) applies himself to seeking until he finds drink. His search takes its bearings: immediately from the correct side, that is to say, the side where he experienced contact.

At 0;0 (20) he bites the breast which is given him, 5 cm. from the nipple. For a moment he sucks the skin which he then lets go in order to move his mouth about 2 cm. As soon as he begins sucking again he stops. In one of his attempts he touches the nipple with the outside of his lips and he does not recognize it. But, when his search subsequently leads him accidentally to touch the nipple with the mucosa of the upper lip (his mouth being wide open), he at once adjusts his lips and begins to suck.

The same day, same experiment: after having sucked the skin for several seconds, he withdraws and begins to cry. Then he begins again, withdraws again, but without crying, and takes it again 1 cm. away; he keeps this up until he discovers the nipple.

Observation 6.—The same day I hold out my crooked index finger to Laurent, who is crying from hunger (but intermittently and without violence). He immediately sucks it but rejects it after a few seconds and begins to cry. Second attempt: same reaction. Third attempt: he sucks it, this time for a long time and thoroughly, and it is I who retract it after a few minutes.

Observation 7.—Laurent at 0;0 (21) is lying on his right side, his arms tight against his body, his hands clasped, and he sucks his right thumb at length while remaining completely immobile. The nurse made the same observation on the previous day. I take his right hand away and he at once begins to search for it, turning his head from left to right. As his hands remained immobile due to his position, Laurent found his thumb after three attempts: prolonged sucking begins each time. But, once he has been placed on his back, he does not know how to coordinate the movement of the arms with that of the mouth and his hands draw back even when his lips are seeking them.

At 0;0 (24) when Laurent sucks his thumb, he remains completely immobile (as though having a nippleful: complete sucking, pantings, etc.). When his hand alone grazes his mouth, no coördination.

Observation 8.—At 0;0 (21): Several times I place the back of my index finger against his cheeks. Each time he turns to the correct side while opening his mouth. Same reactions with the nipple.

Then I repeat the same experiments as those in observation 5. At 0;0 (21) Laurent begins by sucking the teguments with which he comes in contact. He relinquishes them after a moment but searches with open mouth, while almost rubbing the skin with his lips. He seizes the nipple as soon as he brushes against it with the mucosa of his lower lip.

That evening, the same experiment, but made during a nursing which has been interrupted for this purpose. Laurent is already half asleep; his arms hang down and his hands are open (at the beginning of the meal his arms are folded against his chest and his hands are clasped). His mouth is placed against the skin of the breast about 5 cm. from the nipple. He immediately sucks without reopening his eyes but, after a few moments, failure awakens him. His eyes are wide open, his arms flexed again and he sucks with rapidity. Then he gives up, in order to search a little further away, on the left side which happens by chance to be the correct side. Again finding nothing, he continues to change places on the left side, but the rotatory movement which he thus gives his head results in making him let go the breast and go off on a tangent. In the course of this tangential movement he knocks against the nipple with the left commissure of his lips and everything that happens would seem to indicate that he recognizes it at once. Instead of groping at random, he only searches in the immediate neighborhood of the nipple. But as the lateral movements of his head made him describe a tangential curve opposite and not parallel to the curve of the breast, he oscillates in space guided only by light, haphazard contacts with the breast. It takes a short time for these increasingly localized attempts to be successful. This last phase of groping has been noteworthy for the speed with which each approach to it has been followed by an attempt at insertion of the nipple, while the lips open and close with maximum vigor; and noteworthy also for the progressive adjusting of the tangential movements around the points of contact.

At 0;0 (23) a new experiment. Laurent is 10 cm. from the breast, searching for it on the left and on the right. While he searches on the left the nipple touches his right cheek. He immediately turns and searches on the right. He is then moved 5 cm. away. He continues to search on the correct side. He is brought nearer as soon as he grasps the skin; he gropes and finds the nipple.

Same experiment and same result that evening. But, after several swallows, he is removed. He remains oriented to the correct side.

At 0;0 (24) Laurent, during the same experiments, seems much faster. To localize his search it suffices for the nipple to be brushed by the outside of his lips and no longer only by the mucosa. Besides, as soon as he has noticed the nipple, his head's lateral movements become more rapid and precise (less extensive). Finally, it seems that he is henceforth capable not only of lateral movements but also of raising his head when his upper lip touches the nipple.

Observation 9.—At 0;0 (22) Laurent is awakened an hour after his meal, and only cries faintly and intermittently. I place his right hand against his mouth but remove it before he begins to suck. Then, seven times in succession he does a complete imitation of sucking, opening and closing his mouth, moving his tongue, etc.

Observation 10.—Here are two facts revealing the differences in adaptation according to whether the need for nourishment is strong or weak. At 0;0 (25) Laurent is lying on his back, not very hungry (he has not cried since his last meal) and his right cheek is touched by the nipple. He turns to the correct side but the breast is removed to a distance of 5 to 10 cm. For a few seconds he reaches in the right direction and then gives up. He is still lying on his back, facing the ceiling; after a moment his mouth begins to move slightly, then his head moves from side to side, finally settling on the wrong side. A brief search in this direction, then crying (with commissures of the lip lowered, etc.), and another pause. After a moment, another search in the wrong direction. No reaction when the middle of his right cheek is touched. Only when the nipple touches his skin about 1 cm. from his lips does he turn and grasp it.

On reading this description it would seem as though all the practice of the last weeks were in vain. It would seem, above all, that the excitation zone of the reflex stops about 1 cm. from the lips, and that the cheek itself is insensitive. But on the next day the same experiment yields opposite results, as we shall see.

At 0;0 (26) Laurent is lying on his back, very hungry. I touch the middle of his cheek with my index finger bent first to the right, then to the left; each time he immediately turns to the correct side. Then he feels the nipple in the middle of his right cheek. But, as he tries to grasp it, it is withdrawn 10 cm. He then turns his head in the right direction and searches. He rests a moment, facing the ceiling, then his mouth begins to search again and his head immediately turns to the right side. This time he goes on to touch the nipple, first with his nose and then with the region between his nostrils and lips. Then he twice very distinctly repeats the movement observed at 0;0 (24) (see Obs. 8): He raises his head in order to grasp the nipple. The first time he just catches the nipple with the corner of his lips and lets it go. A second or two later, he vigorously lifts his head and achieves his purpose.

The way in which he discerns the nipple should be noted; at 0;0 (29) he explores its circumference with open and motionless lips before grasping it.

The theoretical importance of such observations seems to us to be as great as their triteness.[2] They make it possible for us to understand how a system of pure reflexes can comprise psychological behavior, as early as the systematization of their functioning. Let us try to analyze this process in its progressive adaptational and organization aspects.

§2. THE USE OF REFLEXES.—Concerning its *adaptation*, it is interesting to note that the reflex, no matter how well endowed with hereditary physiological mechanism, and no matter how stable its automatization, nevertheless needs to be used in order truly to adapt itself, and that it is capable of gradual accommodation to external reality.

Let us first stress this element of *accommodation*. The sucking reflex is hereditary and functions from birth, influenced either by diffuse impulsive movements or by an external excitant (Obs. 1); this is the point of departure. In order that a useful

---

[2] We are particularly happy to mention their agreement with those of R. Ripin and H. Hetzer: Frühestes Lernen des Säuglings in der Ernährungssituation, *Zeitschr. f. Psychol.*, 118, 1930, pp. 82–127. Observations of our children, made several years ago, were independent of the latter which makes their convergence a real one.

function may result, that is to say, swallowing, it often suffices to put the nipple in the mouth of the newborn child, but, as we know (Obs. 1), it sometimes happens that the child does not adapt at the first attempt. Only practice will lead to normal functioning. That is the first aspect of accommodation: contact with the object modifies, in a way, the activity of the reflex, and, even if this activity were oriented hereditarily to such contact, the latter is no less necessary to the consolidation of the former. This is how certain instincts are lost or certain reflexes cease to function normally, due to the lack of a suitable environment.[3] Moreover, contact with the environment not only results in developing the reflexes, but also in coördinating them in some way. Observations 2, 3, 5 and 8 show how the child, who first does not know how to suck the nipple when it is put in his mouth, grows increasingly able to grasp and even to find it, first after direct touch, then after contact with any neighboring region.[4]

How can such accommodations be explained? It seems to us difficult to invoke from birth the mechanism of acquired associations, in the limited sense of the term, or of "conditioned reflexes," both of which imply systematic training. On the contrary, the examining of these behavior patterns reveals at once the respects in which they differ from acquired associations: Whereas with regard to the latter, including conditioned reflexes, association is established between a certain perception,

[3] Thus Larguier des Brancels (*Introduction à la Psychologie*, 1921, p. 178), after recalling Spalding's famous experiments concerning the decline of instincts in newly hatched chickens, adds: "The sucking instinct is transitory. A calf which has been separated from its mother and fed by hand for a day or two and then is taken to another cow, more often than not refuses to nurse. The child behaves somewhat similarly. If he is first spoon-fed, he subsequently has great difficulty in taking the breast again."

[4] See Preyer (*L'Âme de l'Enfant*, translated by Variguy, 1887, pp. 213–217), in particular the following lines: "To be sure, sucking is not as fruitful the first as the second day and I have often observed in normal newborn children (1869) that attempts at sucking were completely vain in the first hours of life: when I made the experiment of putting an ivory pencil in their mouth, they were still uncoördinated" (p. 215). Also: "It is well known that newborn children, when put to the breast do not find the nipple without help; they only find it by themselves a few days later (in one case only on the eighth day), that is to say, later than animals" (pp. 215–216). And: "When the child is put to the breast the nipple often does not enter his mouth and he sucks the neighboring skin; this is still evident in the third week . . ." (p. 216).

foreign to the realm of the reflex, and the reflex itself (for example, between a sound, a visual perception, etc., and the salivary reflex), according to our observations, it is simply the reflex's own sensibility (contact of the lips with a foreign body) which is generalized, that is to say, brings with it the action of the reflex in increasingly numerous situations. In the case of Observations 2, 3, 5 and 8, for example, accommodation consists essentially of progress in the continuity of the searching. In the beginning (Obs. 2 and 3) contact with any part of the breast whatever sets in motion momentary sucking of this region, immediately followed by crying or a desultory search, whereas after several days (Obs. 5), the same contact sets in motion a groping during which the child is headed toward success. It is very interesting, in the second case, to see how the reflex, excited by each contact with the breast, stops functioning as soon as the child perceives that sucking is not followed by any satisfaction, as is the taking of nourishment (see Obs. 5 and 8), and to see how the search goes on until swallowing begins. In this regard, Observations 2 to 8 confirm that there is a great variety of kinds of accommodation. Sucking of the eider-down quilt, of the coverlet, etc., leads to rejection, that of the breast to acceptance; sucking of the skin (the child's hand, etc.) leads to acceptance if it is only a matter of sucking for the sake of sucking, but it leads to rejection (for example when it involves an area of the breast other than the nipple) if there is great hunger; the paternal index finger (Obs. 6) is rejected when the child is held against the breast, but is accepted as a pacifier, etc. In all behavior patterns it seems evident to us that learning is a function of the environment.

Surely all these facts admit of a physiological explanation which does not at all take us out of the realm of the reflex. The "irradiations," the "prolonged shocks," the "summations" of excitations and the intercoördination of reflexes probably explains why the child's searching becomes increasingly systematic, why contact which does not suffice to set the next operation in motion, does suffice in doing so a few days later, etc. Those are not necessarily mechanisms which are superposed on the reflex such as habit or intelligent understanding will be, later. But it remains no less true that the environment is indispensable to this operation, in other words, that reflex adaptation is partly accommodation. Without previous contact with the nipple and the experience of imbibing milk, it is very likely that the eider-down quilt, the wool coverlet, or the paternal index finger, after setting in motion the sucking reflex, would not have been so briskly rejected by Laurent.[5]

But if, in reflex adaptation, allowances must be made for accommodation, accommodation cannot be dissociated from progressive *assimilation,* inherent in the very use of the reflex. In a general way, one can say that the reflex is consolidated and strengthened by virtue of its own functioning. Such a fact is the most direct expression of the mechanism of assimilation. Assimilation is revealed, in the first place, by a growing need for repetition which characterizes the use of the reflex (functional assimilation) and, in the second place, by this sort of entirely practical or sensorimotor recognition which enables the child to adapt himself to the different objects with which his lips come in contact (recognitory and generalizing assimilations).

The need for repetition is in itself alone very significant; in effect, it is a question of a behavior pattern which shows a history and which proceeds to complicate the simple stimuli connected with the state of the organism considered at a given moment in time. A first stimulus capable of bringing the reflex into play is contact with an external object. Preyer thus set in motion the sucking movements of a newborn child by touching his lips, and Observation 1 shows us that children suck their hand a quarter of an hour or half an hour after birth. In the second place, there are internal stimuli, connected with the somato-affective states: diffuse impulsive movements (Obs. 1) or excitations due to hunger. But to these definite excitations, connected with particular moments in the life of the organism, there is added, it seems to us, the essential circumstance that the very repetition of the reflex movements constitutes a cynamogeny for them. Why, for instance, does Lucienne suck her fingers soon after birth for ten minutes in succession? This could not be

[5] In animals every slightly complicated reflex mechanism occasions reactions of the same kind. The beginnings of copulation in the mollusks, for example, give way to very strange gropings before the act is adapted.

because of hunger, since the umbilical cord had just been cut. There certainly is an external excitant from the moment the lips touch the hand. But why does the excitation last, in such a case, since it does not lead to any result except, precisely, to the use of the reflex? It therefore seems that, from the start of this primitive mechanism, a sort of circular process accompanies the function, the activity of the reflex having augmented due to its own use. If this interpretation remains doubtful, in so far as the point of departure is concerned, it obtains increasingly, on the other hand, with regard to subsequent behavior patterns. After the first feedings one observes, in Laurent (Obs. 2), sucking-like movements, in which it is difficult not to see a sort of autoexcitation. Besides, the progress in the search for the breast in Observations 2–5 and 8 seems also to show how much the function itself strengthened the tendency to suck. The counterproof of this is, as we have seen, the progressive decay of reflex mechanisms which are not used. How to interpret these facts? It is self-evident that "circular reaction," in Baldwin's sense of the term, could not yet be involved, that is to say, the repetition of a behavior pattern acquired or in the process of being acquired, and of behavior directed by the object to which it tends. Here it is only a matter of reflex and not acquired movements, and of sensibility connected with the reflex itself and not with the external objective. Nevertheless the mechanism is comparable to it from the purely functional point of view. It is thus very clear, in Observation 9, that the slightest excitation can set in motion not only a reflex reaction but a succession of seven reactions. Without forming any hypothesis on the way of conserving this excitation, or *a fortiori,* without wanting to transform this repetition into intentional or mnemonic behavior, one is compelled to state that, in such a case, there is a tendency toward repetition, or, in objective terms, cumulative repetition.

This need for repetition is only one aspect of a more general process which we can qualify as assimilation. The tendency of the reflex being to reproduce itself, it incorporates into itself every object capable of fulfilling the function of excitant. Two distinct phenomena must be mentioned here, both equally significant from this particular point of view.

The first is what we may call "generalizing assimilation," that is to say, the incorporation of increasingly varied objects into the reflex schema. When, for example, the child is hungry but not sufficiently so to give way to rage and to crying, and his lips have been excited by some accidental contact, we witness the formation of this kind of behavior pattern, so important due to its own future developments and the innumerable analogous cases which we shall observe in connection with other schemata. Thus, according to chance contacts, the child, from the first two weeks of life, sucks his fingers, the fingers extended to him, his pillow, quilt, bedclothes, etc.; consequently he assimilates these objects to the activity of the reflex.

To be sure, we do not claim, when speaking of "generalizing" assimilation, that the newborn child begins by distinguishing a particular object (the mother's breast) and subsequently applies to other objects the discoveries he has made about this first one. In other words, we do not ascribe to the nursling conscious and intentional generalization with regard to transition from the particular to the general, especially as generalization, in itself intelligent, never begins by such a transition but always proceeds from the undifferentiated schema to the individual and to the general, combined and complementary. We simply maintain that, without any awareness of individual objects or of general laws, the newborn child at once incorporates into the global schema of sucking a number of increasingly varied objects, whence the generalizing aspect of this process of assimilation. But is it not playing on words to translate a fact so simple into the language of assimilation? Would it not suffice to say "the setting in motion of a reflex by a class of analogous excitants?" And, if one sticks to the term assimilation, must the conclusion then be reached that the nonhabitual excitants of any reflex (for example the aggregate of objects capable of setting in motion the palpebral reflex when they approach the eye) give rise to an identical phenomenon of generalizing assimilation? There is nothing to it. What does present a particular and truly psychological problem, in the case of the sucking reflex, is that the assimilation of objects to its activity will gradually be generalized until, at the stage of acquired circular reactions and even at the stage of intentional movements, it gives birth to a very complex and strong schema. From the end of the second month the child will suck his thumb systematically (with acquired coördination and not by chance), then at nearly five months his hands will carry all objects to his mouth and he will end by using these behavior patterns to recognize bodies and even to compose the first form of space (Stern's "buccal space"). It is thus certain that the first assimilations relating to sucking, even if they reveal a lack of differentiation between contact with the breast and contact with other objects, are not simple confusion destined to disappear with progress in nutrition, but constitute the point of departure for increasingly complex assimilations.

How to interpret this generalizing assimilation? The sucking reflex can be conceived as a global schema of coördinated movements which, if it is accompanied by awareness, certainly does not give rise to perception of objects or even of definite sensorial pictures but simply to an awareness of attitudes with at most some sensorimotor integration connected with the sensibility of the lips and mouth. Now this schema, due to the fact that it lends itself to repetitions and to cumulative use, is not limited to functioning under compulsion by a fixed excitant, external or internal, but functions in a way for itself. In other words, the child does not only suck in order to eat but also to elude hunger, to prolong the excitation of the meal, etc., and lastly, he sucks for the sake of sucking. It is in this sense that the object incorporated into the sucking schema is actually assimilated to the activity of this schema. The object sucked is to be conceived, not as nourishment for the organism in general, but, so to speak, as aliment for the very activity of sucking, according to its various forms. From the point of view of awareness, if there is awareness, such assimilation is at first lack of differentiation and not at first true generalization, but from the point of view of action, it is a generalizing extension of the schema which foretells (as has just been seen) later and much more important generalizations.

But, apart from this generalizing assimilation, another assimilation must be noted from the two first weeks of life, which we can call "recognitory assimilation." This second form seems inconsistent with the preceding one; actually it only reveals progress over the other, however slight. What we have just said regarding the lack of differentiation which characterizes generalizing assimilation is, in effect, true only with respect to states of slight hunger or of satiety. But it is enough that the child be very hungry for him to try to eat and thus to distinguish the nipple from the rest. This search and this selectivity seem to us to imply the beginning of differentiation in the global schema of sucking, and consequently a beginning of recognition, a completely practical and motor recognition, needless to say, but sufficient to be called recognitory assimilation. Let us examine, from this point of view, the way in which the child rediscovers the nipple. Ever since the third day (Obs. 3), Laurent seems to distinguish the nipple from the surrounding teguments; he tries to nurse and not merely to suck. From the tenth day (Obs. 4), we observe the alacrity with which he rejects the eider-down quilt or the coverlet which he began to suck, in order to search for something more substantial. Furthermore, his reaction to his father's index finger (Obs. 6) could not be more definite: disappointment and crying. Lastly, the gropings on the breast itself (Obs. 5 and 8) also reveal selectivity. How is this kind of recognition to be explained?

Of course there could be no question, either here or in connection with generalizing assimilation, of the recognition of an "object" for the obvious reason that there is nothing in the states of consciousness of a newborn child which could enable him to contrast an external universe with an internal universe. Supposing that there are given simultaneously visual sensations (simple vision of lights without forms or depth), acoustic sensations and a tactile-gustatory and kinesthetic sensibility connected with the sucking reflex, it is evident that such a complexus would in no way be sufficient to constitute awareness of objects: the latter implies, as we shall see,[6] characteristically intellectual operations, necessary to secure the permanence of form and substance. Neither could there be a question of purely perceptive recognition or recognition of sensorial images presented by the external world, although such recognition considerably precedes the elaboration of objects (recognizing a person, a toy or a linen

6 Volume II, *La Construction du Réel chez l'Enfant.*

cloth simply on "presentation" and before having a permanent concept of it). If, to the observer, the breast which the nursling is about to take is external to the child and constitutes an image separate from him, to the newborn child, on the contrary, there can only exist awareness of attitudes, of emotions, or sensations of hunger and of satisfaction. Neither sight nor hearing yet gives rise to perceptions independent of these general reactions. As H. Wallon has effectively demonstrated, external influences only have meaning in connection with the attitudes they arouse. When the nursling differentiates between the nipple and the rest of the breast, fingers, or other objects, he does not recognize either an object or a sensorial picture but simply rediscovers a sensorimotor and particular postural complex (sucking and swallowing combined) among several analogous complexes which constitute his universe and reveal a total lack of differentiation between subject and object. In other words, this elementary recognition consists, in the strictest sense of the word, of "assimilation" of the whole of the data present in a definite organization which has already functioned and only gives rise to real discrimination due to its past functioning. But this suffices to explain in which respect repetition of the reflex leads by itself to recognitory assimilation which, albeit entirely practical, constitutes the beginning of knowledge.[7] More precisely, repetition of the reflex leads to a general and generalizing assimilation of objects to its activity, but, due to the varieties which gradually enter this activity (sucking for its own sake, to stave off hunger, to eat, etc.), the schema of assimilation becomes differentiated and, in the most important differentiated cases, assimilation becomes recognitory.

In conclusion, assimilation belonging to the adaptation reflex appears in three forms: cumulative repetition, generalization of the activity with incorporation of new objects to it, and

[7] Let us repeat that we do not claim to specify the states of consciousness which accompany this assimilation. Whether these states are purely emotional or affective, connected with the postures accompanying sucking, or whether there exists at first conscious sensorial and kinesthetic discrimination, we could not decide by studying behavior of the first two or three weeks. What this behavior simply reveals is the groping and the discernment which characterizes the use of the reflex, and these are the two fundamental facts which authorize us to speak of psychological assimilation at this primitive stage.

finally, motor recognition. But, in the last analysis, these three forms are but one: The reflex must be conceived as an organized totality whose nature it is to preserve itself by functioning and consequently to function sooner or later for its own sake (repetition) while incorporating into itself objects propitious to this functioning (generalized assimilation) and discerning situations necessary to certain special modes of its activity (motor recognition). We shall see—and this is the sole purpose of this analysis—that these processes are again found, with the unwedging accounted for by the progressive complexity of the structures, in the stages of acquired circular reactions, of the first voluntary schemata and of truly intelligent behavior patterns.

The progressive adaptation of the reflex schemata, therefore, presupposes their *organization*. In physiology this truth is trite. Not only does the reflex arc as such presuppose an organization but, in the animal not undergoing laboratory experimentation, every reflex system constitutes in itself an organized totality. According to Graham Brown's theories, the simple reflex is, in effect, to be considered as a product of differentiation. From the psychological point of view, on the other hand, there is too great a tendency to consider a reflex, or even a complex instinctive act such as sucking, to be a summation of movements with, eventually, a succession of conscious states juxtaposed, and not as a real totality. But two essential circumstances induce us to consider the sucking act as already constituting psychic organization: The fact that sooner or later this act reveals a meaning, and the fact that it is accompanied by directed searching.

Concerning the meanings, we have seen how much sucking acts vary according to whether the newborn child is hungry and tries to nurse, or sucks in order to calm himself, or whether in a way he plays at sucking. It seems as though they have a meaning for the nursling himself. The increasing calm which succeeds a storm of crying and weeping as soon as the child is in position to take nourishment and to seek the nipple is sufficient evidence that, if awareness exists at all, such awareness is from the beginning awareness of meaning. But one meaning is necessarily relative to other meanings, even on the elementary plane of simple motor recognitions.

Furthermore, that organization exists is substantiated by the fact that there is directed search. The precocious searching of the child in contact with the breast, in spite of being commonplace, is a remarkable thing. Such searching, which is the beginning of accommodation and assimilation, must be conceived, from the point of view of organization, as the first manifestation of a duality of desire and satisfaction, consequently of value and reality, of complete totality and incomplete totality, a duality which is to reappear on all planes of future activity and which the entire evolution of the mind will try to abate, even though it is destined to be emphasized unceasingly.

Such are, from the dual point of view of adaptation and organization, the first expressions of psychological life connected with hereditary physiological mechanisms. This survey, though schematic, we believe suffices to show how the psyche prolongs purely reflex organization while depending on it. The physiology of the organism furnishes a hereditary mechanism which is already completely organized and virtually adapted but has never functioned. Psychology begins with the use of this mechanism. This use does not in any way change the mechanism itself, contrary to what may be observed in the later stages (acquisition of habits, of understanding, etc.). It is limited to strengthening it and to making it function without integrating it to new organizations which go beyond it. But within the limits of this functioning there is room for a historical development which marks precisely the beginning of psychological life. This development undoubtedly admits of a physiological explanation: if the reflex mechanism is strengthened by use or decays through lack of use, this is surely because coördinations are made or unmade by virtue of the laws of reflex activity. But a physiological explanation of this kind does not exclude the psychological point of view which we have taken. In effect, if, as is probable, states of awareness accompany a reflex mechanism as complicated as that of the sucking instinct, these states of awareness have an internal history. The same state of awareness could not twice reproduce itself identically. If it reproduces itself it is by acquiring in addition some new quality of what has already been seen, etc., consequently some meaning. But if, by chance, no state of awareness yet occurred, one could nevertheless speak of behavior or of behavior patterns, given, on the one hand, the *sui generis* character of their development and, on the other, their continuity with those of subsequent stages. We shall state this in precise terms in our conclusion.

The true character of these behavior patterns involves the individual utilization of experience. In so far as the reflex is a hereditary mechanism it perhaps constitutes a racial utilization of experience. That is a biological problem of which we have already spoken (Introduction, §3) and which, while of highest interest to the psychologist, cannot be solved by his particular methods. But, inasmuch as it is a mechanism giving rise to use, and consequently a sort of experimental trial, the sucking reflex presupposes, in addition to heredity, an individual utilization of experience. This is the crucial fact which permits the incorporation of such a behavior pattern into the realm of psychology, whereas a simple reflex, unsubordinated to the need for use or experimental trial as a function of the environment (sneezing for example) is of no interest to us. Of what does this experimental trial consist? An attempt can be made to define it without subordinating this analysis to any hypothesis concerning the kinds of states of consciousness which eventually accompany such a process. Learning connected with the reflex or instinctive mechanism is distinguished from the attainments due to habits or intelligence by the fact that it retains nothing external to the mechanism itself. A habit, such as that of a 2- or 3-month-old baby who opens his mouth on seeing an object, presupposes a mnemonic fixation related to this object. A tactile-motor schema is formed according to the variations of the object and this schema alone explains the uniformity of the reaction. In the same way the acquisition of an intellectual operation (counting, for instance) implies memory of the objects themselves or of experiments made with the objects. In both cases, therefore, something external to the initial mechanism of the act in question is retained. On the other hand, the baby who learns to suck retains nothing external to the act of sucking; he undoubtedly bears no trace either of the objects or the sensorial pictures on which later attempts have supervened. He merely records the series of attempts as simple acts which condition each other. When he recognizes the nipple, this does not involve recognition of a thing or of an image but rather the assimilation of one sensori-motor and postural complex to another. If the experimental trial involved in sucking presupposes environment and experience, since no functional use is possible without contact with the environment, this is a matter of a very special kind of experimental trial, of an autoapprenticeship to some extent and not of an actual acquisition. This is why, if these first psychological behavior patterns transcend pure physiology—just as the individual use of a hereditary mechanism transcends heredity—they still depend on them to the highest degree.

But the great psychological lesson of these beginnings of behavior is that, within the limits we have just defined, the experimental trial of a reflex mechanism already entails the most complicated accommodations, assimilations and individual organizations. Accommodation exists because, even without retaining anything from the environment as such, the reflex mechanism needs the environment. Assimilation exists because, through its very use, it incorporates to itself every object capable of supplying it with what it needs and discriminates even these objects thanks to the identity of the differential attitudes they elicit. Finally, organization exists, inasmuch as organization is the internal aspect of this progressive adaptation. The sequential uses of the reflex mechanism constitute organized totalities and the gropings and searchings apparent from the beginnings of this period of experimental trial are oriented by the very structure of these totalities.

But if these behavior patterns transcend pure physiology only to the very slight extent in which individual use has a history independent of the machine predetermined by heredity (to the point where it could seem almost metaphorical to characterize them as "behavior patterns" as we have done here), they nevertheless seem to us to be of essential importance to the rest of mental development. In effect, the functions of accommodation, of assimilation and of organization which we have just described in connection with the use of a reflex mechanism will be found once more in the course of subsequent stages and will acquire increasing importance. In a certain sense, we shall even see that the more complicated and refined intellectual structures become, the more this functional nucleus will constitute the essence of these very structures.

§3. ASSIMILATION: BASIC FACT OF PSYCHIC LIFE.— In studying the use of reflexes we have ascertained the existence of a fundamental tendency whose manifestations we shall rediscover at each new stage of intellectual development: the tendency toward repetition of behavior patterns and toward the utilization of external objects in the framework of such repetition. This assimilation—simultaneously reproductive, generalizing, and recognitory—constitutes the basis of the functional use which we have described with respect to sucking. Assimilation is therefore indispensable to reflex accommodation. Moreover, it is the dynamic expression of the static fact of organization. From this double point of view it emerges as a basic fact, the psychological analysis of which must yield genetic conclusions.

Three circumstances induce us to consider assimilation the fundamental fact of psychic development. The first is that assimilation constitutes a process common to organized life and mental activity and is therefore an idea common to physiology and psychology. In effect, whatever the secret mechanism of biological assimilation may be, it is an empirical fact that an organ develops while functioning (by means of a certain useful exercise and fatigue). But when the organ in question affects the external behavior of the subject, this phenomenon of functional assimilation presents a physiological aspect inseparable from the psychological aspect; its parts are physiological whereas the reaction of the whole may be called psychic. Let us take for example the eye which develops under the influence of the use of vision (perception of lights, forms, etc.). From the physiological point of view it can be stated that light is nourishment for the eye (in particular in primitive cases of cutaneous sensibility in the lower invertebrates, in whom the eye amounts to an accumulation of pigment dependent on environing sources of light). Light is absorbed and assimilated by sensitive tissues and this action brings with it a correlative development of the organs affected. Such a process undoubtedly presupposes an aggregate of mechanisms whose start may be very complex. But, if we adhere to a global description—that of behavior and consequently of psychology— the things seen constitute nourishment essential to the eye since it is they which impose the continuous use to which the organs owe their development. The eye needs light images just as the whole body needs chemical nourishment, energy, etc. Among the aggregate of external realities assimilated by the organism there are some which are incorporated into the parts of the physico-chemical mechanisms, while others simply serve as functional and general nourishment. In the first case, there is physiological assimilation, whereas the second may be called psychological as-similation. But the phenomenon is the same in both cases: the universe is embodied in the activity of the subject.

In the second place, assimilation reveals the primitive fact generally conceded to be the most elementary one of psychic life: repetition. How can we explain why the individual, on however high a level of behavior, tries to reproduce every experi-ence he has lived? The thing is only comprehensible if the be-havior which is repeated presents a functional meaning, that is to say, assumes a value for the subject himself. But whence comes this value? From functioning as such. Here again, functional as-similation is manifest as the basic fact.

In the third place, the concept of assimilation from the very first embodies in the mechanism of repetition the essential ele-ment which distinguishes activity from passive habit: the co-ördination of the new with the old which foretells the process of judgment. In effect, the reproduction characteristic of the act of assimilation always implies the incorporation of an actual fact into a given schema, this schema being constituted by the repeti-tion itself. In this way assimilation is the greatest of all intellec-tual mechanisms and once more constitutes, in relation to them, the truly basic fact.

But could not this description be simplified by eliminating a concept which is so fraught with meaning that it might seem equivocal? In his remarkable essays on functional psychology Claparède[8] chooses without adding anything as a point of de-

[8] See *l'Education fonctionnelle*, Delachaux and Niestlé, 1931.

parture of all mental activity the very fact of need. How can it be explained that certain behavior patterns give rise to spontaneous repetition? How does it happen that useful acts reproduce themselves? Because, says Claparède, they answer a need. Needs thus mark the transition between organic life, from which they emanate, and psychic life, of which they constitute the motive power.

The great advantage of this phraseology is that it is much simpler than that of assimilation. Besides, on the basis of what Claparède maintains, it is very difficult not to agree with him. Since need is the concrete expression of what we have called the process of assimilation, we could not raise doubts concerning the ground for this conception to which we personally owe much. But the question is to know whether, precisely because of its simplicity, it does not bring up initial problems which the concept of assimilation permits us to refer to biological study. There seems to us to be two difficulties.

In the first place, if need as such is the motive power for all activity, how does it direct the movements necessary to its satisfaction? With admirable analytical acuteness, Claparède himself has raised the question. Not only, he says, does one not understand why the pursuit of a goal coördinates useful actions, but furthermore, one does not see how, when one means fails, others are attempted. It transpires, in effect, especially when acquired associations are superimposed on the reflex, that an identical need releases a succession of different behavior patterns, but always directed toward the same end. What is the instrument of this selection and of this coördination of advantageous reactions?

It is self-evident that it would be useless to try to resolve these fundamental problems now. But does not the question arise because one begins by dissociating the need from the act in its totality? The basic needs do not exist, in effect, prior to the motivating cycles which permit them to be gratified. They appear during functioning. One could not say, therefore, that they precede repetition: they result from it as well, in an endless circle. For example empty sucking or any similar practice constitutes training which augments need as well as the reverse. From the psychological point of view, need must not be conceived as being independent of global functioning of which it is only an indication. From the physiological point of view, moreover, need presupposes an organization in "mobile balance" of which it simply indicates a transitory imbalance. In both kinds of terminology, need is thus the expression of a totality momentarily incomplete and tending toward reconstituting itself, that is to say, precisely what we call a cycle or a schema of assimilation: Need manifests the necessity of the organism or an organ to use an external datum in connection with its functioning. The basic fact is therefore not need, but the schemata of assimilation of which it is the subjective aspect. Henceforth it is perhaps a pseudo question to ask how need directs useful movements. It is because these movements are already directed that need sets them in motion. In other words, organized movements, ready for repetition, and need itself constitute only one whole. True, this conception, very clear with regard to the reflex or any innate organization, ceases to seem so with respect to acquired associations. But perhaps the difficulty comes from taking literally the term "associations," whereas the fact of assimilation makes it possible to explain how every new schema results from a differentiation and a complication of earlier schemata and not of an association between elements given in an isolated state. This hypothesis even leads to an understanding of how a sole need can set in motion a series of successive efforts. On the one hand, all assimilation is generalizing and, on the other hand, the schemata are capable of intercoördination through reciprocal assimilation as well as being able to function alone. (See stages IV–VI concerning this.)

A second difficulty seems to us to appear when one considers need as the basic fact of psychic life. Needs are supposed, in such a case, to insure the transition between organism and psyche; they constitute in some way the physiological motive power for mental activity. But if certain corporeal needs play this role in a large number of lower behavior patterns (such as the search for food in animal psychology), in the young child the principal needs are of a functional category. The functioning of the organs engenders, through its very existence, a psychic need *sui generis,* or rather a series of vicarious needs whose complexity transcends, from the very beginning, simple organic satisfaction. Furthermore, the more the intelligence develops and strengthens, the more the assimilation of reality to functioning itself is transformed into real comprehension, the principal motive power of intellectual activity thus becoming the need to incorporate things into the subject's schemata. This vicariousness of needs, which unceasingly transcend themselves to go beyond the purely organic plane, seems to show us anew that the basic fact is not need as such but rather the act of assimilation, which embodies in one whole functional need, repetition and that coördination between subject and object which foretells discrepancy and judgment.

To be sure, invoking the concept of assimilation does not constitute an explanation of assimilation itself. Psychology can only begin with the description of a basic fact without being able to explain it. The ideal of absolute deduction could only lead to verbal explanation. To renounce this temptation is to choose as a principle an elementary fact amenable to biological treatment simultaneously with psychological analysis. Assimilation answers this. Explanation of this fact is in the realm of biology. The existence of an organized totality which is preserved while assimilating the external world raises, in effect, the whole problem of life itself. But, as the higher cannot be reduced to the lower without adding something, biology will not succeed in clarifying the question of assimilation without taking into account its psychological aspect. At a certain level life organization and mental organization only constitute, in effect, one and the same thing.

CHAPTER II

THE SECOND STAGE:

The First Acquired Adaptations and the Primary Circular Reaction

The hereditary adaptations are doubled, at a given moment, by adaptations which are not innate to which they are subordinated little by little. In other words, the reflex processes are progressively integrated into cortical activity. These new adaptations constitute what are ordinarily called "acquired associations," habits or even conditioned reflexes, to say nothing of intentional movements characteristic of a third stage. Intent, which is doubtless imminent to the more primitive levels of psychological assimilation, could not, in effect, be aware of itself, and thus differentiate behavior, before assimilation through "secondary" schemata, that is to say, before the behavior patterns born of the exercise of prehension and contemporaneous with the first actions brought to bear on things. We can therefore ascribe to the present stage intentional movements as the higher limit and the first nonhereditary adaptations as the lower limit.

In truth it is extremely precarious to specify when acquired adaptation actually begins in contradistinction to hereditary adaptation. From a theoretical point of view, the following criterion can be adopted: in every behavior pattern of which the adaptation is determined by heredity, assimilation and accommodation form one entity and remain undifferentiated, whereas with acquired adaptation they begin to dissociate themselves. In other words, hereditary adaptation does not admit of any apprenticeship outside its own use, whereas acquired adaptation implies an apprenticeship related to the new conditions of the external environment simultaneously with an incorporation of the objects to the schemata thus differentiated. But if one proceeds from theory to the interpretation of particular facts, great difficulties arise in distinguishing real acquisition from simple preformed coördination.

In effect, how is it possible to have a clear idea of the moment whence there is retention of some other condition external to the reflex mechanism itself? In the use of the reflex, as we have seen, there is only fixation of the mechanism as such, and it is in this respect that accommodation of a hereditary schema, while presupposing experience and contact with the environment, forms only one entity with assimilation, that is to say, with the functional use of this schema. At a given moment, on the other hand, the child's activity retains something external to itself, that is to say, it is transformed into a function of experience; in this respect there is acquired accommodation. For instance, when the child systematically sucks his thumb, no longer due to chance contacts but through coördination between hand and mouth, this may be called acquired accommodation. Neither the reflexes of the mouth nor of the hand can be provided such coördination by heredity (there is no instinct to suck the thumb!) and experience alone explains its formation. But if this is clear with regard to that kind of behavior pattern, in how many others is it impossible to draw a clear boundary between the pure reflex and the utilization of experience? The multiple aspects of visual accommodation, for example, comprise an inseparable mixture of reflex use and true acquisition.

There is the same difficulty from the point of view of assimilation. Psychological assimilation characteristic of the reflex consists, as we have seen, in a cumulative repetition with progressive incorporation of the objects into the cycle which has thus been reproduced. But nothing, in such a behavior pattern, yet implies that it is directed by the new results to which it leads. To be sure, in the sucking act, there is from the beginning directed searching and, in case of hunger, success alone gives meaning to the series of gropings. But the result sought yields nothing new in relation to the primitive sensorimotor field of the reflex itself. On the contrary, in the realm of acquired adaptation toward a new result (new either through the character of the sensorial pictures which define it, or through the procedures set in motion to obtain it), this directs repetition. Whereas, in the reflex, assimilation only formed one entity with accommodation, henceforth the reproduction of the new act, or the assimilation of objects to the schema of this act, constitutes a process distinct from accommodation itself. Such a process can be very slightly differentiated when the acquired adaptation merely prolongs the reflex adaptation, but it is the more distinct from accommodation as the new act is more complex. Thus it is that, in the acquisition of prehension, it is one thing to repeat indefinitely a maneuver which has been successful and quite another thing to attempt to grasp an object in a new situation. The repetition of the cycle which has been actually acquired or is in the process of being acquired is what J. M. Baldwin has called the "circular reaction": this behavior pattern will constitute for us the principle of assimilation *sui generis* characteristic of this second stage. But if such a distinction between the simple repetition of the reflex and the "circular reaction" is theoretically clear, it goes without saying that here again the greatest difficulties confront concrete analysis.

Now let us proceed to examining the facts, first grouping them according to separate and distinct realms of activity.

§1. ACQUIRED SUCKING HABITS.—Superimposed on the reflex behavior patterns, which we have described in the first chapter, are, from the second or third month, certain forms of sucking which are unquestionably new. We shall begin by describing the two principal circular reactions—the systematic protrusion of the tongue (later with the action of saliva, of the lips, etc.), and the sucking of the thumb. These two activities will provide us with the type of that which is spontaneous acquired habit, with active assimilation and accommodation. Thereupon we shall discuss some facts concerning accommodation, commonly called "association transfers" or "sensorimotor associations" (setting in motion of sucking by various signals: position, noises, optical signals, etc.) and we shall see that these partial accommodations, however mechanical and passive they may appear to be, in reality constitute simple, isolated and abstract links of the

cycles inherent in circular reaction. Finally we shall speak of
certain coördinations between sucking and vision.

Here are examples of the first group of facts (circular reactions):

Observation 11.—Laurent at 0;0 (30) stays awake without crying, gazing ahead with wide open eyes. He makes sucking-like movements almost continually, opening and closing his mouth in slow rhythm, his tongue constantly moving. At certain moments his tongue, instead of remaining inside his lips, licks the lower lip; the sucking recommences with renewed ardor.

Two interpretations are possible. Either at such times there is searching for food and then the protrusion of the tongue is merely a reflex inherent in the mechanism of sucking and swallowing, or else this marks the beginning of circular reaction. It seems, for the time being, that both are present. Sometimes protrusion of the tongue is accompanied by disordered movements of the arms and leads to impatience and anger. In such a case there is obviously a seeking to suck, and disappointment. Sometimes, on the other hand, protrusion of the tongue is accompanied by slow, rhythmical movements of the arms and an expression of contentment. In this case the tongue comes into play through circular reaction.

Observation 12.—At 0;1 (3) Laurent puts out his tongue several times in succession. He is wide awake, motionless, hardly moves his arms and makes no sucking-like movements; his mouth is partly open and he keeps passing his tongue over the lower lip.—At 0;1 (5) Laurent begins sucking-like movements and then the sucking is gradually replaced by the preceding behavior.—At 0;1 (6) he plays with his tongue, sometimes by licking his lower lip, sometimes by sliding his tongue between his lips and gums.—The following days this behavior is frequently repeated and always with the same expression of satisfaction.

Observation 13.—At 0;1 (24) Lucienne plays with her tongue, passing it over her lower lip and licking her lips unceasingly. Observation is made of the existence of a habit acquired a certain number of days previous. The behavior is extended to sucking the thumb and beyond.

Observation 14.—During the second half of the second month, that is to say, after having learned to suck his thumb, Laurent continues to play with his tongue and to suck, but intermittently. On the other hand, his skill increases. Thus, at 0;1 (20) I notice he grimaces while placing his tongue between gums and lips and in bulging his lips, as well as making a clapping sound when quickly closing his mouth after these exercises.

Observation 15.—During the third month he adds to the protrusion of his tongue and finger sucking new circular reactions involving the mouth. Thus from 0;2 (18) Laurent plays with his saliva, letting it accumulate within his half-open lips and then abruptly swallowing it. About the same period he makes sucking-like movements, with or without putting out his tongue, changing in various ways the position of his lips; he bends and contracts his lower lip, etc.—These exercises subsequently become increasingly varied and do not deserve more detailed examination from the point of view we have taken in this study.

Finger sucking also gives rise to evident acquisition.

Observation 16.—At 0;1 (1) Laurent is held by his nurse in an almost vertical position, shortly before the meal. He is very hungry and tries to nurse with his mouth open and continuous rotations of the head. His arms describe big rapid movements and constantly knock against his face. Twice, when his hand was laid on his right cheek, Laurent turned his head and tried to grasp his fingers with his mouth. The first time he failed and succeeded the second. But the movements of his arms are not coördinated with those of his head; the hand escapes while the mouth tries to maintain contact. Subsequently, however, he catches his thumb; his whole body is then immobilized, his right hand happens to grasp his left arm and his left hand presses against his mouth. Then a long pause ensues during which Laurent sucks his left thumb in the same way in which he nurses, with greed and passion (pantings, etc.).

There is therefore a complete analogy with Observation 7 of Chapter I. But it is more firmly established that nothing external forces the child to keep his hand in his mouth; the arms are not immobilized by the reclining position of the subject but by a spontaneous attitude. Nevertheless the fact observed lends itself to two interpretations: either, as may be the case from the first consecutive days after birth, sucking immobilizes the whole body and consequently the hands—the arms remain tight against the torso while the newborn child nurses, and it is conceivable that it may be the same when he sucks his thumb which he has found by chance—or else there is direct coördination between sucking and the arm movements. Subsequent observations seem to show that actual behavior foretells this coördination.

Observation 17.—At 0;1 (2) Laurent in his crib cries with hunger. He is lifted to an almost vertical position. His behavior then goes through four sequential phases quite distinct from one another. He begins by calming himself and tries to suck while turning his head from left to right and back again while his arms flourish without direction. Then (second phase) the arms, instead of describing movements of maximum breadth, seem to approach his mouth. Several times each hand brushes his lips; the right hand presses against the child's cheek and clasps it for a few seconds. Meanwhile the mouth is wide open and unceasingly attempts to grasp something. The left thumb is then caught and the two arms become rigid, the right arm against the chest under the left arm which is held by the mouth. During a third phase, the arms again wave about in space without direction, the left thumb leaving the mouth after a few minutes. During this time the child becomes angry, his head thrown back and his cries alternating with attempts to suck. Finally a fourth phase begins during which the hands again approach the mouth which tries to seize the fingers which touch it. These last attempts meet with no success and crying ensues.

Can coördination be mentioned this time? Each of these phases finds its parallel in the behavior of the preceding weeks: from the first days of life babies are seen slashing their faces with their fingers while the mouth seems to try to grasp something. Nevertheless the sequence of the four phases seems to indicate a beginning of a connection between the movements of the arms and the sucking attempts.

Observation 18.—At 0;1 (3) Laurent (same position) does not seem to reveal any coördination between hands and mouth before nursing. On the other hand, after a meal, when he was still wide awake and trying to suck, his arms, instead of gesticulating aimlessly, constantly move toward his mouth. To be more precise, it has occurred to me several times that the chance contact of hand and mouth set in motion the directing of the latter toward the former and that then (but only then), the hand tries to return to the mouth. Laurent succeeded in sucking his fingers four times, his hand and arms immediately becoming immobilized. But that has never lasted more than a few seconds.—The evening of the same day Laurent, after nursing, remained wide awake and continued to try to suck, interspersing his attempts with vigorous cries. I then grasped his right arm and held it until his mouth began to suck his hand. As soon as the lips were in contact with the hand, the arms stopped resisting and remained still for several moments. This phenomenon has been confirmed since I made the experiment—since 0;0 (15)—but as a rule the position is not maintained. Only when the thumb is sucked does immobility result (see Obs. 7 and 16). This time, on the contrary, the arm remained immobile for a moment, although the back of the hand only was in contact with the lips; the latter obviously tried to explore the whole hand. After a moment, the hand lost the contact but rediscovered it. It is no longer the mouth that seeks the hand, but the hand which reaches for the mouth. Thirteen times in succession I have been able to observe the hand go back into the mouth. There is no longer any doubt that coördination exists. The mouth may be seen opening and the hand directing itself toward it simultaneously. Even the failures are significant. It thus happens that the fingers are planted on the cheek while the open mouth is ready to receive them.

Observation 19.—At 0;1 (4) after the 6 P.M. meal Laurent is wide awake (as was not the case at the preceding meals) and not completely satisfied. First he makes vigorous sucking-like movements, then his right hand may be seen approaching his mouth, touching his lower lip and finally being grasped. But as only the index finger was grasped, the hand fell out again. Shortly afterward it returned. This time the thumb was in the mouth while the index finger was placed between the gums and the upper lip. The hand then moves 5 cm. away from the mouth only to reënter it; now the thumb is grasped and the other fingers remain outside. Laurent then is motionless and sucks vigorously, drooling so much that after a few moments he is removed. A fourth time the hand approaches and three fingers enter the mouth. The hand leaves again and reënters a fifth time. As the thumb has again been grasped, sucking is resumed. I then remove the hand and place it near his waist. Laurent seems to give up sucking and gazes ahead, contented and satisfied. But after a few minutes the lips move and the hand approaches them again. This time there is a series of setbacks; the fingers are placed on the chin and lower lip. The index finger enters the mouth twice (consequently the sixth and seventh time this has succeeded). The eighth time the hand enters the mouth, the thumb alone is retained and sucking continues. I again remove the hand. Again lip movements cease, new attempts ensue, success results for the ninth and tenth time, after which the experiment is interrupted.

Observation 20.—At 0;1 (5) and 0;1 (6) Laurent tries to catch his thumb as soon as he awakes but is unsuccessful while he is lying on his back. His hand taps his face without finding his mouth. When he is vertical, however (held by the waist, his arms and torso free), he quickly finds his lips.—At 0;1 (7) on the other hand, I find him sucking his thumb while he is lying down. But it keeps escaping him because it does not go far into his mouth but between the upper lip and the gum. Progress ensues, however, because the thumb, after leaving the mouth, returns to it several times in succession. Unfortunately, between these successful attempts, Laurent taps his nose, cheeks and eyes. Finally he becomes angry as the result of an unsuccessful attempt.—The following days, coordination is accomplished. At 0;1 (9), for example, Laurent sucks his thumb while lying on his back. I take it out of his mouth and, several times in succession, he puts it back into his mouth again almost immediately (having at most groped between nose and mouth) and only grasping the thumb, his other fingers remaining outside the mouth.

Observation 21.—At the end of the second month Laurent sucked his left thumb as well as his right. At 0;1 (21), for example, while lying on his left side, he tries to suck his left thumb. After failure due to his position, he raises his right arm. Unable to grasp the thumb he then turns to the right, manages to lie on his back and continues searching. He almost reaches his right thumb but, happening to fail, he returns to his left hand and directs it toward his mouth. Failing once more, he again turns to the right and this time succeeds in seizing the right thumb.—This example reveals that Laurent is equally adept at sucking both thumbs. Subsequently, however, he became more accustomed to sucking the left thumb so that he injured it slightly and it had to be bandaged with his hand attached. After some anger and groping he then resumed sucking his right thumb (0; (7) and the days following).

Observation 22.—During the third month thumb sucking grew less important to Laurent due to the pressure of new interests, visual, auditory, etc. From 0;2 (15) I note that Laurent now sucks his thumb only to assuage his hunger and chiefly to put himself to sleep. This is an interesting example of specialization of the habit, also observable in Jacqueline. When Laurent cries his thumb goes to the rescue. At 0;2 (19) I note that he even closes his eyes and turns on his right side to go to sleep at the moment his thumb touched his lips.—During the third month the thumb is opposite the fingers at the moment sucking takes place. At the end of the second month Laurent began by sucking the back of his hand and of his fingers, or several fingers together, or the thumb and index finger, before finding the thumb alone. During the third month, on the contrary, the thumb gradually placed itself opposite the other fingers and Laurent managed to grasp it at the first attempt and suck it alone.

Observation 23.—In the case of Lucienne who did not undergo the sort of training to which I subjected Laurent, the coördination between arm movements and sucking was only definitely established at 0;2 (2). At 0;1 (25) and 0;1 (26) the hands touch the mouth constantly but I still observe Lucienne's incapacity to hold her thumb between her lips for a long time and above all to find it again once it has left. On the other hand, at 0;2 (2) I was able to make the two following observations. At 6 P.M., after the meal, her hands wandered around her mouth and she alternately sucked her fingers (chiefly the index finger), the back of her hand and her wrist. When her hand escapes her mouth it approaches it again and coördination is reëstablished. At 8 P.M. Lucienne is awakened and again sucks her fingers: her hand remains still for long moments and then the mouth opens to grasp it at the same time as the hand approaches the mouth. The following day, the same observations: coördination was reëstablished during the whole morning and for several moments in the evening. I particularly noted the following: the hand groping in the right direction, then an abrupt movement of the fingers into the mouth which was already open and motionless. The rest of the observations confirmed the fact that co-ordination had become permanent.

Observation 24.—In the case of Jacqueline the first sure signs date from 0;1 (28) and the days following. She puts her left hand in her mouth when she is very hungry, a few moments before nursing. After the meal she often puts her fingers in her mouth again, to prolong sucking. From approximately 0;4 (5) the habit becomes systematic and she must suck her thumb in order to go to sleep.

In addition it is to be noted that the objects grasped are carried to the mouth from approximately 0;3 (15).

Putting out the tongue and finger sucking thus constitute the first two examples of a behavior pattern which prolongs the functional use of the reflex (sucking-like movements), but with the acquisition of some element external to the hereditary mechanisms. The new use of the tongue seems to go beyond the simple reflex play involved in sucking. With regard to the thumb, let us repeat that no instinct to suck the fingers exists and, even if the act of bringing food to the mouth were a hereditary be-havior pattern, it is evident that the late appearance of this act indicates the interdiction of acquired associations, superimposed on ultimate reflex coördination. In characterizing these acquisi-tions it must also be noted that they imply an active element. It is not a question of associations imposed by the environment, but rather of relationships discovered and even created in the course of the child's own searchings. It is this twofold aspect of acquisition and activity which characterizes what we shall hence-forth call "circular reactions" not in the rather loose sense of the term as used by Baldwin, but in Mr. Wallon's limited sense;[1] the functional use leading to the preservation or the rediscovery of a new result.

Along with actual circular reactions sucking also gives rise to behavior patterns in which accommodation is predominant. Here are involved those acquired associations which are often called "associative transfers" when one does not wish to go so far as to speak of "conditioned reflexes." Let us first note that circular reaction brings such transfers with it. In the course of progressive coördination between sucking and hand and arm

[1] *L'enfant turbulant,* p. 85.

movements it is evident that associations are established which direct the thumb to the mouth. The contact of the fingers with the covers, with the face, lips, etc., thus serves sooner or later as a signal which directs the hand. But, outside these mnemonic acquisitions or transfers inherent in circular reaction, there are some which seem to result from single automatic training without the appearance of the element of activity characteristic of the preceding reactions. What must we think of this?

It is appropriate to recall here the fine observations of two of Charlotte Bühler's collaborators, M. Hetzer and R. Ripin,[2] on the nursling's training as a function of feeding conditions (*Ernährungssituation*). According to these authors, three stages in the child's behavior may be distinguished. The first stage comprises the first week: the nursling attempts to suck only when his lips are in contact with the breast or the bottle. This we have seen in Chapter I (§§ 1 and 2). The second stage extends from the second to the eighth or ninth week: the nursling seeks the breast as soon as he finds himself in situations which regularly precede the meal (dressing, diaper changing, a stretched-out position, etc.). Finally the third stage begins between 0;3 and 0;4 and can be recognized by the appearance of visual signals. It is enough that the child sees the bottle or the objects which remind him of the meal for him to open his mouth and cry. Let us examine separately the second and third of these behavior patterns; both of them are in the category of acquired associations, but under different headings.

The behavior patterns characteristic of these stages seem to constitute the prototype of passive association (*Signalwirkung*). Contrary to the transfers characteristic of active circular reaction, the former seem due to the pressure of external circumstances subject to repetition. But, as we shall see, this is only a probability and such accommodations presuppose an element of activity. Concerning the reality of the facts observed we obviously agree with Charlotte Bühler and her collaborators. It is certain that, at a given moment in development, relationships are established between the position of the child, tactile and

[2] H. Hetzer, and R. Ripin, *op. cit.*; and Ch. Bühler, *Kindheit und Jugend*, 3rd edition, Jema: Fischer, 1931, p. 14 f.

acoustic signals, etc., and the release of sucking movements. On the other hand, the date of the appearance of these behavior patterns as well as their interpretation both seem to us to be subjects for discussion. First, here are two observations which will clarify the meaning of our remarks:

Observation 25.—I tried to determine with respect to Laurent when there began to be association between the position of the baby and the seeking of the breast. But it seemed to me impossible to affirm the existence of the association before the second month. At 0;0 (6) and the days following, Laurent, it is true, sought to nurse as soon as he was put on the scale, the dressing table, or his mother's bed, whereas previously he sought nothing and cried in his crib. At 0;0 (9) Laurent is half asleep in his crib; he sought nothing as long as he was being carried, but as soon as he was placed on the bed he opened his mouth and turned his head from side to side with more rapid arm movements and tension of the whole body. At 0;0 (10) he no longer seeks while in his crib but as soon as he is in the nurse's arms, etc. This was his behavior until the end of the first month. But is it a matter of pure coincidence or of an actual association beteween position and sucking? It is impossible for us to decidè this question, because the facts can be interpreted quite independently from the existence of an associative transfer. It is sufficient to state, as we have done in Chapter I, how precocious sucking-like movements and the groping characteristic of the reflex are, to understand that the child will try to nurse as soon as he is neither crying, nor asleep, nor distracted by movement. In his crib he does not seek because nothing distracts him from his cries of hunger, and these cries engender others through this sort of reflex repetition of which we have already spoken; so long as he is carried he seeks nothing because the rocking motion absorbs him; but as soon as he is placed on the scale, on the dressing table where his diapers are changed, or in his nurse's or his mother's arms, he tries to suck before recommencing to cry because neither his weeping nor the excitements of motion prevent him any longer from sucking. Does this mean there is a connection between *Trinklage* and sucking? Nothing authorizes us to deny it, or to affirm it either as yet. Besides, when one knows the difficulty of establishing a conditioned reflex in animals and especially the necessity to "strengthen" it all the time in order to preserve it, one can only be prudent in invoking such a mechanism in so far as the behavior patterns of the first weeks are concerned.[3]

[3] We do not mean to deny that certain conditioned reflexes may be constituted at birth, as D. P. Marquis succeeded in proving this with babies from 3 to 10 days old by associating certain sounds with sucking reflexes

On the other hand, from the moment Laurent knows how to find his thumb (beginning of the second month), the seeking of the breast may be differentiated from the other tendencies and one thus succeeds in establishing a connection between the *Trinklage* and this seeking. Before the meal the child is only inclined to suck his fingers in the crib when he is not crying or is not too sleepy; but, as soon as he is in position to eat (in his mother's arms or on the bed, etc.) his hands lose interest, leave his mouth, and it becomes obvious that the child no longer seeks anything but the breast, that is to say, contact with food. At 0;1 (4) for instance, no experiment involving finger sucking was possible before the meal as Laurent turned his head from side to side as soon as he was in position to eat.

During the second month coördination between position and seeking the breast has made considerable progress. Thus at the end of the month Laurent only tries to nurse when he is in his mother's arms and no longer when on the dressing table.

Observation 26.—In correlation with this progressive accommodation to the situation as a whole, it seemed to us that accommodation to the breast itself made some progress during the second month and went beyond the reflex accommodation of the first weeks. We noted in Jacqueline from 0;1 (14) and in Lucienne from 0;1 (27) the natural disposition to turn the head to the correct side when the breast was changed; whereas their body's rotation should have directed the head to the outside, they themselves turned it in the direction of the breast. Such behavior does not of course imply in any way correct orientation in space; it only indicates that henceforth the child knows how to utilize the contacts with his mother's arms as signals enabling him to mark the location of the food. Now if this is the case, there is obviously acquired association, that is to say, accommodation which transcends simple reflex accommodation.

From the second month we again find the correlations observed by Charlotte Bühler and her collaborators. But do these correlations between the situation as a whole and sucking necessarily presuppose the hypothesis of the "associative transfer" ("*Signalwirkung*")?

That is a general problem to which we shall return in §5.

(*Journ. of Genet. Psychol.*, XXXIX, 1931, p. 479) and W. S. Ray was even able to provoke conditioned reflexes in the fetus (*Child Development*, III, 1932, p. 175). We only claim that, granted the difficulties of the question of conditioning which increase daily, caution compels us whenever possible to have recourse to more satisfactory explanations than those which one sometimes hopes to draw from the existence of the conditioned reflex.

Let us limit ourselves to emphasizing from now on the fact that the association acquired between the signals characteristic of the *Trinklage* and the sucking reflex was not imposed on the child in a wholly mechanical way. There is not only passive recording. Through the constant seeking which characterizes the sucking instinct it is always in connection with the efforts and gropings of the subject himself that the association is acquired. Here again let us beware of too simple a comparison with the conditioned reflex. As we understand it, if association is established between *Trinklage* and sucking, it is not through mere training, otherwise one would not see why optic signals would not also give rise to training of the same kind from the second month. It is simply that the sucking schema—that is to say, the organized totality of the movements and attitudes peculiar to sucking—comprises certain postures which extend beyond the buccal sphere. Now these attitudes are not entirely passive and sooner or later involve the compliance of the whole body: the limbs become rigid, the hands clenched, etc., as soon as the nursling adopts the position characteristic of nursing. Thenceforth the simple recall of these attitudes sets in motion the whole cycle of the sucking act because the kinesthetic sensations and postural sensibility thus released are immediately assimilated to the schema of this act. Therefore association between an independent signal and a given sensorimotor schema does not exist, nor coördination between two groups of independent schemata (as will be the case between vision and sucking, etc.), but rather the constitution and progressive enlargement of a single schema of accommodation and assimilation combined. At most can it be said, in such a case, that accommodation prevails over assimilation.

Let us now come to the most complex acquisitions pertaining to sucking (the third of the stages of Hetzer and Ripin)—the associations between sucking and vision. From the third and fourth month, according to Hetzer and Ripin, the child may be observed getting ready to eat as soon as he sees the bottle or any object connected with food. In such a behavior pattern there is no longer simple, more or less passive, association between a signal and the act but recognition of an external image and of meanings attributed to this image.

We have been able to make similar observations:

Observation 27.—Jacqueline, at 0;4 (27) and the days following, opens her mouth as soon as she is shown the bottle. She only began mixed feeding at 0;4 (12). At 0;7 (13) I note that she opens her mouth differently according to whether she is offered a bottle or a spoon.

Lucienne at 0;3 (12) stops crying when she sees her mother unfastening her dress for the meal.

Laurent too, between 0;3 (15) and 0;4 reacts to visual signals. When, after being dressed as usual just before the meal, he is put in my arms in position for nursing, he looks at me and then searches all around, looks at me again, etc.—but he does not attempt to nurse. When I place him in his mother's arms without his touching the breast, he looks at her and immediately opens his mouth wide, cries, moves about, in short reacts in a completely significant way. It is therefore sight and no longer only the position which henceforth is the signal.

Such behavior patterns are surely superior to those which are governed only by coördination between position and sucking. They imply, in effect, actual recognition of visual images and the attribution of a meaning to these images through reference to the sucking schema. Is this tantamount to saying that the bottle, etc., already constitute "objects" for the child, as Ch. Bühler maintains?[4] We would not dare to go so far.[5] Sensorial images can be recognized and endowed with meaning without by the same token acquiring the characteristics of the substantial and spatial permanence inherent in the object. But we recognize that such images are evidently perceived by the child as "external"; that is to say, they are projected in a coherent whole of images and relationships. In effect, through the very fact that for the nursling the bottle belongs to two series of schemata capable of giving rise to adaptations and functions independent of each other (vision and sucking) and through the fact that it realizes the coördination of these two schemata, it is necessarily endowed with a certain externality. On the other hand, thumb sucking does not realize this condition. Even though this sucking presupposes for the observer coördination between the move-

4 *Op. cit.*, p. 18.
5 We shall see why in the course of Volume II.

ments of the hand and those of the mouth, the thumb is at first only known by the child to the extent that it is sucked and there is no coördination between two independent schemata for the subject himself. We shall speak, therefore, in the case of the release of sucking through visual signals, of recognition as function of the coördination of two schemata of assimilation (sucking and vision).

In conclusion, the acquisitions which characterize the sucking mechanism past the stage of purely hereditary adaptations, are three in number. In the first place there is actual "circular reaction"—playing with the tongue, systematic thumb sucking, etc. This reaction constitutes an essentially active behavior pattern which prolongs the reflex use described in the first chapter but with, in addition, an acquired element of accommodation to the facts of experience. Passivity increases, on the other hand, in the accommodations which are constituted more or less automatically as a function of the external environment, but these accommodations, too, presuppose, at their point of departure, activity of the subject. Finally, the behavior is complicated by the coördination of heterogeneous schemata at the time of the recognition of the visual signals for sucking.

Without wanting to anticipate the theoretical conclusions which we shall try to draw from the facts in §5, it is possible at the beginning to ask ourselves what these three types of conduct represent from the point of view of the mechanisms of adaptation. Circular reaction is surely to be conceived as an active synthesis of assimilation and accommodation. It is assimilation to the extent that it constitutes a functional use prolonging the assimilation reflex described in the first chapter: to suck thumb or tongue is to assimilate these objects to the very activity of sucking. But circular reaction is accommodation to the extent that it realizes a new coördination, not given in the hereditary reflex mechanism. With regard to the so-called associative transfer, it is chiefly accommodation in so far as it presupposes associations suggested by the external environment. But it implies an element of assimilation of earlier circular reactions, to the extent that it proceeds by differentiation. Between its own accommodation and that of the circular reaction there is only a difference of degree: the latter is more active and the former more passive. Finally, the coördination of the schemata in which the recognition of the visual signals for sucking consists, is only a complication of these same mechanisms: it is assimilation to the second degree inasmuch as it is coördination of two schemata of assimilation (vision and sucking) and it is accommodation to the second degree inasmuch as it prolongs the chain of acquired associations.

§2. VISION.—We are here not at all going to study perceptions and visual accommodations in themselves but only attempt, in accordance with the aim of this work, to distinguish in the behavior patterns pertaining to vision the different aspects applying to the development of intelligence. We shall resume consideration of the particulars of certain visual accommodations connected with the formation of the idea of space.

As with sucking, we shall distinguish in the behavior patterns controlled by vision a certain number of types proceeding from the pure reflex to the circular reaction and from there to the acquired coördinations between the visual schemata and those of other activities.

The reflexes should have been dealt with in the first chapter. But, as they are far from interesting inasmuch as the sucking reflexes, we can limit ourselves to mentioning them here as a memorandum. Perception of light exists from birth and consequently the reflexes which insure the adaptation of this perception (the pupillary and palpebral reflexes, both to light). All the rest (perception of forms, sizes, positions, distances, prominence, etc.) is acquired through the combination of reflex activity with higher activities. But the behavior patterns connected with the perception of light imply—as they do with sucking, but to a much lesser degree—a sort of reflex apprenticeship and actual searching. I noted, for example, from the end of the first week how much Laurent's expression changed when he was near luminous objects and how he sought them, as soon as they were moved, without of course being able to follow them with his glance. His head alone followed their movement for an instant, but without continuous coördination. Preyer (op. cit., p. 3) notes during the first days the child's expression of satisfaction at soft light; from the sixth day, his son turned his head toward the window when he was moved away from it. It seems as though such behavior patterns are explainable in the same way as the reflex behavior pertaining to sucking. Light is an excitant (consequently a functional aliment) for visual activity, whence a tendency to preserve perception of light (assimilation) and a groping to rediscover it when it vanishes (accommodation). But nothing acquired is doubtless yet superimposed on this reflex adaptation and, if it is already possible to speak of activity at this level, since there is searching, this activity does not necessarily imply apprenticeship as a function of the external environment.

On the other hand, toward the end of the first month the situation changes, as the result of progress in directing the glance. It is known that there is surface participation as early as the motor accommodation of the eye to the moving of objects. From the point of view of psychological accommodation, the stage thus surmounted during the fourth week is extremely significant. As Preyer says, the child begins "really to look, instead of contemplating vaguely" and the face assumes "a definitely intelligent expression" (op. cit., p. 35) this is the time when the baby stops crying in order to look before him for long minutes in succession without even making sucking-like movements. Here are a few examples:

Observation 28.—Jacqueline at 0;0 (16) does not follow with her eyes the flame of a match 20 cm. away. Only her expression changes at the sight of it and then she moves her head as though to find the light again. She does not succeed despite the dim light in the room. At 0;0 (24), on the other hand, she follows the match perfectly under the same conditions. The subsequent days her eyes follow the movements of my hand, a moving handkerchief, etc. From this date she can remain awake without crying, gazing ahead.

Observation 29.—Lucienne also has directed her glance since the fourth week and is able to rediscover the object when it has escaped her sight and it follows its previous movement. She also finds the object by fits and starts, moving her eyes slightly, then losing sight of the object, then readjusting her head, then following the object with her eyes only, etc.

Observation 30.—Laurent, until 0;0 (21) has only been capable of badly coördinated movements of the head previously reported in connection with the perception of light and simply revelatory of an attempt to make the excitement last. At 0;0 (21) on the other hand, for the first time his eyes follow a match in a dimly lit room, 20 cm. from his eyes.—At 0;0 (23) he is lying down, his head resting on his right cheek; I show him my fingers 20 cm. away and he follows them so that he turns all the way to the left.—At 0;0 (25) same experiment with a handkerchief: I make his head describe an angle of 180° moving backward and forward, so attentively does he follow the object.

Observation 31.—Laurent at 0;0 (24) watches the back of my hand which is motionless, with such attention and so marked protrusion of the lips that I expect him to suck it. But it is only visual interest.—At 0;0 (25) he spends nearly an hour in his cradle without crying, his eyes wide open. At 0;0 (30) same observation. He stares at a piece of fringe on his cradle with continuous little readaptive movements as though his head had difficulty in not changing position and his gaze brought it to the right place. So long as he gazes thus his arms are still, whereas when sucking-like movements are paramount, his arms swing to and fro again.—At 0;1 (6) Laurent stops crying when I put my handkerchief 10 cm. away from his eyes. He looks at it attentively, then follows it; but when he loses sight of it, he does not succeed in catching sight of it again.

Observation 32.—Laurent at 0;1 (7) begins to look at immobile objects with direction, naturally without much coördination. But for this it is essential that a previous movement excite his curiosity. He is, for example, lying in his bassinet, looking at a certain place in the hood. I pull down the hood to the other end of the bassinet so that instead of having over his head the usual material, he finds an empty space, limited by the edge of the hood. Laurent immediately looks at this, seeking from side to side. Thus he follows, roughly, the line of a white fringe which edges the hood and he finally fixes his gaze on a particularly visible point of this fringe. At 0;1 (8) same experiment and same result. But when he looks at the fringe he sees my motionless face (I stood there in order to observe his eyes). He then gazes alternately at the fringe and my head, directing his gaze himself, without having any external movement distracting his attention.

How can such behavior patterns be classified? There is not involved, it goes without saying, any interest of the child in the objects themselves that he tries to watch. These sensorial images have no meaning, being coördinated neither with sucking, grasping or anything which could constitute a need for the subject. Moreover, such images have neither depth nor prominence (the first accommodations to distance are exactly contemporaneous to the beginnings of the directing of the glance). They therefore only constitute spots which appear, move, and disappear without solidity or volume. They are, in short, neither objects, independent images, nor even images charged with extrinsic meaning. What then is the motivating force of the child's behavior? There only remains the very need to look which can play this role. Just as, from the earliest days, the newborn child reacts to light and seeks it to the extent that the reflex use concomitant with this perception makes of the latter a need, so also, as soon as the glance is able to follow a moving spot, the use of the glance suffices to confer a functional value on objects which can be followed with the eyes. In other words, if the child looks at moving objects it is simply because, at the beginning, they constitute an aliment for the activity of the glance. Later, when the various accommodations to distance, prominence, etc., enrich visual perception, the objects looked at serve as more differentiated nourishment for these multiple operations. Still later, or concurrently, the visual images acquire meanings connected with hearing, grasping, touching, with all the sensorimotor and intellectual combinations. Thus they support increasingly subtle functions. The rough initial assimilation of the object to the very activity of the glance gradually becomes recognition and organization of images, projecting in space and, to sum it up, "objective" vision. But, before reaching this state of solidification the visual perception of the nursling is only a functional exercise. The object is, in the true sense, assimilated to the subject's activity. The perseverance and searching characteristic of the beginnings of looking are therefore of the same kind as the functional exercise of sucking activity, to take an example which has already been analyzed. At first purely reflex, this exercise is doubled by an acquired exercise or "circular reaction." At the second or third month level circular reaction seems to us definitely to exist. The direction of the look itself depends on the play of reflexes but these, being cortical, can from the beginning be extended into acquired reactions—that is to say, from the very beginning there is apprenticeship as a function of the objects themselves.

Having stated this, let us now try to analyze these circular reactions. Circular reaction is, therefore, an acquired functional exercise which prolongs the reflex exercise and has the effect of fortifying and maintaining, no more only a completely assembled mechanism, but a sensorimotor whole with new results pursued for their own sake. Inasmuch as it is adaptation, circular reaction involves, according to the rule, a pole of accommodation and a pole of assimilation.

Accommodation is the whole of the associations acquired at the contact of objects due to the increasingly complex play of the "reflexes of accommodation": accommodation of the crystalline lens, pupillary reflex to distance, and binocular convergence. The instruments of this accommodation are certainly reflex and are contained in the hereditary structure of the eye itself. But the instruments only achieve effective utilization in the course of exercise in which experience is a factor. In other words, it is only in exerting himself to perceive forms, prominence, depth, in measuring distances, in seeing things in perspective, in short in making his accommodation reflexes function with respect to things that the child arrives at the correct handling of these instruments. It is useless to emphasize here the particulars of these mechanisms since we shall come across some of them again when dealing with space (Vol. II). Let us limit ourselves to one remark. It is an observed fact that the child at the stage under present consideration does not yet know how to measure distances. Not only are pupillary accommodation and binocular convergence not stabilized with regard to all distances at the age of 4–5 months, but the child makes all sorts of mistakes when he wishes to grasp objects (see Vol. II, Chapter II). Does this mean that the sense of depth is entirely due to acquired experience? Obviously no, because the existence of "accommodation reflexes'" shows that, even if the subject's first evaluations are erroneous, he is necessarily led, by means of his hereditary constitution, sooner or later to attribute depth to space. Is this to say henceforth that accommodation to depth is a pure reflex exercise comparable to the exercise by means of which the newborn child learns to suck —an apprenticeship presupposing the external environment because every function is relative to the environment but owing nothing to it because retaining nothing of the things themselves?

This could be maintained if space were independent of the objects it contains. But it is apparent that depth is nothing independent of concrete evaluations of the distances of objects. To say that a certain subject possesses the sense of depth necessarily means that he perceives a particular object as being farther away or nearer than another. But it is precisely in the acquisition of these particular perceptions that experience plays a role. For the baby to discover that the handle of his bassinet is farther removed in depth than the edge of the same bassinet, it is not enough that he possess the sense of depth by heredity, but he must put things in perspective, compare his perceptions, in short, make experiments. Therefore no accommodation reflex to depth in itself exists; there are only accommodations peculiar to the different objects perceived which presuppose, in addition to hereditary adaptation, acquired "circular reactions." It is in this respect that the functional exercise of looking, of which we are now speaking in general, involves an element of acquired accommodation and not only reflex use.

But the circular reaction proper to looking also presupposes an element of *assimilation*. First, as we have already said, there is essentially reproductive assimilation. If the child looks constantly, and more each day, at the objects surrounding him, this is not, at the beginning, because he is interested in them as objects nor as signals devoid of external meaning, nor even (at the very beginning) as sensorial images capable of being recognized, but simply because these moving, luminous spots are an aliment for his glance and permit it to develop while functioning. Objects are therefore first assimilated to the very activity of looking; their only interest lies in being objects of vision.

How shall we proceed from this purely functional assimilation (through pure repetition) to objective vision—that is to say, to an assimilation which presupposes the precise adaptation of the structure of the subject to the structure of things and vice versa? Three steps must be considered here: generalizing assimilation, recognitory assimilation, and the coördination of the schemata of visual assimilation with the other schemata of mental assimilation.

We can use the term "generalizing assimilation" (in the

same sense as in the first chapter dealing with the sucking system) to designate the fact—which is as important as it is trite —that from the fourth and fifth week the child looks at an increasing number of things but by proceeding through concentric waves. In the beginning, as revealed by the above observations, the nursling limits himself to watching objects which are slowly moved at a distance of 20–30 cm. from his face (Obs. 30) or to staring in front of him (Obs. 31). Then (Obs. 32) he applies himself to directing his glance to certain objects. From now on it becomes possible to make a general appraisal of the child's spontaneous visual interests. Then one observes that the subject looks neither at what is too familiar, because he is in a way surfeited with it, nor at what is too new because this does not correspond to anything in his schemata (for instance, objects too remote for there yet to be accommodation, too small or too large to be analyzed, etc.). In short, looking in general and the different types of visual accommodation in particular are put to use progressively in increasingly varied situations. It is in this sense that the assimilation of objects to visual activity is "generalizing."

Here are a few examples:

Observation 33.—Having learned to direct his glance (Obs. 32), Laurent explores his universe little by little. At 0;1 (9), for example, as soon as he is held vertically in the arms of his nurse, he examines successively the various images before him. First he sees me, then raises his eyes and looks at the walls of the room, then turns toward a dormer window, etc. At 0;1 (15) he systematically explores the hood of his bassinet which I shook slightly. He begins by the edge, then little by little looks backward at the lowest part of the roof, although this had been immobile for a while. Four days later he resumes this exploration in the opposite direction. He begins with the hood itself and then examines a piece of veiling which extends beyond the edge of the roof, a part of the coverlet (in the same position), my face which he finds before him and finally empty space. Subsequently he constantly resumes examining the cradle but, during the third month, he only looks at the toys hanging from the hood or at the hood itself when an unwonted movement excites his curiosity or when he discovers a particular new point (a pleat in the material, etc.).

Observation 34.—His examination of people is just as marked, especially after 0;1 (15); that is to say, after his first smiles. When one leans over him, as when dressing him, he explores the face section by section: hair, eyes, nose, mouth, everything is food for his visual curiosity. At 0;1 (10) he alternately looks at his nurse and at me and, in examining me, his eyes oscillate between my hair and face. At 0;1 (21) he watches his nurse enter and leave the room. At 0;1 (25) he looks in turn at his nurse, his mother, and myself with a change of attitude when confronted by each new face and a abrupt and spontaneous moving of his glance from one face to the other.

But, quickly enough, his interest in faces is no longer a purely visual one. Through coördination with the schemata of hearing in particular and with the global situations of eating, dressing, etc., the familiar faces become fraught with meaning. Thus we leave the realm of purely generalizing assimilation. This reappears, on the other hand, as soon as an unfamiliar feature appears, to alter his visual image of people. Thus at 0;2 (4) Laurent notices his mother wearing a pearl necklace in which he is more interested than in her face. At 0;2 (13) my béret catches his attention. At 0;2 (18) the shaving soap on my chin, then my pipe; the following days it is my tongue which I stick out at him having in mind experiments concerning imitation, etc. At 0;2 (29) he watches me eat most attentively. He successively examines the bread I hold and my face, then my glass and my face. He watches my hand when I raise it to my mouth, my mouth, etc.

Observation 35.—There is generalizing assimilation, not only with respect to the successive objects which the child sees, but also in connection with the successive positions which the subject assumes in order to look. The acquisition of the "alternate" glance may be cited in this connection. During the second month we have seen Laurent look in turn at various objects or different parts of the same object, as example (Obs. 34) three motionless people next to his bassinet or the hair and face of the same person. But in this case he looks at each image irregularly. On the other hand, during the third month, the emergence of the following behavior pattern may be observed: the glance compares, so to speak, two distinct objects while alternately examining them. For example, at 0;2 (11) Laurent is looking at a rattle suspended from the hood of his bassinet when I hang a handkerchief parallel to the rattle. He then looks alternately at the handkerchief and at the rattle and smiles. At 0;2 (17) he explores a part of the hood of his bassinet when I shake it slightly. Laurent then looks at a certain place in the hood, then observes the moving rattle, then returns to the hood and so on, six times in succession. I repeat the experiment a moment later and count nine more alternate glances.[6] Such behavior surely constitutes the beginning of comparison, but as yet, it seems to us, purely

[6] See also Observations 92, at 0;3 (13), the example of the case and the chain.

visual comparison. It is inconceivable that Laurent should already give a causal interpretation to the relationship he observes between the movement of the hood and that of the rattle; he simply compares two things seen.

Observation 36.—Here is another example of generalization due to the subject's position. At 0;2 (21), in the morning, Laurent spontaneously bends his head backward and surveys the end of his bassinet from this position. Then he smiles, returns to his normal position and then begins again. I observed this several times. As soon as Laurent awakens after the short naps to which he is accustomed, he resumes this activity. At four o'clock in the afternoon after a long sleep he has barely awakened before he bends his head backward and bursts out laughing. Such behavior reveals all the characteristics of a typical circular reaction. The days following he continues to explore and the next week his interest is almost as keen.

Thus it may be seen how the child's spontaneous looking develops through being exercised. The bassinet hood, having at first only been the object of "looking for the sake of looking," arouses growing interest through its particularities as well as through its successive modifications (the objects hanging from it). Interest in certain faces adduces interest in all others and in everything which complicates the original appearance of the former. New perspectives due to positions fortuitously discovered, arouse immediate interest through comparison with habitual perspectives, etc. In short, practice of looking brings with it the generalization of its activity.

But this growing generalization of the schema of sight is accompanied by a complementary differentiation of the global schema in particular schemata, this differentiation leading to "recognition." The purely functional assimilation which prevailed in the beginning (looking for the sake of looking) is thus transformed into an assimilation of objects to limited schemata which is tantamount to saying that sight is on the way to objectification (looking in order to see). For example, among the things which the child contemplates all the time are some which are immobile (the hood of the bassinet), some which sometimes move slightly (the fringe of the hood), some which constantly change position, appear and disappear, remain stationary for a while and suddenly disappear (human faces). Each of these categories of visual images gives rise to progressive exercises (generalization) but, at the same time, to differentiations in functioning. Each one presupposes, in effect, an exercise *sui genesis* of vision, just as the breast, the thumb, the pillow, etc., actuate sucking in different ways: so generalizing assimilation brings with it the formation of particular schemata. The child, in assimilating to these schemata the objects which appear in his field of vision, "recognizes" them through this very act. This recognition is therefore probably global in the beginning. The child does not recognize a certain face as such, but at first recognizes this face in a given situation. Only, the more generalizing assimilation permits the subject to incorporate the visual environment into his schemata, the more the latter dissociate themselves and permit precise recognition.

But if purely functional and generalizing assimilation can be observed thanks to the mere behavior of the child, how can what we have just said about recognitory assimilation be verified? From the time when the nursling is able to smile and thus to differentiate his gestures and the expression of his emotions, the analysis of recognition becomes possible without too great a risk of error. Let us try, from this point of view, to analyze the first smiles produced in the presence of visual images and to collect what they can teach us about the beginnings of recognition.

The smile is, as we know, a reflex mechanism whose association with pleasurable states makes it possible sooner or later to make a social sign assuming varied meanings but always related to contact with people. Must it be said, therefore, that the smile is a hereditary social behavior pattern which from the beginning constitutes, as Ch. Bühler maintains, a "reaction to people" or is it possible to think that the smile only becomes specialized progressively in its functions as a social sign and consists during the first months of a simple pleasurable reaction to the most varied excitants, even though it begins in the presence of the voice or movements of the human face? Ours is the second interpretation which is why the smile seems to us a good indication of the existence of recognition in general. Ch. Bühler's interpretation does not seem to us to withstand factual examination as has been already elucidated by C. W. Valentine.[7] In a somewhat categorical note[8] Ch. Bühler has. answered him by presenting statistics which contradict his observations. But an acute observation, especially when made by as good an observer as C. W. Valentine, surpasses all statistics. As for us, examining our three children has left us no doubt concerning the fact that the smile is primarily a reaction to familiar images, to what has already been seen, inasmuch as familiar objects reappear suddenly and release emotion, or again inasmuch as a certain spectacle gives rise to immediate repetition. It is only very gradually that people monopolize the smile precisely in so far as they constitute familiar objects most inclined to this kind of reappearances and repetitions. But in the beginning anything at all can give rise to the emotional recognition which elicits the smile.

Observation 37.—Laurent smiled for the first time at 0;1 (15) at 6 o'clock, 10 o'clock and 11:30 while looking at his nurse who is wagging her head and singing. Apparently there is a global impression involving visual recognition, perception of a rhythmic movement, and hearing. The following days the voice remains necessary to produce the smile but at 0;1 (25) merely seeing the nurse suffices. Same observation at 0;1 (30). On the other hand, it is not until 0;2 (2) that he smiles at his parents when they do not make noises. At 0;2 (3) he refuses to smile at his grandmother and an aunt despite all their advances, but he finally smiles at the latter when she removes her hat. At 0;2 (4) he smiles a lot at his mother (while she remains silent) but a few moments later refuses to smile at a woman of the same age. During this third month I do not succeed in making him smile only on seeing me if I remain immobile (without head movements) or if I appear at a distance (of 1 meter or more). On the other hand, during the fourth month these conditions are no longer inhibiting. At 0;2 (26) Laurent does not recognize me in the morning before I am groomed. He looks at me with a frightened expression and drooping mouth, then he suddenly rediscovers me and smiles. Seeing his systers does not cause him to smile as quickly as seeing his parents, but the reaction became identical after the middle of the third month. During the fourth month he even seems already to prefer children to adults when his acquaintance with both is equally slight. Thus, at 0;3 (7) Laurent is afraid of a neighbor but reveals great interest, with smiling eyes, in the man's 12-year-old son (blond with a very youthful appearance comparable to Laurent's sisters).

[7] C. W. Valentine, British Assoc. 1930, *The Foundations of Child Psychology.*
[8] Ch. Bühler, *op. cit.*

Observation 38.—With regard to inanimate objects, from the beginning of the third month Laurent revealed great interest in the cloth and celluloid toys hanging from the hood of his bassinet. At 0;2 (5) he looks at them as yet unsmilingly but emitting periodically the sound *aa* with an expression of enchantment. At 0;2 (11) he smiles broadly when he sees his toys move. He has not seen or heard anyone either previously or when confronted by this spectacle, for I move the toys from a distance with a stick. Besides, the toys have no human appearance; they are little balls of wool or celluloid. The sound of the toys which could have played a role in this first smile, does not do so subsequently; five times in succession on the same day Laurent smiles at these motionless toys. The evening of the same day I hung a handkerchief next to the toys. Laurent compares them (see above, Obs. 35) then smiles (he has not seen or heard me). The following days the reaction is just as definite and frequent. At 0;2 (15) I notice seven smiles at things (the motionless toys and hood of the bassinet, the movements of the bassinet when it is carried without the person making noise or showing himself to Laurent, etc.), and three smiles at people (his mother). At 0;2 (18) he smiles five times in succession while looking at the mosquito net (I observe this through the bassinet hood). The same day he laughs and babbles with great excitement while watching the toy. As soon as he is naked he laughs loudly, gesticulating and looking at the objects surrounding him including the brown wall of the balcony. At 0;2 (19) he did not smile at people a single time in a whole day; on the other hand, he smiled at all the familiar objects. In particular he smiles for the first time (five times during the day) at his left hand which he looks at since about fifteen days before (see Obs. 62). At 0;2 (21) he even smiles beforehand while drawing his hand toward his face. The same day he learns to look backward (as seen in Obs. 36) and almost infallibly smiles at this new perspective. From 0;2 (25) he smiles during his experiments with grasping; in shaking a toy, etc. At 0;3 (6 and 7) for example, he manifests a certain astonishment and even anxiety in the presence of new objects which he would like to grasp (shiny paper, tinfoil, medical tubes, etc.) but smiles (or smiles only with his eyes) while taking familiar objects (cloth and celluloid toys, package of tobacco, etc.).

Observation 39.—Lucienne likewise expresses with smiles certain definite recognitions of things and people. She too begins by smiling at a person—at 0;1 (24)—as the result of head movements and sounds. Then she smiles at her mother merely at the sight of her, at 0;1 (27) before smiling at her father. Then from 0;2 (2) she smiles at familiar objects attached to the bassinet or its hood. At 0;2 (13) for example, she smiles at the hood. She looks attentively at a particular place, then smiles while wriggling all over, then returns to this place, etc. At 0;2 (19) the ribbon which always hangs from this hood arouses her hilarity; she looks at it, laughs while twisting herself about, looks at it again, etc. At 0;2 (27) same reactions with, in addition, broad smiles at the toys which are swinging. At 0;3 (0) smile at the hood which is being replaced in position (without Lucienne's seeing or hearing the person).

Thus may be seen the extent to which smiles evidence subtle differences in recognition. The reactions differ with respect to different people and to the same person, to different situations (according to distances, movements, etc.). If, then, primitive recognition is "global"—that is to say, related to varied situations and to different types of looking becoming differentiated as a function of generalizing assimilation and of accommodation combined—nevertheless this recognition becomes more and more precise. The reaction is exactly the same with regard to things.

In conclusion, visual circular reaction or acquired adaptation in the realm of looking requires a component of accommodation of the function to the object and a component of assimilation of the object to the function. Such assimilation, at first simply functional and reproductive (repetition or pure circular reaction), becomes simultaneously generalizing and recognitory. It is when it attains a certain level of recognition that visual perception may be considered as perception of images distinct from one another and no longer only as a simple exercise of which the sensorial image constitutes the aliment without exciting interest in itself.

But the process is far from adequate to explain the growing objectification of visual adaptation. It is not enough that a sensorial image be recognized when it reappears for it to constitute by itself an external object. Any subjective state can be recognized without being attributed to the action of objects independent of the ego. The newborn child who nurses recognizes the nipple by the combination of sucking and swallowing reflexes without making the nipple a thing. So also a month-old child can recognize certain visual images without, however, really exteriorizing them. What is the next condition necessary for the solidification of such images? It seems to us essential that the visual schemata be coördinated with other schemata of assimilation such as those of prehension, hearing, or sucking. They

must, in other words, be organized in a universe. It is their insertion in a totality which is to confer upon them an incipient
objectivity.

This leads us to the third aspect of visual circular reactions
—their *organization.* It may be stated that the visual images to
which the child adapts himself are, through the very fact of this
adaptation, coördinated among themselves and also in relation
to other kinds of schemata. The organization of visual images
among themselves can itself give rise to a distinction. First there
are the coördinations of distance, size, etc., which constitute visual
space and which we shall not mention here because the matter
deserves special study (see Vol. II). Then there are the wholly
qualitative coördinations (relationships of color, light, etc., and
the sensorimotor relationships), whose activity is made manifest
in generalizing and recognitory assimilation. Thus it may be
said that, independently of any coördination between vision and
the other schemata (prehension, touch, etc.), the visual schemata
are organized among themselves and constitute more or less well-
coördinated totalities. But the essential thing for this immediate
question is the coördination of the visual schemata, no longer
among themselves, but with the other schemata. Observation
shows that very early, perhaps from the very beginnings of orientation in looking, coördinations exist between vision and hearing
(see Obs. 44–49). Subsequently the relationships between vision
and sucking appear (see Obs. 27), then between vision and prehension, touch, kinesthetic impressions, etc. These intersensorial
coördinations, this organization of heterogeneous schemata will
give the visual images increasingly rich meanings and make
visual assimilation no longer an end in itself but an instrument
at the service of vaster assimilations. When the child seven or
eight months old looks at unknown objects for the first time before swinging, rubbing, throwing and catching them, etc., he no
longer tries to look for the sake of looking (pure visual assimilation in which the object is a simple aliment for looking), nor
even to look for the sake of seeing (generalizing or recognitory
visual assimilation in which the object is incorporated without
adding anything to the already elaborated visual schemata), but
he looks in order to act, that is to say, in order to assimilate the

new object to the schemata of weighing, friction, falling, etc. There is therefore no longer only organization inside the visual schemata but between those and all the others. It is this progressive organization which endows the visual images with their meanings and solidifies them in inserting them in a total universe.

From the point of view of the functional categories of thought which correspond to the biological invariants of mental development, it is interesting to note the extent to which this element of organization is, here as everywhere, the source of totalities and of values. In so far as the organization of the visual schemata forms a more or less closed totality, vision constitutes a value in itself and the assimilation of things is an assimilation to vision itself. On the other hand, in so far as the visual universe is coördinated to the other universes—that is to say, where there is reciprocal organization and adaptation between the visual and other schemata—visual assimilation becomes a simple means at the service of higher ends, and consequently a value derived in relation to principal values (the latter being constituted by the totalities pertaining to hearing, prehension and the activities proceeding from it). This is what we shall see in the following pages.

§3. PHONATION AND HEARING.—As is the case with sucking and vision, phonation and hearing give rise to acquired adaptations superimposing themselves on hereditary adaptations and, again in this case, the first acquired adaptations consist in circular reactions to the breast in which it is possible to distinguish the processes of accommodation, assimilation, and organization.

Phonation is evidenced at birth by the cry of the newborn child and his whining in the first weeks. That this reflex behavior might from the beginning be subject to some complications analogous to those we have noted in connection with vision and especially sucking, is not impossible if one considers these two observations, both unfortunately to be received with caution. The first is this sort of rhythm which appears very early in the child's cries. Laurent has hardly ever cried at night during the first three weeks but almost every day between 4 and 6 P.M.; Lucienne cries mostly in the morning, etc. The second is the possibility of a contagious spreading of crying beginning the first week. When a baby cries in the room shared by the newborn babies in a clinic, several seem to copy him; furthermore it seemed to me that my voice (I said, "Aha, aha," etc.) made Laurent cry beginning 0;0 (4 and 5). But the rhythm in question may be due to an organic rhythm (particularly digestive) without any reflex involvement, and the supposed contagious spreading of crying may be due to coincidence or to the simple fact that the others' voices awaken the child and a newborn child cries almost immediately upon awaking. Let us therefore conclude nothing.

On the other hand, circular reaction is superimposed on reflex phonation as soon as, at one or two months, the little wail which precedes crying is kept up for its own sake and gradually gives rise to modulations. This is the point of departure for our analysis of phonation in so far as it is acquired adaptation.

With regard to hearing, an interest in sound may be observed in the first days of life. At the end of the second week, for instance, Laurent stopped crying for a moment in order to listen to a sound coming from near his pillow. But it cannot be called acquired adaptation until the second month from the time the heard sound provokes a somewhat prolonged interruption of the action in progress and an actual search.

If we study phonation and hearing simultaneously, we observe that, from the stage when circular reaction prolongs, in these two realms, hereditary adaptation, to the child hearing and voice are connected. Not only does the normal child regulate his own phonation primarily according to the acoustic effects he notices, but also the voices of others seem to react on his own voice. Is such a connection between hearing and phonation partly hereditary and consolidated by acquired adaptation, or is it only acquired? It is very difficult to decide. If from birth the cries were really imitative there would definitely exist a hereditary connection. But, as we have just seen, even if the fact of a contagious spreading of crying were established, it could be explained otherwise than by imitation. Let us therefore

not form hypotheses concerning the heredity of connections between phonation and hearing and limit ourselves to studying the
behavior patterns related to these functions from the time when
acquired adaptation exists.

First, here are some observations concerning phonation:

Observation 40.—Jacqueline, until the middle of the second month, has
only used her voice for daily wails and certain more violent cries of
desire and anger when hunger became persistent. Around 0;1 (14) it
seems as though crying stops simply expressing hunger or physical dis-
comfort (especially intestinal pains) to become slightly differentiated.
The cries cease, for example, when the child is taken out of the crib
and resume more vigorously when he is set down for a moment before
the meal. Or again, real cries of rage may be observed if the feeding is
interrupted. It seems evident, in these two examples, that crying is connected with behavior patterns of expectation and disappointment which
imply acquired adaptation. This differentiation of mental states concomitant with phonation is soon accompanied by a differentiation in
the sounds emitted by the child. Sometimes crying is imperious and
enraged, sometimes plaintive and gentle. It is then that the first "circular reactions" related to phonation may definitely be observed. Sometimes, for instance, the wail which precedes or prolongs the crying is
kept up for its own sake because it is an interesting sound: 0;1 (22).
Sometimes the cry of rage ends in a sharp cry which distracts the child
from his pain and is followed by a sort of short trill: 0;2 (2). The smile
may be accompanied by indistinct sounds: 0;1 (26). Finally, the sounds
thus produced as prolongations of crying or of smiles are immediately
rediscovered and sustained as such: at 0;2 (12) Jacqueline prattles for
a moment without smiling or wailing. At 0;2 (13) she emits a sort of
trill. At 0;2 (15) the crying is transformed into playing with the voice,
"aha," "ahi," etc. At 0;2 (15) she even interrupts her meal to resume her
babbling. Finally, at 0;2 (18) playing with her voice becomes routine
when she is awake.

It is to be noted, as we shall see concerning imitation, that these
first circular reactions are almost immediately accompanied by vocal
contagion and then, at 0;2, by definite imitation.

Observation 41.—Until 0;1 (8) I noticed nothing in Laurent resembling
a vocal circular reaction. His phonation only consists of cries of hunger
and pain or in wails preceding and prolonging the cries. True, at 0;0
(9) Laurent makes a sound similar to *aha,* without crying, but only
once; usually this sound precedes crying. On the other hand, beginning
0;1 (8) vague voice exercises may be observed, but these could be the
beginning of a wail interrupted by a visual or auditory interest. At 0;1
(9) on the other hand, the wailing is maintained for its own sake, for

several seconds before the crying. As soon as the first cry ensues I imitate Laurent's wailing; he then stops crying and begins to wail again. This first vocal imitation seems to me to substantiate the existence of circular reaction. If imitation of others exists, there also exists, in effect and *a fortiori,* imitation of oneself, that is to say "circular reaction." At 0;1 (15) I note a sort of fleeting *arr* or *rra,* and at 0;1 (20) a sound resembling *en* indicating contentment interspersed with sucking-like movements in which he indulges, alone and wide awake. The latter sound reappears intermittently at 0;1 (22) and at 0;1 (26) in the same situations, whereas the sound *aa* or *rra* which I emit in Laurent's presence in order to copy him releases analogous sounds, after a smile, at 0;1 (22). At 0;1 (28) circular reaction begins with the sounds *aha, enhen,* etc., and at the third month vocalizations are produced. At 0;2 (7) Laurent babbles in the twilight and at 0;2 (16) he does this on awakening early in the morning often for half an hour at a time.

Observation 42.—In certain special cases the tendency to repeat, by circular reactions, sounds discovered by pure chance, may be observed. Thus at 0;2 (12) Lucienne, after coughing, recommences several times for fun and smiles. Laurent puffs out his breath, producing an indefinite sound. At 0;2 (26) he reproduces the peals of his voice which ordinarily accompany his laughter, but without laughing and out of pure phonetic interest. At 0;2 (15) Lucienne uses her voice in similar circumstances, etc.

It is useless to continue this description since phonation does not interest us for its own sake but simply inasmuch as it is subject to adaptations of general form. In this respect it is easy to find in circular vocal reactions of which we have just spoken, the processes of accommodation, assimilation and organization to which sucking and vision have already accustomed us. Accommodation, first, because circular reaction is an effort to rediscover the new sound discovered by chance. There is thus perpetual accommodation of the vocal organs to phonic reality perceived by hearing (see for example Obs. 42) even though this reality is the product of their own activity. Very early too, vocal accommodation will consist in the imitation of new sounds made by others, but we can remit study of this question to the volume on "Imitation." The use of the voice is then assimilation in the triple sense of the term. There is assimilation through repetition, to the extent that each vocal system is consolidated while functioning. There is generalizing assimilation to the extent that circular reaction progressively diversifies the phonic material in indefinite combinations which the authors have noted in detail. There is recognitory assimilation to the extent that circular reaction and beginning imitation entail the discrimination of one sound in relation to another. Finally phonation is organization in two complementary senses, first inasmuch as the totality of the sounds produced constitutes a system of interdependent articulations and then inasmuch as phonation is immediately coördinated with other schemata and in particular with the auditory schemata.

This leads us to hearing. The first acquired adaptations related to hearing date from the second month, from the time when two essential coördinations are established—coördination with phonation and coördination with vision. Until then the only reaction observed is the child's interest in the voice. But as this reaction is accompanied by no other visible accommodation except the smile and the coördinations of which we have just spoken, it is very difficult to fix the boundary of reflex adaptation and of acquired adaptation.

Observation 43.—At 0;1 (0) Jacqueline still limits herself to interrupting her crying when she hears an agreeable voice or sound but she does not try to mark the sound. At 0;1 (6 and 13), same reaction. At 0;1 (10) on the other hand, she begins to smile at the voice. From now on it is possible in a general way to distinguish the sounds which she recognizes and which make her smile (vocalizations, singing intonations, etc., resembling her own phonations) from those which astonish, worry, or interest her. The same is true of Lucienne, beginning 0;1 (13). The sound *rra* which is a copy of her own vocalizations almost invariably makes her smile for three or four weeks, beginning at 0;1 (25) and produces a vague imitation beginning 0;1 (26).—Laurent smiles at the voice alone beginning 0;1 (20), but at 0;0 (12) the voice sufficed to interrupt his crying and this interest in sound gave rise to attempts at localization from 0;1 (8). As a rule high-pitched sounds in a childish intonation make him smile; deep tones surprise and disturb him. The sound *bzz* is sure to make him smile during the third month (before he himself emits it) provided that it is sung on a sufficiently high key. At 0;1 (22) he easily recognizes the sound of the metal rattle in his celluloid balls and he immediately looks in the right place as soon as he hears them.

These facts suffice to make us state that the child behaves with respect to sounds as with respect to vision. On the one hand, he progressively accommodates himself to them; on the other hand, he assimilates them. This assimilation is at first the simple pleasure of hearing (circular reaction to the sound or assimilation through repetition). Then, to the extent that there is discrimination of the sounds heard, there is simultaneously generalizing assimilation (that is to say, interest in increasingly varied sounds) and recognition of certain sounds (*rra*, *bzz*, etc.).

Let us proceed to the coördinations between sound and sight:

Observation 44.—At 0;2 (12) Jacqueline turns her head to the side whence the sound comes. For example, hearing a voice behind her, she turns in the right direction. At 0;2 (26) she localizes the source of the sound quite accurately. It seems she searches until she finds the person who is speaking but it is of course difficult to say whether she identifies the source of the sound and the original image or whether there is simply accommodation to the sound.

Observation 45.—At 0;1 (26) Lucienne, whose head is turned to the left when I call her from the right, turns her head at once and seeks by looking. At 0;1 (27) she is carried under my window whence I call her; she turns her head left and right and finally above her at an angle 45° too much to the left but revealing obvious control. In this last example it seems as though she tries to see what has produced the sound and not only to accommodate herself to the sound. At 0;2 (12) also, she turns her head when I call her and looks until she has seen me, even if I remain motionless.

Observation 46.—At 0;1 (8) Laurent reveals an incipient localization of sound. He lies on his back without seeing me and looks at the roof of the cradle while moving his mouth and arms. Then I call him softly, "Aha, aha." His expression immediately changes, he listens, motionless, and seems to try to locate the sound by looking. His head oscillates slightly from right to left without yet finding the right location and his glance, instead of remaining fixed as previously, also searches. The following days Laurent better directs his head toward the sound and of course he then looks in the right direction, but it is impossible to decide whether the child tries to see the source of the sound or whether his looking simply accompanies pure auditory accommodation.

Observation 47.—At 0;1 (15), on the other hand, it seems that on hearing my voice Laurent tries to see the face that goes with it but with two conditions which we shall try to specify. That morning Laurent smiled for the first time, three times, and, as we have seen, it is probable that the smile was started by a global impression, auditory as well as visual. That afternoon I stand at Laurent's left while he is lying in his cradle and looks to the right. I call, "Aha, aha." Laurent then slowly turns his head to the left and suddenly sees me after I have stopped singing. He looks at me at length. Then I move to his right (without his being able to follow me with his eyes) and I call. Laurent again turns in my direction and his eyes seem to search. He sees me and looks at me but this time without an expression of understanding (I am immobile at this moment). I move back to the left, call, and he turns back again. As a counterproof I repeat the same experiment but I tap the window panes with my hand (the cradle is between the two leaves of a French window). Each time Laurent turns to the correct side and looks in the direction of my face which, however, he perceives in passing. It appears therefore that he associates the sound of the voice with the visual image of the human face and that he tries to see something else upon hearing a new sound.—But the rest of the observation shows that two conditions are still necessary for Laurent to look at a face when he has heard a voice: he must have seen this face shortly beforehand and it must be in motion. For example at 0;1 (20) I enter unobserved by Laurent and say. "Aha." He looks and searches most attentively (his arm movements stop completely) but limits himself to exploring the visual field exposed to him through his initial position (he examines the hood of the bassinet, the ceiling of the room, etc.). A moment later I appear in front of Laurent, then disappear and call him sometimes at the left sometimes at the right of the bassinet. Henceforth he searches in the right direction every time. The next day, same experiment and same result; furthermore I note that if I remain immobile he looks at me without interest and without even recognizing me, whereas if I move he looks at me and his searching ends as though he knew it was I who sang. At 0;1 (22) in the same way he searches anywhere at all although manifesting much attention to my voice; then he perceives me while I am immobile and continues searching without attributing importance to my visual image; after this I shake my head and thereafter he turns toward me whenever I call and seems satisfied as soon as he has discovered me. The following days, same phenomenon.

Observation 48.—From 0;1 (26) on the other hand, Laurent turns in the right direction as soon as he hears my voice (even if he has not seen me just before) and seems satisfied when he has discovered my face even when it is immobile. At 0;1 (27) he looks successively at his father, his mother, and again at his father after hearing my voice. It therefore seems that he ascribes this voice to a visually familiar face. At 0;2 (14) he observes Jacqueline at 1.90 to 2 meters, at the sound of her voice; same observation at 0;2 (21). At 0;3 (1) I squat before him while he is in his mother's arms and I make the sound *bzz* (which he likes). He looks to his left, then to his right, then ahead, then below him; then he catches sight of my hair and lowers his eyes until he sees my motionless face. Finally he smiles. This last observation may be considered as definitely indicating identification of the voice and visual image of the person.

Observation 49.—Regarding the noises made by things, it seems as though Laurent acquired his auditory-visual coördination around the same time as that relating to persons. At 0;1 (22) for example, he turns immediately in the direction of a celluloid ball in which there is a rattle. True, it is moving, but at 0;1 (26) he finds it again when it is immobile.—At 0;2 (6) he looks at an electric kettle as soon as I produce a sound by means of its lid. At 0;2 (11) he is sucking his thumb while looking to the right when I shake a celluloid rattle which has been attached to the hood of his bassinet for several days only (two weeks at most). He immediately lets go his thumb to look up at the right place, thus showing that he knows where the sound came from. That evening, same reaction, very rapid even though he was half asleep after a long nap. The next day and the following days: same phenomena. At 0;2 (14) Laurent observes, one meter away, my pipe which I knock lightly on wood; he stops looking at the place of contact when the sound stops and immediately finds it again when I resume. Same reactions at 0;2 (15), with a cane (at 1.50 to 2 meters), then he rediscovers the cane in various places when I change the point of contact.

It is therefore permissible to regard as certain the existence of coördination between sight and hearing from the third month on, whereas the facts observed during the second month can be due to a simple accommodation of the head to the direction of the sound. These ideas coincide with the results obtained by B. Löwenfeld.[9]

This coördination between sound and vision poses an interesting question. The coördinations which we have hitherto encountered oscillate between two extreme types. On the one hand, there is the more or less passive association imposed by the environment; thus the special position at mealtime is accompanied in the 1- or 2-month-old nursling by a search for the breast. True, such associations have seemed to us only capable of being constituted through accommodations and searchings, indicating a certain activity. But, granted this element of active accommodation, it must be recognized that it is reduced to its simplest expression and that the environment imposes the content of these accommodations before the child really assimilates

---

[9] Berthold Löwenfeld, Systematisches Studium der Reaktionen der Säuglinge auf Klange und Gerausche, *Zeitschr. f. Psychol.* CIV, 1927, pp. 62–96.

them in detail (through recognition, etc.). At the other extreme we have the active recognition of a sign charged with meaning. It is thus that the 3- to 4-month-old nursling recognizes his bib by visual perception and knows that it announces the coming meal. With regard to the coördination between hearing and sight, we are now confronted by behavior patterns contemporaneous with coördinations of position and of sucking (first type), but behavior patterns which resemble the later coördinations of vision and of sucking (second type). How should they be interpreted? Must we state that the sound of the voice is a simple signal forcing the baby to search with his eyes for the face corresponding to this voice in the manner in which the sound of the bell sets in motion salivation in the dog by conditioned reflex, or must we think that the sound of the voice constitutes a sign charged with meaning and is recognized by the child as going with the visual perception of someone's face? If, in the coördinations of position and sucking, we admit the existence of an element of active accommodation, however small, then it is evident that a series of intermediaries will link the two extreme types (active and passive coördination) and that the coördination between sight and hearing will be located midway between these extremes. In other words, the association between a sound and a visual perception is never a purely passive association, but it is not at the outset a relationship of understanding (recognition of meanings). How then can this intermediary state and the progress of understanding be explained?

In view of all we have seen regarding assimilation we may hypothesize that every assimilatory schema tends to conquer the whole universe including the realms assimilable by means of other schemata. Only the resistances of the environment or the incompatibilities due to the conditions of the subject's activity curb this generalization. So it is that the child sucks everything that touches his mouth or face and learns to coördinate the movements of his hands with those of sucking as a function of his pleasure in sucking his thumb. When he will know how to grasp he will suck everything he will have in his hands. Concerning what he sees or hears, if the nursling does not try to suck this from the outset it is perhaps less because these realms have no connection with sucking (it often happens that he makes sucking-like movements as soon as he hears a sound) than because it is difficult for the child to do two things at once (looking attentively and making sucking-like movements, etc.). But instead of immediate coördination between sucking and sight it is possible that there exists nevertheless excitation of the sucking cycle in the presence of especially interesting visual images. The remarkable protrusion of the lips observed in the youngest children (see Obs. 31) in states of great attention could not be other than sucking-like movements if it cannot be explained by a purely automatic or tonic postural mechanism.[10] In the same way, with regard to the visual, hearing and grasping schemata, etc., the child will try little by little to see everything, hear everything, take everything, etc. This is well put by Ch. Bühler when she says with regard to the first sensorial reactions that the response to an excitant during the first months depends more on the subject's functional needs than on the nature of this excitant.[11] Consequently it is natural that the nursling should try in the course of his first auditory adaptations to look at the same time as listen, at least from the time when he has learned to direct the movement of his eyes [at 0;1 (7) in Laurent's case (see Obs. 32)]. This beginning of coördination between hearing and sight does not necessarily presuppose a passive association but can be explained by active assimilation. It is true that, when he turns his head to accommodate himself to the sound, the child comes automatically, in the case of the human voice, to perceive an interesting visual image (the corresponding face); the element of passive association is not to be entirely excluded. But simple associations would never give rise to actual searching in the coördination between sight and hearing (looking for the face which corresponds to the voice and later for the sounds which correspond to the objects seen) if the schemata of visual and audi-

[10] Preyer, op. cit., p. 251–252, construes this protrusion of the lips as being a hereditary association between sucking and sight (his son evidenced it the tenth day while looking at a candle). But it goes without saying that, if association exists, it can be explained by reflex assimilation without recourse to heredity.

[11] Op. cit., p. 26.

tory assimilation did not succeed in reciprocally directing their respective realms by assimilating them in an active way.

More precisely, if at a given moment the child applies himself to searching systematically for the visual images which correspond to the sounds heard, this is so in the first place because he forces himself to look at everything. Without yet knowing that a sound necessarily comes from a visible object, the child is visually excited by the sound as well as through hearing it. Thus in Observation 46 the sound *aha* releases a need in Laurent to look as well as to listen; and this is true, probably, not because Laurent already knows that this sound emanates from a precise visual image but simply because the excitant arouses all his needs at once; in other words, because the child tries to integrate the new reality into all the available schemata of assimilation. In the second place, the child turns his head in the direction of the sound through an accommodation to the sound comparable to the movements of the eye following an object. It is self-evident, consequently, that the glance is directed to the same side as the head, whence the observer's impression that the baby tries to see what he hears (see end of Obs. 46), whereas he undoubtedly only tries to see at the same time he hears. In the third place, in certain cases success confirms the searching. The sound of the voice of others in this respect constitutes a privileged example; such a sound nearly always gives rise to double assimilation, auditory and visual. In other words, the human face has the almost unique property, in the universe of the child of 1 to 2 months, of lending itself to a totality of simultaneous assimilation. This face is at the same time recognizable and mobile, thus exciting visual interests to the highest degree; it is this face that the baby contemplates or rediscovers when he fixes his attention on the sound of the voice; again it is this face which is central in the most interesting moments of existence (coming out of the bassinet, dressing, meal, etc.). In the case of the appearance of other people it is possible to speak, not of association between various assimilations, but of global assimilation, and it is apparently this fact which explains why the smile occurs more frequently in the presence of persons than with respect to things. As far as coördination between hearing and sight is concerned it is thus evident that the child early identifies someone's face inasmuch as it is a visual image of this same face, inasmuch as it is a sonorous image. It is self-evident that, to the child, another person is not yet an object conceived as cause of the voice. But it cannot be said, inversely, that sound and vision are simply associated. This is why it must be asserted that visual and auditory schemata are reciprocally assimilated. The child tries, in a sense, to listen to the face and to look at the voice. It is this reciprocal assimilation that constitutes the identification of visual and sonorous images prior to the more complex solidifications which are to give rise to the object and to the causality.[12] In other words, the human face is one entity with regard to looking, listening, etc., and once he has acquired, in this case and some other privileged examples (rattles, etc.), coördination between hearing and sight, the child will search systematically and everywhere for correlations between sounds and visual images.

Let us finally proceed to the coördination between hearing and phonation. This coördination seems much simpler since every phonation is accompanied from the outset by auditory perception and is controlled by it. It seems therefore that here there is not intersensorial coördination, but pure circular reaction; a series of movements culminating in a sensorial effect and maintained by the interest of this result. But if that is true of simple phonation, the inverse process may also be observed: the action of hearing on phonation. In effect, as we have seen (Obs. 41) vocal contagion is almost as precocious as the first circular reactions which are the basis of phonation; the wailing of another person maintains that of the child, etc. What does this mean, if not that the schemata of phonation and hearing are reciprocally assimilated and in the same way as those of hearing and sight? Just as the child comes to listen to the sound of his voice instead of merely crying and thus inaugurates acquired circular reactions, so also he listens to the voice of another and, inasmuch as the sounds heard are analogous to the sounds he himself makes, he can only perceive them by means of corresponding auditory-vocal schemata. The imitation of sounds, in the beginning, is thus only

[12] This explains why attributing the voice to a face is only achieved by relatively long stages; see Obs. 47 and 48.

the confusion of one's own voice with that of another, coming from the fact that the voice of others is actively perceived, that is to say, assimilated to the schemata of phonation.

In conclusion, analysis of the schemata of phonation, of hearing and of their coördination completely confirms what we have stated with regard to sucking and vision. Each of these adaptations brings with it a measure of accommodation to the external environment—accommodation to the direction of sounds, to their gradual variety, etc. But each one also involves an element of assimilation. First it is assimilation by pure repetition—listening for the sake of listening, crying or wailing in order to hear these sounds, etc. Then it is generalizing assimilation—listening to or producing increasingly varied sounds. Finally it is recognitory assimilation—rediscovering a definite sound. These perceived or produced sounds at first only present an internal organization. Related to each other they only have meaning in relation to the system they form; it is this system that the child maintains and uses, to which he assimilates the various heard sounds and which he accommodates as much as possible to the new heard sounds. Then this internal organization is itself inserted into a wider organization which gives it new meanings; sound is coördinated with vision, etc. But this coördination involves no new process; it is constituted by reciprocal assimilation of the visual and auditory schemata, etc.

If the latter process is difficult to study at so early an age as 1 to 2 months, analyzing prehension will now afford us the opportunity to extend the description of the mechanism of the coördinations among heterogeneous schemata.

§4. PREHENSION.—With the mouth, the eye, and the ear, the hand is one of the most essential instruments of which the intelligence, once it has been established, will make use. One can even say that the definitive conquest of the mechanisms of grasping marks the beginning of the complex behavior patterns which we shall call "assimilations through secondary schemata" and which characterize the first forms of deliberate action. It is therefore important to analyze fundamentally the way in which this discovery of grasping takes place: here, more even than with the preceding schemata, we find an indispensable connecting link between organic adaptation and intellectual adaptation.

The hand's chief activity is grasping. But it is self-evident that this function cannot entirely be dissociated from touching or the coördinations between kinesthesia and sight, etc. We shall therefore touch on these questions in passing, but only in passing. The aim of this work is not to supply an inventory of behavior patterns of the first year of life and we shall only dwell on examples of use to the analysis of intelligence.

It seems to us five stages may be discerned in the development of grasping. If, as revealed by studying our three children, these stages do not correspond to definite ages, their sequence nevertheless seems necessary (except perhaps with regard to the third stage). Let us therefore examine the facts by classifying them according to the way they succeed one another.

The *first stage* is that of *impulsive movements* and of *pure reflex*. The newborn child closes his hand when the palm is lightly touched. Lucienne, a few hours after birth, closed her fingers around my index finger without resistance of the thumb. But at first it seems as though this reflex were unaccompanied by any search or appreciable use: the child immediately relinquishes that which he grasped. It is only while nursing when his hands are tightened and almost clenched, before the general relaxation of tonicity, that the child is able to hold on to a solid object for a few minutes (pencil, etc.). But it would be rash to conclude that this is due to a pure automatism and thus to contrast the grasping reflexes to those of sucking whose use we have seen presupposed to a great extent active accommodation and assimilation. In effect when the child closes his hand around the object which touched his palm, he reveals a certain interest. Laurent, at 0;0 (12) stops crying when I put my finger in his hand and recommences shortly afterward. The grasping reflex is thus comparable to sight or hearing during the first two weeks and not at all comparable to reflexes such as sneezing, yawning, etc., which do not attract the subject's attention in any way. True, things remain thus for a long time and prehension does not from the outset lend itself to systematic use as does sucking But we may ask ourselves whether the impulsive movements of arms, hands, and fingers, which are almost continuous during the first weeks (waving the arms, slowly opening and closing the hands, moving the fingers, etc.) do not constitute a sort of functional use of these reflexes.

The *second stage* is that of *the first circular reactions related to hand movements, prior to any actual coördination between prehension and sucking or vision.* We shall group here the whole of the circular reactions léading to prehension for its own sake (grasping and holding objects without seeing them or attempting to carry them to the mouth), tactile and kinesthetic reactions (scratching a body, moving the fingers, hands or arms, etc.), the coördinations between sucking and hand movements (finger sucking, etc.) and finally the coördination between sucking and actual prehension (grasping an object in order to carry it to the mouth), the coördination which characterizes the third stage and realizes notable progress in the way of systematic prehension and the coördinations between sight and grasping (grasping in order to look, grasping objects perceived in the visual field), which will be formed during the fourth and fifth stages and indicate definitive success in grasping.

Thus defined, the first circular reactions related to hand movements and to prehension begin by autonomous activities of hands or fingers which prolong in a continuous way the impulsive movements and reflexes of the first stage. We have stated, in effect, that from birth certain impulsive movements seem to constitute an empty use of the grasping mechanism. From the second month it becomes evident that some of these movements are so systematized that they give rise to true circular reactions, capable of gradual accommodation and assimilation.

Observation 50.—At 0;1 (8) Laurent's arm is stretched out and almost immobile while his hand opens, half closes and then opens again, etc. When the palm of his hand strikes the covers, he grasps them, lets them go in unceasing oscillating motion. It is difficult to describe these vague movements, but it is also difficult not to see in them grasping for the sake of grasping, or even empty grasping analogous to the phenomena described in connection with sucking, vision, etc. But there does not yet exist, in such behavior patterns, either true accommodation to the object or even any continuity.

Observation 51.—Until 0;1 (19) I did not observe in Laurent any accommodation, even momentary, of the hand to the object outside of reflex accommodation. It seems, on the contrary, that today the contact of my hand with his little finger or of a handkerchief with the outer surface of his finger sets in motion a certain searching. True, his hand does not remain on the spot as it will do later on. There are attempts, back and forth, and each time his hand touches my fingers or the handkerchief and seems more ready to grasp (the palm seems to be directed toward the object). But it is self-evident that the interpretation of such movements remains a very delicate one. At 0;1 (20) also, contact of his closed left hand with a rolled up handkerchief which I hold produces this result: the hand moves away while opening, then returns, open, to strike the object, grasps it feebly, then moves away again, returns to grasp it, etc. The hand seems to be stimulated by contact with the object, a beginning of accommodation. But the hand comes and goes instead of remaining immobile and really searching.

Observation 52.—Beginning at 0;1 (22), on the other hand, there seems to be more continuity in the grasping movements. Thus at 0;1 (22) Laurent holds in his hand four and a half minutes an unfolded handkerchief which he grasped by chance (his arm is occasionally immobile and occasionally in slow movement). At 0;1 (23) he holds about two minutes a toy which I placed on his palm. When he half lets it go he grasps it again by himself (twice). But soon complete lack of interest ensues. Same observation at 0;1 (26) and 0;1 (29). At 0;1 (25) he opens his hand and grasps my index finger when I touch the back of his fingers. This observation seems doubtful at first but seems to be confirmed on the following days. In particular, at 0;1 (30) for a few moments Laurent pulls my thumb without letting it go, having by chance knocked it with the back of his hand.

Observation 53.—From 0;2 (3) Laurent evidences a circular reaction which will become more definite and will constitute the beginning of systematic grasping; he scratches and tries to grasp, lets go, scratches and grasps again, etc. On 0;2 (3) and 0;2 (6) this can only be observed during the feeding. Laurent gently scratches his mother's bare shoulder. But beginning 0;2 (7) the behavior becomes marked in the cradle itself. Laurent scratches the sheet which is folded over the blankets, then grasps it and holds it a moment, then lets it go, scratches it again and recommences without interruption. At 0;2 (11) this play lasts a quarter of an hour at a time, several times during the day. At 0;2 (12) he scratches and grasps my fist which I placed against the back of his right hand. He even succeeds in discriminating my bent middle finger and grasping it separately, holding it a few moments. At 0;2 (14) and 0;2 (16) I note how definitely the spontaneous grasping of the sheet reveals the characteristics of circular reaction—groping at first, then regular rhythmical activity (scratching, grasping, holding and letting go), and finally progressive loss of interest.

But this behavior grows simpler as it evolves in that Laurent scratches less and less, and instead really grasps after a brief tactile exploration. Thus already at 0;2 (11) Laurent grasps and holds his sheet or handkerchief for a long time, shortening the preliminary scratching stage. So also at 0;2 (14) he pulls with his right hand at a bandage which had to be applied to his left. The following days his tactile interest is entirely absorbed by reciprocal hand grasping and tactile exploration of the face to which we shall return. With regard to object grasping Laurent (whose precocity has been noted with regard to thumb sucking) begins, at the end of the third month, to grasp in order to suck. He thus passes from the second to the third stage.

Observation 54.—Lucienne manifested the same vague reactions as Laurent (see Obs. 50–52) until about the age of 2 and ½ months. About 0;2 (12) I note agitation of her hands when in contact with the covers—grasping and releasing, scratching the material, etc. Same reactions on the following days. At 0;2 (16) she pulls at a pillow. At 0;2 (20) she opens and shuts her hands in space, and scratches a piece of material. At 0;2 (27) she holds her cover for a few moments, then a corner of the sheet which she grasped by chance, then a small doll which I placed against her right palm. At 0;3 (3) she strikes her quilt with her right hand; she scratches it while carefully watching what she is doing, then lets it go, grasps it again, etc. Then she loses contact with it, but as soon as she feels it again, she grasps it without scratching it first. Same reaction several times in succession. There exists therefore a quite systematic circular reaction directed by touch and not by sight.

It is not difficult to find in these reactions the first behavior patterns pertaining to sight or hearing: assimilation by pure repetition (grasping for the sake of grasping) and the beginning of accommodation (orientation of hand and fingers as a function of the object when they are in contact with this object). But there are not yet subtler accommodations or recognitory or generalizing assimilations.

From the onset of these primitive behavior patterns, on the other hand, a coördination between hand movements and those of sucking may be observed. Actually, with regard to our three children, the systematic sucking of the fingers either preceded or accompanied the first acquired activities involving only the hand or the fingers. It is also possible to find other very precocious reactions of the fingers coördinated not only with sucking but also with all the tactile sensibility of the face and discovered parts of the body:

Observation 55.—Jacqueline, while learning to suck her fingers [achieved at 0;1 (28)] constantly moved her hand over her face without appearing to explore it systematically but undoubtedly learning to recognize certain contacts. For instance at 0;2 (77) she puts her right hand on her nose when it is being cleaned. So also, during the third month, she rubs her eyes several times in succession so that they become irritated.

Observation 56.—At 0;2 (17) and the days following, Lucienne more or less systematically puts the fingers of her right hand on her right eye and goes to sleep in this position. Perhaps the irritation of the eye before her nap provoked this repeated reaction. At 0;2 (25) she scratches her eye with the back of her hand and recommences momentarily so that the whole eyelid is reddened.

Observation 57.—Beginning 0;2 (8) Laurent constantly pulls at his face before, during, or after sucking his fingers. This behavior slowly gains interest for its own sake and thus gives rise to two distinct habits. The first consists in holding his nose. Thus at 0;2 (17) Laurent babbles and smiles without any desire to suck, while holding his nose with his right hand. He begins this again on 0;2 (18) while sucking (he holds his nose with four fingers while sucking his thumb), then continues later. At 0;2 (19) he grasps his nose sometimes with his right, sometimes with his left hand, rubs his eye in passing but constantly returns to his nose. That evening he holds his nose with both hands. At 0;2 (22) he seems to raise his right hand to his nose when I pinch it. At 0;2 (24) and the following days he touches his nose again.

Observation 58.—The second habit acquired by Laurent at the same period consists in rubbing his eyes sometimes with the back of his hand, sometimes with the fingers. This may be observed when he awakens and is stretching but not only a particular reflex must be involved for stretching is present from birth but eye rubbing has just occurred and only sporadically. Furthermore and more important, Laurent rubs his eyes all the time independently of his nap as though he has made the tactile discovery of his eyes and kept returning to it through circular reaction. At 0;2 (16) I even note that he closes his eye before his right hand approaches it and while he does not yet see it. At 0;2 (18), same reaction: both of his eyes close before he scratches the right eye. At 0;2 (19) he turns his head to the left as his left hand is being directed toward his eye. Then he rubs both eyes simultaneously with both hands At 0;2 (20) he makes fists in order to rub his eyes, again closes his eyes beforehand and smiles with joy; there is no connection with stretching The following days, same reactions.

Observation 59.—The activity of the hands with respect to the body itself is not limited to the nose and eyes. Sometimes the whole face is covered by both hands joined together. Sometimes—in Laurent's case at 0;2 (24) —the chest receives regular blows. But it is chiefly the hands which discover and touch one another. This phenomenon was particularly important with respect to Laurent not only because it gave rise to an especially tenacious habitual schema but also because this schema subsequently set in motion very precocious behavior patterns of prehension coördinated with sucking and above all with vision. It is noteworthy in the first place that already during the acquisition of thumb sucking (Obs. 6–21) Laurent often clasped his hands while he sucked the fingers of one of them. This pattern was revealed sporadically until the end of the second month. At the beginning of the third month it gave rise to a very systematic habit. I note that at 0;2 (4) and 0;2 (10) he seems to touch his hands. At 0;2 (14) his right hand pulls a bandage on his left. At 0;2 (17) I draw away his left hand by means of a string (attached to it to prevent Laurent from sucking his left thumb), he catches this hand several times by means of his right hand. The precision with which he performs this function while his left hand tries to overcome the resistance of the string and to enter his mouth, shows that a solidly constructed schema has already been formed. At 0;2 (19) Laurent clasps his hands several times and toward evening does it almost continuously. He touches them, then sucks them together, lets them go, grasps them again, etc. The interest is primarily in grasping and only secondarily in sucking. The following days this behavior is increasingly frequent but here we must interrupt our description of it because looking intervenes and begins to modify this "schema of junction." Beginning 0;2 (24) Laurent is observed to examine his clasped hands so attentively that their movement is transformed by this, which is characteristic of the third stage. Primarily, the systematization of this habit of joining results in hastening the moment when Laurent will grasp with both hands some object in order to keep it in his mouth which is also typical of this third stage (it is even by this last characteristic that we shall arrive at defining the transition from the second to the third stage of prehension).

These coördinations between the movement of hands and face (Obs. 55–58) do not raise any particular question. They are not, like the coördination between sight and hearing, for example, reciprocal assimilations of independent schemata; they only actually constitute an extension of the primitive and purely tactile schemata of prehension (Obs 50–54). The clasping of the hands on the contrary, is in one sense a mutual assimilation, but not outside the realm of tactile prehension. Until now the above-mentioned coördination of the thumb and of sucking (Obs. 16–24) involves a beginning of reciprocal assimilation between independent schemata; but if the mouth sucks the hand and the hand directs itself to the mouth, the hand is not yet able to grasp everything that the mouth sucks.

Let us now proceed to the coördinations between vision and hand movements. Preyer and Tournay observed that during the seventeenth week the child looked at his hands for the first time in a systematic way. Wallon[13] who quotes this, seems to envisage it as an indication of a general truth.

Observation of our children unfortunately does not corroborate these dates; rather it seems to show that coördination between vision and hand movements is a continuous process depending on functional use more than on acquisitions which can definitely be placed in time. The only date which is easy to determine is that of the appearance of the following behavior pattern: at a given moment the child grasps the objects which he has perceived in the same visual field as his hand and before grasping them he alternately looks at his hand and the objects. Now this occurrence (fixed by Preyer at the 17th week) took place in Jacqueline's case at 0;6 (1), in Lucienne's at 0;4 (15) and in Laurent's at 0;3 (6). It characterizes what we shall call the fourth stage of prehension. But earlier all sorts of coördinations between vision and hand movements may be observed, coördinations which begin at the present stage and continue through the third. Here are those which we have observed during the second stage:

Observation 60.—Lucienne, at 0;2 (3), that is to say, the day after the day she began systematically to suck her thumb, twice looked at her fingers as they came out of her mouth (see above, Obs. 23). This glance was fleeting, but with accommodation of the eye to distance. At 0;2 (12), on the other hand, and the next day she looked at her hand more attentively. At 0;2 (15) I watch her while she lies on her right side and sucks her bib. Her hands move in front of her (the fingers constantly moving), grasping and letting go the sheets, scratching the cover, and the right hand or both hands momentarily enter her mouth. Lucienne's eyes seem to follow the movements of her hands (her glance rises and falls correctly, etc.) but her hands do not yield to the exigencies of the visual field. Vision, therefore, adapts itself to the movements of the hand but the converse is not yet true.—At 0;2 (16) Lucienne is lying on

13 *Op. cit.,* pp. 97–98.

her left side, her right hand pulling at the pillow; she attentively looks at this hand. At 0;2 (17) Lucienne is on her back, her right hand stretched out and the fingers moving slightly; she looks at this hand most attentively and smiles. A moment later she loses sight of it (her hand having lowered); her glance obviously seeks it and, when her hand is raised again, it immediately follows it. At 0;2 (20) Lucienne continues to look at her hands, including the left one. For instance the hands open and close alternately; they do so simultaneously and frequently outside the visual field which surely reveals that an entirely motor circular reaction independent of vision is involved. But as soon as the phenomenon is produced opposite her face, Lucienne directs her glance to her hand and watches it for a long time. She also inspects her right hand which scratches a piece of material. At 0;2 (27) she looks at her right hand which is holding a doll but is unable to keep this spectacle in her visual field. She also looks at her empty hands, the left almost as much as the right, but also without keeping them in the visual field; the glance searches for the hands but they are not subordinated to the glance. At 0;3 (3) she looks attentively at her right hand which scratches a quilt, then relinquishes it, then grasps it again, etc. While her hand loses contact with the quilt she looks at the latter but without coördination with the hand movements. Her hand rediscovers the quilt through tactile accommodation and not through accommodation with sight. That evening, she watches her hand open and close. There is as yet no precise coördination between these movements and sight except that the fingers seem to move more when Lucienne looks at them. At 0;3 (8 and 9) she looks attentively at her clasped hands while sucking the index finger and the back of her right hand.—We shall stop with this observation for, from this date on, Lucienne begins to carry to her mouth the objects she has grasped which marks the beginning of the third stage.

Observation 61.—Jacqueline seems not to have looked at her hands before 0;2 (30). But on this date and the following days she frequently notices her moving fingers and looks at them attentively. At 0;3 (13) she rumples her quilt with both hands. When her hands move into her visual field she looks fixedly at them just as she looks at the folds of the quilt when they appear before her but, if her eyes attempt to see the hands, the hand movements do not yet depend on vision at all. At 0;3 (21) likewise, her eyes follow her hands. At 0;3 (22) her glance follows her hands which turn aside and she seems very much surprised to see them reappear.

Observation 62.—At 0;2 (4) Laurent by chance discovers his right index finger and looks at it briefly. At 0;2 (11) he inspects for a moment his open right hand, perceived by chance. At 0;2 (14), on the other hand, he looks three times in succession at his left hand and chiefly at his raised index finger. At 0;2 (17) he follows its spontaneous movement for a moment, then examines it several times while it searches for his nose or rubs his eye. Next day, same observation. At 0;2 (19) he smiles at the same hand after having contemplated it eleven times in succession (when it has been untied); I then put this hand in a bandage again; as soon as I detach it (half an hour later) it returns to the visual field and Laurent again smiles at it. The same day he looks very attentively at his two clasped hands. At 0;2 (21) he holds his two fists in the air and looks at the left one, after which he slowly brings it toward his face and rubs his nose with it, then his eye. A moment later the left hand again approaches his face; he looks at it and touches his nose. He recommences and laughs five or six times in succession while moving the left hand to his face. He seems to laugh before the hand moves, but looking has no influence on its movement. He laughs beforehand but begins to smile again on seeing the hand. Then he rubs his nose. At a given moment he turns his head to the left but looking has no effect on the direction. The next day, same reactions. At 0;2 (23) he looks at his right hand, then at his clasped hands (at length). At 0;2 (24) at last it may be stated that looking acts on the orientation of the hands which tend to remain in the visual field. Thus we reach the third stage.

It may thus be seen of what the coördinations between vision and the first circular reactions of the hand and fingers consist. We can say that the visual schemata tend to assimilate the manual schemata without the converse being yet true. In other words, the glance tries to follow what the hand does but the hand does not tend in any way to realize what the glance sees; it does not even succeed in remaining in the visual field! Later, on the contrary, the hand will be regulated by vision, and vice versa; this will enable the child to grasp the objects seen. But, for the time being, the hand moves independently of the glance, the few vague circular reactions to which it gives rise being only directed by touch, kinesthetic sensations, or sucking. The relations between sight and hand movements are therefore different from those which exist between sucking and these movements; in the case of sucking, the schemata external to the hand movements control them and incorporate them (sucking entails circular reaction of the arms and hands) while in the case of vision hand movements are autonomous and the glance is limited to assimilating without controlling them. It is therefore clear that from this point of view sucking is ahead of vision. Thus at the third stage we shall see the hands grasp objects to carry them to the mouth and not yet in order to look at them.

In a general way we may conclude the following with regard to the second stage. During this stage the hand movements are no longer controlled only by reflex and impulsive mechanisms but give rise to some acquired circular reactions. The reactions certainly remain indefinite and it seems as though with respect to the most primitive of them (opening and closing the hands, scratching with the finger tips, grasping and letting go, etc.) that a simple impulsive automatism were always involved. But the question is to know if these behavior patterns are indeterminate because they are still entirely "impulsive" or because as yet they only constitute empty circular reactions without interest in the object grasped. The case of prehension is, in effect, exactly analogous to that of sucking, vision, or hearing. Just as there exists empty sucking, tongue sucking, etc., so also the nursling can wave his arms, open and close his hands, clench them, move the fingers, etc., for weeks without an object and without true contact with a reality which resists. And just as vision passes through a stage during which objects are aliments for the glance without assuming interest as external images, so also the first contacts of the hand with the things it grasps, touches and scratches by chance, bear witness to a purely functional phase of assimilation (grasping for the sake of grasping) by repetition and not yet by combined generalization and recognition. It is to this phase that Observations 50–52 apply. On the other hand, Observation 53 and Observations 55–58 are evidence of a generalizing assimilation and a beginning of tactile recognition in addition to this primitive functioning. On the one hand, as soon as the child learns to scratch and pull at objects (Obs. 53) he extends this behavior to everything, including his face and his own hands (Obs. 55–58). On the other hand, through the very fact of the extension of the schema it becomes differentiated and gives rise to a recognitory assimilation. This is why the child recnizes his nose, eyes and hands by touch, when he is searching for them. In correlation with the progress of assimilation there is gradual accommodation to objects. The hand takes the form of a thing, the thumb gradually is opposed to the other fingers, beginning the third month (or even shortly before) it is enough to touch the back of the hand to make the hand attempt to grasp, etc. With regard to coördinating organizations there is, as we have seen, a beginning of coördination with sucking and with vision but without reciprocal assimilation of the schemata. The mouth sucks the hands but the hands do not try to carry to the mouth everything they grasp nor to grasp everything that the mouth sucks, and the eye looks at the hands but the hands do not try to feel or to grasp everything the eyes see. These two essential coördinations will develop during the three succeeding stages. The coördination between sucking and grasping is more precocious and thus characterizes the third stage. But there is no logical necessity for this order of succession and it is possible to conceive of the existence of a partial reversal in the case of certain exceptional subjects.

During a *third stage* notable progress is revealed: henceforth there is *coördination between prehension and sucking.* In other words, the hand grasps objects which it carries to the mouth and reciprocally it takes hold of objects which the mouth sucks.

Let us first describe the facts in order later to analyze their various aspects.

Observation 63.—At 0;3 (8) Lucienne grasps her coverlet in her right hand and sucks it. I then place a pencil in her hand; her hand moves slightly toward her mouth and stops. As yet it is impossible to decide between chance and coördination. But that evening three times in succession I place a soft collar in her right hand which is stretched out on the coverlet and each time she carries it to her mouth. No attempt at seeing. At 0;3 (9) I place a wooden object in her hand; she brings it toward her mouth, then lets it go. At 0;3 (13), same experiment: she holds the object, carries it to her mouth and alternately licks the object and her hand without appearing to dissociate these two bodies from one another. At 0;3 (24) she grasps bib, quilt, covers by herself and carries them to her mouth. At 0;4 (4) she grasps a toy by chance (of course without seeing it) and holds it firmly for a few moments. Then a sudden movement to put it in her mouth without trying to look. Same reaction with a part of the coverlet. She does not yet direct the object; she sucks that which comes first. There exists therefore in some way a conjunction of two schemata (grasping and holding) and (putting the hand to the mouth) and not yet the single act of putting the object to the mouth.

Observation 64.—At 0;4 (9) I put a rattle before her eyes: no reaction. Then I place it in her hands: she immediately puts it in her mouth, sucks it, then moves it at random while looking at it. It seems as though this time the act of grasping a substance in order to suck it forms a single organized whole. This is confirmed by the following reaction. That evening I show Lucienne her usual rattle: she looks at it fixedly, opens her mouth, makes sucking movements, opens her mouth again, etc., but she does not grasp it. The sight of the toy, therefore, set in motion movements of sucking and not of prehension. But barely touching her stretched-out hand with the handle of the rattle suffices to produce movements of prehension: successive attempts with the fingers until the opposition of the thumb leads to success. The rattle, as soon as it is grasped, is carried to the mouth. At 0;4 (10) same reactions: the object, as soon as it is grasped, regardless of the visual field, is carried to the mouth. If it falls to the side groping ensues until success is attained.

Observation 65.—At 0;4 (10) Lucienne is lying on her back. I put a doll in front of her mouth. She manages to suck it while moving her head, but with difficulty. She then moves her hands but without bringing them together appreciably. A moment later, on the other hand, I place the rattle in her mouth, the handle lying on her chest; she immediately brings her hand to it and grasps it. The experiment is repeated three times: same reactions. At 0;4 (15) as soon as the rattle is in contact with the mouth, the hand moves in this direction. But Lucienne does not persevere. That evening, however, she grasps it immediately. This behavior seems to be definitely acquired and coördinated. To accomplish this Lucienne does not look at her hands at all and as soon as she touches the rattle she succeeds in grasping it. She does this with her left as well as with her right hand, but less often. From this observation on, Lucienne begins to coördinate her grasping movements with vision, and thus enters the fourth stage.

Observation 66.—At 0;3 (2) Lucienne carries to her mouth what she has grasped at random, opposing her thumb to the other fingers. At 0;4 (8) too, she carries to her mouth ribbons, corners of pieces of material, her bib, etc.

Observation 66 repeated.—Already at 0;2 (17) Laurent, after grasping his sheet, sucks it at the same time as his hand. There is therefore a chance connection between the schema of prehension and that of finger sucking. The next day he sucks the bandage on his left hand while holding it with his right. The following days the relations between prehension and sucking remain at random. On the other hand, at 0;2 (28) it is enough for me to place his rattle in his left hand (outside the visual field and the extended arm) to cause Laurent to introduce this object into his mouth and suck it. The experiment succeeds a series of times, with the right hand as well as the left, and the systematization of the reaction shows that this new schema was constituted several days before. Same result on the following days. At 0;3 (4) he carries to his mouth ribbons, fringes of covers, cloth dolls, etc., and, at 0;3 (5) he does the same with unfamiliar objects (package of tobacco, cigarette lighter, tobacco pouch, etc.) which I put in front of his face and which he grasps after having touched them while putting his hands together. So also it suffices that I place in his outstretched hand, outside the visual field, an object which is unfamiliar (visually and tactilely) such as a clothes pin, for Laurent to carry it immediately to his mouth and not to his eyes.

Thus it may be seen that from the second half of the third month there exists, in Laurent, coördination between sucking and grasping but, as we shall see later, this third stage was shortened in his case by a certain precocity in coördination between vision and prehension. Moreover the sequential order of the acquisition of coördinations was almost reversed in the case of this child.

Such observations are interesting inasmuch as they indicate how systematic prehension is acquired. Following the circular reactions of the second stage (pure, generalizing, and recognitory assimilations) the child begins to interest himself in the objects themselves which his hand has touched. Here the same phenomenon is produced as with respect to vision or hearing. After having looked for the sake of looking the child becomes interested in the objects he looks at, because the assimilation of reality to vision is completed through coördination between vision and the other schemata. So also, after having practiced in space various hand movements and having grasped for the sake of grasping, after having used his prehension with respect to all the solid objects he encounters and having thus acquired an increasingly precise accommodation to objects concomitant to generalizing assimilation, after having even developed a sort of tactile-motor recognition of things, the child finally becomes interested in the objects he grasps inasmuch as prehension, which has thus become systematic, is coördinated with an already completed schema, such as that of sucking. How can this coördination be explained? In the beginning (Obs. 63) it seems that there is only partial coördination—that is to say, simple conjunction of two partially independent schemata. The hand takes hold of the objects and the mouth attracts the hand. Thus at 0;4 (4) Lucienne still indifferently sucks hand or object when the hand brings the objects to the mouth. At a given moment, on the other hand, coördination becomes total. But here as with regard to sight and hearing, it clearly appears that this coördination results from a reciprocal assimilation of the schemata under consideration. The mouth seeks to suck what the hand grasps just as the hand seeks to grasp what the mouth sucks. In effect, in Observation 64, the mouth is ready to suck before the hand has discovered the object and then what the child grasps is at once brought to the mouth. Inversely, at 0;4 (10) (Obs. 65) Lucienne seeks to grasp the object which her mouth sucks when this object has not previously passed through manual prehension. Thus it may once more be seen of what the progressive organization of schemata consists: a mutual adaptation with reciprocal accommodation and assimilation.

This leads us to the coördination between vision and prehension. We recall that during the second stage the glance already follows the hand movements but the latter are not governed by the former. During the fourth stage we shall see that prehension itself is controlled by vision. With regard to the third stage which concerns us at the moment, it may be said that vision, without yet controlling prehension (which still only depends on touch and sucking) already exerts an influence on hand movements. The act of looking at the hand seems to augment the hand's activity or on the contrary to limit its displacements to the interior of the visual field.

Observation 67.—Lucienne, at 0;3 (13) looks at her right hand for a long time (her arm is outstretched) and opens and closes it. Then her hand moves quite suddenly toward her left cheek. Her eyes follow this movement with exactitude, her head moving continuously as though there were prevision. The hand then resumes its position. Lucienne looks at it again and smiles broadly while shaking herself, then the same game begins again. The following days her visual interest in hand movements or the hand holding an object remains constant, but vision does not seem to have any effect other than a vague dynamogenization of these movements.

Observation 68.—At 0;4 (9) Lucienne makes no motion to grasp a rattle she is looking at. But when she subsequently brings to her mouth the rattle she has grasped independently of sight and sees the hand which holds this object, her visual attention results in immobilizing the movement of her hands; however, her mouth was already open to receive the rattle which is 1 cm. away from her. Then Lucienne sucks the rattle, takes it out of her mouth, looks at it, sucks again, and so on.—The same day, a new experiment: I place a case in her left hand. Lucienne carries it directly to her mouth, but, as she is about to put it in (her lips already open) she perceives it, moves it away and holds it before her eyes at a distance of about 10 cm. She looks at it most attentively while holding it almost motionless for more than a minute. Her lips move and she carries the object to her mouth and sucks it for several seconds but she removes it to look at it.—The same day, Lucienne engages in the same play with her coverlet, but as yet there is no coördination between the sight of an object or of the hand and prehension as such.

Observation 69.—At 0;4 (10) Lucienne looks at her rattle with the same reactions of buccal desire. She opens her mouth, makes sucking-like movements, raises her head slightly, etc. But she does not stretch out her hands although they make grasping-like movements. A moment later, her right hand being outstretched, I place a rattle next to her. Lucienne looks alternately at her hand and the rattle, her fingers constantly moving, but she does not move her hand closer. However, when the rattle touches her hand she grasps it immediately.

Observation 70.—Jacqueline, at 0;4 (1) looks attentively at her right hand which she seems to maintain within the visual field. At 0;4 (8) she sometimes looks at the objects which she carries to her mouth and holds them before her eyes, forgetting to suck them. But there does not yet exist prehension directed by sight nor coördinated adduction of objects in the visual field. It is when the hand passes at random before her eyes that it is immobilized by the glance.—Sometimes, too, she looks attentively at her hands which happen to be joined.—At 0;5 (12) I observe that she constantly looks at her hands and fingers but always without coördination with prehension. At 0;6 (0) she has not yet established this coördination. She watches her hand move; her hand moves toward her nose and finally hits her eye. A movement of fright and retreat: her hand still does not belong to her! Nevertheless the hand is maintained more or less successfully within the visual field.

Observation 71.—At 0;3 (23) Lucienne's right arm is outstretched, her hand remaining outside the visual field. I grasp this hand. She tries to free it but does not look in this direction at all. Same result at 0;4 (9), etc. It is only during the following stages that Lucienne will search with her eyes for the hand which is held.

Observation 72.—Jacqueline still reacts in the same way at 0;5 (12)— that is to say, during the present stage. She is on her back and I alternately hold her right and left hands which are lying flat on the mattress.

She makes vain attempts to face her hand but without looking in the right direction although she tries to see what is going on. At a given moment while wriggling about Jacqueline happens to perceive my hand which is holding her right hand. She looks attentively at this unfamiliar image but without making an effort to free herself at this exact moment. Then she resumes the struggle while looking all around her head but not in the right direction. The consciousness of effort is therefore not localized in the visual image of the hand, but in the absolute. At 0;5 (25) same reaction.

Observation 73.—Laurent has revealed, with regard to the coördination of vision and hand movements, remarkable precociousness which must, we feel, be attributed to his development acquired by the schema of joining the hands (see Obs. 59). In effect, through clasping of the hands which necessarily takes place in front of the face in a reclining child, Laurent eventually studied them by looking at them attentively [see Obs. 52 at 0;2 (19) and 0;2 (23)]. This regular connection, although its cause is fortuitous, results quite naturally in leading to the influence of the glance on the movement of the hand. Thus at 0;2 (24) Laurent rubs his hands, 5 to 10 cm. from his mouth, without sucking them. He separates them and then grasps them again at least twenty times in succession while looking at them. It would appear, in such an instance, that visual pleasure alone were the cause of the repetition of the phenomenon. An hour later this impression is strengthened when Laurent, having grasped his right hand with his left and having removed the bandage (placed on the right thumb) holds the bandage within the visual field and looks at it with curiosity. At 0;2 (25) Laurent looks at his motionless left hand, after having rubbed his eye. At 0;2 (26 and 28) he looks at a rattle which he has in his hands and at 0;2 (29) I observe a new combination derived from differentiation of this schema of clasping the hands. Laurent holds his hands with the tips of his fingers only, and 10 to 15 cm. away, exactly opposite his eyes. He obviously keeps them within the visual field and reveals no tendency to suck or even actually to grasp for at least a quarter of an hour. There is only involved playing with the fingers discovered tactilely and agreeable to the eye. The next day, same observation.

Observation 74.—The significance of the preceding behavior patterns is that, with regard to Laurent, they give rise to a very curious reaction which particularly facilitated access to the definitive coördination characteristic of the fourth and fifth stages of prehension. Beginning 0;3 (3) Laurent began to grasp my hand as soon as it appeared before his face because my hand was visually assimilated to one of his hands and so set in motion the schema of hand clasping.

At 0;3 (3), around 2 P.M. I place my motionless hand opposite his face, 10 to 15 cm. from his mouth. He looks at it and immediately makes

sucking-like movements while looking at it, as though he were assimilating it to his hand which he constantly examines before or after
sucking. But he looks at my hand without trying to grasp it. Then,
without changing its location, I open my hand more and manage to
touch his left hand very lightly with my little finger. Laurent immediately grasps this finger without seeing it. When I withdraw it, Laurent
searches for it until he rediscovers it (which is the first example of a
reaction important to the development of prehension: recapturing
that which escaped the hands). Finally this use of prehension passes
into the visual field and Laurent looks at my finger most attentively.
The same day, at 6 P.M. if I display my hand in the same position this
is enough to make Laurent grasp it! I touched his hand (with my little
finger) just once, then five times in succession he grasps my hand
without my having previously touched his nor his having seen his
hand at the same time as mine! At first I assumed this phenomenon to
be a coördinated act of prehension regulated by sight of the object
alone (hence an act characteristic of the fifth stage) but the rest of the
observation suggested a simpler interpretation. The sight of my hand
simply set in motion the habitual cycle of movements of bringing the
hands together (the schema of clasping) and as my hand was in the
trajectory of his hands, he met and grasped it.

The next day, at 0;3 (4) he at once grasps my hand even though
I have not touched his at all. I find, moreover, confirmation of the preceding interpretation in the following three facts. In the first place,
when I present Laurent with some objects instead of my hand, he does
not attempt to grasp them and confines himself to looking at them. In
the second place, when I present my hand at a certain distance (20 to 30
cm.) and not just in front of his face, he is content to grasp his hands
without trying to reach my hand. In the third place, when I separate
and clasp my hands, at a distance of about 50 cm., Laurent imitates me,
as we shall see later. These three combined facts seem well to demonstrate that, if Laurent grasps my hand in front of his face, this is
through assimilating my hand to the schema of clasping his own.

At 0;3 (5) Laurent imitates less well my clasping movement when
I am at a distance. As soon as I bring my hand closer to his face, he
joins his hands and, at the proper distance, grasps them. When I again
move my hands away, he joins his. That afternoon, I present my motionless hand: he grasps it and laughs. Then I replace my hand with a
package of tobacco, a cigarette lighter and finally my tobacco pouch: he
grasps all three in sequence! By means of my hand and the schema of
joining, Laurent thus arrives at the beginning of the fourth stage.

Observation 75.—At 0;3 (5)—that is to say, the third day of the preceding observation—I immobilize Laurent's hands outside the visual field:
he does not look (see Obs. 71 and 72).

Observation 76.—Finally here is an example of the conjunction of the combined schemata of vision, prehension and sucking. At 0;4 (4) I show Lucienne my motionless hand. She looks at it attentively, then smiles, then opens her mouth wide and finally puts her own fingers into it. Same reaction many times. It appears that Lucienne assimilates my hand to hers and thus the sight of my fingers makes her put hers into her mouth. It is noteworthy that shortly afterward she looks at her own index finger, sucks it, looks at it again, etc. So also Laurent, at 0;3 (6), while looking at my hand in the same position, opens wide his mouth. Then he grasps my hand and draws it toward his open mouth while staring at my fingers.

It may thus be seen in what these coördinations between vision and hand movements consist. It is not yet possible to speak of coördination between vision and prehension, since the child knows neither how to grasp what he sees (he does not grasp what he touches or sucks) nor how to hold before his eyes that which he has grasped (he carries things to the mouth and not to the eyes), nor even how to look at his own hand when it is held by the hand of someone else (Obs. 71, 72 and 75). It can no longer be said, however, that the child is limited to looking at his hands without having them react to his looking. When the hand by chance enters the visual field it tends to remain there. It even happens that the child postpones sucking the grasped object through pure visual interest (Obs. 68 and 70). In short, there is a beginning of true coördination—that is to say, of reciprocal adaptation. The hand tends to conserve and repeat the movements that the eye looks at, just as the eye tends to look at everything the hand does. In other words the hand tends to assimilate to its schemata the visual realm just as the eye assimilates to its schemata the manual realm. Henceforth when the child perceives certain visual images (sees the fingers move, the hands hold an object, etc.) this is enough to make his hand tend to conserve them through reproductive assimilation to the extent that these images are assimilated to manual schemata.

How is this reciprocal assimilation to be explained? We understand the meaning of the assimilation of the motor realm by the visual schemata, since the hand and its movements can be seen and watched. But what does the assimilation of the visual by the manual mean? In what follows this will be tantamount to saying that the hand tries to grasp everything that the eye sees. But this coördination will only be exactly produced later, during the fourth or fifth stage. For the time being the manual schemata only assimilate the visual realm to the extent that the hand conserves and reproduces what the eyes see of it. Now how is this possible? Associationism simply responds: the visual image of the hand, through being associated to the movements of this hand, acquires by transfer the value of a signal and governs sooner or later these very movements. Concerning the fact, as such, of this associative transfer, everyone is of course in agreement. Every accommodation involves putting into relationship known quantities imposed by experience, and the child discovers the connection between the visual image of the hands and their movements quite a while before attributing this image and the corresponding kinesthetic impressions to a unique and substantial "object." But the problem is to find out whether this relation between the visual and the motor is established by "association." On the contrary, we place in opposition to the passive concept of association the active concept of assimilation. That which is fundamental and without which no relationship between sight and hand movements could be established is that the hand's activity constitutes schemata which tend to conserve and reproduce themselves (opening and closing, grasping bodies and holding them, etc.). Through the very fact of this tendency toward conservation such activity incorporates in itself every reality capable of supporting it. This explains why the hand grasps that which it encounters, etc. Now comes the moment when the child looks at his hand which is moving. On the one hand, he is led, by visual interest, to make this spectacle last—that is to say, not to take his eyes off his hand; on the other hand, he is led, by kinesthetic and motor interest, to make this manual activity last. It is then that the coördination of the two schemata operates, not by association, but by reciprocal assimilation. The child discovers that in moving his hand in a certain way (more slowly, etc.) he conserves this interesting image for his sight. Just as he assimilates to his glance the movement of his hands, so also he assimilates to his manual activity the corresponding visual image. He moves with his hands the image he contemplates just as he looks with his eyes at the movement he produces. Whereas until now only tactile objects served as aliments for the manual schemata, visual images now become material for exercises of the hands. It is in this sense that they may be called "assimilated" to the sensorimotor activity of the arms and hands. This assimilation is not yet an identification: the visual hand is not yet a tactile-motor hand. But the substantial identification will result from assimilation as the geometric point of the crossing of lines. The intersection of the assimilating activities will define the object, in proportion as these activities applied to the outside world will constitute causality.

An excellent illustration of this process is supplied by Observations 73 and 74. After watching his hands join for several days, at 0;3 (3) Laurent manages to grasp a privileged object as represented by my hand. How can this precocious prehension be explained, if not precisely as being due to the fact that this visual image of my hand is assimilated to the visual image of his hands, and that this latter image is already incorporated in the schema of joining the hands.[14] Here we see at work, in the most definite way, the play of assimilation in its dual reproductive and recognitory character. If the coördination of vision and prehension were a matter of pure physiological maturation of the nervous system, the differences in dates of acquisitions as revealed by three normal children such as Jacqueline, Lucienne and Laurent could not be understood. On the other hand, by following in detail Laurent's psychomotor assimilations (the use of the cycle

[14] It may be thought strange that we should assert with regard to Observation 74 that at 0;3 (3) Laurent manages to assimilate my hand to his, despite differences in size and position. But a good reason impels us to this interpretation. Beginning 0;3 (4) I have been able to establish that Laurent imitates my hand movements; he separates, then joins his hands in response to my suggestions. This imitative reaction recurred at 0;3 (5), 0;3 (6), at 0;3 (8), at 0;3 (23), etc. Now if there is imitation of such a movement, to the exclusion of so many others, it is obvious that there is assimilation. That this assimilation is entirely synthetic, without objective identification, is evident; it does not yet involve either the distinguishing of another's body and his own body or the concept of permanent and comparable objects grouped in categories, and it is doubtless even based upon a confusion rather than an actual comparison. But no more than this is needed to enable us to speak of assimilation. Assimilation, which is the source of imitation as it is of recognition, is an earlier mechanism than objective comparison and, in this sense, there is no obstacle to asserting that a 3-month-old child can assimilate another's hand to his own.

to the joining of the hands, the assimilation to this schema of the visual image of the hands and finally the assimilation of my hand to his hands) the reason for his precocity may be understood.

The same applies to the still more complex example of as-similation of the visual to the manual furnished by observation 76. At 0;4 (4) Lucienne sucks her hand while looking at mine. Before that time Lucienne has already coördinated the grasping of objects to sucking movements. She carries to her mouth everything that she grasps, regardless of the visual field. In addition she visually recognizes the objects she sucks or is going to suck and thus a coördination between vision and sucking is established which we have analyzed in connection with the latter. Now, among these objects the hand plays a central role, since Lucienne is visually acquainted with it at about two months, that she knows how to suck from a still earlier date and knows how to carry her hand to her mouth after having looked at it. There exists, therefore, as far as the hand is concerned, a conjunction of at least three schemata—sucking, vision, and motor activity to the exclusion of actual prehension. Lucienne looks at my hand; her reaction is to suck it immediately and perhaps to move it. But, either she confuses it at first with her own and then sucks her own, or else, what is more likely, she has the impression, due to global assimilation, of an object capable of being carried to the mouth more easily than the others, and, not knowing how to grasp what she sees, it is her own hand that she brings between her lips. In this second case, there was only semiconfusion; but in both cases the visual image of my hand is assimilated to the simultaneously visual, motor, and buccal schema of her own hand.

Regardless of these last examples, the coördination between vision and hand movements until the present only affect the latter to the exclusion of prehension. In other words, except in Observations 74 and 76, the child still only grasps objects when he touches them by chance, and, if he looks at his hands when they are holding the object, vision does not yet help at all in the actual act of grasping. During the fourth and fifth stage, the coördination between vision and hand movements will be extended until it arrives at actual prehension.

The *fourth stage* is that during which *there is prehension as soon as the child simultaneously perceives his hand and the desired object.* I have been able to observe, in effect, in the most definite way with respect to my three children that the grasping of objects which have simply been looked at only begins to become systematic in cases in which the object and the hand are perceived in the same visual field.

Observation 77.—At 0;6 (0) Jacqueline looks at my watch which is 10 cm. from her eyes. She reveals a lively interest and her hands flutter as though she were about to grasp, without however discovering the right direction. I place the watch in her right hand without her being able to see how (the arm being outstretched). Then I again put the watch before her eyes. Her hands, apparently excited by the contact just experienced, then proceed to move through space and meet violently, subsequently to separate. The right hand happens to strike the watch: Jacqueline immediately tries to adjust her hand to the watch and thus manages to grasp it. The experiment is repeated three times: it is always when the hand is perceived at the same time as the watch that the attempts become systematic.—The next day, at 0;6 (1) I resume the experiment. When the watch is before her eyes Jacqueline does not attempt to grasp it although she reveals a lively interest in this object. When the watch is near her hand and she happens to touch it, or it is seen at the same time as her hand, then there is searching, and searching directed by the glance. Near the eyes and far from the hands, the watch is again simply contemplated. The hands move a little but do not approach each other. I again place the object near her hand: immediate searching and again, success. I put the watch a third time a few centimeters from her eyes and far from her hands: these move in all directions but without approaching each other. In short, there are still two worlds for Jacqueline, one kinesthetic and the other visual. It is only when the object is seen next to the hand that the latter is directed toward it and manages to grasp it.—That evening, the same experiments with various solid objects. Again and very regularly, when Jacqueline sees the object facing her without perceiving her hands, nothing happens, whereas the simultaneous sight of object and of hand (right or left) sets prehension in motion. Finally it is to be noted that, that day, Jacqueline again watched with great interest her empty hand crossing the visual field: The hand is still not felt to belong to her.

Observation 78.—Lucienne, at 0;4 (12) looks attentively at her mother's hand while taking the breast. She then moves her own hand while looking at her mother's. Then she perceives her own hand. Her glance then oscillates between the aforementioned hands. Finally she grasps her mother's hand.—The same day, in the same situation, Lucienne again perceives her mother's hands. She then lets go the breast to stare at this hand while moving her lips and tongue. Then she puts forward her own hand in the direction of the maternal hand and suddenly, she puts her own between her lips, sucks it a moment and takes it out, the while looking at her mother's hand. There ensues a reaction analogous to that of Observation 65. As she did a week earlier, Lucienne sucks her own hand out of confusion with the hand she perceives. But this time the confusion does not last; after having removed her hand from between her lips she moves it about at random, haphazardly touches her mother's hand and immediately grasps it. Then, while watching this spectacle most attentively, she lets go the hand she was holding, looks alternately at her own hand and the other one, again puts her hand in her mouth, then removes it while contemplating the whole time her mother's hand and finally grasping it and not letting it go for a long moment.

Observation 79.—Lucienne, at 0;4 (15) looks at a rattle with desire, but without extending her hand. I place the rattle near her right hand. As soon as Lucienne sees rattle and hand together, she moves her hand closer to the rattle and finally grasps it. A moment later she is engaged in looking at her hand. I then put the rattle aside; Lucienne looks at it, then directs her eyes to her hand, then to the rattle again, after which she slowly moves her hand toward the rattle. As soon as she touches it, there is an attempt to grasp it and finally, success.—After this I remove the rattle. Lucienne then looks at her hand. I put the rattle aside. She looks alternately at her hand and at the rattle, then moves her hand. The latter happens to leave the visual field. Lucienne then grasps a coverlet which she moves toward her mouth. After this her hand goes away haphazardly. As soon as it reappears in the visual field, Lucienne stares at it and then immediately looks at the rattle which has remained motionless. She then looks alternately at hand and rattle after which her hand approaches and grasps it.

Observation 80.—The same day progress is revealed after the facts related in Observation 65 (taking the rattle placed against the mouth). I put the rattle above Lucienne's face. The immediate reaction consists in trying to suck it; she opens her mouth, makes sucking-like movements, pulls her tongue, pants with desire. Thereupon her hands approach her mouth and seem to stretch toward the object. As soon as the right hand is seen, it directs itself toward the rattle and grasps it. It is therefore the desire to suck the object which set the hand in motion; therein is progress toward the fifth stage.—I then place the rattle higher up. Same expression of buccal drive. The hand tries to grasp, in space. As soon as Lucienne perceives her hand she looks alternately at the rattle and at her hand, then tries to grasp, which she achieves after some groping.—At 0;4 (19) same reactions with my finger: she makes sucking-like movements while looking at it, then moves her hand toward her mouth and when she sees the hand, grasps.

Observation 81.—At 0;3 (6)—that is to say following Observation 73 and 74—Laurent looks at my watch which I hold not in front of his face, but to his right. This spectacle sets in motion activity of both hands, but not a joining movement. The right hand remains in the zone of the watch, as though he were searching for it. As soon as Laurent sees watch and hand together, he grasps! The hand was well oriented, open, with the thumb opposite.—A moment later, I present a cloth doll on the left side. The reaction is the same: Laurent looks at the doll, then perceives his left hand, looks at it, then his eyes return to the doll. He then grasps it, carries it to his mouth and sucks it.

That evening, an essential observation. Laurent's hands are outstretched and he looks ahead of him, wide awake. I present to him the customary objects (rattle, cloth doll, package of tobacco, etc.): he grasps nothing and looks at them as though he knew nothing whatever about grasping. Thereupon I place my motionless hand in front of his face, in the same place as the objects: he grasps it immediately; my hand is barely in position when his hands move and with one motion seize my hand.—It seems that, through lack of seeing a hand, Laurent did not have the idea of grasping the objects presented at first, and that the sight of my hand (in its role of hand and not of object) immediately stimulated his schema of prehension.

A little later I present to Laurent a cloth doll (on the left side): he looks at it attentively without moving his hand (except for a few vague movements). But, as soon as he sees his hand (I observe his glance through the hood of the bassinet), he grasps. Same experiment with the customary series of objects and same reactions.

Observation 82.—At 0;3 (7), the following day, Laurent is motionless, his hands outstretched, engaged in babbling, when I begin the day's first experiment. I present to him on the left side (without showing myself) a roll of tinfoil (to him an unfamiliar object). Three definite reactions succeed one another. In the first place, his hands immediately move, open and tend to approach one another. Meanwhile Laurent looks at the object without looking at his hands. His left hand passes near the paper, very slowly, but instead of bifurcating in the direction of the object, it pursues its trajectory toward the other hand which comes to meet it. The hands then meet while Laurent continues to look at the object. The sight of the object has therefore set in motion the cycle of the functioning of the hands, without modifications. In the second place, while Laurent's hands are joined, I put the tinfoil opposite him. He looks at it but does not react at all. In the third place, I put the paper in the same visual field as his hands. He then looks at his hands, losing sight of the object for a moment, then again looks at the object; then he separates his hands and directs them toward the object which he manages to grasp. The simultaneous viewing of hands and object is therefore still necessary for prehension.

The next day, same observations, in the morning. In the afternoon I present one of his rattles to Laurent; when the rattle is in the trajectory of his hands, he grasps it immediately. Otherwise he looks alternately at his hand and the object. In particular, when I place the rattle on his quilt, before his face at a distance of about 10 cm., he looks at length at his hand and the rattle before attempting to grasp; his hand remains 5 cm. from the rattle. Then at last he makes an attempt and succeeds.

Same reaction for two more days, then Laurent enters the fifth stage.

Observation 83.—During this fourth stage I was able to observe in Laurent a beginning of the reciprocal relation between vision and actual prehension. But it is only a beginning. At 0;3 (7) when he has succeeded in grasping the tinfoil, Laurent lets it go soon after (with his left hand). He then turns his head to look at his empty hand. Same observation a moment later. I then hold each of his hands in succession, outside the visual field, to see whether he takes notice of the position. In seven attempts Laurent succeeds twice on the left side, but not at all on the right. Then I place an object in his right hand (tinfoil). He at once carries it to his mouth. But, before introducing it between his lips, he perceived it and then maintains it in his visual field.

At 0;3 (8) after the experiment with the rattle (Obs. 82) he loses it on the right side (but he has let it go with his left hand while he was shaking it from side to side). Laurent then looks four or five times in succession at his empty left hand. He even shakes his hand very markedly, at a certain moment, as though this shaking would start the sound of the rattle! Regardless of this last point, in any case he marks with his glance the position of his hand.

The importance of this fourth stage is evident. Henceforth the child grasps the objects which he sees, and not only those he touches or those he sucks. It is thus the beginning of the essential coördination which will aid prehension. The only limitation which still exists and which thus makes the fourth stage stand in the way of the fifth is that the child only tries to grasp the objects seen to the extent that he perceives, in the same visual field, his own hand. It is even, as is clearly apparent from examining the facts, the simultaneous sight of hand and object which induces the child to grasp; neither the sight of the object nor of the hand alone leads to this result. It might appear that an ex-

ception should be made of Observation 80. Lucienne tries to
grasp the rattle or the finger that she wants to suck. But the ex-
ception is only ostensible. Either Lucienne simply brings her
hand to her mouth and it is on seeing it that she tends to grasp
the object, or else from the outset it is in order to grasp that she
simply prolongs the behavior patterns recorded in Observation
65 (grasping objects placed against her mouth) which was revealed several minutes before those of Observation 80 which is in
question.

How can we explain this tendency to grasp objects when
they are perceived in the same visual field as the hand? It is possible to waver between two extreme solutions: the associative
transfer and the Gestalt. Concerning associationism, as the sight
of the hand holding the object has been associated to the act of
grasping a certain number of times, it suffices, at a given moment,
for the hand and the object to be visually perceived separately
but simultaneously, in order that this perception may set prehension in motion. But, as we have already seen with regard to
the third stage, such an explanation overlooks the element of
activity peculiar to such establishing of relationships. The visual
image of the hand is not only a signal which sets prehension in
motion; it constitutes, with the grasping movements a total
schema, in the same way that, during the third stage, the visual
schemata of the hand are coördinated with the motor schemata
other than that of prehension. Is it then necessary to speak of
Gestalt and to say that the simultaneous sight of the hands and
of the object causes a "structure" to appear which neither the
sight of the hands nor of the object was sufficient to give rise to?
About the fact itself we are certainly in agreement, and Observations 77–83 may be compared to those of W. Köhler according to
which the monkey uses the cane when he perceives it at the same
time as the objects to be drawn to him and not when the cane has
been seen outside of the same visual field. Only it must be noted
that this "structure" did not appear suddenly, but in close relation to a whole series of earlier searchings and of coördinations
between sight and hand movements. Once the child has learned,
during the third stage, to conserve and reproduce by means of
movements of the hand that which the eye has been able to see

of these same movements, he becomes able to grasp under the influence of the glance. In other words, it is not so much the new "structure" which is of importance here as the process leading to this structure. This is why we speak of active assimilation.

Actually, once the visual schemata and the sensorimotor schemata of the hand have been mutually assimilated during the third stage (the eye looks at the hand just as the hand reproduces those of its movements which the eye sees), this kind of coördination is applied sooner or later to the very act of grasping. Looking at the hand which grasps an object, the child tries, with the hand, to maintain the spectacle which the eye contemplates as well as continuing, with his eye, to look at what his hand is doing. Once this double schema has been constituted, it is self-evident that the child will try to grasp an object while he looks at the same time at his hand when he is not yet capable of this behavior when he does not see his hand. Grasping the object when he sees the object and the hand at the same time is therefore, for the child, simply assimilating the sight of the hand to the visual and motor schema of the act consisting in "looking at grasping."

Proof that this act of "looking at grasping" simply constitutes a double schema of assimilation and not a "structure" independent of the effort and progressive activity of the subject is that this act was revealed at 0;3 (6) by Laurent, at 0;4 (12 to 15) by Lucienne and at 0;6 (0–1) by Jacqueline—that is to say, with a distance of nearly three months between the extremes. Now this difference between one child and another is explained by the whole history of their ocular-manual coördinations. Lucienne looked at her fingers since 0;2 (3), Laurent since 0;2 (4) whereas Jacqueline waited until 0;2 (30) and 0;3 (0), etc. However, nothing justifies us in considering Jacqueline retarded in relation to Lucienne. The explanation is very simple: Jacqueline, born January 9th and spending her days outdoors on a balcony, was much less active in the beginning than Lucienne and Laurent, born in June and in May. Furthermore and by virtue of this very fact, I made many fewer experiments on her during the first months, whereas I was constantly busy with Laurent. Regarding the latter, his precocity can be explained, as we have seen, first by the fact that he sucked his fingers much earlier than the others (partly because of my experiments), and chiefly by the fact that this finger sucking gave rise to a very firm schema, that of joining the hands (Obs. 59). Constantly joining his hands, he applied himself to watching them function (Obs. 73). Once accustomed to this spectacle, he precociously grasped my hands through assimilation with his own (Obs. 74), and he thus arrived quite naturally at grasping objects (see Obs. 81: he only grasps objects, at a given moment, after having seen and grasped my hand). It seems therefore that the appearance of the essential coördinations between sight and grasping depends upon the whole psychological history of the subject and not on structures determined by an inevitable physiological unfolding. It is therefore the history, the assimilating process itself, which is of the essence and not the isolated "structure" of this history. It even appears as though a certain chance intervenes in the child's discoveries and the assimilating activity which utilizes these discoveries is thus more or less slowed down or accelerated, as the case may be.

During the *fifth stage,* at last, *the child grasps that which he sees* without limitations relating to the position of the hand.[15] First here are the facts:

Observation 84.—At 0;6 (3)—that is to say, three days after the beginning of the fourth stage—Jacqueline, at the outset, grasped pencils, fingers, neckties, watches, etc., which I present to her at a distance of about 10 cm. from her eyes, regardless of whether or not her hands are visible.

Observation 85.—The same day Jacqueline brings before her eyes the objects I put into her hand outside the visual field (pencils, etc.). This reaction is new and did not appear on the previous days.

Observation 86.—Finally, the same day, Jacqueline instantaneously looks in the right direction when I hold her hand outside the visual field. This too is new (see Obs. 72). These three behavior patterns which appeared simultaneously (grasping what one sees, carrying the objects to the eyes, and looking at the hand which is being held) were maintained and established the following days.

Observation 87.—Lucienne, at 0;4 (20), looks at my finger and opens her mouth in order to suck. Meanwhile her right hand touches mine,

15 See in this connection H. Hetzer, with H. H. Beaumont and E. Wiehe-meyer, Das Schauen und Greifen des Kindes, *Zeitschr. f. Psychol.,* 113, 1929, p. 239 (see in particular pp. 257 and 262–263).

feels it and climbs little by little toward the finger, while her glance is lowered and looks for the hand. This coördination of the direction of the glance with a gesture made by the hand outside the visual field is new in connection with the fourth stage and presages the fifth stage. —So also, a moment later, Lucienne looks at a rattle located above her face. Without seeing her hand, she raises it toward the rattle. As soon as she perceives the hand, prehension follows (left hand). When the rattle is higher, Lucienne wavers between putting her hands in her mouth and trying to grasp. The sight of the hand stimulates prehension. At 0;4 (21) in the same situation, Lucienne brings her hand at once into the visual field, looks alternately at this hand and at the rattle and grasps. When I place the rattle higher up, on the other hand, she gesticulates without bringing the hand nearer and it is necessary for her to have perceived the hand for her to attempt to grasp the object. When the rattle is lower down, the hand is then brought into the visual field and then the simultaneous sight of hand and object induces grasping. Likewise, when the rattle is high up, but Lucienne has just touched it (without seeing it), she tries to grasp while steering her hand in the right direction.—All these facts, therefore, indicate an intermediary behavior pattern between the fourth and the fifth stage. Sight of the hand remains adjuvant to prehension, but sight of the object suffices to bring the hand into the visual field.

Observation 88.—Beginning at 0;4 (26), on the other hand, it seems that sight of the object at once sets prehension in motion in the case of Lucienne; all the day's attempts are positive. At 0;4 (28) she seems at first to have regressed; simultaneous sight of hand and object is necessary, at the beginning of the day. But that evening she immediately tries to grasp what she sees. For instance, I place my slide rule above her eyes. She looks for a moment at this unfamiliar object, then both her hands simultaneously direct themselves toward it. From 0;5′ (1) there is no longer any hesitation; Lucienne attempts to grasp everything she sees.

Observation 89.—At 0;5 (1) also, Lucienne immediately brings to her eyes the object she grasps or which is placed in her hands, regardless of the visual field. Then she sometimes sucks the object, but not always. It is only on an average of 3 out of 10 times that she sucked before looking. Furthermore, at the moment that she brings the object toward the visual field she expects to see something and searches with her glance even before seeing.

Observation 90.—At 0;5 (1) Lucienne looks in the direction of her hand which is being held. For example, I clasp her right hand while she looks to the left; she immediately turns in the right direction. Until now such an experiment yielded negative results.—A moment later, I place in her left hand (outside the visual field) a bulky object (a gourd), which she immediately tries to grasp but which I retain. She then definitely looks for this hand, even though her arm is outstretched beside her body and thus her hand is hard to see.

At 0;5 (18), Lucienne corroborates these last acquisitions: taking what she sees, bringing the object before her eyes when she has grasped it outside the visual field, and looking in the direction of the hand which is being held.

Observation 91.—At 0;3 (11) Laurent is pulling toward himself sheets, covers, etc., to suck them (he does this a part of each day since he has learned how to grasp). When I hold out directly in front of him a package of tobacco, he grasps it immediately, without looking at his hand. Same reaction with an eraser. At 0;3 (12) under the same conditions he grasps my watch chain which is on his left and outside the trajectory of the joining of his hands. That evening, same reaction with this chain and with a roll of cardboard. At 0;3 (13) he immediately grasps a case which I hold out to him. He does not look at his hands or attempt to join them but at once directs the right hand toward the case. When he has grasped it, he does not suck, but examines it.

Observation 92.—At 0;3 (12) when I put a key in his hand, outside the visual field, he carries it to his mouth and not to his eyes. But he is very hungry (five hours have elapsed since his last meal). That evening same reaction with the case with which he is familiar but, when I place my watch chain in his hand, he looks at it before attempting to suck it.

The next day he swings a hanging chain in order to move his rattle (see below, Obs. 98). He has grasped it without looking at it, but twice he looks at his hand while it is holding the chain. In the same way, he rolls part of his sheet into a ball before sucking it and from time to time he looks at what he is doing (with both his hands).

At 0;3 (13) likewise, while he still holds in his left hand the case which he grasped (see Obs. 91) and looks straight at me, I slip into his right hand without his noticing it, my watch chain rolled into a knot (his hand is outstretched beside him). Then I withdraw and observe through the hood of the bassinet. He immediately brings the chain before his eyes (and not to his mouth) and, as he still holds the case in his left hand, he looks alternately at case and chain.—At a certain moment he loses his case. He searches for it (without seeing and still with his left hand), then he touches it without succeeding in extricating it from the_folds of the coverlet. A long attempt. As soon as he succeeds in grasping it, he brings it before his eyes!

Observation 93.—At 0;3 (12) Laurent's left hand is outstretched. I then hold it outside the visual field: he immediately looks at it. The experiment fails with his right hand, but he seems unnerved. That evening, when I hold his right hand, he looks at it at once.

We see what comprises the acquisitions belonging to the fifth stage which denote the definitive triumph of prehension. The coördination between vision and prehension is now sufficient for each object which meets the eye to give rise to a grasping movement even when the hand is not yet perceived in the same visual field as the object.

How can this final coördination be explained? It can be conceived as being the simple result of the effort of reciprocal assimilation which the visual and manual schemata have hitherto revealed. As early as the second stage the glance attempts to follow (hence to assimilate itself) everything that the hand performs. During the third stage the hand attempts, in return, to reproduce those of its movements which the eye sees; that is to say, as we have seen, to assimilate the visual realm to the manual schemata. During the fourth stage this assimilation of the visual to the manual is extended to prehension itself when the hand appears in the same field of observation as the object to be grasped. The hand thus takes hold of what the eye observes, just as the eye tends to look at that which the hand grasps. During the fifth stage reciprocal assimilation is finally complete. All that is to be seen is also to be grasped and all that is to be grasped is also to be seen. It is natural that the hand should seek to grasp everything that the eye looks at, since the behavior patterns characteristic of the fourth stage have taught the child that this was possible when the hand is perceived at the same time as the object. The behavior belonging to the fifth stage is in this respect only a generalization of the coördinations belonging to the fourth stage. With regard to looking at everything that is grasped, it is remarkable that this tendency appears precisely at the same time as the complementary tendency. Observations 85 and 89 show that Jacqueline at 0;6 (3) and Lucienne at 0;5 (1) bring to their eyes that which they grasp, on the very date when they begin to grasp systematically what they see. The same day they also tend to look at their hand when it is held outside the visual field (Obs. 86 and 90). Such facts adequately demonstrate how much the coördination of vision and prehension is a matter of reciprocal assimilation and not of simple and irreversible associative transfer.

In conclusion, the conquest of prehension, while much more complex than that of sucking and the other elementary acquired adaptations, confirms what we have observed of the latter. All adaptation is a putting in equilibrium of a complementary accommodation and assimilation and is itself correlative to an internal and external organization of the adaptational systems. In the realm of prehension, the *accommodation* of the hand to the object is what has chiefly held writers' attention. Pure reflex in its beginnings, it subsequently involves an apprenticeship during which the accomplishment of hand movements and the opposing of the thumb are on a par with the coördination of these movements as a function of sucking and of the tactile and visual characteristics of the object. This aspect of the question is important, particularly in regard to the elaboration of the concept of space. With respect to the *assimilation* of the real to the grasping schemata, this develops analogously to what we have seen in the other realms. The child begins by moving his hand for the sake of moving it, to grasp for the sake of grasping, and hold for the sake of holding, without any interest in the objects themselves. This purely functional or reproductive assimilation (assimilation through simple repetition) is seen in the course of the reflex stage and of the second stage. How will the subject proceed from this purely functional interest (denoting an elementary assimilation of the real to the activity) to an interest in the objects grasped? Through a dual process of complication of assimilation and coördination among the sensorimotor schemata. As far as an assimilation itself is concerned, it becomes complicated through generalization. In the beginning the nursling limits himself to grasping immobile objects of a certain consistency which come in contact with the palm of the hand or the inside of the fingers; then through very repetition of the act of prehension he applies the same schemata to objects of various consistencies, animated by different movements and which the hand approaches in different ways. There exists, therefore, "generalizing" assimilation and through that very thing, the constitution of differentiated schemata, that is to say, "recognitory" assimilation. But the manifestations of the latter are less clear in the realm of prehension than in that of sight, hearing, etc., because prehension is too quickly subordinated to external ends, such as sucking or sight. Nevertheless tactile recognition exists as revealed by the different ways in which a child grasps a handkerchief or a pencil, for example: from the first contacts the accommodation is different. This diversification of schemata during which generalizing and recognitory assimilation are on a par with the progress of accommodation explains in part how interest in the objects grasped follows purely functional interest. But it is chiefly the coördination of prehension with sucking and vision that accounts for the progressive objectifying of the universe in its relations to the activity of the hands.

Here we reach the *organization* of the grasping schemata. These schemata become organized among themselves through the fact that they adapt themselves to the external world. Thus every act of prehension presupposes an organized totality in which tactile and kinesthetic sensations and arm, hand and finger movements intervene. Hence such schemata constitute "structures" of a whole, although they were elaborated in the course of a slow evolution and over a number of attempts, gropings, and corrections. But above all these schemata are organized in coördination with schemata of another kind, chief of which are those of sucking and of vision. We have seen in what this organization consists: it is a reciprocal adaptation of the schemata in view, naturally with mutual accommodation but also with collateral assimilation. Everything that is looked at or sucked tends to be grasped and everything that is grasped tends to be sucked and then to be looked at. This coördination which crowns the acquisition of prehension also indicates an essential progress in objectification. When an object can be simultaneously grasped and sucked or grasped, looked at and sucked, it becomes externalized in relation to the subject quite differently than if it could only be grasped. In the latter case it is only an aliment for the function itself and the subject only attempts to grasp through the need to grasp. As soon as there is coördination, on the contrary, the object tends to be assimilated to several schemata simultaneously. It thus acquires an ensemble of meanings and consequently a consistency, which endow it with interest.

§5. THE FIRST ACQUIRED ADAPTATIONS: CONCLU-SIONS.—After having analyzed in detail the first adaptations which are superimposed on the reflex adaptations, it is appropriate to draw some general conclusion which can subsequently guide us in our study of actual intelligence. The behavior patterns which we have described in the foregoing chapters in effect form the transition between the organic and the intellectual. They cannot yet be described as intelligent behavior patterns because intention is lacking (the differentiation between means and ends) and also mobility, which allows adaptation to continue in new circumstances. But certain intersensorial coördinations, such as those of prehension with vision, are not far removed from intelligent connection and already presage intention. On the other hand, these adaptations can no longer be characterized as purely organic because they add to the simple reflex an element of accommodation and asimilation related to the subject's experience. It is therefore important to understand how the behavior patterns of this second stage prepare intelligence.

Expressed in ordinary language, the problem which confronts us here is that of acquired association or habit and the role of these mechanisms in the genesis of intelligence. Sucking thumb or tongue, following with the eyes moving objects, searching for where sounds come from, grasping solid objects to suck or look at them, etc., are the first habits which appear in the human being. We have described their appearance in detail but the question may be asked in a general way, what sensorimotor habit is and how it is constituted. Furthermore, and it is with this sole aim that we have studied the first acquired adaptations, it may be asked in what way habitual association prepares the intelligence and what the relationships are between these two types of behavior patterns. Let us begin with this last point.

In psychology there has always been a tendency to trace back the active operations of intelligence to the passive mechanisms arising from association or habit. To reduce the causal link to a matter of habit, to reduce the generalization characteristic of the concept to the progressive application of habitual systems, to reduce judgment to an association, etc.—such are the common positions of a certain psychology dating from Hume and Bain. The idea of the conditioned reflex, which is perhaps misused today, undoubtedly revives the terms of the problem, but its application to psychology certainly remains in the prolongation of this tradition.—Habit, too, has always seemed to some people to be the antithesis of intelligence. Where the second is active invention, the first remains passive repetition; where the second is awareness of the problem and an attempt at comprehension, the first remains tainted with lack of awareness and inertia, etc. The solution we shall give to the question of intelligence thus partly depends on that which we shall choose in the realm of habit.

Now at the risk of sacrificing precision to a taste for symmetry, we believe that the solutions between which one may waver with regard to the relationships between habit and intelligence are five principal ones and that they are parallel to the five solutions (delineated in our Introduction) regarding the genesis of the morphological reflex structures and their relationship to intelligence. Let us examine these various solutions.

The first consists in asserting that habit is a primary fact from which, through progressive complication, intelligence is derived. This is the associationist solution and the doctrine of conditioned reflexes insomuch as the latter attempts to be an instrument of general explanation in physiology. We have seen (Introduction, §3) to which Lamarckian attitude this first solution in biology proper corresponds.

The second solution which is on a par with vitalism in biology and the doctrine of "intelligence faculty" in psychology, consists in considering habit as being derived, through automatization, from higher operations involving intelligence itself. Thus to Buytendijk, the formation of habits, in animal psychology, presupposes something quite different from association: "Not only are the phenomena much more complicated, but here we see appear, in the sensitive-motor realm, phenomena which bear considerable analogy to the higher process of thought."[16] This analogy, according to this writer, rests upon the fact that "the center whence emanate all the functions of the soul . . . is an

16 Buytendijk, *Psychologie des animaux*, Paris, Payot, p. 205.

immaterial cause, as much of sensorial activities as of the motor (activities) of the animal's psychic function."[17]

A third and a fourth solution, which are on a par with the theories of preformation and mutation in biology and with apriority and pragmatism would be tantamount to saying that habit is absolutely or relatively independent of intelligence and in some ways even its opposite. Although this point of view has not yet been systematically supported with regard to the theory of habit itself, many indications of it may be found in connection with intelligence in the work of writers whose chief common preoccupation is to emphasize the originality of the intellectual act. Thus it is that the Gestalt theory (third solution) radically opposes the putting into structures fitted to understanding and the simple automatism due to habit. Among the French psychologists H. Delacroix is also very decisive: "Far from necessarily depending on habit, it seems on the contrary as though it (generalization) were connected with the power to free oneself of it. . . . Thus, even while asserting the importance of habit as a means of grouping, all generalization remains irreducible to it."[18] So also when Claparède (fourth solution) describes intelligence to us as a searching arising on the occasion of the defeats of instinct and of habit, he partially puts the latter in opposition to the former.[19]

A fifth solution is, finally, conceivable: this is to consider the formation of habits as being due to an activity whose analogies with intelligence are purely functional, but which will be found again at the point of departure of intellectual operations when the suitable structures will permit it to go beyond its initial structure. As we understand the very important work of J. M. Baldwin, it seems to us that the concept of "circular reaction" is precisely destined to express the existence of this active factor, the principle of habit, and at the same time the source of an adaptational activity which intelligence will prolong by means of new techniques. It is through being inspired by this kind of tradition that we have, for our part, interpreted the genesis of

17 *Ibid.,* pp. 290–291.
18 Delacroix, in Duman, *Traité,* 1st edition, II, p. 135.
19 Claparède, *op. cit.,* pp. 137–161.

the first habits of the nursling in terms of active assimilation and accommodation. This is not to say that this adaptational activity of which habit is only an automatization is already intelligence. For this it lacks the structural characteristics (intention, systems of mobility, etc.) whose advent we shall describe in connection with the following stage. But it does present all the functional characteristics of intelligence which will arise from it through reflexive progress and a differentiation of the relationships between subject and object more than by simply being placed in opposition to acquired habits.

Having distinguished these five solutions, let us try to discuss them in the light of the facts previously established. This will provide us with an opportunity to state precisely the meaning of the general concepts of conditioned reflex, associative transfer, habit, and circular reaction to which we have alluded without sufficient criticism, and finally to elaborate upon the concepts of accommodation, assimilation and organization which will subsequently aid us in analyzing intelligence itself.

The *first solution* is tantamount to explaining the formation of habits by the hypothesis of training or of passive association. Do the facts which we have analyzed in the course of §§1–4 lend themselves to such an interpretation? We do not think so. Neither the physiological concept of the "conditioned reflex" transposed into psychology without addenda, nor the concept of "associative transfer" seems adequate to account for the formation of the first habits which we have described.

As far as the conditioned reflex is concerned it is certain that this concept corresponds to facts which have been well established in physiology. But are these facts of sufficient importance in that field to support on themselves alone the whole weight of psychology, as some people demand of them today? In the second place, assuming that they are utilized in psychology, should they then be translated into the language of association as desired by the new associationism born of reflexology, or else have they a quite different meaning? To the first of these two questions we shall reply that the conditioned reflex is essentially fragile and unstable if it is not constantly "confirmed" by the external environment. And to the second, we shall reply that, to the extent that the conditioned reflex is "confirmed" it ceases to be a simple association and is inserted in the more complex schema of the relationships between need and satisfaction, consequently the relationships of assimilation. That the conditioned reflex is fragile—that is to say, that the results of training are soon lost if not constantly confirmed by new training—has been brought to light by the physiologists. Moreover, they have remained much more prudent than psychologists in employing this concept. In order that a conditioned reflex may become stabilized it is, in effect, necessary either that it cease to be conditioned and become hereditarily fixed, or else that it be "confirmed" by experience itself. But the hereditary fixing of conditioned reflexes, maintained at first by Pavlov who subsequently withdrew his assertion, and then by MacDougal, seems improbable and we have seen why in our Introduction. Therefore there only remains stabilization by the environment itself and this brings us back to psychology.

A conditioned reflex can be stabilized by experience when the signal which sets the reflex in motion is followed by a confirmation—that is to say, a situation in which the reflex has the opportunity to function effectively. Hence in order to confirm the association between a sound and the salivary reflex, the animal is periodically given real food which gives the signal back its first meaning. So also could many of our observations be interpreted in terms of conditioned reflexes confirmed by experience. When the nursling makes ready to nurse when in his mother's arms and then actually finds the breast; when he turns his head to follow with his eyes a moving object and indeed finds it; when he searches with his eyes for a person whose voice he has heard and succeeds in discovering his face; when the sight of an object excites his movements of prehension and he subsequently manages to grasp it, etc.; it might be said that the reflexes of sucking, of visual and auditory accommodation and of prehension have been conditioned by signals of a postural, visual, etc., nature and that these conditioned reflexes have been stabilized because of being constantly confirmed by experience itself. But such a manner of speaking would elude the main question: How does experience confirm an association; in other words, what are the psychological conditions necessary in order that success may consolidate a behavior pattern? It is in order to answer this question that we have invoked combined assimilation and accommodation and this is why the term pure conditioned reflex seems to us inadequate.

In effect, when a conditioned reflex is confirmed by experience, through this very fact it enters a whole schema—that is to say, it ceases to be isolated and becomes an integral part of a real totality. It is no longer a simple term in the series of acts leading to satisfaction and it is this satisfaction which becomes the essential. In effect a series of movements resulting in gratifying a need cannot be interpreted as a juxtaposition of associated elements: it constitutes a whole—that is to say, the terms which compose it only have meaning in relation to the act which regulates them and to the success of this act. It is because the objects perceived by the child are thus assimilated to the act of grasping —that is to say, because they have set in motion the need to grasp and allow it to be gratified—that the hand reaches for them, and not because an association has been established between a visual image and the reflex of prehension. The latter association, in the capacity of a conditioned reflex, is only an abstraction, only a movement artificially cut in the series itself which also presupposes an initial need and a final satisfaction. Judgment has long been explained by the association of images or of sensations. Today we know that the simplest association already presupposes some activity which participates in the judgment. In the same way the act of grasping objects visually perceived may be explained by a chain of conditioned reflexes. But the links will never be coördinated except insomuch as a single act of assimilation will confer on the object seen the meaning of an object to be grasped.

What we say about the conditioned reflexes is all the more acceptable in that this is already true of the simple reflexes themselves. It is known to what extent the story of reflexes has been renovated by Sherrington's fine works. We became aware that the classic reflex arc is an abstraction rather than a reality. In the living organism, the reflexes form organized totalities and not juxtaposed mechanisms. According to Graham Brown, a rhythm of the whole always precedes the differentiation in reflexes: "The reflex does not explain the rhythm. In order to understand the reflex, the rhythm itself must first be invoked." And Herrick and Coghill, in studying the embryological development of the locomotor reflexes in the batrachians, speak of a "total" locomotor reaction which is subsequently dissociated into a particular reflex.[20] If all this is true of the reflexes themselves there is all the more reason to accept it as true of the conditioned reflexes. Let us be careful not to make of the conditioned reflex a new psychological element through whose combinations we shall reconstruct complex acts, and let us wait until the biologists have defined its real meaning rather than use it inordinately to explain that which is most elementary and consequently most obscure in mental phenomena.

In short, wherever we may speak of conditioned reflexes being stabilized as the result of experience, we always perceive that a schema of the whole organizes the parts of the associations. If the nursling seeks the breast when he is in position to nurse, follows moving objects with his eyes, tends to look at the people whose voice he hears, grasps objects he perceives, etc., it is because the schemata of sucking, vision, and prehension have assimilated increasingly numerous realities, through this very fact endowing them with meaning. Accommodation and assimilation combined, peculiar to each schema, insure its usefulness and coördinate it to the others, and it is the global act of complementary assimilation and accommodation which explains why the relationships of the parts which presuppose the schema are confirmed by experience.[21]

But is that not a completely verbal explanation and would not things be clarified if, for the concepts of assimilation and accommodation, the apparently clearer concept of "associative transfer" were substituted? The concept of the associative trans-

[20] Concerning all these points see Larguier, *Introduction à la psychologie*, pp. 126–138.

[21] This continuous subordination of the conditioned reflexes to organized totalities or global schemata of assimilation is demonstrated experimentally in the realm of the conditioned motor behavior patterns by a series of studies which M. André Rey, Chief of the work at our Institute, is pursuing at the present time and which will soon be published.

fer is more general than that of the conditioned reflex: association is involved, no longer only between a signal and some movement. Thus the sight of stairs suffices to set in motion appropriate movements of the legs and feet in the subject accustomed to climbing a staircase, etc. The associative transfer is thus regarded as the basis of the habit, by the first of the five above-mentioned solutions. According to this hypothesis our schemata of assimilation would not be anything other than the totalities of associative transfers whereas, according to us, every associative transfer presupposes a schema of assimilation in order to be constituted. It is therefore fitting to discuss this point closely; only this discussion is able to elucidate the true nature of sensorimotor assimilation and accommodation.

Let us first distinguish the two principal cases in which the associative transfer seems to intervene—the associations which are constituted within the same schema and the associations between heterogeneous schemata. The criterion of this distinction is the following. When the sensorial movements and elements are associated which do not yet present themselves, by another road, in the isolated state, we shall say that there is a single schema. We shall say, on the contrary, that coördination between schemata exists when they are able to function separately in other situations. For example, putting the thumb in the mouth constitutes a single schema and not a coördination between the sucking schema and the manual schemata because, at the age at which the child learns to suck his thumb he knows, it is true, how to suck something other than his thumb, but he does not know how to accomplish in other circumstances, by means of his hand, the action which he performs in putting it into his mouth (the few spontaneous movements of the hands which we have noted at about 1 to 2 months cannot even yet be definitely considered as independent schemata for it is not certain that they already constitute circular reactions distinct from impulsive movements). On the other hand, the behavior pattern consisting in grasping objects seen (4 to 5 months) may be cited as an example of coördination between heterogeneous schemata, for grasping objects independently of sight constitutes, as early as the fourth month, an autonomous schema and looking at objects independently of prehension is prevalent from 1 to 2 months. Hence we see how the two cases are different: in the first association appears as constitutive of the schema itself, whereas in the second it superadds itself to already existing schemata. The concept of the associative transfer must therefore be discussed separately in each case.

Concerning the first case, the doctrine of the associative transfer is tantamount to saying that each of our schemata is constituted by virtue of a sequence of independent associations. For example, if the child has acquired the habit of sucking his tongue, then his thumb, and then seeking the breast when he is in position to nurse, this would be for the following reasons: certain sensations of lips and tongue having regularly preceded the movements of the latter, and these movements having led to agreeable sucking sensations, the first sensations (contact of the tongue and the lips, etc.) would become a sort of signal automatically starting tongue movements and leading to the desirable result. In the same way that certain sensations of empty sucking have preceded the introduction of the thumb into the mouth a sufficient number of times and this has been followed by agreeable sensations of thumb sucking, it would suffice for the child to make sucking-like movements or to have just finished his meal in order that the sensorial elements peculiar to this situation serve as a signal and set in motion by association the putting of the thumb into the mouth. Finally if these sensations peculiar to the nursing situation set in motion the search for the breast, it is because they would be associated to these movements in the capacity of a signal regularly preceding them. So also, in the realm of vision, if the glance follows objects it is because, the perception of the initial displacements having regularly preceded the movements of the muscles of the eye permitting it to rediscover the displaced object, this perception would have become a signal regulating the movements of the eye itself: hence there would be in the act of following with the glance, a chain of associative transfers. Such an interpretation thus applies to everything: it is not one of the schemata, which we have delineated, which could not be conceived of as being a combination of associative transfers.

But such a manner of speaking seems to us more convenient

than precise. The same criticisms can be applied to the associationist explanation thus renovated as can be applied to the generalization of the conditioned reflex. As the essential in every behavior pattern seems to result from an associative transfer, the essential is not the association itself; it is the fact that the association leads to a favorable or unfavorable result: without the relationship *sui generis* existing between this result and the subject himself, the association would not be consolidated in anything. When the hand is retracted when confronted by fire or the foot is raised at the step of a staircase, the precision of the sensorimotor accommodations which constitute these behavior patterns depends entirely on the meaning which the subject attributes to the flame or to the staircase. It is this active relationship between the subject and the objects that are charged with meanings which creates the association and not the association which creates this relationship. So also, when the child sucks his tongue and his thumb, seeks the breast when he is in nursing position, follows with his eyes moving objects, etc.; it goes without saying that such habits presuppose regulated associations between sensorial elements and movements, but these associative transfers were only able to be constituted and consolidated thanks to a fundamental relationship between the activity of the subject (sucking, vision, etc.) and the sensorial subject endowed with meanings because of this very activity. It may therefore be said, in a general way, that if the association of ideas presupposes judgment instead of constituting it, so also the associative transfer presupposes a relation *sui generis* between the act and its result instead of constituting it.

What, then, is this relation between the act and its objective? Here intervene the concepts of assimilation, accommodation and organization, outside of which the associative transfer seems to us meaningless. The point of departure of all individual activity is, in effect, one or several reflexes already hereditarily organized. There are no elementary habits which do not graft themselves upon reflexes; that is to say, upon an already existing organization, capable of accommodation to the environment and of assimilation of the environment to its own functioning. Now, where a habit begins—that is to say where the associative transfers begin to constitute themselves—there may always be observed this relationship of combined assimilation and accommodation between the reflex activity of the subject and the new result which the nascent habit tends to attain and conserve. It is, in effect, the relation between the act and its result which alone permits the establishing of associative transfers. Now, such a relationship involves assimilation, for what makes the interest or the meaning of the new result pursued by the subject is precisely the fact that it can be assimilated to the reflex activity upon which the habit information grafts itself: hence the tongue and thumb are sucked because they serve as aliments for sucking, objects are followed by the eye because they serve as aliments for looking, etc. In short, the result of the acts, which alone gives to these acts their direction and thus "confirms" the associative transfers, sustains, with the initial reflex schemata, a functional relation of gratifying need, consequently of assimilation. Besides, and by virtue of that very fact, the assimilation of new objects to schemata preformed by the reflexes presupposes an accommodation of these schemata to the situation insomuch as it is new. Thus it is that in order to suck his tongue and his thumb the newborn child is obliged to incorporate into the movements constituting his hereditary sucking schema new movements, discovered in the course of individual experience: pulling the tongue, bringing the hand to the mouth, etc. It is precisely this incorporation of movements and of sensorial elements into the schemata which have already been constituted that is called in associationist terminology conditioned reflex or associative transfer. Only this accommodation is inseparable from assimilation and in this resides the fact that it is much more than an association. It is an insertion of new sensorimotor elements into a totality which has already been organized, which totality constitutes precisely the schema of assimilation. Hence, in sucking his tongue or his fingers, the child incorporates the new sensations he experiences into those of former sucking (sucking the breast, etc.)—therein is assimilation—and, at the same time, he inserts movements of putting out his tongue or putting his thumb into his mouth into the already organized totality of sucking movements—and this is what constitutes accommodation. It is this progressive extension of the total schema that enriches itself while remaining organized which constitutes accommodation. That is not "association" but progressive differentiation. Thus when the child seeks the breast when he is in nursing position, it cannot simply be said that the attitudes peculiar to this position are henceforth associated to sucking. It must be said that the global schema of sucking movements has incorporated into itself these attitudes and that from this moment they form a whole with the schema itself. In short, the associative transfer is only a moment, artificially cut, in the act of accommodation, which proceeds by differentiation from an earlier schema and by the incorporation of new elements into this schema, and not by association; furthermore, this accommodation is inseparable from assimilation, since it presupposes a total schema and this schema only functions in assimilating to itself new realities. This assimilation alone can explain the satisfaction to which the act leads and which determines the so-called "associative transfers."

As far as the associations producing themselves within an identical schema are concerned, it is therefore illusory to speak of associative transfer. Only the result of an act determines its contexture, which is tantamount to saying, in associationist terminology, that sanction is necessary to consolidate training and stabilize associations. The relationship between an activity and its object cannot be dissociated from the assimilation of the objective result to this activity and of accommodation of the activity to this result. This being so, it necessarily follows that the activity proceeds by global schemata of organization and not by associations. Not only, in effect, does assimilation presuppose such schemata, but further, it unceasingly reconstitutes their unity.

If we now go on to the second possible case—that is, the coördination between two separate schemata—we do not find more associative transfers in the pure state. When the child coördinates his hearing with his vision (and tries to see what he hears) or his prehension with sucking and vision, etc., it cannot be said that this is simple association between a sensorial signal (acoustic, visual, or tactile) and the movements of eye, mouth, or hand. In effect, all the reasons previously involved with regard to the single schemata apply here. The only difference is that in the present case there is no relationship of simple assimilation and accommodation between the activity of the subject and the object of this activity, but rather reciprocal assimilation and accommodation between two already existing schemata. Between the coördination of schemata and their internal constitution, there is therefore only a difference of degree and not of quality.

In conclusion, the first solution could not account for the facts which we have analyzed in this chapter, for reasons analogous to those which prevent simple Lamarckism from explaining the hereditary morphological reflex variations and which prevent associationism from exhausting intelligence itself. In the three realms of reflexes, sensorimotor acquisitions and intelligence, the primacy of habit or of passive association, leads to a neglect of the factor of organization, hence of combined assimilation and accommodation which is irreducible to automatism. Habit, as such, is certain only an automatization, but in order to be constituted it presupposes an activity which goes beyond simple association.

Then is it necessary to adopt the *second solution* and to consider, as do vitalism or spiritualistic intellectualism that every habit is derived from intelligence itself? The preceding remarks on the complementary relationships of assimilation and accommodation which connect the act to its result bring to mind Buytendijk's arguments concerning the intelligent finality inherent in every activity giving rise to habits, even in the animal. Must the conclusion be drawn from this that habit presupposes intelligence? For our part we would refrain from going that far. It seems indisputable, in effect, that the formation of habits precedes all truly intelligent activity. It is functionally, and not from the point of view of structure, that the behavior patterns described in this chapter can be compared to those we shall subsequently analyze as characterizing the beginnings of intelligence itself. Furthermore the workings of assimilation and accommodation do not necessitate any recourse to finalism or to "immaterial" activities. In yielding to a realism useless to psychology one deduces from the fact of psychological organization the hypothesis of a special force of organization, or one projects into assimilatory activity the structure of an implicit intelligence. Pseudopsychological realism of which one is thus the victim simply springs from the twofold illusion of philosophical common sense according to which we can grasp in ourselves our own intellectual activity as a known datum of internal experience (whence the ideas of synthetic "reason," of spiritual energy, etc., which extend the *Geist* or the "soul" itself) and according to which this given activity is structurally preformed at the most primitive stages (whence the ideas of vital force, of *a priori* reason, etc.). Quite different is the meaning which we would attribute to the concepts of organization, assimilation, and accommodation. Those are functional processes and not forces. In other words, these functions crystallize in sequential structures and never give rise to an *a priori* structure which the subject would discover directly within himself. In this respect nothing is more instructive than the comparison of the picture of the first infantile activities with the renowned studies by Maine de Biran. Probably no writer has observed better than Maine de Biran the contrast between activity and passive associations in the individual's elementary acquisitions. Concerning hearing and the voice, vision, touch and prehension and many other primordial functions, Maine de Biran always emphasizes the factors of effort and of active motive power which are contrary to the passivity of "affective sensibility" and he concludes the impossibility of an associationistic explanation. In this respect the concepts of assimilation and accommodation which we have employed could be conceived as hypotheses extending, without adding anything, Biran's doctrine of activity. But an obstacle remains, which seems to us to be the following: Biran's "effort" which is found at all levels of psychological activity and explains the "living intelligence" of the adult reflected in the formation of the first habits, is the emanation of a self which apprehends directly in the capacity of substance. It is therefore a force remaining identical to itself in the course of its history and opposing itself to the environmental forces which it comes to know by their resistance. Quite different is active adaptation such as the analysis of assimilation and accommodation obliges us to conceive it. Neither assimilation nor accommodation is a force which presents itself just as it is to consciousness and which furnishes in the capacity of immediate data the experience of a "self" and of an external world. On the contrary, through the very fact that assimilation and accommodation are always on a par, neither the external world nor the self is ever known independently of the other. The environment is assimilated to the activity of the subject at the same time as the latter accommodates itself to the former. In other words, it is through a progressive construction that the concepts of the physical world and of the internal self will become elaborated as a function of each other, and the processes of assimilation and accommodation are only instruments of this construction without ever representing the actual result of it. Regarding this result, it is always relative to the construction as such, and besides there does not exist, at any level, direct experience either of the self or of the external environment. There only exist "interpreted" experiences and this is true precisely thanks to this double play of correlative assimilation and accommodation. In short, the organization peculiar to intellectual becoming is not a faculty which would form intelligence itself nor a force which would form the "self": it is only an operation of which the sequential structural crystallizations never realize intelligence as such. All the more reason why it is unlikely that the most elementary acquisitions—that is to say the subject's first habits which are under discussion, derive from the higher intellectual processes as spiritualism would have it.

But if habit does not derive from intelligence, without adding anything, it cannot be said, as in the *third* and the *fourth* solution that it does not have, or almost does not have, any relationships to intellectual activity. If association and habit are considered not in their automatized form, but to the extent that they become organized at the level at which we have considered them in analyzing the facts, it seems indisputable that they reveal close functional analogies to intelligence. The same is true, in effect, of habit as of imitation. Its automatic form is not the primitive form and the primitive form presupposes a more complex activity than the evolved forms. In the case of habit, this elementary activity is that of the sensorimotor organizations whose schemata function in the same way as intelligence itself, through complementary assimilations and accommodations. We shall see in what follows that there are present all the transitions between these schemata and those of intelligence. Besides, it is too early to show now in which respect the Gestalt theory has exaggerated the contrast between the higher structures and the more fluctuating behavior of the elementary stages, and in which respect the schema of assimilation is to be conceived of as a system of relations less rigid than a Gestalt and itself involving an organizing activity of which it is only the expression. Let us limit ourselves to recalling that schemata such as those of sucking thumb or tongue, grasping seen objects, the coördination of hearing and of vision, etc., never arise *ex abrupto* but constitute the point of arrival of a long effort of gradual assimilation and accommodation. It is this effort which foretells intelligence. Besides, when Delacroix tells us that intellectual generalization is in a sense the opposite of habit, that is true of habit which has been formed and is degenerating in passivity, but that is not certain concerning the assimilation which is at the point of departure of this habit. There is, as we have seen, a generalizing assimilation which works in the same way as intelligence, through a sequence of choices and corrections. Even groping, which Claparède regards as the characteristic of nascent intelligence is therefore not excluded from the formation of habits which does not mean that the latter are already intelligent, but rather that there is a continuous organizing activity connecting organic adaptation to intellectual adaptation through the intermediary of the most elementary sensorimotor schemata.

It is therefore the *fifth solution* which we shall adopt. Association and habit form the automatization of an activity which functionally prepares intelligence while yet differing from it by a more elementary structure. Let us try to state these assertions precisely and to do so let us first recall the general characteristics of the stage under consideration, contrasting them to those of the preceding stage and those of the following one.

In general it may be said that the behavior patterns studied in §§1–4 consist in searchings which prolong reflex activity and which are as yet devoid of intention but which lead to new results of which the mere discovery is fortuitous and whose conservation is due to a mechanism adapted from combined sensorimotor assimilation and accommodation. These behavior patterns prolong those of the first stage in that the needs connected with the reflex (sucking, looking, listening, crying, grasping, etc.) are still their only motive power without there yet being needs connected with derived and deferred aims (grasping in order to throw, in order to swing to and fro, etc.). But, contrary to purely reflex searching, the searching peculiar to the present stage is displayed in gropings which lead to new results. Contrary to the subsequent stage, these results are not pursued intentionally. They are therefore the product of chance, but, resembling intelligent behavior patterns, the behavior patterns of which we are speaking tend, as soon as the result is obtained, to conserve it by correlative assimilation and accommodation.

This conservation of advantageous results obtained by chance is, of course, what Baldwin has called "circular reaction." This concept of which we have made use in describing the facts seems to us exactly to define the position of the present stage. Circular reaction involves the discovery and the conservation of the new, and in that it differs from the pure reflex; but it is anterior to intention, and in that it precedes intelligence. Only, such a concept requires interpretation. If one limits oneself, as is frequently done, to explaining repetition by the "reaction of excess" and tracing, one returns to automatism to account for what is, on the contrary, preëminently active searching. If the child tends to rediscover an advantageous result, this is not because that is the course of least effort, but on the contrary, it is because the result is assimilated to an earlier schema and the question is to accommodate this schema to the new result. The "circular reaction" is, accordingly, only a global concept, embracing in reality two distinct processes. Let us try, in conclusion, to summarize what we know about these processes.

First there is *accommodation*. The great novelty inherent in circular reaction and habit compared to the reflex, is that accommodation begins to be differentiated from assimilation. At the heart of the reflex, in effect, accommodation mingles with assimilation. The use of the reflex is at once pure repetition (that is to say, assimilation of the object to an already constructed schema) and accurate accommodation to its object. On the other hand, from the moment when the sensorimotor schema is applied to new situations and thus dilates to embrace a larger realm, accommodation and assimilation tend to be differentiated. Take, for example, thumb sucking. During the reflex stage this behavior pattern consisted in a simple, occasional animated application of the sucking schema to a new object but without having this circumstance transform the schema in any way whatever. The new object was assimilated to the old schema and this generalizing assimilation had no other effect than to exercise the reflex in general; at most it permitted it to discriminate in future breast sucking from what was not breast sucking. During the present stage, on the contrary, application of the sucking schema to a new object such as the thumb or tongue transforms the schema itself. This transformation constitutes an accommodation and this accommodation is consequently distinct from pure assimilation. In a general way, contact of some schema with a new reality results, during the present stage, in a special behavior pattern, intermediate between that of the reflex and that of intelligence. In the reflex the new is entirely assimilated to the old and accommodation thus mingles with assimilation; in intelligence, there is interest in the new as such and accommodation is consequently definitely differentiated from assimilation; in the behavior patterns of the intermediary stage, the new is still only of interest to the extent that it can be assimilated to the old, but it already cracks the old frameworks and thus forces them to an accommodation partly distinct from assimilation.

How does this accommodation work? We have seen in the above: not through association, but through differentiation of an existing schema and insertion of new sensorimotor elements among those which already form it. In effect, with the reflex activity a series of already constructed schemata are hereditarily given and their assimilatory function thus represents an activity directed toward performance dating from the very beginning of life and prior to all association. When these schemata are differentiated by accommodation—in other words, in physiological terminology, when a reflex connection is subordinated to a cortical connection and with it forms a new totality—it cannot be said that a given reaction is simply associated to new signals or to new movements. It must be said that an activity which has already been organized from the beginnings is applied to new situations and that the sensorimotor elements connected with these new situations were comprised in the primitive schema in thus differentiating it. There is no subordination of the reflex schema to new associations nor inverse subordination. There is continuity of a single activity with complementary differentiation and interpretation.

Accommodation, then, presupposes *assimilation* as, in reflective intelligence, empirical association presupposes judgment. It is this factor of functional assimilation which forms the organizing and totalizing activity insuring the continuity between the schema considered before accommodation and the same schema after the insertion of new elements due to this accommodation. What, then, is assimilation?

Assimilation is first of all purely functional—that is to say, cumulative repetition and assimilation of the object to the function: sucking for the sake of sucking, looking for the sake of looking, etc. As such psychological assimilation prolongs without adding anything to organic functional assimilation and does not require any special explanation. Then, to the extent that assimilation of the object to the function extends to include increasingly varied objects, assimilation becomes "generalizing"; that is to say (as regards the present stage), combines with multiple accommodations. Finally, and through the very fact of this differentiation, assimilation becomes "recognitory"; that is to say, perception of objects—or more precisely, of sensorial images—as a function of the multiple activities delineated by the generalizing assimilation. Therein resides a first principle of exteriorization which combines with the exteriorization due to the coördination between heterogeneous schemata.

To describe this assimilation clearly one can do so either from the point of view of consciousness or from that of behavior. What can the consciousness of the infant be concerning the thumb he sucks, the object he looks at, the object he will grasp after having perceived it, the sounds he makes, etc.? Stern[22] as-

22 W. Stern, *Psychologie der frühen Kindheit bis zum sechsten Lebensjahre,* Leipzig, Quelle & Meyer, 1927.

serts that an impression is only individualized if it is connected with a movement experienced as being active or at least connected with the context of the activity itself. One could, at first, object to this way of seeing the 2-month-old baby's attention to things and people (Lucienne, at 0;1 (28) looks at the trees above her, laughs when people move about in front of her). But, in order to look, there exists accommodation of the eyes and of the head and this accommodation is probably experienced as a real activity much more by the nursling than by us. Mimicry denotes unceasing effort, tension, expectation, satisfaction or disappointment, etc. Besides, perception is already extended into imitation, as we shall see later. We therefore fully concede Stern's remark.[23] Now, the following, it seems to us, results from this, from the point of view of the states of consciousness concomitant to assimilation. During the elementary stages of consciousness things are much less apprehended in their own form than is the case with the adult or the child who talks. There is not a thumb, a hand, a ribbon about to be grasped, etc. There is a variety of tactile, visual, gustatory, etc., images which are not contemplated but rather operated—that is to say, produced and reproduced, impregnated, so to speak, with the need to be supported or rediscovered. Hence this conclusion which must always be borne in mind in order to avoid the associationist error constantly reappearing under cover of the law of transfer: the new objects which are introduced to consciousness have no peculiar and separate qualities. Either they are at once assimilated to an already existing schema: a thing to suck, to look at, to grasp, etc. Or else they are vague, nebulous, because of being unassimilable and then they create an uneasiness whence comes sooner or later a new differentiation of the schemata of assimilation.

From the point of view of behavior, assimilation is revealed in the form of cycles of movements or of acts bringing each other along and closing up again on themselves. This is clearly true of the reflex whose various forms of use we have studied. This is again true of circular reaction: the performed act leaves a vacuum

[23] Ch. Bühler, *op. cit.*, adds that the child's interest in a situation culminates at the moment that actual activity begins to triumph over his difficulties.

which, in order to be filled, leads to the repetition of the same act. Hence there exists the form of an ensemble or cycle of organized movements, to the extent that the act gratifies a real need. Each activity forms a whole. To be sure, the ensemble is not perfect from the outset. There is groping in its performance and it is in the course of this groping that it is easy to dissociate the sequential movements in order to describe them in terms of associative transfer. But the so-called signal which would determine the movements constitutes more of an indication in comparison with an activity which tries to gain satisfaction for itself than a trigger starting up movements. The true cause of movement is need; that is to say, the total act of assimilation. This is not to say yet that the movement is intentional. Need is nothing other, for the moment, than the vacuum created by the preceding performance of the act and, at the beginning, by the chance discovery of an interesting result, interesting because directly assimilable.

In short, the uniting of accommodation and assimilation presupposes an *organization*. Organization exists within each schema of assimilation since (we have just recalled it) each one constitutes a real whole, bestowing on each element a meaning relating to this totality. But there is above all total organization; that is to say, coördination among the various schemata of assimilation. Now, as we have seen, this coördination is not formed differently from the simple schemata, except only that each one comprises the other, in a reciprocal assimilation. At the point of departure we are in the presence of needs which attain satisfaction separately. The child looks for the sake of looking, grasps in order to grasp, etc. Then there is an accidental coördination between one schema and another (the child looks by chance at the hand which grasps, etc.) and finally, fixation. How does this fixation work? It seems at first that this might be by association. Contact of the hands with an object or of an object with the lips seems to be the signal which sets in motion the movement of the object to the lips and sucking. But the opposite procedure is also possible. The need to suck sets in motion the movement of the hand to the mouth, etc. The possibility of the two complementary actions shows sufficiently that they form but one unit. All the more reason why this is so when the coördination of the schemata is reciprocal, when, for instance, the child grasps what he sees and brings before his eyes that which he grasps. In short, the conjunction of two cycles or of two schemata is to be conceived as a new totality, self-enclosed. There is neither association between two groups of images nor even association between two needs, but rather the formation of a new need and the organization of earlier needs as a function of this new unity.

It is then, let us remember, that assimilation becomes objectified and perception is externalized. A sensorial image which is at the point of intersection of several currents of assimilation is, through that very fact, solidified and projected into a universe where coherence makes its first appearance.

In conclusion it may be seen to what extent the activity of this stage, activity from which the first sensorimotor habits proceed, is identical, from the functional point of view, with that of intelligence, while differing from it in structure. Functionally speaking, the accommodation, assimilation and organization of the first acquired schemata are altogether comparable to those of the mobile schemata of which sensorimotor intelligence will make use and even to those of the concepts and relationships which reflective intelligence will employ. But, from the structural point of view, the first circular reactions lack intention. As long as action is entirely determined by directly perceived sensorial images there can be no question of intention. Even when the child grasps an object in order to suck or look at it, one cannot infer that there is a conscious purpose. The goal of the action is one with the point of departure only by virtue of the fact of the unity of the schema of coördination. It is with the appearance of secondary and mobile schemata and of deferred reactions that the purpose of the action, ceasing to be in some way directly perceived, presupposes a continuity in searching, and consequently a beginning of intention. But, to be sure, all gradations exist between these evolved forms of activity and the primitive forms of which we have spoken hitherto.

PART II

The Intentional Sensorimotor Adaptations

THE INTENTIONAL SENSORIMOTOR
ADAPTATIONS

The coördination of vision and prehension, which we have studied in Chapter II, inaugurates a new series of behavior patterns: the intentional adaptations. Unfortunately, nothing is more difficult to define than intention. Shall it be said, as is frequently done, that an act is intentional when it is determined by representation, contrary to the elementary associations in which the act is controlled by an external stimulus? But if representation is taken in the strict sense of the word, there would not then be intentional acts prior to language—that is to say, before the faculty of thinking of reality by means of signs making up the deficiency of action. Now intelligence presupposes intention. If, on the other hand, one extends the term representation so that it comprises all consciousness of meanings, intention would exist ever since the simplest associations and almost since the beginning of reflex use. Shall it be said that intention is connected with the power of evoking images and that searching for the fruit in a closed box, for instance, is an intentional act to the extent that it is determined by the representation of the fruit in the box? But, as we shall see, it appears according to all probabilities that even this kind of representations, by images and individual symbols, makes a tardy appearance. The mental image is a product of the internalization of the acts of intelligence and not a datum preliminary to these acts. Since then we see only one method of distinguishing intentional adaptation from the simple circular reactions peculiar to sensorimotor habit: this is to invoke the number of intermediaries coming between the stimulus of the act and its result. When a 2-month-old baby sucks his thumb this cannot be called an intentional act because the coördination of the hand and of sucking is simple and direct. It therefore suffices for the child to maintain, by circular reaction, the favorable movements which satisfy his need, in order that this behavior become habitual. On the other hand, when an 8-month-old child sets aside an obstacle in order to attain an objective, it is possible to call this intention, because the need set in motion by the stimulus of the act (by the object to be grasped) is only satisfied after a more or less lengthy series of intermediary acts (the obstacles to be set aside). Intention is thus determined by consciousness of desire, or of the direction of the act, this awareness being itself a function of the number of intermediary actions necessitated by the principal act. In a sense, there is therefore only a difference of degree between the elementary adaptations and the intentional adaptations. The intentional act is only a more complex totality subsuming the secondary values under the essential values and subordinating the intermediary movements or *means* to the principal steps which assign an end to the action. But, in another sense, intention involves a reversing in the data of consciousness. There is henceforth the influence of recurrent consciousness of direction impressed on the action or no longer only on its result. Consciousness arises from dis-adaptation and thus proceeds from the periphery to the center.

In practice, we can acknowledge—provided we bear in mind that this division is artificial and that all the transitions connect the acts of the second stage to those of the third—that intentional adaptation begins as soon as the child transcends the level of simple corporal activities (sucking, listening and making sounds, looking and grasping) and acts upon things and uses the interrelationships of objects. In effect, to the extent that the subject is limited to sucking, looking, listening, grasping, etc., he satisfies in a more or less direct way his immediate needs, and, if he acts upon things, it is simply in order to perform his own functions. In such a case it is hardly possible to speak of ends and means. The schemata serving as means become mingled with those which assign an end to the action and there is no occasion for this influence of consciousness *sui generis* which determines intention. On the contrary, as soon as the subject, possessing the coördinated schemata of prehension, vision, etc., utilizes them in order to assimilate to himself the totality of his universe, the multiple combinations which then present themselves (by generalizing assimilation and accommodation, combined) bring with them the momentary hierarchies of ends and means; that is to say, there is the influence of consciousness of the direction of the act or of its intention.

From the theoretical point of view, intention therefore denotes the extension of the totalities and relationships acquired during the preceding stage and, by the fact of their extension, their greater dissociation into real totalities and ideal totalities in relationships of fact and relationships of value. As soon as there is intention, in effect, there is a goal to reach and means to use, consequently the influence of consciousness of values (the value or the interest of the intermediary acts serving as *means* is subordinated to that of the goal) and of the ideal (the act to be accomplished is part of an ideal totality or *goal,* in relation to the real totality of the acts already organized). Thus it may be seen that the functional categories related to the function of organization will henceforth become more precise, from the time of the global schemata of the preceding stage. Concerning the functions of assimilation and accommodation, intentional adaptation also brings with it a more pronounced differentiation of their respective categories, ever since the relatively undifferentiated state of the first stages. Assimilation, after having proceeded as hitherto, by nearly rigid schemata (the sensorimotor schemata of sucking, prehension, etc.) will henceforth engender more mobile schemata, capable of various involvements and in which we shall find the functional equivalent of the qualitative concepts and of the quantitative relationships peculiar to reflective intelligence. With regard to accommodation, by clasping more tightly the external universe, it will clarify the space-time relationships as well as those of substance and causality, hitherto enveloped in the subject's psycho-organic activity.

In other words, we now arrive at the problem of intelligence which we shall study with regard to stages III to VI. Hitherto we have stayed on this side of actual intelligence. During the first stage this was self-evident, since pure reflexes were involved. Concerning the second stage it was not known how, despite the functional resemblances, to identify habit and intelligent adaptation, since it is precisely intention that separates them. This is not the place to define this structural difference which analyzing the facts alone will permit us to fathom and which we shall take up again at the conclusion of this book. Let us say only that the sequence of our stages corresponds in the main to the system outlined by Claparède in a remarkable article on intelligence published in 1917.[1] To Claparède intelligence is an adaptation to new situations as opposed to reflexes and habitual associations which also constitute adaptations, either hereditary or due to personal experience, but adaptations to situations which repeat themselves. Now these new situations to which the child will have to adapt himself appear precisely when the habitual schemata, elaborated during the second stage, will be applied for the first time to the external environment in its complexity.

Furthermore, there may be distinguished, among the intentional acts which constitute intelligence, two relatively opposite types, corresponding in the main to what Claparède calls empirical intelligence and systematic intelligence. The first consists in operations controlled by the things themselves and not by deduction alone. The second consists in operations controlled from within by the consciousness of relationships and thus marks the beginning of deduction. We shall consider the first of these behavior patterns as characteristic of the stages III to V and shall make the appearance of the second behavior patterns the criterion of a sixth stage.

On the other hand, the concept of "empirical intelligence" remains a little vague as long as one does not put into effect, in the sequence of facts, some divisions intended, not to make discontinuous an actual continuity, but to permit analysis of the increasing complication of the behavior patterns. This is why we shall distinguish three stages between the beginnings of the action upon things and those of systematic intelligence: stages III to IV.

The third stage appearing with the prehension of visual objectives is characterized by the appearance of a behavior pattern which is already almost intentional, in the sense indicated before, which also foretells empirical intelligence but which nevertheless remains intermediary between the acquired association belonging to the second stage and the true act of intelligence. This is the

[1] Republished in *Education fonctionnelle, op. cit.*

"secondary circular reaction," that is to say, the behavior which consists in rediscovering the gestures which by chance exercised an advantageous action upon things. Such a behavior pattern, in effect, goes beyond acquired association to the extent that almost intentional searching is necessary to reproduce the movements until then performed fortuitously. But it does not yet constitute a typical act of intelligence since this searching simply consists in rediscovering that which has just been done and not in inventing again or in applying the known to new circumstances: the "means" are hardly yet differentiated from the "ends" or at least they are only differentiated after the event, at the time the act is repeated.

A fourth stage begins at around 8 to 9 months and lasts until the end of the first year. It is characterized by the appearance of certain behavior patterns which are superimposed on the preceding ones and their essence is "the application of known means to new situations." Such behavior patterns differ from the preceding ones both in their functional meaning and in their structural mechanism. From the functional point of view for the first time they fully correspond to the current definition of intelligence: adaptation to new circumstances. Given a habitual goal temporarily thwarted by unforeseen obstacles, the problem is to surmount these difficulties. The simplest procedure consists in trying out different known schemata and in adjusting them to the goal pursued: in this consist the present behavior patterns. From the structural point of view they therefore constitute a combination of schemata among themselves, so that some are subordinated to others in the capacity of "means"; hence two results: a greater mobility of the schemata and a more accurate accommodation to external conditions. If this stage is to be distinguished from the preceding one with respect to the functioning of intelligence, it is to be distinguished still more with regard to the structure of objects, space and causality: it marks the beginnings of the permanence of things, of "objective" spatial "groups" and of spatial and objectified causality.

At the beginning of the second year a fifth stage makes itself manifest, characterized by the first real experimentations; hence the possibility of a "discovery of new means through active

experimentation." This is the impetus of the instrumental behavior patterns and the acme of empirical intelligence.

Finally this totality of the behavior patterns, the application
of which determines the beginning of the sixth stage, will be
crowned by the "invention of new means through mental combination."

CHAPTER III

THE THIRD STAGE:

The "Secondary Circular Reactions" and the Procedures Destined to Make Interesting Sights Last

From the simple reflex to the most systematic intelligence, the same method of operation seems to us to continue through all the stages, thus establishing complete continuity between increasingly complex structures. But this functional continuity in no way excludes a transformation of the structures being on an equal footing with an actual reversal of perspectives in the subject's consciousness. At the beginning of intellectual evolution, in effect, the act is set in motion all at once and by an external stimulus and the individual's initiative consisted merely in being able to reproduce his action when confronted with stimuli analogous to the normal stimulus, or by simple empty repetition. At the end of the evolution, on the other hand, every action involves an organization versatile in making dissociations and unlimited regroupings, the subject thus being able to assign to himself goals which are increasingly independent of instigation by the immediate environment.

How does such a reversal work? Due to the progressive complication of the schemata: by constantly renewing his acts through reproductive and generalizing assimilation, the child surpasses simple reflex use, discovers circular reaction and thus forms his first habits. Such a process is obviously capable of unlimited extension. After applying it to his own body, the subject will utilize it sooner or later in order to adapt himself to the unforeseen phenomena of the external world, whence the behavior patterns of exploration, experimentation, etc. Wherefore the possibility, subsequently, of decomposing and recomposing the same schemata: gradually as the schemata apply themselves to more varied external situations the subject is, in effect, led to dissociate their elements and to consider them as means or as ends, while at the same time regrouping them among themselves in all sorts of ways. It is this distinction of means and ends which sets intention free and so reverses the act's direction. Instead of being turned toward the past—that is to say, toward repetition— the action is directed toward new combinations and actual invention.

Now the stage which we are about to describe forms exactly the transition between the behavior patterns of the first type and those of the second. The "secondary circular reactions" prolong, in effect, without adding anything to, the circular reactions under examination hitherto; that is to say, they essentially tend toward repetition. After reproducing the interesting results discovered by chance on his own body, the child tries sooner or later to conserve also those which he obtains when his action bears on the external environment. It is this very simple transition which determines the appearance of the "secondary" reactions; accordingly it may be seen how they are related to the "primary" reactions. But it is necessary immediately to add that, the more the effort of reproduction bears upon results removed from those of reflex activity, the clearer becomes the distinction between means and ends. To the extent that it is a hereditary assembly the reflex schema forms an indissociable totality. The repetition belonging to "reflex use" would only know how to make the machine go by activating it completely without distinction between the transitive terms and the final terms. In the case of the first organic habits (thumb sucking, for example) the complexity of the schema augments since an acquired element is inserted among the reflex movements; repeating the interesting result therefore will involve a coördination between terms not necessarily united with each other. But, as their union, although an acquired one, was in a way imposed by the conformation of the body itself and sanctioned by a strengthening of reflex activity, it is still easy for the child to rediscover through simple repetition the result obtained without distinguishing the transitive terms and the final term of the act. On the other hand, as soon as the result to be reproduced is connected with the external environment—that is to say, with independent objects (even if their mutual relationships and their permanence are still unknown to the child)—the effort to rediscover a propitious gesture will lead the subject, after the event, to distinguish in his action the transitive terms or "means" and a final term or "end." It is from this time on that it is possible really to speak of "intention" and of a reversal in acquiring consciousness of the act. But this reversal will only be definitive when the different terms will be sufficiently dissociated so that they may recombine among themselves in various ways; that is to say, when there will be a possibility of applying known means to new ends or, in a word, when an intercoördination of the schemata will exist (fourth stage). The "secondary circular reaction" is not yet at this level; it tends simply to reproduce every advantageous result obtained in relation to the external environment, without the child's yet dissociating or regrouping the schemata thus obtained. The goal is therefore not set ahead of time, but only when the act is repeated.—Therein the present stage forms the exact transition between preintelligent operations and truly intentional acts. The behavior patterns which characterize it still owe a great deal to repetition while being superior to it from the point of view of complexity and they already possess intelligent coördination while remaining inferior to it from the point of view of dissociation of means and ends.

This intermediary characteristic will be found again, as we shall see in Volume II, in all the behavior patterns of the same stage, whether it is a matter of the content of intelligence or of real categories (object and space, causality and time) as well as of its form (which we shall study).

With regard to the object, for example, the child at this stage arrives at a behavior pattern exactly intermediary between those of nonpermanence, belonging to the lower stages, and the new behavior relating to objects which have disappeared. On the one hand, in effect, the child knows henceforth how to grasp the objects he sees, bring to sight those he touches, etc., and this coördination between vision and prehension indicates notable progress in the solidification of the external world: acting upon things, he considered them unyielding and permanent to the extent that they prolong his action or thwart it. On the other hand, to the extent that objects leave the perceptual field and consequently, the child's direct action, the child no longer reacts and does not apply himself to active searching to find them again, as he will do during the next stage. If there is permanence of the object it is still relative to the action in progress and not a fact in itself.

Concerning space, the actions brought to bear on things by the child at the third stage result in forming a perception of "groups"; that is to say, of schemata of displacements capable of returning to their point of departure. In this sense, the behavior patterns of this stage mark important progress in relation to the preceding ones in fixing securely the intercoördination of the various practical spaces (visual, tactile, buccal spaces, etc.). But the "groups" thus formed remain "subjective" for, beyond the immediate action, the child does not yet take into consideration the spatial interrelations of objects. Causality, too, takes form to the extent that the child acts upon the external environment: henceforth it unites certain separate phenomena to the acts which correspond to them. But, precisely because the schemata belonging to this stage are not yet dissociated in their elements, the child only gets a confused and global feeling of the causal connection and does not know how to objectify or spatialize causality.

The same is true *a fortiori* of the temporal series which will link the different phases of the act but not yet the different events produced in an environment independent of the self.

In short, during the first two stages—that is to say, so long as the child's activity consists in mere repetitions without intention—the universe is not yet at all dissociated from the action itself and the categories remain subjective. As soon as the schemata become, on the other hand, capable of intentional decompositions and recombinations—that is to say, of really intelligent activity—the consciousness of the relations thus implicated by distinguishing means and ends will necessarily bring with it the elaboration of a world independent of the self. From this point of view of the contents of intelligence, the third stage, therefore, also marks a turning point. Its particular reactions remain midway between the solipsist universe of the beginning and the objective universe belonging to intelligence. Without being requisite to the description of the facts which follows, such thoughts nevertheless clarify many aspects of them.

§1. THE "SECONDARY CIRCULAR REACTIONS"— I. THE FACTS AND REPRODUCTIVE ASSIMILATION.— We can call the circular reactions of the second stage "primary." Their character consists in simple organic movements centered on themselves (with or without intercoördination) and not destined to maintain a result produced in the external environment. So it is that the child grasps for the sake of grasping, sucking, or looking, but not yet in order to swing to and fro, to rub, or to reproduce sounds. Moreover the external objects upon which the subject acts are one with his action which is simple, the means being confused with the end. On the other hand, in the circular reactions which we shall call "secondary" and which characterize the present stage, the movements are centered on a result produced in the external environment and the sole aim of the action is to maintain this result; furthermore it is more complex, the means beginning to be differentiated from the end, at least after the event.

Of course, all the intermediaries are produced between the primary circular reactions and the secondary reactions. It is by convention that we choose, as criterion of the appearance of the latter, the action exerted upon the external environment. Henceforth if they make their appearance, for the most part, after the definitive acquisition of prehension, it is nevertheless possible to find some examples of this phenomenon prior to that.

First here are some examples of circular reactions relating to the movements the child gives to his bassinet and to the hanging objects:

Observation 94.—At 0;3 (5) Lucienne shakes her bassinet by moving her legs violently (bending and unbending them, etc.), which makes the cloth dolls swing from the hood. Lucienne looks at them, smiling, and recommences at once. These movements are simply the concomitants of joy. When she experiences great pleasure Lucienne externalizes it in a total reaction including leg movements. As she often smiles at her knick-knacks she caused them to swing. But does she keep this up through consciously coördinated circular reaction or is it pleasure constantly springing up again that explains her behavior?

That evening, when Lucienne is quiet, I gently swing her dolls. The morning's reaction starts up again, but both interpretations remain possible.

The next day, at 0;3 (6) I present the dolls: Lucienne immediately moves, shakes her legs, but this time without smiling. Her interest is intense and sustained and there also seems to be an intentional circular reaction.

At 0;3 (8) I again find Lucienne swinging her dolls. An hour later I make them move slightly: Lucienne looks at them, smiles, stirs a little, then resumes looking at her hands as she was doing shortly before. A chance movement disturbs the dolls: Lucienne again looks at them and this time shakes herself with regularity. She stares at the dolls, barely smiles and moves her legs vigorously and thoroughly. At each moment she is distracted by her hands which pass again into the visual field: she examines them for a moment and then returns to the dolls. This time there is definite circular reaction.

At 0;3 (13) Lucienne looks at her hand with more coördination than usually (see Obs. 67). In her joy at seeing her hand come and go between her face and the pillow, she shakes herself in front of this hand as when faced by the dolls. Now this reaction of shaking reminds her of the dolls which she looks at immediately after as though she foresaw their movement. She also looks at the bassinet hood which also moves. At certain times her glance oscillates between her hand, the hood, and the dolls. Then her attention attaches itself to the dolls which she then shakes with regularity.

At 0;3 (16) as soon as I suspend the dolls she immediately shakes them, without smiling, with precise and rhythmical movements with quite an interval between shakes, as though she were studying the phenomenon. Success gradually causes her to smile. This time the circular reaction is indisputable. Same reaction at 0;3 (24). Same observations during the succeeding months and until 0;6 (10) and 0;7 (27) at sight of a puppet and at 0;6 (13) with a celluloid bird, etc.

Observation 94 repeated.—At 0;3 (9) Lucienne is in her bassinet without the dolls. I shake the bassinet two or three times without her seeing me. She looks very interested and serious and begins again, for a long stretch of time, rough and definitely intentional shaking.—That evening I rediscover Lucienne in the act of shaking her hood spontaneously. She laughs at this sight.

Here is involved, therefore, the schema described in the foregoing observation, but applied to a new object. Same observation on the following days.

At 0;4 (4) in a new bassinet, she moves her loins violently in order to shake the hood. At 0;4 (13) she moves her legs very rapidly while looking at the festoons on the bassinet hood; as soon as she sees them again, after a pause, she begins once more. Same reaction with regard to the hood in general. At 0;4 (19) she recommences by examining each part of the hood in detail. At 0;4 (21) she does the same in her carriage (and no longer in the bassinet): she studies the result of her shaking most attentively. Same observations at 0;5 (5) etc., until 0;7 (20) and later.

Observation 95.—Lucienne, at 0;4 (27) is lying in her bassinet. I hang a doll over her feet which immediately sets in motion the schema of shakes (see the foregoing observations). But her feet reach the doll right away and give it a violent movement which Lucienne surveys with delight. Afterward she looks at her motionless foot for a second, then recommences. There is no visual control of the foot, for the movements are the same when Lucienne only looks at the doll or when I place the doll over her head. On the other hand, the tactile control of the foot is apparent: after the first shakes, Lucienne makes slow foot movements as though to grasp and explore. For instance, when she tries to kick the doll and misses her aim, she begins again very slowly until she succeeds (without seeing her feet). In the same way I cover Lucienne's face or distract her attention for a moment in another direction: she nevertheless continues to hit the doll and control its movements.

At 0;4 (28), as soon as Lucienne sees the doll she moves her feet. When I move the doll toward her face she increases her movements and thus resumes the behavior described in the preceding observations. So also at 0;5 (0) she oscillates between the global reaction and specific foot movements, but at 0;5 (1) she resumes the latter movements only and even seems to regulate them (without seeing them) when I raise the doll a little. A moment later she gropes until she has felt contact between her naked foot and the doll: she then increases her movements. Same reaction at 0;5 (7) and the days following.

At 0;5 (18) I place the doll at different heights, sometimes to the left, sometimes to the right: Lucienne first tries to reach it with her feet, and then, when she has succeeded, shakes it. The schema is therefore definitely acquired and begins to be differentiated through accommodation to various situations.

Observation 96.—At 0;5 (8) Jacqueline looks at a doll attached to a string which is stretched from the hood to the handle of the bassinet. The doll is at approximately the same level as the child's feet. Jacqueline moves her feet and finally strikes the doll whose movement she immediately notices. A circular reaction ensues comparable to that in the foregoing observation but less coördinated in view of Jacqueline's retarded development as she was born in winter and had less physical exercise than Lucienne. The feet move, first without conscious coordination, then certainly by circular reaction. The activity of the feet grows increasingly regular whereas Jacqueline's eyes are fixed on the doll. Moreover, when I remove the doll Jacqueline occupies herself quite differently, and when I replace it, after a moment, she immediately recommences to move her legs. But, contrary to Lucienne, Jacqueline does not understand the necessity for contact between feet and doll. She limits herself to noting the connection between the movement of the object and the total activity of her own body. This is why, as soon as she sees the doll, she places herself in the situation of total movement in which she has seen the doll swing. She moves her arms, her torso and her legs in a global reaction without paying particular attention to her feet. The counterproof is easy to furnish. I place the doll above Jacqueline's face, outside the range of any possible contact: Jacqueline recommences to wriggle her arms, torso, and feet, exactly as before, while staring only at the doll (and not at her feet). Jacqueline accordingly establishes a connection between her movements in general and those of the object and not between her feet and the object. I do not observe any tactile control either.

The objection might then be raised that Jacqueline establishes no connection and limits herself to manifesting her joy at the doll's movements without attributing them to her own activity. The child's wriggling would thus be only an attitude accompanying pleasure and not a circular reaction tending toward an objective result. But, without having proofs in the particular case, we can conclude that there is an intentional connection by analogy with the foregoing and following observations in which the child's much more precocious reactions permitted us to make quite a different interpretation.

Observation 97.—Laurent, from the middle of the third month, revealed global reactions of pleasure, while looking at the toys hanging from the hood of his bassinet, or at the hood itself, etc. He babbles, arches himself, beats the air with his arms, moves his legs, etc. He thus moves the bassinet and recommences more vigorously. But it is not yet possible to speak of circular reaction: there is no connection felt between the movements of his limbs and the spectacle seen, but only an attitude of joy and of physical exertion. Again, at 0;2 (17) I observe that when his movements induce those of the toys, he stops to contemplate them, far from grasping that it is he who produces them; when the toys are motionless, he resumes, and so on. On the other hand, at 0;2 (24) I made the following experiment which set in motion a beginning of secondary circular reaction. As Laurent was striking his chest and shaking his hands which were bandaged and held by strings attached to the handle of the bassinet (to prevent him from sucking), I had the idea of using the thing and I attached the strings to the celluloid balls hanging from the hood. Laurent naturally shook the balls by chance and looked at them at once (the rattle made a noise inside them). As the shaking was repeated more and more frequently Laurent arched himself, waved his arms and legs—in short, he revealed increasing pleasure and through this maintained the interesting result. But nothing yet authorizes us to speak of circular reaction; this could still be a simple attitude of pleasure and not a conscious connection.

The next day, at 0;2 (25) I connect his right hand to the celluloid balls but leave the string a little slack in order to necessitate ampler movements of the right arm and thus limit the effect of chance. The left hand is free. At first the arm movements are inadequate and the rattle does not move. Then the movements become more extensive, more regular, and the rattle moves periodically while the child's glance is directed at this sight. There seems to be conscious coördination but both arms move equally and it is not yet possible to be sure that this is not a mere pleasure reaction. The next day, same reactions.

At 0;2 (27), on the other hand, conscious coördination seems definite, for the following four reasons: (1) Laurent was surprised and frightened by the first shake of the rattle which was unexpected. On the other hand, since the second or third shake, he swung his right arm (connected to the rattle) with regularity, whereas the left remained almost motionless. Now the right could easily move freely without moving the rattle, the string being loose enough to permit Laurent to suck his thumb, for instance, without pulling at the balls. It therefore seems that the swinging was intentional. (2) Laurent's eye blinks beforehand, as soon as his hand moves and before the rattle moves, as though the child knew he was going to shake it. (3) When Laurent temporarily gives up the game and joins his hands for a moment, the right hand (connected to the rattle) alone resumes the movement while the left stays motionless. (4) The regular shakes that Laurent gives the rattle reveal a certain skill; the movement is regular and the child must stretch his arm backward sufficiently to make the rattle sound.—The reaction is the same on the following days: the right arm connected to the rattle is always more active than the left. Moreover the interest is growing and Laurent swings his right arm as soon as he has heard the rattle (while I fasten the string) without waiting to shake it by chance.

At 0;3 (0) I attached the string to the left arm after six days of experiments with the right. The first shake is given by chance: fright, curiosity, etc. Then, at once, there is coördinated circular reaction: this time the right arm is outstretched and barely mobile while the left swings. Now Laurent has plenty of room to do something else with his left arm than shake the rattle, but he does not try at all to free his hand from the string and his glance is directed at the result.—This time it is therefore possible to speak definitely of secondary circular reaction, even though Laurent only learned a week later to coördinate his prehension with his vision. The fact is all the more certain because at 0;2 (29) I observed the following. Putting my middle finger in his left hand I made his arm swing in a movement analogous to that required to set the rattle in motion: when I stopped, Laurent continued this movement by himself and directed my finger. Such a movement therefore lends itself to intentional coördination beginning at this age.

At 0;3 (10), after Laurent has learned to grasp what he sees, I place the string, which is attached to the rattle, in his right hand, merely unrolling it a little so that he may grasp it better. For a moment nothing happens but, at the first shake due to chance movements of his hand, the reaction is immediate: Laurent starts when looking at the rattle and then violently strikes his right hand alone, as if he felt the resistance and the effect. The operation lasts fully a quarter of an hour during which Laurent emits peals of laughter. The phenomenon is all the more clear because, the string being slack, the child must stretch his arm sufficiently and put the right amount of effort into it.

Observation 98.—Subsequently, at 0;3 (12) Laurent is subjected to the following experiment. I attach to the rattles (hanging from the bassinet hood) my watch chain and let it hang vertically until it almost reaches his face in order to see whether he will grasp it and thus shake the celluloid balls. The result is completely negative: when I put the chain in his hands and he shakes it by chance and hears the noise, he immediately waves his hand (as in the foregoing observation) but lets the chain go without understanding that he must grasp it in order to shake the rattle. The following day, however, he discovers the procedure. At first, when I place the chain in his hand (I only do so in order to start the experiment as this act of prehension would in any case be produced, sooner or later and fortuitously), Laurent waves his hand, then lets the chain go, while looking at the balls. Then he strikes great blows at random which shake the chain (and the rattle) without his grasping it. Then, without looking, he takes hold of the sheet in front of him (doubtless to suck it, as he does a part of the day) and at the same time grasps the chain without recognizing it. The chain then moves the rattle and Laurent again is interested in this sight. Little by little, Laurent thus arrives at discriminating tactilely the chain itself: his hand searches for it and as soon as the outer side of his fingers strikes it, he lets go the sheet or coverlet in order to hold the chain alone. Then he immediately swings his arm while looking at the rattle. He therefore seems to have understood that it is the chain, and not his body movements in general, that shakes the rattle. At a certain moment he looks at his hand which holds the chain; then he looks at the chain from top to bottom.

That evening, as soon as he hears the sound of the rattle and sees the chain hanging, he tries to grasp it without looking either at his hand or at the lower end of the chain (he only looks at the rattle). It happened exactly as follows: while looking at the rattle, Laurent let go with his right hand the sheet which he was sucking (he keeps it in his mouth with his left hand) and searched for the chain, his right hand open and the thumb opposed; as soon as he made contact with the chain he grasped and shook it. After a few moments of this, he resumes sucking his fingers. But when the chain touches him lightly he at once removes his right hand from his mouth, grasps the chain, pulls it very slowly while looking at the toys and apparently expecting a noise: after a few seconds during which he still pulls the chain very gently, he shakes much harder and succeeds. He then bursts into peals of laughter, babbles and swings the chain as much as possible.

At 0;3 (14) Laurent looks at the rattle at the moment I hang up the chain. He remains immobile for a second. Then he tries to grasp the chain (without looking at it), brushes it with the back of his hand, grasps it but continues to look at the rattle without moving his arms. Then he shakes the chain gently while studying the effect. Afterward he shakes it more and more vigorously. A smile and expression of delight.

But, a moment later, Laurent lets go the chain, unawares. He then keeps his left hand (which thitherto held the chain) tightly closed whereas his right hand is open and immobile and he continues to shake his left arm as though he held the chain, while looking at the rattle. He continues thus for at least five minutes.—This last observation shows that, although Laurent knows how to coördinate his grasp movements and the shaking of the rattle, he little understands the mechanism of these connections.

The following days, Laurent grasps and shakes the chain as soon as I hang it up and thus shakes the rattle, but he does not look at the chain before grasping it: he limits himself to searching for it with his hand (right or left, as the case may be) and to grasping it when he touches it. At 0;3 (18) on the other hand, he looks first at the rattle, then at the chain which he grasps after having seen it. The chain has therefore acquired a visual and no longer only a tactile meaning: Laurent knows henceforth that this visual obstacle is simultaneously a thing to be grasped and a means of shaking the rattle. But this tactile-visual coördination relating to the chain in no way implies that Laurent has understood the particulars of the mechanism. There is simply an efficient connection between the grasping of the chain, followed by the adaptation of the arm, and the movements of the rattle. The rest of the observation (see below, Obs. 112) will show us, in effect, to what extent this schema remains phenomenalistic: the chain is not conceived as the extension of the rattle, it is simply a thing to be grasped and shaken when one desires to see and hear the rattle in motion.

Observation 99.—After having thus discovered the use of the chain hanging from the toys, Laurent generalizes this behavior pattern by applying it to everything that hangs from the hood of his bassinet.

For example, at 0;3 (23) he takes hold of the string attaching a rubber doll to the hood and shakes it immediately. This gesture, simple assimilation of the perceived string to the habitual schema, has of course the effect of shaking the hood and the toys attached to it. Laurent, who did not seem to expect this result, considers it with growing interest and his vigor increases, this time apparently in order to make the spectacle last. After an interruption, I myself shake the hood (from behind): Laurent then looks for the string, grasps and shakes it. He then succeeds in grasping and shaking the doll itself.

The following evening: identical reactions. I observe that Laurent, when he pulls the string, looks at it from top to bottom: he therefore is expecting the result of his act. He also looks at it before grasping it, but not in general: he does not need to do so, since he knows the visual meaning of this object and how to guide his arm by using his kinesthetic sense.

At 0;4 (3) he pulls at will the chain or the string in order to shake the rattle and make it sound: the intention is clear. I now attach a paper knife to the string. The same day I attach a new toy half as high as the string (instead of the paper knife): Laurent begins by shaking himself while looking at it, then waves his arms in the air and finally takes hold of the rubber doll which he shakes while looking at the toy. The coördination is clearly intentional.

At 0;4 (30) Laurent, seeing the doll hang from the rattles at the hood at once looks at these and then shakes the doll only: it is clearly in order to shake the rattles that he grasps the doll.

At 0;5 (25) the same reactions on seeing the string. Furthermore, if I shake the hood (from behind, without being seen) this suffices to make Laurent pull the string in order to make this movement continue.

Observation 100.—At 0;7 (16) Jacqueline reveals a circular reaction analogous to that in Observation 99, but with the delay explained by the three-month retardation which separate her from Laurent from the point of view of prehension of seen objects. She is presented with a doll suspended from the string which connects the hood to the handle of the bassinet. In grasping this doll she shakes the bassinet hood; she immediately notices this effect and begins again at least twenty times in succession, more and more violently and while watching the shaken hood laughingly.

At 0;7 (23) Jacqueline looks at the hood of her bassinet which I shake several times while I remain unseen. As soon as I have finished she grasps and pulls a cord hanging where the doll had been. My movement of course reminds her of the familiar schema and she pulls the string at the usual place without having necessarily understood the mechanism in detail. Same reaction, but entirely spontaneous, at 0;8 (8), 0;8 (9), 0;8 (13), 0;8 (16), etc.

Observation 100 repeated.—Lucienne, similarly, at 0;6 (5) pulls a doll hanging from the hood in order to make it move; she even looks at the hood ahead of time while grasping the doll, thus revealing accurate foresight. Same observation at 0;6 (10), 0;8 (10), etc.

Observation 101.—Finally two other procedures were employed by Jacqueline, Lucienne, and Laurent in order to shake their bassinet or the objects hanging from the hood. At 0;7 (20) Lucienne looks at the hood and the hanging ribbons; her arms are outstretched and slightly straightened, at an equal distance from her face. She gently opens and closes her hands, then more and more rapidly with involuntary arm movements which thus gently shake the hood. Lucienne then repeats these movements with increasing speed. Same reaction at 0;7 (27), etc. I again observe the phenomenon at 0;10 (27): she moves her bassinet while waving her hands.

At 0;8 (5), Lucienne shakes her head from side to side in order to shake her bassinet, the hood, ribbons, fringes, etc.

Jacqueline, in the same way, shakes her bassinet, at 0;8 (19) while swinging her arms. She even succeeds in differentiating her movements in order to conserve certain effects obtained by chance. She waves her right arm in a certain way (obliquely to her trunk) in order to make the bassinet grate while shaking it all over. In case of failure she corrects herself and gropes, places her arms perpendicularly to her trunk, then places them more and more obliquely until she succeeds. At 0;11 (16) she shakes at a distance (at the end of her bassinet) a jack-in-the-box, while swinging her arms.

At the end of the fourth month Laurent discovered these same two circular reactions which shows that they are general. Thus at 0;3 (23) I find him shaking his head spontaneously (a lateral movement) when confronted by the hanging toys, before grasping the cord which enables him to shake them. Actually this head movement sufficed to shake the whole cradle slightly.

With regard to the arm movements, they are partly the result of the reactions learned in Observations 97 and 98, but partly also of the movements of the whole body which the child sometimes performs in order to shake his bassinet. At 0;3 (25), for example, and at 0;4 (6) he begins by shaking himself all over when confronted by hanging objects, then he shakes his right arm in space. The reaction becomes general during the following days.

Here are some observations concerning secondary circular reactions relating to objects, usually not hanging, that the child grasps in order to move, swing, shake, rub them against others, cause them to make a noise, etc.

Observation 102.—The simplest example is doubtless that of the objects the child simply shakes as soon as he has grasped them. From this elementary schema, which is almost "primary," the following is immediately derived: if the objects brandished produce a sound this is enough to make the child attempt to reproduce it.

As early as 0;2 (26) Laurent, in whose right hand I have put the handle of a rattle, shakes it by chance, hears the noise and laughs at the result. But he does not see the rattle and looks for it in the direction of the hood, at the place from which such a sound usually comes. When he finally sees the rattle he does not understand that this is the object which is making the noise nor that he himself makes it move. He nevertheless continues his activity.

At 0;3 (6), during the fourth stage of prehension, he grasps the rattle after having seen his hand in the same visual field, then brings it to his mouth. But the sound thus produced arouses the schema of the hanging rattle: Laurent shakes himself all over, especially moving his arm, and finally only moves the latter, astonished and slightly worried by the increasing noise.

From 0;3 (15)—that is to say, the present stage—it suffices for Laurent to grasp an object to make him shake it and that he observe the rattle with the handle to cause him to grasp and shake it properly. But subsequently the reaction becomes complicated through the fact that Laurent tries rather to strike it with one hand while holding it with the other, to rub it against the edges of the bassinet, etc. We shall return to this in connection with these latter schemata.

At 0;4 (15) Lucienne grasps the handle of a rattle in the shape of a celluloid ball. The movements of the hand in grasping the rattle result in shaking it and producing a sudden and violent noise. Lucienne at once moves her whole body, and especially her feet, to make the noise last. She has a demented expression of mingled fear and pleasure, but she continues. Hitherto the reaction is comparable to that of Observations 94–95 repeated, and the movement of the hands is not yet maintained for itself, independently of the reaction of the whole body. This reaction lasts a few days but then Lucienne, when she is in possession of the rattle, limits herself to shaking it with the hand that holds it. But—a curious thing—at 0;5 (10) and again at 0;5 (12) she accompanies this movement of the hands with shakes of the feet analogous to those she makes to shake a hanging object (see Obs. 95).

Jacqueline, too, at 0;9 (5) shakes while holding a celluloid rattle in the form of a parrot which she has just been given. She smiles when the noise is slight, is anxious when it is too loud and knows very well how to gradate the phenomenon. She progressively increases the noise until she is too frightened and then returns to the soft sounds. Furthermore, when the rattle is stuck at one of the ends, she shakes the parrot by turning it in another direction and thus knows how to reëstablish the noise.

Observation 103.—A second classic schema is that of "striking." At 0;4 (28) Lucienne tries to grasp the rattle in Observation 102 when it is attached to the bassinet hood and hangs in front of her face. During an unlucky attempt she strikes it violently: fright, then a vague smile. She brings her hand back with a doubtless intentional suddenness: a new blow. The phenomenon then becomes systematic: Lucienne hits the rattle with regularity a very great number of times.

At 0;5 (0) the same happens to her hanging dolls which she strikes violently.

At 0;6 (2) she looks at a wooden Pierrot which I have hung before her and with which she has rarely played. Lucienne at first tries to grasp it. But the movement she makes in holding out her hand shakes the Pierrot before she has touched it: Lucienne at once shakes her legs and feet in a regular and rapid rhythm in order to maintain the swinging of the object (see Obs. 94). Then she grasps and pulls it. The Pierrot again escapes her and swings; Lucienne reacts by shaking her legs again. Finally she rediscovers the schema of 0;4 (28) and 0;5 (0): she strikes the toy more and more vigorously, without trying to grasp it, and bursts out laughing at the Pierrot's antics. Same reactions at 0;6 (3). At 0;6 (10) she begins by striking the puppet that I hang up, and so makes it swing, then she maintains the movement by shakes of the legs. At 0;6 (19) she strikes the hanging dolls in order to make them swing.

Jacqueline in the same way strikes her toys, from 0;7 (15); at 0;7 (28) strikes her duck, at 0;8 (5) a doll, at 0;9 (5) her cushions, from 0;8 (5) to 0;9 (0) her parrot, etc.

With regard to Laurent the schema of striking arose in the following way. At 0;4 (7) Laurent looks at a paper knife attached to the strings of a hanging doll. He tries to grasp the doll or the paper knife, but, at each attempt, the clumsiness of his movements results in causing him to knock these objects. He then looks at them with interest and recommences.

The next day, at 0;4 (8) same reaction. Laurent still does not strike intentionally but, trying to grasp the paper knife, and noting that he fails each time, he only outlines the gesture of grasping and thus limits himself to knocking one of the extremities of the object.

At 0;4 (9), the next day, Laurent tries to grasp the doll hanging in front of him; but he only succeeds in swinging it without holding it. He then shakes it altogether, while waving his arms (see Obs. 101). But he thus happens to strike the doll: he then begins again intentionally a series of times. A quarter of an hour later, as soon as he is confronted by the same doll in the same circumstances he begins to hit it again.

At 0;4 (15), faced by another hanging doll, Laurent tries to grasp it, then he shakes himself in order to make it swing, happens to knock it and then tries to strike it. The schema is therefore almost differentiated from the preceding ones but it does not yet constitute a principal and independent behavior pattern.

At 0;4 (18) Laurent strikes my hands without trying to grasp them, but he has begun by simply waving his arms in the air and only "hit" subsequently.

At 0;4 (19), at last, Laurent directly strikes a hanging doll. The schema is therefore completely differentiated. At 0;4 (21) he strikes the hanging toys in the same way and thus swings them as much as possible. Same reaction on the following days.

From 0;5 (2) Laurent strikes the objects with one hand while holding them with the other. Thus he holds a rubber doll in the left hand and strikes it with his right. At 0;5 (6) he grasps a rattle with a handle and strikes it immediately. At 0;5 (7) I hand him different objects which are new to him (a wooden penguin, etc.): he hardly looks at them but strikes them systematically.

It may thus be seen how the schema of striking hanging objects became differentiated little by little from simpler schemata and gave rise to the schema of hitting objects held in the hands. It is noteworthy, however, that though the 4- to 7-month-old child thus learns to swing hanging objects by hitting them as hard as possible, he does not attempt simply to start their swinging to observe it, but often achieves this by chance. It is only at about 0;8 (10) that I observed the latter behavior pattern in Lucienne and Jacqueline and about 0;8 (30) in Laurent. But it definitely differs from the preceding one both from the point of view of causality and that of the intellectual mechanism. The child who strikes in order to swing is, in effect, active himself, whereas he who limits himself to starting the swinging transfers this activity to the object as such. Therefore that is no longer a simple secondary circular reaction but an exploration and almost a sort of experimentation. For this reason we shall not speak of this behavior here but shall study it in connection with the next stage.

Observation 104.—A final noteworthy example is the behavior pattern consisting in rubbing objects against hard surfaces such as the wicker of the bassinet. Lucienne, from 0;5 (12), and Jacqueline a little later, about 0;7 (20) used the toys they held in their hands to rub the surfaces of the bassinet. Laurent discovered this at 0;4 (6) in circumstances which it is worthwhile to analyze.

At 0;3 (29) Laurent grasps a paper knife which he sees for the first time; he looks at it a moment and then swings it while holding it in his right hand. During these movements the object happens to rub against the wicker of the bassinet: Laurent then waves his arm vigorously and obviously tries to reproduce the sound he has heard, but without understanding the necessity of contact between the paper knife and the wicker and, consequently, without achieving this contact otherwise than by chance.

At 0;4 (3) same reactions, but Laurent looks at the object at the time when it happens to rub against the wicker of the bassinet. The same still occurs at 0;4 (5) but there is slight progress toward systematization.

Finally, at 0;4 (6) the movement becomes intentional: as soon as the child has the object in his hand he rubs it with regularity against the wicker of the bassinet. He does the same, subsequently, with his dolls and rattles (see Obs. 102), etc.

These few examples of secondary circular reactions thus constitute the first behavior patterns involving an action brought to bear upon things and no longer a utilization, in some way organic, of reality. Such a question again raises the whole problem of mental assimilation.

When the nursling takes the breast for the first time and then immediately begins to suck and swallow or, even earlier, when he impulsively moves his lips and then continues empty sucking, one might suppose that this reproductive assimilation as well as the recognitions and generalizations which prolong it are themselves dependent for their conditioning upon an earlier need: the organic need to take nourishment and to suck. So also, when the child learns to look, listen, or grasp, it could be asserted that this functional activity is only assimilatory because it constitutes first of all a satisfaction of physiological needs. If such were the case, it would not be possible to understand how the child's activity can become centered beginning at 4 to 6 months on results such as those of the secondary circular reactions which do not correspond, in their externality, to any internal, definite and particular need.

But, as we have seen (Chapter I, §3) the retention in consciousness of a physiological need is not a simple fact nor an immediate condition, and it is fitting to distinguish two distinct series in the humblest act of repetition, by which reflex use or acquired association begin: the organic series and the psychic series. From the physiological point of view it is certain that need explains repetition: it is because sucking corresponds to a need that the nursling does not stop sucking, and it is because of the connection established between thumb sucking and satisfying this need that the 1- to 2-month-old child puts his thumb back into his mouth as soon as he is capable of this coördination. But it is noteworthy, from this strictly physiological point of view, that all needs depend, either immediately or remotely, upon a fundamental need which is that of the organism's development; that is to say precisely, upon assimilation: it is due to the subordination of the organs to this chief tendency—which defines life itself—that the functioning of each one gives rise to a particular need. Now, from the psychological point of view, it proceeds in exactly the same way. The need sets in motion the act and its functioning, but this functioning itself engenders a greater need which from the very first goes beyond the pure satisfaction of the initial need. It is therefore fruitless to ask if it is need that explains repetition or the reverse: together they form an inseparable unity. Hence the primary fact is neither the need anterior to the act nor repetition, the source of satisfaction, but it is the total relation of the need to the satisfaction. From the point of view of behavior, this relation is none other than the operation by which an already organized mechanism becomes established by functioning and functions by utilizing a condition external to itself: it is therefore functional assimilation. From the point of view of consciousness, this relation is also of an operative nature, and this is why one cannot seek the fundamental truth of psychology either in a state of simple consciousness or in an isolated tendency. Need and satisfaction are, in effect, vicarious, and oscillate between the purely organic and the functional; moreover, they are experienced relatively to one another. Consequently they are both connected to a fundamental operation— of which they are only the influence of variable and approximative consciousness—by which the behavior pattern puts its own functioning into relationship with the conditions of the environment. The relation of need and satisfaction thus reveals a relation anterior to assimilation, according to which the subject only apprehends the object relatively to his own activity. Consequently, just as all physiological needs depend on a main tendency—that of the organism's development through assimilation to the environment—so also every elementary psychic function, however subordinated it may seem to be to the satisfaction of a precise physiological need, involves an activity which will gradually integrate the whole of the behavior patterns: the assimilation of the object to the subject in general.

When these principles are remembered it is easy to understand how needs which were at first chiefly organic can be subordinated little by little to functional needs and how the latter can give rise to operations concerning the interrelations of things and no longer the relations of things to the organs of the body. For example, how does it happen that the child, instead of merely grasping the doll hanging from the hood of his bassinet, makes use of it in order to shake the hood (Obs. 100)? Until then, in effect, the doll was an object to be looked at, grasped, sucked, heard, etc., but not at all a thing to produce extrinsic results such as the shaking of the hood. The transition from the first state to the second must therefore be explained. With regard to the movements of the hood, either they are perceived for the first time, and then it must be understood why from the very first they give rise to an attempt at repetition, or else they have already been a thing to look at, to hear, etc., and it must be understood how they are transformed into a result to be maintained by new means.

The question is simplified as soon as one sees the essential fact that, among the unknown phenomena observed by the child only those which are experienced as dependent on the activity itself give rise to a secondary circular reaction. But let us note that this is not as natural as it might seem. One might very well think that the child, confronted by any new spectacle at all, even one independent of him from the observer's point of view, tries from the very first to reproduce it or make it continue. This is exactly what is subsequently revealed when, accustomed to repeat everything through circular reaction, the child generalizes this behavior pattern and tries to discover "procedures to make interesting sights last" (see Obs. 112–118). But observation shows that that is derived behavior and that, before practicing the secondary circular reaction, the child, in order to assimilate new sights, limits himself to utilizing the primary reactions. For instance, when he sees the hanging toys move without yet knowing that it is he who sets them going, or when he sees the rattle with a handle without yet realizing that he is the cause of the effect produced, Laurent is already interested in these phenomena; that is to say, he tries to assimilate them but he tries to conserve them only by looking at or listening to them without yet attempting to reproduce them by means of hand or arm movements. This, however, does not mean that these phenomena are conceived by him as "objective" and independent of his activity in general. It is very possible, on the contrary, that when looking at an object or turning his head to listen to it, etc., the subject may have the impression of participating in the repetition or continuation of the sensorial image. But, to be precise, such a relationship must be experienced in order that the attempt at repetition which constitutes the secondary circular reaction may begin.

Hence it cannot be said that the present behavior pattern consists in repeating everything which happens to appear in the child's visual field. The secondary circular reaction only begins when a chance effect of the action itself is understood to be the result of this activity. Thereafter it is easy to grasp the continuity which exists between the primary and secondary reactions. Just as, in the first, the objective is aliment for sucking, vision or prehension, so also, in the second, it becomes aliment for any movement produced by differentiation of prehension and the movements of the forearm. True, the difference is great between the somewhat centripetal interest of sucking, or even of sight, and the centrifugal interest of the present level, an interest directed at the external result of the acts. But this contrast is modified if it is recalled that a sensorial image is the more objectified and externalized because it coördinates within itself more schemata and because all the intermediaries between the primary and secondary reactions therefore exist. A visual objective, for example, is much nearer the actual "object" if it is simultaneously a thing to see, to hear and to touch than if it is only an image to contemplate. Consequently the movement of the hood or the sound of a stick against the wicker of the bassinet will give rise to an externalization all the greater because they are simultaneously to be seen, heard, and reproduced by means of hand movements. Through a paradox analogous to that of the development of the sciences, it happens that reality is objectified in proportion as it is elaborated by the thinking and working of the subject's schemata, whereas the phenomenalism of immediate perception is only subjectivism. Furthermore, while incorporating in his activity results so remote from himself, the child introduces into his proceedings a series of intermediaries. For instance, when he shakes the hood of his bassinet by grasping a hanging doll he is obliged, even without any understanding of the relations which exist between the two states, to see in the hood's movement the prolongation of the act of grasping the doll. The assimilation of the movements of the hood to the schema of prehension thus presupposes putting these movements into relationship with those of the doll. Such a process explains why every reproductive assimilation of a remote spectacle brings with it an active elaboration of relationships. The action ceases to be simple in order to introduce a beginning of differentiation between means and ends, and the assimilation of things to the self becomes construction of relationships between things.

The assimilation characteristic of secondary circular reaction is, in short, only the development of assimilation at work in the primary reactions. Just as everything, in the child's primitive universe, is for sucking, looking, listening, touching, and grasping, everything gradually becomes something to be shaken, swung, rubbed, etc., according to differentiations of the manual and visual schemata. But before discerning the mechanism according to which these progressive accommodations operate, there remains to be explained how a remote spectacle can thus be conceived as produced by the action itself (which is, as we have just noted, the condition for the advent of the secondary reaction). This question can be answered in one word: this discovery is made through reciprocal assimilation of the present schemata. We recall, in this connection, how coördination such as that of vision or hearing is established: by seeking to see that which he hears and to hear that which he sees, the child perceives little by little that a same given object is simultaneously the source of sounds and visual image. It is in an analogous way that the co-ordination of vision and prehension subsequently is brought about. After having looked at his hands and at the objects grasped, the child tries to move the visual image which he also sees; in that way he discovers that one may grasp what one sees as well as look at what one grasps. Now in the case of the beginnings of secondary circular reaction a phenomenon of the same kind ensues. For instance when Laurent unwittingly starts a movement of the toys by pulling a chain or rubs a paper knife against the wicker of his bassinet he is looking at, listening to, etc., the effect thus produced without trying to conserve it by other means. But, precisely because he is in the act of shaking the chain or the paper knife while he looks at or listens to the result of these movements, the two kinds of schemata sooner or later end by being reciprocally assimilated. The child then applies himself to moving with his hand the image that he looks at, just as formerly he was led intentionally to move the visual image of his own limbs. This does not yet mean that he tries to reproduce the objective phenomenon as such (which will constitute the secondary circular reaction), but simply that his visual and manual schemata, being simultaneously active, tend to assimilate each other according to a general law. But as soon as this reciprocal assimilation has been formed the child understands that the external result which he has observed (the movements of the toys or the sound of the paper knife against the wicker) depends upon his manual as well as his visual or auditory activity, and this understanding thereafter gives rise to an immediate circular reaction; that is to say, to an act of reproductive assimilation. From the point of view of assimilation itself, secondary circular reaction thus prolongs the primary reaction, and the child's interest only becomes externalized on the interrelations of things as a function of the increasing coördination of the present schemata (the primary schemata).

§2. THE SECONDARY CIRCULAR REACTIONS—II. ACCOMMODATION AND ORGANIZATION OF THE SCHEMATA.—Until the present behavior patterns—that is, during the entire stage of the pure primary reactions—accommodation remained relatively subordinated to assimilation. Sucking, looking, grasping, consisted in incorporating observed objects into corresponding schemata of assimilation, free to accommodate these schemata to a variety of things. So it is that the movements and positions of hands, eyes, and mouth vary as a function of the objectives, in a continuous accommodation concomitant to assimilation, although of opposite direction. At the other extreme of sensorimotor behavior patterns—that is to say, in the tertiary circular reactions, we shall see—on the contrary, that accommodation precedes assimilation, in a sense. Confronted by new objects the child intentionally seeks to find out in what way they are new and so experiments upon them before assimilating them to a schema constructed on their effect. Hence accommodation evolves from the simple differentiation of schemata, peculiar to the primary reactions, to the search for the new, peculiar to the tertiary reactions. What of the secondary circular reaction?

In its point of departure the latter reveals no accommodation other than that of the primary reactions: a simple differentiation of schemata as function of the object. So it is that Laurent discovers the possibility of hitting a hanging doll, simply while trying to grasp it (Obs. 103), and that Lucienne and Laurent learn to rub a toy against the side of the bassinet simply while swinging it (Obs. 104, etc.). But, contrary to that which occurs in the primary reactions, this initial differentiation of the schema does not, without adding something, lead to its application to new objects, precisely since Laurent does not succeed in grasping the doll nor in moving the rattle as he intends to, but discovers an unforeseen phenomenon due to this very defeat: the doll swings when one strikes it and the rattle rubs the wood of the bassinet. It is then that the specific accommodation of the secondary circular reaction is produced: the child tries to rediscover the movements which lead to the result observed. As we have previously demonstrated, the child begins, in effect, by trying to assimilate this new result while limiting himself to looking at it, etc. (primary schemata). Then, as soon as he has discovered, through reciprocal assimilation of the schemata, that this result depends on his manual activity, he tries to reproduce it by assimilation to this activity. But, as it is just in differentiating the latter that the subject has by chance obtained the new result, the question is to establish this differentiation intentionally and it is in this that the accommodation peculiar to the secondary reactions consists: rediscovering the movements which have given rise to the result observed. This accommodation, without preceding assimilation as is the case in the tertiary reaction, or simply doubling it, as is the case in the primary reaction, consists, then, in completing it at the moment when the new schema is formed. Therefore accommodation is no longer an almost automatic differentiation of the schemata, nor yet an intentional search for novelty as such, but it is a voluntary and systematic fixation of the differentiations imposed by new realities which arise by chance. A concrete example will enable us to understand:

Observation 105.—Laurent, from 0;4 (19) as has been seen (Obs. 103) knows how to strike hanging objects intentionally with his hand. At 0;4 (22) he holds a stick; he does not know what to do with it and slowly passes it from hand to hand. The stick then happens to strike a toy hanging from the bassinet hood. Laurent, immediately interested by this unexpected result, keeps the stick raised in the same position, then brings it noticeably nearer to the toy. He strikes it a second time. Then he draws the stick back but moving it as little as possible as though trying to conserve the favorable position, then he brings it nearer to the toy, and so on, more and more rapidly.

The dual character of this accommodation may be seen. On the one hand, the new phenomenon makes its appearance by simple fortuitous insertion in an already formed schema and hence differentiates it. But, on the other hand, the child, intentionally and systematically, applies himself to rediscovering the conditions which led him to this unexpected result.

It goes without saying that the use of the stick described in this example was only episodical: it has nothing to do with the "behavior pattern of the stick" which we shall describe in connection with the fifth stage.

This analysis of the accommodation peculiar to the secondary circular reactions makes it possible to understand why the child's activity, which hitherto seemed to us essentially conservative, henceforth appears to be indefinitely diversified.

That activity should be conservative at the reflex stage is

only natural. The schemata belonging to the reflexes having already been hereditarily elaborated, reflex behavior simply consists in assimilating the datum to these schemata and in accommodating them to reality by simple use without transforming them. With regard to the primary circular reactions and the habits which derive from them the same is true fundamentally, despite the obvious acquisitions characteristic of these behavior patterns. When the child learns to grasp, to look, to listen, to suck for the sake of sucking (and no longer only in order to eat), he assimilates to his reflex schemata an increasing number of realities and, if acquired accommodation to these realities exists, they remain nevertheless simple aliments for the conservation of the schemata. With regard to acquisitions through the coördination of schemata, the question is, as we have seen, only one of reciprocal assimilation, that is to say, again of conservation. This assimilation, consequently, does not exclude enrichment and cannot be reduced to identification pure and simple—this goes without saying—but it nevertheless remains essentially conservative.

How, then, can it be explained that at a given moment the circle of conservation seems to break and the reproduction of new results prolongs the primary reaction by thus creating multiple relations between the things themselves? Is it reality alone which makes the framework of assimilation crack by confining the child's activity to a progressive diversification, or can this diversification be considered as a function of assimilation and as always depending on conservation?

There is no doubt that both are present. On the one hand, reality forces the child to make indefinite accommodations. As soon as the child knows how to grasp that which he sees, the objects he manipulates put him brutally in the presence of the most varied experiences. The rattles which swing while producing disturbing sounds, the bassinet which shakes while producing the movement of the hanging toys, the boxes which offer opposition by reason of their weight and shapes, the coverlets or strings held back or attached in an unpredictable way, everything is an opportunity for new experiments, and the content of these experiments cannot give rise to assimilation without a continuous accommodation which opposes it in a way.

But, on the other hand, this accommodation is never pure, and secondary circular reaction would not be explainable if the child's behavior did not remain basically assimilatory and conservative. As we have just seen, each of the secondary circular reactions which appear in the child is derived by differentiation from a primary circular reaction or a secondary reaction grafted upon a primary reaction. Everything thus goes back to movements of legs or feet, arms or hands, and it is these "circular" movements of prehension which become differentiated in movements directed at pulling, shaking, swinging, displacing, rubbing, etc. When Lucienne, at 3 to 4 months, shakes her bassinet and her dolls (Obs. 94–95) she limits herself to moving feet and legs, in conformity to a primary schema. When Laurent at 0;2 (24)– 0;3 (0) shakes a rattle attached to his arm (Observation 97) before knowing how to grasp, he is only prolonging the spontaneous circular movements of that arm. And when at 0;3 (13) he learns to shake the rattle by means of a chain, this is simply because he uses his nascent schema of prehension (Obs. 98). The same applies to all the secondary circular reactions: each is the prolongation of an already existing schema. With regard to "procedures to make interesting sights last" of which we shall speak later on, they in turn prolong these circular reactions. The only difference between the secondary reactions and the primary reactions is, therefore, that henceforth the interest is centered on the external result and no longer only on the activity as such. But that is not contradictory to the conservative character of this function: in effect, the external result, arising suddenly at the very center of the child's activity, interests him at one and the same time inasmuch as it is related to his essential schemata and inasmuch as it is unforeseen and baffling. If it were only new it would merely deserve momentary attention; but on the contrary, it appears to the subject as being connected with his most familiar acts or with his schemata in actual use. Moreover this unforeseen result leads astray all that of which these schemata habitually admit. The attention is, therefore, perforce centered on the exterior and no longer only on the function. In short, the secondary circular reactions are essentially conservative and as-similatory since they prolong without adding anything to the primary reactions and, if the child's interest is displaced and externalized on the material result of the acts, it is simply be-cause this result is function of an increasingly rich assimilatory activity.

What do these acquisitions mean now from the point of view of organization?

Organization, we recall, is the internal aspect of the func-tioning of the schemata to which assimilation tends to reduce the external environment. It is therefore, one might say, an internal adaptation of which accommodation and assimilation combined form the external expression. Actually each schema, or each en-semble of schemata, consists in a "totality" independently of which no assimilation would be possible and which in turn rests upon a number of interdependent elements (see Introduction, §2). Furthermore, to the extent that these totalities are not en-tirely realized but are in process of elaboration, they involve a differentiation between "means" and "ends," between "values" subordinated to the formation of the whole, this whole not com-plete for an "ideal' totality. This fundamental mechanism of organization accompanies internally the external manifestations of adaptation. How then does it function, during this stage, and in what form is it made manifest in the child's behavior?

It is not difficult to see, in effect, that the secondary sche-mata, once they have been elaborated through complementary assimilation and accommodation, consist in organized schemata: in the capacity of a practical concept in which the schema thus constitutes a "totality," whereas the "relations" on which it rests determine the reciprocal relationships which constitute this totality.

With regard to the interorganization of the schemata—that is to say, the coördination of the secondary schemata—it only manifests itself during the following stage. We shall therefore speak of it again in connection with that fourth stage. But it is apparent that the different schemata of this stage, without inter-coördination in intentional series conscious of their unity, have already reached balance among themselves and constitute a system of unconsciously interdependent relationships. Without this total subjacent organization it would be impossible to explain how any object which is presented to a child is immediately classified, that is, assimilated through a simultaneously reproductive and recognitory act of assimilation suitable to this object and no other.

The totalities in process of being constituted or reconstituted remain to be examined. An original totality is constituted, in effect, every time that a new schema is elaborated by contact with things, and this contact is reconstituted every time the subject again finds himself confronted by suitable objects and assimilates them to the schema in question. The organization of these totalities marks progress over that of the "primary" schemata in this sense that, for the first time, and to the extent that the "relations" of which we shall presently speak are formed, the "means" begin to be distinguished from the "ends": consequently the movements made and the objects used henceforth assume different "values" subordinated to an "ideal" totality, that is to say, not yet realized. For instance when, in Observation 98, Laurent discovers that the hanging chain can be used to shake the rattle to which it is attached, it is certain that the action of pulling the chain is conceived as a "means" toward the "end" of reproducing the interesting result, although the means have been supplied at the same time as the end in the initial action reproduced by circular reaction. It is after the event, and when the subject seeks the result for himself, that he distinguishes between means and ends. Now, such a distinction is certainly new to the child's consciousness. It is true that one could in the same way analyze any primary schema such as that of thumb sucking. The action of introducing the thumb into the mouth could be conceived as a means at the service of the end which consists in sucking. But it is clear that such a description does not correspond to anything from the point of view of the subject himself, since the thumb is not known independently of the act which consists in sucking it; on the contrary, the chain serving to shake the rattle has been perceived and manipulated before being conceived as a "means" and does not cease to be regarded as distinct from the rattle. With regard to the coördinations among primary schemata (grasping in order to suck, etc.) they make manifest, it is true, the present distinction between means and ends, precisely since "secondary circular reaction" is only made possible by this kind of coördination (that of prehension and vision and, in the elementary cases, that of foot movements with vision). But, as we have seen, they consist in simple reciprocal assimilations, resulting in the formation of new global entities in which, consequently, the difference of which we speak is immediately obliterated.

But, if the distinction between means and ends is only established in the course of the elaboration of secondary schemata, we must not allow ourselves to believe that it is thus achieved and to identify it with that which it will become during the next stage—that is to say, at the time of the coördination of the same schemata. In effect, we have just seen that, during the present stage, the secondary schemata are not yet intercoördinated; each one constitutes a more or less self-enclosed totality instead of arranging itself in series analogous to that which in reflective thought is reason or the implication of concepts. From the fourth stage, on the contrary, these schemata will become intercoördinated when it will be a question of adapting themselves to unforeseen circumstances, thus giving rise to behavior patterns which we shall call the "application of known schemata to new situations." It is only in this connection that the "means" will be definitely dissociated from the "ends": the same schema being capable of serving as "means" to different ends will therefore assume an instrumental value which is much clearer than that which can be offered, during the present stage, by a movement (such as pulling the chain) always connected to the same end (shaking the rattle) and whose function of "means" has been discovered fortuitously.

In conclusion, it can be said that the secondary circular reactions make intelligent adaptation manifest, without, however, constituting true acts of intelligence. If compared to primary circular reactions they reveal intelligence because they elaborate an ensemble of almost intentional relations between things and the subject's activity. In effect these relations with the environment being at the outset complex, they give rise, as we have just seen, to a beginning of differentiation between means and ends and thereby to a rudiment of intention. When the child pulls the chain in order to shake a rattle, he carries out a much higher behavior pattern than simply grasping an object which he sees.

But, furthermore, the secondary circular reactions do not yet constitute complete acts of intelligence for two reasons. The first is that the relations utilized by the child (shaking himself in order to move the bassinet, pulling a chain in order to shake a rattle, etc.) were discovered fortuitously and not for the purpose of resolving a problem or satisfying a need. The need arises from the discovery and not the discovery from the need. On the contrary, in the true act of intelligence there is pursuit of an end and only subsequently discovery of means. The second reason, closely connected with the first, is that the only need involved, in the secondary circular reactions, is a need of repetition. For the child, the question is simply to conserve and reproduce the beneficial result discovered by chance. It is need that sets the act in motion at each new turn of the circle of circular reaction and it can surely be said, in this sense, that need is anterior to the act; in any case it is this fact which makes it possible to speak of intention and of intelligence. But, this need being only a desire for repetition, the means put to work in order to reproduce the desired result are already found. They are entirely contained in the fortuitous action which is at the point of departure of the ensemble of the reaction and which it is simply a question of repeating. The role of intelligence involved in such behavior patterns therefore consists simply in rediscovering the series of movements which have given rise to the beneficial result and the intention of these behavior patterns merely consists in trying to reproduce this result. Therein, let us repeat, is an outline of an intelligent act, but not a complete act. In effect, in a true act of intelligence, the need which serves as motive power not only consists in repeating, but in adapting, that is to say, in assimilating a new situation to old schemata and in accommodating these schemata to new circumstances. It is to this that secondary circular reaction will lead by extension; but, in this respect, it is not yet there.

All the more reason why it is impossible to attribute to such behavior patterns the capacity to engender or to utilize representations. There could be no question, at first, of a representation of the means employed: the child does not know in advance that he will perform a certain movement, since he simply tries to rediscover the motor combination which succeeded and since he subsequently limits himself to repeating his acts. With regard to the goal, does the child, for example, keep the memory of the shaken rattle in the form of visual or auditory images and does he try to reproduce something which conforms to this representation? There is no need for so complicated a mechanism to account for such behavior patterns. It is enough that the sight of the rattle created a sufficiently powerful interest for this interest to orient the activity in the direction already followed an instant before. In other words, when the rattle stops moving, there ensues a vacuum which the child immediately tries to fill and he does so by utilizing the movements which have just been performed. When these movements lead to a result which resembles the earlier spectacle, there is certainly recognition, but recognition does not presuppose the existence of representation. Recognition simply requires that the new result embrace entirely the structure of the assimilatory schema outlined at the beginning of circular reaction. Of course, if this mechanism repeats itself indefinitely, there can be a beginning of representation but, without being able to determine precisely when this appears, it can be said that it is not pristine and that it is useless to the formation of the present behavior patterns.

On the other hand, the secondary schemata constitute the first outline of what will become "classes" or concepts in reflective intelligence: perceiving an object as being something "to shake," "to rub," etc. This is, in effect, the functional equivalent of the operation of classification peculiar to conceptual thought. We shall return to this, in connection with the fourth stage, when the secondary schemata will have become more "mobile," but the observation arises now.

Furthermore, just as the logic of classes is correlative to that of "relations," so also the secondary schemata involve putting things into conscious interrelationships. Herein resides, as we have seen, their chief novelty in relation to the primary schemata. What are these relationships? It is apparent, since they are established within the same schema and not due to coördinations between separate secondary schemata, that they remain essentially practical and, consequently, global and phenomenalistic, without yet involving the elaboration of really "objective" substantial, spatial, or causal structures. When, in the example already commented upon, the child pulls a chain in order to shake a rattle, the relation he establishes between the chain and the rattle is not yet a spatial, causal and temporal relation between two "objects," it is a simple practical relationship between the act of pulling and the result observed. It is during the fourth stage, with the coördination of the secondary schemata and the implications which result, that these relations begin to become objectified, with the sole disadvantage of not being really objectified until the fifth stage.

But, however empirical these relations remain, they nevertheless constitute, from the formal point of view, the beginning of a system separate from that of "classes" which will later become increasingly differentiated. Furthermore, this elementary elaboration of relations, like the "logic of relations" of reflective intelligence, leads, at the outset, to the discovery of quantitative relations as distinguished from simple qualitative comparisons inherent in the classification as such.

We know, in effect, that if the concepts or "classes" only structure reality as a function of the qualitative resemblances or differences of the beings so classed, the "relations," on the other hand, involve quantity and lead to the elaboration of mathematical series. Even the relations with qualitative content, such as "darker" or "brother of" constitute, in effect, a "seriation" of a kind other than the relations of appurtenance or of inherence and hence presuppose either the concepts of "more" and "less" which are frankly quantitative, or a discrimination and ordering of individuals, which relationships envelop number.

Now this is precisely what happens on the sensorimotor plane as soon as the first relations are elaborated. For instance, the relations established by the child between the act of pulling the chain and the movements of the rattle (Obs. 98) at the outset leads the subject to the discovery of a quantitative connection immanent in this relation: the more the chain is shaken the more violently the rattles move.

Observation 106.—In the evening of 0;3 (13) Laurent by chance strikes the chain while sucking his fingers (Obs. 98): he grasps it and slowly displaces it while looking at the rattles. He then begins to swing it very gently which produces a slight movement of the hanging rattles and an as yet faint sound inside them. Laurent then definitely increases by degrees his own movements: he shakes the chain more and more vigorously and laughs uproariously at the result obtained.—On seeing the child's expression it is impossible not to deem this gradation intentional.

At 0;4 (21) as well, when he strikes with his hand the toys hanging from his bassinet hood (Obs. 103) he visibly gradates his movements as function of the result: at first he strikes gently and then continues more and more strongly, etc.

These gradations are found in nearly all the preceding observations as well as in the use of "procedures to make interesting sights last" (see below, Obs. 112–118).

Thus it may be seen how the secondary schemata constitutes not only a kind of concept or practical "class" but also a system of relationships enveloping the quantity itself.

§3. RECOGNITORY ASSIMILATION AND THE SYSTEM OF MEANINGS.—The facts hitherto studied constitute essentially phenomena of reproductive assimilation: through repetition rediscovering a fortuitous result. Before seeing how this behavior is extended into generalizing assimilation and thus gives rise to "procedures to make interesting sights last," let us once more emphasize a group of facts, which no longer constitute circular reactions in themselves but which are derived from secondary reactions, in the capacity of recognitory assimilations. What happens, in effect, is that the child, confronted by objects or sights which habitually set in motion his secondary circular reactions, limits himself to outlining the customary movements instead of actually performing them. Everything takes place as though the child were satisfied to recognize these objects or sights and to make a note of this recognition, but could not recognize them except by working, rather than thinking, the schema helpful to recognition. Now this schema is none other than that of the secondary circular reaction corresponding to the object in question.

Here are some examples:

Observation 107.—At 0;5 (3) Lucienne tries to grasp spools suspended above her by means of elastic bands. She usually uses them in order to suck them, but sometimes she swings them while shaking herself when they are there (see Obs. 94 and 94 repeated). She manages to touch but not yet to grasp them. Having shaken them fortuitously, she then breaks off to shake herself a moment while looking at them (shakes of the legs and trunk), then she resumes her attempts at grasping.

Why has she broken off in order to shake herself a few seconds? It was not in order to shake the spools because she did not persevere and was busy with something else at the moment when she made this movement: neither was it in order to facilitate her attempts at grasping. Is it a question of a purely mechanical movement started by the sight of their chance swinging? It would seem so, but the rest of the observation shows that this behavior pattern was renewed too often to be automatic: it therefore certainly has a meaning. Neither is it a question of a sort of ritual analogous to those we shall study in connection with the beginnings of play because the child, far from seeming to amuse herself, was perfectly serious. Everything transpires as though the subject, endowed for a moment with reflection and internal language, had said to himself something like this: "Yes, I see that this object could be swung, but it is not what I am looking for." But, lacking language, it is by working the schema that Lucienne would have thought that, before resuming his attempts to grasp. In this hypothesis, the short interlude of swinging would thus be equivalent to a sort of motor recognition.

Such an interpretation would remain completely hazardous when confronted by a single fact. But its probability increases along with the following observations. For instance at 0;5 (10) Lucienne again relapses into states identical to those vis-à-vis a rattle. So also, at 0;6 (5) she shakes herself several times in succession, very briefly each time, as soon as she has caught sight of her hand (which comes out of her mouth or by chance enters the visual field, etc.). One cannot see what this movement might mean if not that it is the outline of some action suggested by this sight.

At 0;6 (12) Lucienne perceives from a distance two celluloid parrots attached to a chandelier and which she had sometimes had in her bassinet. As soon as she sees them, she definitely but briefly shakes her legs without trying to act upon them from a distance. This can only be a matter of motor recognition. So too, at 0;6 (19) it suffices that she catches sight of her dolls from a distance for her to outline the movement of swinging them with her hand.

From 0;7 (27) certain too familiar situations no longer set in motion secondary circular reactions, but simply outlines of schemata. Thus when seeing a doll which she actually swung many times, Lucienne limits herself to opening and closing her hands or shaking her legs, but very briefly and without real effort. At 0;10 (28) she is sitting in her bassinet. With my hand I slightly shake the whole apparatus by touching the handle. Lucienne laughs and responds by gently shaking her hand, but this is not an attempt to make me continue; it is only a sort of acknowledgment.

Observation 107 repeated.—Laurent, too, at 0;4 (21) has an object in his hands when, in order to distract him, I shake the hanging rattles which he is in the habit of striking. He then looks at the rattles without relinquishing his toy and outlines with his right hand the movement of "striking." From 0;5 I often note such outlines of acts when confronted by familiar objectives; they are similar to Lucienne's.

It may be seen how such behavior patterns constitute a separate class. It is no longer a question of a simple secondary circular reaction, since the child reveals no effort to arrive at a result. It is true that there might be a simple automatization of earlier reactions. But, on the one hand, the child's expression does not give the impression that he acts mechanically and, on the other hand, we do not see at all why an automatic reproduction of useless acts would last so long (we have only chosen one or two examples from among innumerable ones). In the second place, these behavior patterns cannot be identified with the "procedures to make an interesting spectacle last," of which we shall speak presently. These "procedures . . ." appear at the moment when a sight contemplated by the child is interrupted, and their purpose is to act upon the things themselves, while the present behavior patterns arise at simple contact with an object, regardless of whether this is immobile or mobile, and without an attempt at acting upon it. In the third place, neither is it possible to reduce these behavior patterns to "explorations" and "tertiary circular reactions" of which we shall speak subsequently. The latter relate to new objects whereas the present behavior patterns are set in motion by familiar objects.

We therefore only see one interpretation for Observations 107–107 (repeated): they are acts of recognitory assimilation. Confronted by a familiar object or event, but whose sudden appearance was not foreseen by the child, the latter needs to adapt himself to the unexpected. This is what occurs, for example, when Lucienne sees a spool swing at the moment she wishes to grasp it, or perceives her hand, the parrots, etc., at a moment and in a place she did not expect them, etc. To adapt oneself means, in such cases, simply noting the event, in so far as it is known and of no use at present: it is then, without adding anything, a matter of recognizing and classing the thing. The subject will subsequently do this in enunciated words or in internal language but, due to his present lack of such symbolic instruments, the child is limited to outlining the gestures of the corresponding schema, used thus in the capacity of a recognitory schema. In other words, instead of saying: "Oh! the spool is swinging," or: "There is my hand. . . . There is the parrot. . . There is the bassinet which is moving," the child assimilates these facts by means of motor concepts, not yet verbal, and, by shaking his own legs or hands, so indicates to himself that he understands what he perceives.

The existence of this recognitory assimilation might seem doubtful if it had not been prepared by all the reproductive assimilation of the secondary circular reaction. Two circumstances show that reproductive assimilation brings with it at the outset the formation of a sensorimotor recognition. In the first place, the very fact of rediscovering an interesting result—that is, the definition of secondary circular reaction—entails an increasingly accurate recognition. In the second place, once the schema has been constituted, it is reactivated by each new contact with the objects due to which it arose. Each time, for example, the child sees the doll hanging he is in the habit of swinging by shaking himself or striking it, etc., of his own accord he resumes shaking himself, striking, etc. This activation of the schema by immediate assimilation of the object to its function is simultaneously a recognitory and reproductive fact of assimilation, these two aspects of the assimilatory process being as yet undifferentiated during this initial phase. It is therefore very natural that simply recognitory assimilation should dissociate itself at a given moment from reproductive or purely active assimilation. At first, as revealed by the beginning of Observation 107, it can happen that the child finds himself incited by external facts to activate a schema at the exact moment when his interest is elsewhere and is already acting there according to a different schema. In this case the schema which interferes with the main action will simply be outlined whereas the activity in progress will be pursued normally. Then, it can happen, as revealed by the end of the same Observation 107, that the schema excited by the external events is too familiar to give rise to a real action and so is again limited to a short and simple indication of it. In both cases the outline of activity, replacing real activity, is consequently equivalent to a step which is more contemplative than active; in other words, to an act of simple recognition or simple classification rather than to effective action. So it may be seen that recognitory assimilation, at first involved in reproductive assimilation, detaches itself from it little by little, to remain in the half-active, half-verifying state which is the state nearest to the pure judgment of verification of which the sensorimotor intelligence is capable.

These remarks lead us to the analysis of "meanings" and to the study of the signals or signs characteristic of this third stage. To understand the nature of the following facts it behooves us first to remind ourselves briefly how the problem of meaning arises.

To assimilate a sensorial image or an object, whether through simple assimilation, recognition, or generalizing extension, is to insert it in a system of schemata, in other words, to give it a "meaning." Regardless of whether these schemata are global and vague or, as in the recognition of an individual factor, they are circumscribed and precise, consciousness does not know any state except in reference to a more or less organized totality. Ever since then it is necessary to distinguish, in every mental element, two indissolubly bound aspects whose relationship constitutes meaning: the signifier and the signified. With regard to "meanings" of a higher order, which are also collective meanings, the distinction is clear: the signifier is the verbal expression, that is, a certain articulated sound to which one has agreed to attribute a definite meaning, and the signified is the concept in which the meaning of the verbal sign consists. But with regard to elementary meanings (significations) such as that of the perceived object, or even, in the small child and prior to the formation of substantial objects, that of the simply "presented" sensory images, the same applies. The "signified" of objective perceptions such as that of the mountain I see from my window or the inkwell on my table is the objects themselves, definable not only by a system of sensorimotor and practical schemata (climbing a mountain, dipping pen in ink) or by a system of general concepts (an inkwell is a container which . . ., etc.), but also by their individual characteristics: position in space, dimensions, solidity and resistance, color in different lights, etc. Now the latter characteristics, although perceived in the object itself, presuppose an extremely complex intellectual elaboration; for example, in order to attribute real dimensions to the little spots which I perceive to be a mountain or an inkwell, I must place them in a substantial and causal universe, in an organized space, etc., and accordingly construct them intellectually. The signified of a perception —that is to say, the object itself—is therefore essentially intellectual. No one has ever "seen" a mountain or even an inkwell from all sides at once in a simultaneous view of their different aspects from above and below, from East and West, from within and without, etc. In order to perceive these individual realities as real objects it is essential to complete what one sees by what one knows. Concerning the "signifier," it is nothing other than the few perceptible qualities recorded simultaneously and at the present time by my sensory organs, qualities by which I recognize a mountain and an inkwell. Common sense, which prolongs in each of us the habits of infantile realism, certainly considers the signifier as being the object itself and as being more "real" than any intellectual construction. But when one has understood that every concrete object is the product of geometric, kinematic, causal, etc., elaborations, in short, the product of a series of acts of intelligence, there no longer remains any doubt that the true signified of perception is the object in the capacity of intellectual reality and that the apprehensible elements considered at a fixed moment of perception serve only as signs, consequently as "signifiers."

With regard to the simplest sensory images which are assimilated by the nursling and which are anterior to the permanent and substantial object, the same distinctions can be made, though to a lesser degree. Thus when the baby gets ready to grasp the rattle which he sees, the visual appearance of this toy is only a "signifier" in relation to the "signified" which the other qualities of the same object constitute and which are not given simultaneously but are collected by the mind in a unique bundle (in particular its quality of object to be grasped). Here again the signifier refers to a system of schemata (of vision, prehension, hearing, sucking, etc.) and only has meaning, even with regard to the precise image given through perception, in relation to the whole of the system.

But if we interpret the idea of signification in this way, including the complementary ideas of "signifier" and "signified" it is necessary at once to distinguish between three kinds of signifiers, which we shall call the "indication," the "symbol" and the "sign" so as to place in their true perspective the facts of comprehension of significations that we shall presently describe.

The "symbol" and the "sign" are the signifiers of abstract meanings, such as those which involve representation. A "symbol" is an image evoked mentally or a material object intentionally chosen to designate a class of actions or objects. So it is that the mental image of a tree symbolizes in the mind trees in general, a particular tree which the individual remembers, or a certain action pertaining to trees, etc. Hence the symbol presupposes representation. We shall see it made manifest during the child's second year at the time of the appearance of the symbolic game (the game of make-believe) or when the progress, intelligence and use of practical deduction will really evoke absent objects. The "sign," moreover, is a collective symbol, and consequently "arbitrary." It also makes its appearance in the second year, with the beginning of language and doubtless in synchronism with the formation of the symbol. Symbol and sign are only the two poles, individual and social, of the same elaboration of meanings.

Concerning the "indication," this is the concrete signifier connected with direct perception and not with representation. In a general way we shall call indication every sensory impression or directly perceived quality whose signification (the "signified") is an object or a sensorimotor schema. In the strict and limited sense of the word, an indication is a perceptible fact which announces the presence of an object or the imminence of an event (the door which opens and announces a person). But as we have just seen, the concept of indication could be extended to include every sensorimotor assimilation. What I see of an inkwell or of a mountain is an indication of the existence of these objects; the rattle which the baby looks at is an indication of virtual prehension; the nipple which the nursling's lips touch is an indication of possible sucking, etc. The facts belinging to the present stage thus belong in the class of concrete significations of which the signifier is "indication."

But, in order to understand the true nature of these facts, it is fitting first to divide into different types the different varieties of indications and, to do this, to recapitulate the whole of the "significations" hitherto under study.

In the first place, we have been able to speak of recognitory assimilation since the very beginning of the reflex (Chapter I). When the child is hungry and is not limited to sucking for the sake of sucking (reproductive assimilation) nor to sucking the first object that reaches his lips (generalizing assimilation), he well knows how to seek the nipple and discern it in relation to the surrounding teguments. What does this mean if not that the nipple has a meaning for him, in contrast and in relation to other significations (that of empty sucking, etc.)? This first type of signification is the simplest possible. In such a case the signifier is the elementary sensory impression accompanying the play of the reflex (whence the impression which serves as "excitant" to sucking) and the signified is the sucking schema. The proof of such an interpretation has in it nothing artificial; it is that this schema involves, as we have just recalled, a certain number of differentiated subschemata: contact with the nipple entails sucking with swallowing, whereas contact with the surrounding teguments or with an object only entails sucking for the sake of sucking, the erethism of the buccal apparatus entails empty sucking, etc. Each of these sensory impressions is therefore already classed and corresponds to a fixed subschema. At the very least, when a child is hungry and seeks the nipple, it can be said that the impression peculiar to this contact is subject to recognitory

assimilation and consequently that it comprises a precise "signified."

In the second place come the significations peculiar to the
first habits and to assimilation through acquired schemata
(primary). But, as we have seen, the recognition characteristic of
this level presupposes as "signifiers" in addition, simple sensory
impressions identical to those of the preceding level which it has
been agreed to call "signals." The signal is an as yet elementary
indication; it consists in a sensory impression simply associated
to the reaction and to the perceptual images characteristic of any
schema; thereafter it announces these images and sets in motion
these reactions to the extent that it is assimilated to the schema
under consideration. For example, the consciousness of a certain
attitude in the position for nursing sets the sucking schema in
motion. What does this mean if not that this consciousness is a
signal or a signifier for the signified which the feeding constitutes?
Such a signifier is surely more complex than that of the first type
(direct sensory contact with the nipple or the surrounding teguments), since it presupposes an acquired extension of the schema
of assimilation, but the signification which it permits remains
elementary. The consciousness of the position for nursing does
not signify anything more, from the subject's point of view, than
the awaiting and the beginning of the sensory images connected
with sucking. It is therefore necessary to avoid comparing, as is
sometimes done, the signal to the "arbitrary" sign. Doubtless any
signal at all can serve to set any reaction in motion: training
operates in this way, in animals, establishing the most varied associations. But, as we have seen, association only becomes "fixed"
if the signal is incorporated in a schema of assimilation and thus
receives its meaning from the single act connecting the effort
with its result. Thereafter, to the subject's consciousness, the
signal is an indication and not a sign; an indication, that is to
say, a given objective aspect of external reality, as the track of
paws is to the hunter the indication of the passing of the game.
The signal is therefore no more "arbitrary" in the sense that
linguistic scholars give to this word than the association of sound
and sight in perceiving a clock in movement, is arbitrary.

The latter example evokes a particular variety of this second

type: the signals founded on the coördination of heterogeneous
schemata. As we have established in analyzing the different coordinations of sight and hearing, of sight and sucking, of grasping
with sucking and sight, etc., the objects which give rise to such
coördinations through this very fact acquire a complex signification: they begin to assume a certain solid and permanent contexture. In looking at a feeding bottle or a rattle, the child
understands that it is a thing to suck or a thing to grasp; in
listening to a noise the child understands that the thing heard is
to be looked at, etc. An active search then ensues which comprises
progress in foresight. Upon hearing a certain sound the child
prepares himself to see a certain image, etc. But in such significations the signifier is always constituted by sensory impressions
or signals, simply more varied than before, and the signified still
consists in coördinated practical schemata.

Finally there comes the third type of significations which we
shall now emphasize—that of the indication belonging to the
secondary circular reactions.

Whether there is a secondary circular reaction such as pulling a chain or a string in order to shake objects hanging from the
hood (Obs. 99 and 100) or a procedure to make interesting spectacles last, such as pulling the same string in order to swing these
objects from a distance (Obs. 113), it is apparent that the significations involved in such cases are much more complex than the
preceding ones while being derived from them by differentiation.
In effect, the significations of the second type remain essentially
functional and related to the subject's own activity. That which
the sensory signals announce is that a certain thing is to be seen,
heard, grasped, etc. On the contrary, the significations of this
third type comprise from the beginning an element of foresight
related to the things themselves: the string hanging from the
bassinet hood is not only to be seen, grasped, and pulled, it serves
to swing the objects from a distance, etc. There is, accordingly,
in the signification of the string a content related to the foresight
of events. Without yet understanding, of course, the details of
this connection, the child knows that the gesture of pulling the
string brings with it the movement of other objects. But this
foresight is not always independent of the action. The string is

still a signal whose signification is the schema of "pulling in order to shake the hood." The foresight is therefore not yet pure; it is comprised in a motor schema. But, in relation to the significations of the second type, there is certainly progress and, in addition to the merely active "signal," one already anticipates the "indication" in the strict sense of the word: the string is indication of a series of possible movements.

This characteristic of transition between the "signal" belonging to the preceding stages and the "indication" belonging to the fourth stage which will set free foresight of the context of the action in progress is found again in a series of signs which are made manifest between 0;4 and 0;8, independently of the circular reactions under study hitherto.

Observation 108.—From 0;4 (12) to approximately 0;4 (30) Laurent cried with rage when, after his feedings, a handkerchief or napkin was placed under his chin: they announced a few spoonsful of a beverage he disliked.

At 0;7 (10) he cries in the morning as soon as he hears his mother's bed creak. Until then, although awake, he did not show his hunger. But, at the slightest creak, he moans and thus demands his bottle.— The same applies, for a stronger reason, to the noises of the door, but he remains insensible to external sounds (noises in the hall or neighboring rooms).

From 0;7 (15), also in the morning, when I play with him and his mother appears he immediately cries with hunger.

The same applies at 0;9 (20) when a maid and not his mother gives him his morning bottle: at sight of the maid he loses all interest in what is going on, even when he is in his mother's bed.

Observation 109.—At 0;8 (3) Jacqueline smiles and says *aa* as soon as the door to her room opens, before seeing the person who enters. She therefore understands by this sign that someone will appear. At 0;8 (10) she cries from hunger as soon as her mother enters the room; she does not do this for her father. Same reaction in negative form at 0;9 (9): she moans at sight of her mother (due to lack of appetite[1]) when she had been laughing and enjoying herself.

At 0;8 (13) she raises her hand to grasp her mother's face when the latter whispered in her ear from behind her. Without seeing anything, Jacqueline understands that there is someone behind her. Likewise, at 0;9 (27) she laughs and turns when I blow down her neck, even though she has neither seen me nor heard me arrive.

[1] At that time she suffered from anorexia.

At 0;8 (18) she is still not hungry and cries when her bib is put on, knowing that a meal awaits her. Furthermore, she opens her mouth as soon as her forehead is touched by her sponge (which she has not seen) because every day she amuses herself by biting it.

Such recognitions of indications at first appear to be sufficiently detached from the action to give rise to truly objective foresight as will be the case during the fourth stage. But in reality the signs in question here are not yet "mobile" in the sense in which we shall interpret this term in connection with the fourth stage; that is to say, they do not give rise to foresight related to the activities of the objects themselves independently to the subjects. The indications described in Observations 108–109 all make up a part of the global schema: either that of the meal, in which the child is certainly active, or else that of an "interesting spectacle" (such as having his neck or hands blown on, etc.) comparable to those "interesting spectacles" which the child maintains due to procedures which are still "circular" and which we shall study in the next paragraph. If such indications already announce objective foresight, it cannot then be said that they are entirely detached from secondary circular reaction. They are simply inserted in the preëstablished schemata and only acquire meaning as a function of the latter. Like the indications and significations which we have recalled, they merely form a transition between the primary "signals" and the actual indications of the fourth stage.

§4. GENERALIZING ASSIMILATION AND THE CONSTITUTION OF "PROCEDURES TO MAKE INTERESTING SPECTACLES LAST."—The generalization of secondary schemata is produced when the child is confronted by new objects. In such cases the child from the outset makes use of his usual behavior patterns and assimilates the unfamiliar to their schemata, without adding anything. It is a remarkable thing that the younger the child, the less novelties seem new to him. Unfortunately, it is impossible to compare in this respect secondary with primary reactions in the presence of unfamiliar objects for there is no appreciable common gauge for them. But if the reactions of the present stage are compared to those of the following one and above all to the "tertiary circular reactions" of the fifth stage, the difference is all the more striking as the situations become more homogeneous. In the face of a new phenomenon, the child in the fifth stage is capable of adopting the attitude of experimentation (this does not mean that he necessarily adopts it, but he is apt to do so). He seeks novelty and varies the conditions of the phenomenon in order to examine all of its modalities. The child in the fourth stage, without reaching these true "experiments to see," is also interested in the new object in itself. But, in order to "understand" it, he tries to apply to it in turn the whole of the known schemata in order to find which one in particular will be most suitable to it. On the other hand, the child at the present stage, while sometimes feeling surprise in the presence of an unknown object, nevertheless from the outset treats it as a familiar object and employs it in the use of his habitual schemata. Thereafter one has the impression that the child, far from still being interested in the thing in itself and far from appreciating its novelty as such, merely tries to use his secondary schemata by pure functional assimilation, as he did hitherto by means of the primary schemata. Consequently there exists a simple generalization of secondary schemata.

Here are examples of this elementary generalizing assimilation:

Observation 110.—At 0;3 (29) for the first time Laurent sees the paper knife which figured in Observation 104. He grasps and looks at it, but only for a moment. Afterward he immediately swings it with his right hand as he does all the objects grasped (see the schema of Obs. 102). He then rubs it by chance against the wicker of the bassinet and tries to reproduce the sound heard, as though it were a rattle (see Obs. 102). It then suffices that I place the object in his left hand for him to shake it in the same way. He ends by sucking it. The novelty of the object has therefore in no way interested the child, except for the brief glance at the beginning: the paper knife from the outset was used as aliment for the habitual schemata.

At 0;4 (8) I place a large rubber monkey in front of Laurent; the mobile limbs and tail as well as its expressive head constitute an absolutely new entity for him. Laurent reveals, in effect, lively astonishment and even a certain fright. But he at once calms down and applies to the monkey some of the schemata which he uses to swing hanging objects;

he shakes himself, strikes with his hands, etc., gradating his effort according to the result obtained.

Likewise, at 0;5 (25) and the days following, Laurent looks at an unfolded newspaper which I place on the hood of his bassinet. He immediately begins to pull the strings hanging from the hood, to shake himself or his feet and arms. He bursts out laughing on seeing the movements of the newspaper just as he frequently does when the rattles shake.

At 0;6 (0) Laurent at once grasps a big box of lozenges which is unfamiliar to him. He hardly looks at it but immediately uses it to rub against the sides of the bassinet, then he passes it from one hand to the other and rubs the object against the opposite side of the bassinet.

At 0;6 (1) he grasps a new rattle made of three parts: the handle, a middle ball of medium size and the end ball, a large one. Laurent looks at the object quite a long time while passing it from one hand to the other and even seems to palpate the surface which foretells the behavior patterns of the following stage. But he quickly desists in order to move the object in the air, at first slowly, then more and more rapidly, and finally he shakes it, rubs it against the sides of the bassinet, etc.

At 0;6 (7) I offer him various new objects to see if he will resume his attempts at spatial exploration which seemed to appear in connection with the last object. This does not occur; the child utilizes the new object as aliment for his habitual schemata. So it is that a penguin with long feet and a wagging head is only looked at briefly: at first Laurent strikes it, then rubs it against the side of the bassinet, etc., without paying attention to the end by which he grasped it. Several knick-knacks receive the same treatment: he grasps them with one hand and strikes them with the other.

At 0;6 (14) he takes hold of a new doll, looks at it for a moment without investigating either its shape or clothing: he strikes it, rubs it against the wicker, shakes it in the air, etc.

At 0;6 (18) a pipe holds his attention more but is subsequently utilized in the same way. At 0;6 (16) a new swan, encircled by a ring and with a handle is looked at with curiosity and immediately struck, shaken, rubbed, etc. At 0;6 (26) a series of unfamiliar objects (a rattle with a bell, a bear, a lamb, etc.) are barely examined before being struck, shaken, etc.

At 0;7 (2) he only looks a little at an unfamiliar bird of complicated shape mounted on a plank with wheels. He limits himself to shaking and striking it, and rubbing it against the side of the bassinet.

Observation 111.—At 0;5 (3) Lucienne only has one schema at her disposition which she employs in the course of her circular reactions and attempts to make interesting spectacles last: that of shaking her foot or entire body to cause swinging (see Obs. 116). Furthermore, of course, she knows how to grasp, suck, etc. When a new object is presented to her there ensues the curious result that she tries in turn the schemata of prehension and of shaking the feet, but applying the first chiefly to immobile and near objects and the second mainly to objects in motion or hanging before her. Here is the series of attempts:

First of all, before a cross of Malta which hangs above her, Lucienne immediately moves her feet only. Then she slows down her movements and begins empty sucking while looking at the object; after this she grasps it and brings it in front of her eyes in order to examine it.

A pipe, motionless: attempts at prehension, sucking at a distance and foot movements, all simultaneous.

An eraser: surprise, sucking at a distance and prehension. Once the eraser has been grasped, Lucienne looks at it briefly, in her hand, then immediately begins to move her feet.

Again the cross of Malta: immediate and sustained foot movements. Then Lucienne's hand having knocked against the object, there is an attempt at prehension, but this second reaction is obviously due to a fortuitous cause.

A hanging puppet: she grasps it and pulls but, not succeeding in drawing it to her, she periodically desists in order to give hard shakes of the feet. She then resumes, grasping, then moves her legs again: there is constant alternation between these two activities.

A slide rule: exclusive attempts at prehension. No movement of the feet.

A strap which I swing slowly: shakes of the feet, then attempts at prehension.

A stick of sealing wax; only prehension.

A watch placed very near her face: first prehension, then when I raise it too high, shakes of the feet.

This observation consequently shows us how much the new object is immediately assimilated to a schema; that is to say, generically recognized as being able to give rise to a familiar behavior pattern, even when the habitual schemata are very limited in number. In what follows it goes without saying that the more these schemata are multiplied the more the new object is subjected to various attempts.

It may be seen in what such behavior patterns consist. When confronted by new objects the child does not yet try to find out in what way they are new, he limits himself, at the outset or after a short pause, to using them as aliments for his habitual behavior patterns. He therefore generalizes, without adding anything for their use, the schemata he possesses.

But the generalizing assimilation belonging to this stage is not limited to this elementary form. It sometimes happens that the novelty presented to the child does not consist in a particular object but in an event, in an actual spectacle on which the subject has no direct influence. What occurs then? The child, desirous of seeing the spectacle prolonged, also utilizes his habitual schemata which he generalizes without adding anything to this effect. That is what is revealed by Observation 110. When Laurent, at 0;4 (8) and 0;5 (25) cannot grasp the monkey or the newspaper which he sees from afar, he at once applies to them the schemata related to hanging objects and thus seeks to act upon them from a distance. From that to trying to act upon any phenomenon whatever, independently of any real contact, is only a step.

This step is taken as a result of the following behavior pattern: It is a transitional behavior pattern which stems from secondary circular reaction but whose higher forms foretell the combinations of the fourth stage. It is the activity by means of which the child tries to make last the interesting spectacles of which he has just been witness without himself having provoked their first appearance (for example, prolonging the swinging of a watch seen from afar, etc.). Such behavior patterns still partake of circular reaction, since it is simply a matter of conserving and reproducing, but they generalize its principle, since the schemata hitherto inserted in actual circular reactions are henceforth applied to entirely new circumstances. Here are some examples of these behavior patterns:

Observation 112.—The first example will make us understand how the secondary circular reaction is prolonged in procedures to make an interesting spectacle last. Following Observation 98 at 0;3 (20) I make the following experiment on Laurent. I give him a rubber doll, unfamiliar to him and attached to the usual rattle by a string sufficiently loose so that the doll's movements do not shake the rattle. As soon as Laurent sees the doll, he grasps it in his right hand and sucks it. This preliminary phase lasts ten minutes during which the rattle has neither moved nor made a noise. After this Laurent lets his arm drop to the side while keeping the doll in his hand. I then shake the rattle without shaking the string or Laurent's hand; moreover, he did not look at the rattle at this time. Then, as soon as he hears the rattle, he looks at it and stretches out his right arm, while holding the doll in his hand, then he shakes this doll in a perfectly adapted way.

But a moment later Laurent's right hand is in contact with the doll, without holding it. I then shake the rattle again. He immediately moves his right arm, his hand remaining empty and not attempting to grasp the doll.

Thus it may be seen how, as soon as circumstances are changed, the schema becomes dissociated and the efficacious gesture (grasping, and shaking the arm, or simply shaking the arm) is advanced to the rank of procedure to make the interesting spectacle last, in the very absence of the usual intermediaries (of the chain).

The rest of the observation well shows, in effect, that this arm movement has become, for Laurent, a constant "procedure" and has not simply consisted in an episodic effort. At 0;3 (5) for example, Laurent practices grasping my hand when it is within his direct reach; but, when I put it at a distance of 50 cm. or more, he looks at it and then swings his arms rapidly just as he does when confronted by his usual rattle.—At 0;3 (23), I present him (at a distance of 50 cm.) with an unfamiliar doll (in costume) which I swing for a moment. As long as it moves, he looks at it, motionless, but as soon as it stops, he shakes his arm. Same reaction with respect to my watch and my wallet. The same day I saw him behave spontaneously in this way while looking at his hanging doll.

At 0;3 (29) I shake his arm as soon as I stop swinging a paper knife 100 cm. away from him.—At 0;4 (18) he shakes his arm in order to make me continue when I shake his feet. He laughs and waves his arms more and more vigorously until I resume. At 0;5 (26) he does the same as soon as a grating sound stops, a sound which I had made without his seeing me. He definitely gradates his movement according to the variations of the waiting time.

At 0;6 (27) again, he shakes his arm when he does not succeed in grasping a distant object or in order to make an object move at a distance (a sheet of paper placed on a cupboard, at a distance of 150 cm. from him, etc.). Same observation at 0;7 (5).

At 0;7 (7) he looks at a tin box placed on a cushion in front of him, too remote to be grasped. I drum on it for a moment in a rhythm which makes him laugh and then present my hand (at a distance of 2 cm. from his, in front of him). He looks at it, but only for a moment, then turns toward the box; then he shakes his arm while staring at the box (then he draws himself up, strikes his coverlets, shakes his head, etc.; that is to say, he uses all the "procedures" at his disposition). He obviously waits for the phenomenon to recur. Same reaction at 0;7 (12), at 0;7 (13), 0;7 (22), 0;7 (29) and 0;8 (1) in a variety of circumstances (see Obs. 115).

It therefore seems apparent that the movement of shaking the arm, at first inserted in a circular schema of the whole, has been removed from its context to be used, more and more frequently, as a "procedure" to make any interesting spectacle last.

Observation 112 repeated.—Another hand movement of which Laurent has made use as a "procedure" is the act of "striking"; but in contra-distinction to the preceding one, this schema was utilized for the first time as a "procedure," due to a simple association of continuity.

At 0;7 (2), in effect, Laurent is in the process of striking a cushion when I snap my middle finger against the ball of my thumb. Laurent then smiles and strikes the cushion but while staring at my hand; as I no longer move, he strikes harder and harder, with a definite expression of desire and expectation and, at the moment when I resume snapping my fingers, he stops as though he had achieved his object.

A moment later, I hid behind a big curtain and reappeared every few minutes. In the interim, Laurent strikes his covers harder and harder while looking at the curtain.—Same reaction while looking at an electric light. At 0;7 (5) he strikes the side of his bassinet while looking at the hanging rattles and continues for a long time despite failure.

At 0;7 (7) he strikes his coverlets while looking at a tin box on which I have just drummed (see Obs. 112). Same reactions until about 0;8.

At 0;7 (11) he strikes the wrong end of his bottle in the hope of seeing the nipple come up (see Vol. II, Obs. 78).

Observation 113.—Jacqueline, likewise, at 0;7 (16), that is to say, after Observation 100, applies the schema of pulling the strings of the hood to new circumstances. After having moved the hood by moving a hanging doll, Jacqueline looks at my watch which I swing at a certain distance. She begins by trying to grasp my watch, then she happens to graze the string hanging from the hood; then she grasps it and shakes it violently while looking at the watch, as though her movement were going to make the object continue to swing.—That evening, same reaction with regard to a doll which I swing from a distance. At 0;7 (23) after having pulled the same string to shake the hood of the bassinet, Jacqueline looks at a book which I pass back and forth in front of her, at the level of the hood but in the open. As soon as I stop, Jacqueline, who until then was motionless, without hesitation pulls the string hanging from the hood while staring at the book. She shakes the string harder and harder, ten times, then stops. I then recommence to move the book. As soon as I stop doing it, Jacqueline pulls the string, but less energetically and less frequently. And so on, twice more. If the number of shakes she gave the string during these four attempts is counted, the following series is obtained: 8–10; 5–8; 3–4; 2. It is apparent from her countenance and from this series, that Jacqueline hoped to make the book continue to move by pulling the string and that she gave up little by little. At the fifth and sixth attempts Jacqueline limits herself to looking at the book while it moves without attempting anything afterward.

At 0;8 (8) on the other hand, after having used the string to make the hood of the bassinet move, she looks at a bottle which I swing 50 cm. away from her. As soon as I stop, she pulls the string to make it continue while staring at the bottle with a very typical expression of expectation and anxiety. When she notes the failure, she tries another procedure and imitates with her hand the movement of the bottle without trying to grasp it.

At 0;8 (16) Jacqueline looks at me while my lips imitate the mewing of a cat. She holds a little bell suspended from the hood. After some other procedures (see Vol. II, Obs. 132), in order to make me continue, she shakes the little bell she holds. I answer by miauling. As soon as I stop, she again shakes the little bell, and so forth. After a few moments I definitively stop my miaulings. She shakes the bell two or three times more and, confronted by failure, she changes means.

Observation 114.—At 0;7 (29) Jacqueline answered herself by rubbing the wicker side of her bassinet with her right hand. At a given moment, when her hand is outstretched beside her, without her knowledge I shake the hood once or twice. She does not then try to pull the string but again rubs her hand against the wicker while watching the hood as though this were going to move. Same reaction many times. It is true that when the hand movements are sufficiently violent they make the whole bassinet shake slightly, but the rest of the observation will show that this relative success is not enough to explain the use of the procedure.

The next day, at 0;7 (30) I clap my hands in front of Jacqueline. When I have finished she moves her hand against the wicker of the bassinet while looking at my hands. When I recommence she stops as though she had attained her goals and, when I stop, she begins again.

A few hours later, same reaction with regard to my béret which I hold (without showing myself) 100 cm. from his eyes. At the beginning the child's expression leaves no doubt of her desire to prolong the interesting spectacle by this means, but the child progressively slackens with failure. Finally, Jacqueline only moves her hand slightly, then not at all.

Observation 115.—Everyone knows the attitude of nurslings when freely enjoying themselves or when an unexpected sight causes them a lively feeling of pleasure. They draw themselves up by pressing on their feet and shoulder blades and let themselves fall back in a heap. Moreover it is not difficult to note that this movement is often utilized in order to make the bassinet move. It is enough that the child has observed the effect of these shakes for him to draw himself up intentionally while looking at the hood and the hanging objects. Now this schema, once acquired, is subsequently applied to anything at all, in the capacity of a "procedure to make an interesting spectacle last." In the course of Volume II (Obs. 132) we shall cite a long observation made of Jacqueline concerning the development of causality. Here is its equivalent in Laurent.

At 0;4 (2) Laurent simply shakes the bassinet by drawing himself up. But already at 0;4 (7) he utilizes this schema as a "procedure." When I stop humming he waits for a brief moment and then draws himself up, at first very gently, then more and more vigorously, while looking at me. The intention is clear. Same reaction at 0;7 (3).

Between 0;4 and 0;6 he uses the same procedure to prolong the swinging, etc. At 0;6 (6) and 0;7 (2) he makes use of it to cause me to continue to snap my fingers (see Obs. 112 repeated). He visibly gradates his effort as a function of his impatience.

From 0;7 (7) to 0;8 (1) he draws himself up to act upon a tin box on which I drummed or upon a series of similar objects (see Obs. 112).

In short, the action of drawing himself up is promoted to the rank of a magic-phenomenalistic procedure and is used in the most varied circumstances.

Observation 116.—Lucienne revealed exactly analogous behavior patterns but with procedures of course varying as a function of her earlier circular reactions. Now, we recall (Obs. 94–95) that one of her most frequent reactions was to shake her bassinet or the rattles by means of repeated vigorous shakes of legs and feet (movements analogous to pedaling). From the sixth month this behavior pattern gave rise to procedures destined to satisfy desires or make interesting spectacles last. Already at 0;4 (14) Lucienne looks at my hand which I show her from a distance. Her fingers move, but her arms and trunk remain immobile; she has an expression of desire and makes sucking movements; she becomes red with emotion while opening and closing her mouth and she brusquely moves her legs with all possible speed. But is this simply an attitude or already an attempt at action? This remains in doubt until 0;5 (21). At 0;5 (10) she shakes her legs while holding a rattle with a handle, as she does when confronted by the hanging rattle. Then at 0;5 (21) she does it as soon as I stop swinging my hands. Instead of imitating my gesture she shakes her legs to make me continue. At 0;7 (1) she does the same when I move my fingers, wag my head, move my hands, etc., in order to study imitation. She begins by imitating, then shakes her legs, paying great attention to what I do. At 0;8 (5) same reaction in the presence of all sorts of spectacles: a doll that I swing, etc. At 0;8 (13) she watches me open and close my mouth. She begins by examining me with great interest, then tries to grasp, then, not succeeding, she moves her legs slightly; as soon as I stop, she shakes them violently, apparently to make me continue. Same reaction at 0;8 (15). Now this is not a question of a simple receptive attitude but of an active procedure, for Lucienne constantly gradates her effort according to the result. She tries at first prudently and slowly and if I respond by moving my lips, she shakes herself more and more vigorously.

Observation 117.—Here are some more procedures which Lucienne has used. From 0;7 (20) when she shook her bassinet by moving her hands (see Obs. 101) she used this procedure for quite other purposes. Thus, at 0;7 (23) she looks at me with great interest when I unfold a newspaper and rumple it. As soon as I have finished she moves her hands several times in succession. The same day I appear in her visual field, disappear, reappear, etc. She is very much puzzled and (after my disappearance, I see her through the hood) moves her hands while looking in the direction where I should have reappeared. She subsequently applies this schema to everything: at 0;7 (27) to make me continue my gestures, at 0;8 (0) to move a puppet from a distance, at 0;8 (18) to make me repeat a cry, at 0;10 (12) to make me put my index finger back into my mouth, etc.

From 0;8 (5) as we have previously seen (Obs. 101), she shakes her head in order to move the bassinet. The following days she applies this schema to the most varied situations: at 0;8 (12) she tries them in order to make me repeat a cry, at 0;10 (7) in order to make swing a placard hanging in a car and rendered immobile by the stopping of the train, etc.

At 0;9 (28) she puffs through her mouth in analogous situations (to make me repeat my gestures, etc.). At 0;10 (8) she draws herself up, like Jacqueline (Obs. 115) to prolong a gesture, a whistle, a movement of the dolls, etc. At 0;10 (24) she vigorously scratches her coverlet with the same intentions, etc.

Observation 118.—Let us finally mention the manner in which Laurent has come to utilize his head movements as "procedures" charged with efficacity. From 0;3 Laurent is able to imitate a lateral displacement of the head. Now, as early as 0;3 (23) I find him moving his head in this way when confronted by a hanging rattle, as though to give it a real movement (see Vol. II, Obs. 88).

At 0;3 (29) he shakes his head when I stop swinging a paper knife. The following weeks he reacts in the same way as soon as I interrupt a movement he has observed.

At 0;7 (1) he does it to incite me to continue to snap my middle finger against my thumb. At 0;7 (5) same reaction in the presence of a newspaper which I unfolded and which remains motionless. At 0;7 (7) he shakes his head the same as he shakes his arm or draws himself up when he sees a tin box on which I have drummed.

Until toward 0;8 he thus continues to use this schema to make any interesting sight whatever last, whether it is a visually perceived movement, regardless of the direction of this movement, or even a sound (humming, etc.).

Thus it may be seen that it is not an exaggeration to talk of generalization in characterizing such behavior patterns. In the

six observations which we have just summarized there is a question of schemata elaborated in the course of the child's circular
reactions, but applied to new circumstances. These situations
have in common the fact that the child has just witnessed an
interesting spectacle and would like to have an influence upon it
in order to make it last. This desire, not being coördinated with
any adapted mechanism since precisely in such cases the subject
is impatient, is radiated, quite naturally, in movements connected with the circular reactions, that is to say, to situations in
which the child can prolong the desirable result at will. So it is
that the schemata originally related to limited circumstances are
applied at first to all analogous situations, then to any activity
whatever on condition that it is a question of reproducing an
interesting spectacle.

But the latter condition at the same time shows us the limits
of circular reaction. On the one hand, as we have already stressed,
it is only a question of repeating and not of inventing, truly to
adapt oneself to new circumstances. On the other hand, to the
extent that there is generalization, the procedures employed do
not apply in detail to these new situations. There exists, so to
speak, abstract generalization (the effective gesture being applied
to empty space) and not concrete insertion of the means employed
into the context of the situation. Let us remark, moreover, with
regard to this last point, that the same is true at all levels. Not
only the schemata due to secondary circular reactions but also
those due to the most precise discoveries can subsequently be
applied to empty space and give rise to magic-phenomenalistic
connections (see below, Chap. V, Obs. 176). But, at the level
which we are now considering, that is to say, at the beginning of
the action upon things and the interrelations of things, these
connections remain the only possible ones.

Fortunately, there is a second method of generalization of
the secondary schemata: that which we shall study in the next
chapter in trying to find out how the child will intercoördinate
his schemata when it will be a question not only of repeating or
prolonging, but of really adapting himself to new situations.

Before that, let us emphasize the lasting importance of
secondary circular reaction during the last stages of intellectual

development. Secondary circular reaction, in so far as it is a reproduction of an interesting result fortuitously obtained, is, in effect, far from constituting a behavior pattern peculiar to the child. An adult, unacquainted with machinery, does not behave differently from the baby when, having by chance touched part of a motor, he does not understand the effect produced and repeats the action which set it in motion. Like the reflexes of the first stage and the acquired associations or habits of the second, the secondary reactions are behavior patterns whose mere appearance characterizes a given stage but which are conserved as substructures in the last stages.

The peculiarity of the circular reactions of the present stage is that, during this period, they constitute the highest intellectual manifestations of which the child is capable, whereas subsequently they will only fill an increasingly derived role. This point is of a certain importance and justifies the distinction we shall henceforth make between "typical" secondary circular reactions and "derived" secondary circular reactions. In effect, when the child at the present stage tries to reproduce an interesting result, he has never obtained this result except in an entirely fortuitous way; that is to say, without the context of his activity being one of research, of experimentation, etc. On the contrary, when the child at a final stage or an adult discovers a fortuitous result, it is almost always in a context of research or of experimentation and thereafter the action of reproducing the effect obtained only constitutes a "derived" action.

For example we shall observe such "derived" reactions during the fourth stage when, in the presence of new objects, the child applies himself to attempts at "explorations" (see Chap. IV, §5). If in the course of "exploration" the child fortuitously discovers an unforeseen result, he immediately reproduces it. Such behavior is identical to that of the secondary circular reaction, but is "derived." During the fifth stage, too, it happens that in experimenting—that is to say, in organizing what we shall call the "tertiary circular reactions"—the child comes little by little to repeat the movements which engendered an unforeseen effect. He then relapses into secondary circular reaction, but this is, in such a case, once more "derived."

The time has not yet come to study these derivations. Let us limit ourselves to citing an example of these final circular reactions in order to show their structural identity with the preceding ones:

Observation 119.—Jacqueline, at 1;1 (7) continues to reproduce all the new movements which she discovers by chance and everything she is made to do. For instance, I put a stick on her head: she immediately puts it back there. I hold her cheeks in my hands, then let them go: she puts her cheek back into my hand, or grasps my hand in order to press it against her cheek, or she applies her own hand.

At 1;3 (12) she is sitting in her play pen with one leg through the bars. When she tries to lift herself up she does not at first succeed in withdrawing her foot. She moans, almost cries, then tries again. She then painfully succeeds in disengaging herself, but as soon as she has done so she replaces her leg in the same position and begins all over again. This happens four or five times in succession until the situation is completely assimilated.

At 1;3 (13) while walking, she knocks her head on a table so that she has a very noticeable red mark. Nevertheless she immediately grasps a stick which is beside her and strikes her forehead on the same place. Then as this dangerous instrument is taken from her, she again knocks herself intentionally, but with very great prudence, against the arm of a chair.

In conclusion, the deep unity of the behavior patterns of this stage may be seen. Whether it is a question of pure "secondary circular reactions" or of movements of recognitory assimilation or again of generalization of schemata in the presence of new objects or of spectacles to be prolonged, in all these cases the behavior of the child consists in repeating what he has just done or is already used to doing. The action performed by the child therefore always consists in a global and unique action of a single advent and characterized by a single schema. One can, it is true, already distinguish the means and ends in such an action, in the sense that the child's movements are seriate and complex in their interrelations. But means and ends are inseparable from one another and, consequently, produced in the same entity. On the other hand, the behavior patterns of the following stage will furnish us an example of coördinations between separate schemata, some of which will serve as ends and others as means.

Now this need of repetition, which characterizes this stage

and which explains the global aspect of assimilation through secondary schemata, also conditions the accommodation to external environment peculiar to such behavior patterns. Whether it is a question of secondary circular reactions or of the generalization of the same schemata in the presence of new objects or sights, this accommodation always consists in rediscovering with the maximum precision possible, the movements which were effectual. The accommodation characteristic of the fourth stage will be quite different. By virtue of the coördination of the schemata, it will constitute an adjustment of their contexture to the objects themselves and thus will go beyond the simple, confused and whole application.

In short, if the elaboration of the secondary schemata of the third stage marks perceptible progress over that of the primary schemata in the sense that the child begins really to act upon things, it nevertheless prolongs the assimilation and accommodation characteristic of the primary reactions in that the child's activity remains centered on itself more than on objects.

CHAPTER IV

THE FOURTH STAGE:

The Coördination of the Secondary Schemata and Their Application to New Situations

At about 8 to 9 months a certain number of solidary transformations appear concerning at the same time the mechanism of intelligence and the elaboration of objects, of spatial groups as well as of causal and temporal series. These transformations even seem important enough to characterize the appearance of a stage: that of the first actually intelligent behavior patterns.

From the point of view of the functioning of intelligence this fourth stage marks considerable progress over the preceding one. The behavior patterns of the third stage, as we have seen, only consist in "circular reactions." No doubt these reactions are related to the external environment and no longer only to the body itself. Moreover, we have called them "secondary" to distinguish them from the "primary" reactions. No doubt either that the activity of the secondary schemata can start whenever the child wishes to prolong any interesting phenomenon and no longer only the result in connection with which the schemata in question were constituted. But, as we have stated, that is only a simple generalization of schemata without elaboration of the special relations between each of them and the new goal to be reached. In short, the reactions of the third stage therefore constitute the simple prolongation of the primary circular reactions; they owe only to their complexity the fact of drawing, after the event, a distinction between transitive and final states, between means and ends. On the other hand, the behavior patterns of the fourth stage involve such a distinction from the very outset. The criterion of their appearance is, in effect, the intercoördination of the secondary schemata. Now, in order that two schemata, until then detached, may be coördinated with one another in a single act, the subject must aim to attain an end which is not directly within reach and to put to work, with this intention, the schemata thitherto related to other situations. Thereafter the action no longer functions by simple repetition but by subsuming under the principal schema a more or less long series of transitional schemata. Hence there exists simultaneously the distinction between the end and the means, and the intentional coördination of the schemata. The intelligent act is thus constituted, which does not limit itself merely to reproducing the interesting results, but to arriving at them due to new combinations.

From the point of view of the real categories such progress leads, as we shall see in Volume II, to an essential result. By coördinating the schemata which constitute the instruments of his intelligence, the child learns *ipso facto* to put things in relationship to each other. In effect, the concrete connections uniting objects of the external world are constructed at the same time as the formal interrelations of schemata since the latter represent actions capable of being brought to bear on objects. The parallelism of these two series, real and formal, is even so close that, during the first stages, it is very difficult to dissociate action from object. On the other hand, in proportion as the action becomes complicated through coördination of schemata, the universe becomes objectified and is detached from the self.

The phenomenon is apparent, at first, with regard to the concept of "object." It is to the extent that the child learns to coördinate two separate schemata—that is to say, two actions until then independent of each other—that he becomes capable of seeking objects which disappeared and of attributing to them a consistency independent of the self. Searching for the object which has disappeared is, in effect, to set aside the screens which mask it and to conceive it as being situated behind them; it is, in short, to think of it in its relations with things seen at the present time and not only in its relations with the action.

This progress in the formation of the object is on a par with a correlative elaboration of the spatial field. As long as the child's activity is made manifest only in the form of isolated movements —that is to say, of schemata which are not intercoördinated, the "groups" of displacements remain dependent on the movements; in other words, space is only envisaged as a function of the self and not yet as an immobile environment connecting things to one another. With the coördination of the schemata, on the other hand, begins the putting of the bodies themselves into spatial interrelationships, that is to say, the formation of objective space. To be sure, the formation of this space, like that of the "objects" which are correlative to it, is not achieved at one time and at this stage many remnants of the preceding stages are found. But the orientation of the subject's mind is henceforth different and instead of bringing the universe to himself, the child begins to place himself in a universe which is independent of him.

The same is true in the realm of causality and of time. During the present stage the causal series go beyond the purely global relations between the activity and the external movements, to become objectified and made spatial. In other words, the cause of a certain phenomenon is no longer identified by the child with the feeling he has of acting upon this phenomenon. The subject begins to discover that a spatial contact exists between cause and effect and so any object at all can be a source of activity (and not only his own body). Consequently the temporal series begin, for their part, to be set in order as a function of the sequence of events, and not only of the sequence of actions.

Thus one catches a glimpse of how the intercoördination of secondary schemata is accompanied by a correlative progress with regard to the elaboration of the "real" categories of intelligence. But let us save the study of these transformations for Volume II and only analyze at the present time the formal elaboration of the mechanism of intelligence.

§1. THE "APPLICATION OF FAMILIAR SCHEMATA TO NEW SITUATIONS." I. THE FACTS.—The essential novelty of the situation which we shall now study is that: the child no longer merely tries to repeat or prolong an effect which he has discovered or observed by chance; he pursues an end not immediately attainable and tries to reach it by different intermediate "means." As far as these means are concerned it is true that familiar schemata are always involved and not new means; but, granted that the subject no longer limits himself to reproducing that which he has just done but pursues a distant goal, he adapts the familiar schema to the particulars of this situation and so raises it to the level of a true "means." With regard to the "purpose" it goes without saying that the child does not decide about it in advance, in the sense that we manage, through reflection, to impose a plan on our conduct, independently of any external suggestion. It is always under the pressure of perceived facts, or by prolonging a recent reaction, that the child acts. His acts are still, therefore, in this sense, conservative, and have no function other than the use of his earlier schemata. That conforms, moreover, to the fundamental law of assimilation and we do not see how it could be otherwise. But—and it is in this sense that the goal is set in advance and that the situation is "new"— obstacles intervene between the act and its result. Where the child wishes to grasp, to swing, to strike, etc. (as many ends as are consistent with primary and secondary circular reactions), circumstances erect barriers he must clear. Hence it is a question of keeping in mind the "goal" to be reached and of trying different known means of surmounting the difficulty. The act of intelligence properly so called develops in that way, to the extent that it is differentiation of the secondary circular reaction and involves to a higher degree the "reversal" in the consciousness which constitutes intention and of which we have spoken before.

Let us try to analyze some samples of this behavior, beginning by describing three cases intermediate between the secondary circular reactions and the true "applications of familiar means to new situations."

Observation 120.—We believe we have observed in Laurent an elementary example of these behavior patterns as early as 0;6 (1), provided that the facts we have described were observed correctly. If this was the case, the thing has nothing extraordinary about it, for three reasons. The first is that this first manifestation of the "application of familiar schemata to new situations" is not yet typical and forms the transition between the simple "secondary circular reaction" and the freer behavior patterns, the description of which will follow. The second reason is that Laurent has always been ahead of his sisters, after the circumstances previously noted, and that consequently, at 0;6 (1) he has utilized, for three months already, all sorts of secondary circular schemata. Hence it is natural that he arrive at coördinating them to each other in certain exceptional situations. The third reason, which we emphasize strongly, is that the behavior patterns characteristic of a stage appear so much the less at one time, in the form of simultaneous manifestations, according as this stage is more evolved and these behavior patterns are therefore more complex. Thereafter it is perfectly normal that these first behavior patterns of the fourth stage are constituted sporadically from the middle of the third stage, except that these episodic productions are only systematized and consolidated one or two months later. In the same way we shall see that the behavior patterns of the fifth stage are foreshadowed from the apex of the fourth and those of the sixth are foreshadowed at the fifth stage. Inversely, it is evident that the behavior patterns belonging to a given stage do not disappear during the following stages but conserve a role whose importance only diminishes very gradually (and relatively).

Regardless of the application of these remarks to this observation, Laurent, at 0;6 (1) tries to grasp a big piece of paper that I offer him and finally place on the hood of his bassinet (and on the string connecting the hood with the handle of the bassinet). Laurent begins by stretching out his hand; then as soon as the object is placed, he reacts as he always does in the presence of distant objectives: he shakes himself, waves his arms, etc. The desire to grasp the paper seems to inspire such reactions, as I regulated it by removing the objective from the hood for a few seconds in order to move it progressively closer and farther away.—It is when the paper seems inaccessible to the hand alone that Laurent shakes himself. After having behaved thus for a moment, he seems to look for the string hanging from the hood, then pulls it harder and harder while staring at the paper. At the moment when this is ready to fall off the hood, Laurent lets go the string and reaches toward the objective of which he immediately takes possession. Several sequential attempts have yielded the same result.—It goes without saying that it cannot be demonstrated that Laurent pulled the string in order to grasp the paper, but the whole behavior pattern gave me the impression of being performed with this end in view and of being perfectly coördinated.

If such is the case, it can be asserted that the schema of "pulling the string" has momentarily served as means to attain the end assigned by the schema "grasping the objective." This of course does not mean that Laurent has foreseen the object's fall, nor that he has conceived of the string as its extension: He has simply utilized a familiar schema with a new intention, and this is what characterizes the behavior patterns of the fourth stage. But, as the paper was placed in the same situation which habitually sets in motion the schema of "pulling the string," such an example still partakes of the generalizing assimilations of the "secondary circular reaction" (see Obs. 99).

Observation 121.—Here is an analogous example, but easier to interpret. At 0;8 (20) Jacqueline tries to grasp a cigarette case which I present to her. I then slide it between the crossed strings which attach her dolls to the hood. She tries to reach it directly. Not succeeding, she immediately looks for the strings which are not in her hands and of which she only saw the part in which the cigarette case is entangled. She looks in front of her, grasps the strings, pulls and shakes them, etc. The cigarette case then falls and she grasps it.

Second experiment: same reactions, but without first trying to grasp the object directly.

At 0;9 (2) Jacqueline tries directly to grasp her celluloid duck when I put its head between the strings I have just described. Not succeeding, she grasps both strings, one in each hand, and pulls. She looks at the duck who shakes when she shakes. Then she grasps both strings in one hand and pulls, then grasps them in the other hand a little higher up and pulls harder until the duck falls.

I begin over again, but attach the duck more firmly. She then at once pulls the strings, systematically, until she can touch the duck with her finger, but does not succeed in making it fall. She then gives up although I shake the duck several times, which shows that she tries to grasp the duck and not to swing it.

It may be seen that these behavior patterns differ from those in Observation 113, even though in both cases it is a question of shaking the string to exert influence on a distant object. In the case of Observation 113, the child limits himself to utilizing a procedure which he has employed just previously, and to utilizing it in order to prolong a spectacle he has just had before his eyes. On the other hand, in the present case, he tries to grasp an object and to do so he must find the appropriate means. The means to which Jacqueline has recourse is of course borrowed from the schemata of her earlier circular reactions, but the act of intelligence has precisely consisted in finding the right means without limiting herself to repeating that which has already been done.

These behavior patterns must not, however, be overestimated and one must not so soon see in them a utilization of instruments (the behavior pattern of the "stick") or even a utilization of extensions of the object (the behavior pattern of the "string"). There could be no question of instruments for several more months (concerning the "string" we shall return to it in Chap. V, §2). The following observation, which can be cited in the margin of this one, shows that Jacqueline does not yet consider the strings as extensions of the desired object.

Observation 121 repeated.—At 0;9 (8) Jacqueline tries to grasp her parrot which I placed between the entwined strings (in the same position as the duck in the previous observation). She pulls a string from the lower end of which her doll is hanging. She sees the parrot swing and, instead of trying to grasp it, henceforth she merely tries to shake it. It is then that the behavior pattern we shall emphasize here arises and which constitutes a true act of intelligent adaptation. Jacqueline looks for the doll at the other end of the string, grasps it with one hand and hits its head with the other hand while staring at the parrot. She then does this at regular intervals while alternately looking at doll and parrot and each time controlling the result (the parrot swings at each stroke).

Now the genesis of this act is easy to grasp. Three days earlier (see Obs. 102) Jacqueline shook her parrot, while holding it, in order to hear the rattle it contains. Hence when she sees the hanging parrot, she wants to grasp it in order to shake it again. Moreover, she knows how to strike objects and, in particular, has constantly struck her parrot during the preceding weeks (see Obs. 103). Thereafter as soon as she discovers that the parrot is connected to the same string as her doll, she uses the doll as a means to shake the parrot. Here again she does not limit herself to applying a gesture which she made previously (as is the case in Obs. 112–118). She really adapts a schema known earlier to a new situation.

But furthermore, when Jacqueline hits the doll she does not at all have in mind pulling the string (which connects the doll to the parrot) in order to augment the effect. As in the previous observation, the string is not therefore an "extension of the object" and Jacqueline is not yet concerned with spatial and mechanical contacts. Hence the string has no other than a tactile and kinesthetic meaning: it is only a material for manual and muscular schemata, a procedure to obtain a certain result, and not yet a physical object as the "string" and above all the "stick" are later to become.

Let us now proceed to clear cases and begin by the simplest possible: withdrawing the material objects which intervene between the intention and the result. Among the behavior patterns corresponding to this definition the most elementary of all is that which consists in moving away someone's hand or a certain object which one places between the child and the objective at the time the act of grasping is performed. The objective must of course be left entirely visible, hiding it constituting an additional difficulty which we shall only examine at the end of these observations.

Observation 122.—Concerning Laurent, this sort of behavior (the acquiring of which we have just studied closely) was made manifest only at 0;7 (13). It is this coördination between a distinctly differentiated action serving as means (=setting aside the obstacle) and the final action (=grasping the object) which we shall consider as the beginning of the fourth stage.

Until 0;7 (13) Laurent has never really succeeded in setting aside the obstacle; he has simply attempted to take no notice of it, or else to utilize the magic-phenomenalistic "procedures" taken up in Chapter III, §4. For instance at 0;6 (0) I present Laurent with a matchbox, extending my hand laterally to make an obstacle to his prehension. Laurent tries to pass over my hand, or to the side, but he does not attempt to displace it. As each time I prevent his passage, he ends by storming at the box while waving his hand, shaking himself, wagging his head from side to side, in short, by substituting magic-phenomenalistic "procedures" for prehension rendered impossible. Afterward I hold out the box to him while merely holding it by the edge. Laurent pulls, tries to snatch it away from me, but does not push back my hand.

Same reactions at 0;6 (8), 0;6 (10), 0;6 (21), etc. At 0;6 (17) I present a rattle to him while placing my hand in front of it, so that only half the object is visible. Laurent tries to grasp it directly, but not to set aside my hand.

At 0;7 (10) Laurent tries to grasp a new box in front of which I place my hand (at a distance of 10 cm.). He sets the obstacle aside, but not intentionally; he simply tries to reach the box by sliding next to my hand and, when he touches it, tries to take no notice of it. This behavior gives the impression that he pushes the screen away, but there does not yet exist any differentiated schema, any "means" dissociated from the final action (from the schema assigning an end to the action). The behavior pattern is the same when I use a cushion as an obstacle.

Same reactions at 0;7 (12). Finally, at 0;7 (13) Laurent reacts quite differently almost from the beginning of the experiment. I present a box of matches above my hand, but behind it, so that he cannot reach it without setting the obstacle aside. But Laurent, after trying to take no notice of it, suddenly tries to hit my hand as though to remove or lower it; I let him do it to me and he grasps the box.—I recommence to bar his passage, but using as a screen a sufficiently supple cushion to keep the impress of the child's gestures. Laurent tries to reach the box, and, bothered by the obstacle, he at once strikes it, definitely lowering it until the way is clear.

At 0;7 (17) I resume the experiment without there having been intervening attempts. First I present the object (my watch) 10 cm. behind the cushion (the object of course being visible). Laurent tries at first just to grasp the watch, then pauses to hit the cushion. Same thing with his hand: he at once strikes the obstacle.

From the outset it may be seen how this act of pushing back an obstacle by striking it constitutes a new behavior pattern in relation to the behavior patterns of 0;6 (0) to 0;7 (12). Before trying to attain his end (grasping the objective) Laurent henceforth pauses and exerts a completed action on the obstacle (striking it to remove it), definitely differentiated from the final schema and nevertheless subordinated to it.

Moreover, one notes that the intermediate act serving as means (removing the obstacle) is borrowed from a familiar schema: the schema of striking. We recall that Laurent, from 0;4 (7) and above all from 0;4 (19) has the habit of hitting hanging objects in order to swing them and finally, from 0;5 (2) of striking the objects (see Obs. 103). Now, this is the usual schema of which Laurent makes use at the present time, no longer in the capacity of an end in itself (of a final schema) but as a means (a transitional or mobile schema) which he subordinates to a different schema. The need to remove the obstacle arouses, through generalizing assimilation, the simplest of the schemata of displacement which he knows and utilizes: the schema of striking. It is noteworthy, in this respect, that the child does not yet displace the objects from one position to another as he will do later, in order to study experimentally the groups of displacements (see Vol. II, Chap. II, §§ 3 and 4). That is why the act of removing or of displacing the obstacle is so difficult when it seems so simple. The universe of the child of 0;6–0;8 is not yet a world of permanent objects animated by independent movements in space (we shall try to demonstrate this in Volume II in studying the development of the concept of space). Besides, in order to push away the obstacle the child is obliged to call upon his circular schemata of which the most appropriate to the situation is that of "striking in order to swing."

Let us observe, finally, that the procedure thus discovered by Laurent has nothing in common with the behavior pattern which consists in removing annoying objects (pillows, etc.) from in front of him. Laurent, at 0;5 (25) for example, throws aside without hesitation a pillow which I put over his face. But such a reaction, in which there is probably a reflex element, only comes into play if the screen is placed in front of the child. The child no longer removes it if he is in front of the object (see Vol. II, Obs. 27). Therein is not a "means" related to the objective, but simply the elimination of a cause of annoyance related to the subject. Consequently it would be entirely artificial to say that the child removes a screen (= means) in order to see something (= end). The act of ridding himself of the obstructive object forms an entity in itself.—So it is not a question of searching in this behavior pattern for the origin of the one which we are now examining: proof in itself that between 0;6 (0) and 0;7 (12) Laurent has never succeeded in removing the obstacles, in the sense we give to these terms here, when he knew ever since 0;5 and doubtless long before how to push any obstructive screen away from his face or from before him.

Observation 123.—From 0;7 (28) the transitional schema of "pushing the obstacle away" is slightly differentiated in Laurent: instead of simply hitting the things which intercede between his hand and the objective, he has applied himself to pushing them away or even to displacing them.

For example at 0;7 (28) I present to him a little bell 5 cm. behind the corner of a cushion. Laurent then strikes the cushion, as previously, but then depresses it with one hand while he grasps the objective with the other. Same reaction with my hand.

At 0;7 (29) he immediately depresses the cushion with his left hand in order to reach the box with his right. He does the same at 0;8 (1): when my hand intervenes as the obstacle I definitely feel that he depresses it and pushes harder and harder to overcome my resistance.

At 0;8 (1) right after the attempt just described, Laurent swings his box in order to cause the lozenges within to make a noise. I then keep my hand on his arm to prevent him from playing. First he tries to proceed with the very arm whose hand holds the box, then he brings forward his other hand and removes mine. It is the first time he succeeds in this attempt, already made for weeks and days before.

At 0;8 (28), on the other hand, I observe that he does not know how to push my hand away when I hold the object[1] nor when I move my hand closer to the object from behind in order to take it away from him.—Both these behavior patterns appeared simultaneously at 0;9 (15). When I hold one of these rattles by its extremity he pushes my hand away with his left hand while pulling the object with his right, and when I get ready to take the rattle back, he pushes away my hand or forearm before I reach it.

It may thus be seen that these perfections of the transitional schema were constituted by gradual differentiation of the original procedure: "Hitting the object in order to push it away."

Observation 124.—At 0;8 (8) Jacqueline tries to grasp her celluloid duck but I also grasp it at the same time she does. Then she firmly holds the toy in her right hand and pushes my hand away with her left. I repeat the experiment by grasping only the end of the duck's tail: she again pushes my hand away. At 0;8 (17) after taking a first spoonful of medicine, she pushes away her mother's hand which extends to her a second one. At 0;9 (20) she tries to place her duck against the wicker of the bassinet but she is bothered by the string of the bell which hangs from the hood. Then she takes the string in her right hand and moves it to the far side of the left arm (the arm holding the duck), and consequently where the string no longer is an obstacle. Same operation shortly afterward.

Unfortunately, we have been unable to determine precisely with regard to Jacqueline, from which circular schema the action of "re-

---

[1] I started this experiment at 0;6 (10): he simply pulls the object without removing my hand.

moving the obstacle" was differentiated. It was probably not from the schema of "striking" since she only made the latter manifest shortly before. It must be, rather, the act of holding the object in order to shake, swing, or rub it which gave her the idea of displacing the obstacles. It goes without saying that the filiation can vary in each child between the transitional or mobile schemata of the fourth stage and the circular schemata. We merely assert that the subordination of means to ends belonging to the fourth stage begins by a simple coördination of earlier circular schemata.

Observation 125.—If one is still doubtful that this assertion is well founded, in other words, if one considers the act of removing the obstacle as being too simple not to be able to be formed by itself independently of the earlier schemata, the following example is of a nature to furnish a counterproof to the foregoing considerations.

Suppose there is an intentional act, which is performed as a means and which is more elementary than that of "removing the obstacle," this is doubtless the act which consists in relinquishing an object or putting it down, in order to grasp another. In effect, as soon as the child knows how to coördinate prehension with vision (beginning of the third stage), he sometimes lets go voluntarily the objects he was holding. Furthermore, he observes this phenomenon very early, since from the first weeks of the same stage (about 0;4, in Laurent) he seeks the lost object with his hand (see Vol. II, Chap. I, §2), and from the middle of the stage (about 0;6, in Laurent) his eyes follow it (see Vol. II, §1, Obs. 6). Now, far from furnishing, from the outset, a "means" to use in all circumstances, this falling of the grasped object remains unused for a long time. It therefore in no way constitutes a "schema"—that is to say, a positive action—but simply an accident, a failure of the act. (One cannot speak, in this connection, of a negative act, for a negative act is a complex act inasmuch as it is always subordinated to another). It is only at the end of the fourth stage and the beginning of the fifth that the act of relinquishing an object becomes an intentional act (concerning Laurent, see Obs. 140 and 141): This fact obviously constitutes proof that the transitional schema of "relinquishing the object," utilized as a "means," does not merely stem from the chance falling of the object, but is formed as a function of other schemata, such as those of "removing the obstacle." This is what we shall now prove.

At 0;6 (26) Laurent holds a rattle with which he no longer does very much (satiety after use). I then offer him a doll which he immediately tries to grasp with both hands (as he always does). He grasps it with his left hand, holding the rattle in his right, but he brings his hands closer together in the obvious wish to hold only the doll. He remains perplexed, alternately looking at both objects, and does not succeed in relinquishing the rattle.

At 0;6 (29) same reaction with two other objects. I offer him a third toy: he tries to grasp it with his right hand, without letting go what he is holding in it.—Finally of course he fortuitously loses the object in which he is no longer interested, but he does not remove it on purpose.

At 0;7 (0) he has in his hands a small celluloid doll when I offer him a box (more interesting). He grasps the latter with his left hand and tried to grasp it with both hands. He then knocks both objects together, at once separates them (very much surprised at the result), and recommences to knock them again, wishing to surround the box with his hands. He then knocks them several times in succession for fun, which gives him the idea of rubbing the box against the wicker of the bassinet. Then he tries once more to surround the box with both hands; surprised at the resistance due to the doll, he looks for a moment at the two contiguous objects.

At 0;7 (28) I again note the same reaction: he knocks involuntarily the two objects he is holding when he wants to grasp one of them with both hands.—Of course, in order that this experiment have some meaning, it is fitting to choose two objectives of very unequal interest, for otherwise one could always wonder if the child was not trying to keep them both. This objection, moreover, is not theoretical since Ch. Bühler has demonstrated that an 8-month-old baby can very well pay attention to both toys simultaneously. In fact, the look and expression of the child are enough to show which toy he prefers and wishes to conserve.—It is necessary, moreover, to act quickly and to surprise the child by means of the second object before he has let go the first, without realizing it, due to lack of interest. In daily life, that is to say, independently of the experiment under discussion, these things always take place as follows: "When the child whose two hands hold an object, sees a second one and tries to grasp it, he lets go the first involuntarily, out of pure lack of interest, whereas he strains to reach the second one. In order that the experiment succeed it is therefore necessary to offer the object at a distance of several centimeters from the hand so that the child may have no difficulty in taking possession of it nor have time to lose the first one.

Finally at 0;7 (29) Laurent finds the solution. He holds a little lamb in his left hand and a rattle in his right. A small bell is held out to him: he lets go the rattle in order to grasp the bell. The reaction is the same several times in succession but I have difficulty in discerning whether he simply lets the rattle escape him or really discards it. While he holds the bell I offer him a big box: he grasps it with his (free) left hand and with his right (by sticking the bell against the box) but, noticing the difficulty, this time he definitely discards the bell.—Same reaction at 0;7 (30) with a big rattle.

At 0;8 (1) he has a big box in his hands and I present my watch chain to him. He then places the box on his coverlets in order to grasp the chain. Now this gesture is new (hitherto he only performed it by chance): It apparently derives from the act of "discarding" observed for three days.—I again offer him the box while he holds the chain: he removes the box.

Henceforth Laurent knows how either to discard one object in order to grasp another or to place it, or to let it fall intentionally. This transitional schema, given the tardy and complex character of its advent, apparently derives from the preceding schemata which consist in "removing the obstacle" and not in the fortuitous escape of objects held in the hand.

Observation 126.—A final behavior pattern belonging to the present group of schemata ("removing the obstacle") consists in searching under a screen for invisible objectives. We shall closely study this behavior in connection with the development of the concept of the object. But from the point of view of the working of intelligence, it is fitting to show now how such an act is constituted by coördination of independent schemata.

For example Laurent, at 0;8 (29), plays with a box which I remove from his hands in order to place it under a pillow. Although, four days before, he did not react at all in an analogous situation, this time he at once takes possession of the pillow. Though it cannot be stated that he expects to find the box under the pillow (for the behavior is too undecided), it is nevertheless apparent that Laurent is not interested in the pillow as such and that he lifts it in order to try something. The act of lifting the pillow is therefore not a sure means for the child, but it already constitutes a "means" for the attempt, that is to say, a separate action from grasping the box.

Likewise, at 0;9 (17), Laurent lifts a cushion in order to look for a cigar case. When the object is entirely hidden, the child lifts the screen with hesitation, but when one end of the case appears, Laurent removes the cushion with one hand and with the other tries to extricate the objective. The act of lifting the screen is therefore entirely separate from that of grasping the desired object and constitutes an autonomous "means," no doubt derived from earlier analogous acts (removing the obstacle, displacing and pushing away objects which are a barrier, etc.).

This proves that in all these examples, the action of "removing the obstacle" definitely constitutes a transitional schema differentiated from the final schema. As we have seen in each case analyzed, either these transitional schemata derive from earlier circular schemata (Obs. 122), or else they derive from other transitional schemata (Obs. 123–126). The subordination of transitional schemata to final ones—hence of "means" to ends—always takes place by coördination of the independent schemata.

Here, finally, is a third group of examples of the "application of familiar schemata to new situations." Henceforth it is no longer a question of removing obstacles, but of finding intermediates between the subject and the objective. These intermediates are not yet "instruments," as in the fifth stage, but they are more complex than the organized schemata borrowed without change from the secondary circular reactions (as is the case with our first group of examples: Obs. 120–121 repeated).

Observation 127.—If Jacqueline, at 0;8 (8) has shown herself capable of removing a hand which forms an obstacle to her desires, she has not delayed in making herself capable of the inverse behavior pattern: using the other person's hand as an intermediate in order to produce a coveted result. Thus at 0;8 (13) Jacqueline looks at her mother who is swinging a flounce of material with her hand. When this spectacle is over, Jacqueline, instead of imitating this movement, which she will do shortly thereafter, begins by searching for her mother's hand, places it in front of the flounce and pushes it to make it resume its activity.

Certainly it is not a question here of only making last a spectacle which has just been seen. In this respect these cases can be compared to those of Observations 112–118. But notable progress is made by virtue of the fact that Jacqueline mentally decomposes the spectacle she witnessed and utilizes the other person's hand as intermediary. Furthermore, two months later she applies this means to a new situation.

At 0;10 (30) Jacqueline grasps my hand, places it against a swinging doll which she was not able to set going herself, and exerts pressure on my index finger to make me do the necessary (same reaction three times in succession).

We shall later study (Vol. II, Chap. III, §3), these behavior patterns in detail, in connection with making causality spatial, but it behooved us to cite them now from the point of view of the "application of familiar schemata to new situations" to show how they arise from coördination of independent schemata. The great novelty of such a behavior pattern is the following. Until about 0;8 the child, when an interesting result is produced before him, tries to act upon this result directly. He looks at the objective and, according to cases, he draws himself up, waves his hands, etc. (see Obs. 112–118). or else, if he can reach the objective (a rattle, for instance), he strokes it, shakes it, etc. Furthermore it constantly happens that he reacts in the same way solely in the presence of the adult's hand. If I snap my middle finger against my thumb and present my hand to the child, either he draws himself up, etc., if

it is unattainable, or else he strokes it, shakes it, etc., to make me continue. Hence this reveals two kinds of independent secondary circular
schemata: actions upon the objective and action upon the hand (which
is conceived in this case as being an objective). Now, in the observation
which we have just described, Jacqueline uses the other person's hand
as intermediate, in order to act upon the objective. What does this
mean if not that, as with regard to the schemata of "removing the obstacle" or the simpler schemata of the first group, the child begins to
coördinate two kinds of schemata thitherto independent? He tries to act
upon the other person's hand, but inasmuch as this hand can itself act
upon the objective: accordingly he puts one of the two schemata in
relationship with the other.

Observation 128.—Laurent too, from 0;8 (7) uses my hand as an intermediate to make me resume the activities which interest him. For example, I tap my cheek with my left middle finger, then I drum on my
eyeglasses (he laughs). Afterward I put my hand halfway between his
eyes and my face. He looks at my glasses, then at my hands, and ends
by gently pushing my hand toward my face (see the continuation of
these observations, Vol. II, Obs. 144).

As in the preceding observation, for the child it is a question of
prolonging an interesting spectacle. But instead of applying the habitual procedures (Obs. 112–118) without adding anything to them, or of
himself reproducing the thing by imitation, Laurent utilizes as means
an element of the whole which he has just observed and an element
which can be assimilated to his own activity. The other person's hand
is comparable to that of the subject and the child simply prolongs its
action due to an intermediate whose power he knows by analogy to his
own earlier experiences.

Observation 129.—At 0;9 (24) Jacqueline is seated and tries to grasp her
duck which is near her feet. Not succeeding, she draws it toward her
with her right foot. I was not able to see whether there was still groping
or if the reaction was immediate. At 0;11 (21), on the other hand, she
lets fall a celluloid swan from its swinging nest. Unsuccessful in her
attempts to pick it up, she immediately displaces it with her feet and
brings it nearer to her. At 1;0 (7) same immediate reaction with her
parrot. Of course Jacqueline also uses her feet to strike the objects with
which they come in contact, etc.

These behavior patterns can surely be conceived not as acts of intelligence but as simple coördinations analogous to those of manual
prehension. But as soon as they appeared they gave rise to a series of
applications which definitely bear the seal of intelligent generalization.

Thus, at 0;11 (28), Jacqueline is seated and shakes a little bell.
She then pauses abruptly in order delicately to place the bell in front
of her right foot, then she kicks hard. Unable to recapture it, she grasps

a ball which she places at the same spot in order to give another kick. It is therefore apparent that before the act there was intention and utilization adapted from the schema of kicking.

Furthermore, the same day, Jacqueline, while playing with a thimble, struck a wooden box. Interested by this contact, she repeated it two or three times, after which at one leap she struck the thimble against her leather shoe. This gesture was precise and rapid, revealing all the signs of a typical intentional act.

Moreover, at 1;0 (10) she is in the act of striking a piece of wood against the wicker of her bassinet when she suddenly pauses, obviously to look for her shoe. As her feet are covered by a shawl, she immediately removes the shawl (see Obs. 124) and taps her shoe.

These last three observations correspond in the most characteristic way to the definition of the behavior patterns which we shall now analyze: First, the intention preceding the act (increasing the contact of the bell, the thimble, or the piece of wood); second, the search for a "means" capable of being subordinated to such an end; third, the application to that end, of a schema discovered earlier (using the foot to stir up, strike, etc.).

Observation 130.—Laurent, at 0;10 (3) utilizes as a "means" or a transitional schema, a behavior pattern which he discovered the previous day and whose genesis we shall describe in Observation 140.—By manipulating a tin of shaving cream he learned, at 0;10 (2) to let this object fall intentionally. Now, at 0;10 (3) I give it to him again. He at once begins to open his hand to make it fall and repeats this behavior a certain number of times. I then place, 15 cm. from Laurent, a large wash basin and strike the interior of it with the tin in order to make Laurent hear the sound of the metal against this object. It is noteworthy that Laurent, already at 0;9 (0), had, while being washed, by chance struck a small pot against such a basin and immediately played at reproducing this sound by a simple circular reaction. I therefore wanted to see if Laurent was going to use the tin to repeat the phenomenon and how he was going to go about it.

Now, at once, Laurent takes possession of the tin, holds out his arm and drops it over the basin. I moved the latter, as a check. He nevertheless succeeded, several times in succession, in making the object fall on the basin. Hence this is a fine example of the coördination of two schemata of which the first serves as "means" whereas the second assigns an end to the action: the schema of "relinquishing the object" and that of "striking one object against another."

§2. THE "APPLICATION OF FAMILIAR SCHEMATA TO NEW SITUATIONS"—II. COMMENTARY.—These kinds of behavior patterns constitute the first acts of intelligence,

properly so called, that we have hitherto encountered. It is therefore fitting to try to characterize them exactly and, to do this, to
begin by distinguishing them from the different varieties of behavior patterns previously under study.

These behavior patterns at first contrast with the primary
circular reactions and the sensorimotor habits which derive from
them. In the case of these reactions, the contact (tactile, visual,
etc.) with the object immediately sets in motion a global assimilatory act without our being able to distinguish between the end
of the action and the means employed, whereas in the present
case the contact with the external object only releases intention
and the search for appropriate means. Intention exists, that is
to say, consciousness of a desire to the extent that the assimilatory
schema set in motion by contact with the object is opposed by
an obstacle and thereafter only is made manifest in the form of
a tendency and not of immediate realization. This same circumstance explains the search for means: It is, in effect, a question of
overcoming the intervening obstacle. So it is that in Observation
122, the sight of the object merely sets in motion the schema of
prehension but, when obstacles intervene, prehension is promoted to the rank of a distant end and certain means must be
sought in order first to remove these difficulties. When Laurent
tries to grasp the object behind my hand we see, in the simplest
way, how the sensorimotor schema characteristic of the steps of
primary circular reaction and the first habits is differentiated in
an intentional act due to the intervention of intermediate obstacles. When he raises a screen in order to find a hidden object
(Obs. 126), the same thing becomes complicated, but the principle
remains the same: It is therefore the dissociation of means and
ends, due to intervening obstacles, which creates intention and
puts the present behavior pattern in opposition to simple habits.

Perhaps the objection will be raised that the intersensorial
coördinations peculiar to some of the primary circular reactions
seem very early to make us witness seriations of the same kind.
When the child grasps an object in order to suck it, look at it,
etc., he seems to differentiate the means from the ends and, consequently, set a goal in advance. But, for want of an obstacle capable
of attracting the child's attention, nothing warrants attributing

these distinctions to the subject's consciousness. Grasping in order to suck constitutes a single act in which the means and the end are one, and this single act is formed by immediate reciprocal assimilation between the schemata present. It is therefore the observer, and not the subject, who makes divisions in the case of such schemata. It is only when the child seeks to put things in themselves into relationship that the differentiation of means from ends appears—in other words, the acquisition of consciousness characterizing intention and arising when external obstacles are produced.

How are the present behavior patterns thereafter to be distinguished from the secondary circular reactions which also involve the utilization of connections between the things themselves? With regard to the actual circular reactions (Obs. 94–104), first by the way in which they assign a purpose. The circular reaction has no other end, in effect, than that of reproducing a result obtained earlier, or which has just been discovered by chance. This kind of process can be accompanied by intention but after the event, to the extent that there is repetition and when the result to be reproduced presupposes a complex activity. The effect which is to be repeated is then posited in advance, as an end, and the child tries to rediscover the means which have just led him to it (in this, let us recall, these behavior patterns already presage intelligence). But, although intentional, an end of this sort is nevertheless the simple prolongation of an earlier effect. On the contrary, in the present behavior patterns, the end is posited without having been attained beforehand, at least, not in the same situation. When the child tries to grasp his toys by pushing an obstacle away (Obs. 122–124), tries to act upon objects through the intermediary of someone's else hand (Obs. 127–128), tries to shake a parrot from a distance (Obs. 121 repeated) or to knock objects against his shoes (Obs. 129), these are projects which arise in the course of his action, in conformity, it is true, with his earlier circular reactions (the very nature of the end consequently does not differ from one behavior pattern to another), but in an actually new situation. The novelty of this situation pertains, in effect, either to the presence of obstacles or to the unexpectedness of the combinations observed. With regard to the means employed, the difference is just as clear. In the secondary circular reaction, the means utilized were discovered fortuitously and were applied just beforehand; hence it is only a question of rediscovering them. In the behavior patterns now under study, on the other hand, it is necessary to improvise means and remove obstacles which separate the intention from its final result. It goes without saying that before inventing new means (which he will do later), the child at first limits himself to applying the schemata with which he is familiar. Moreover the means which are found are borrowed, like the ends themselves, from the schemata of earlier circular reactions. But the chief point was to remember them at the right time and adapt them to the current situation.

Finally, if we compare these behavior patterns to the "procedures to make an interesting spectacle last" the differences are approximately the same, although less accentuated (these "procedures" form, in effect, the transition between the circular reaction and the true act of intelligence). On the one hand, the contrast remains, from the point of view of ends, between "making last" that which one has just seen and pursuing an end in a new situation. Besides, from the point of view of means, the following difference exists. In the case of procedures to make spectacles last, the means utilized are borrowed either from a circular reaction immediately preceding which was interrupted by the interesting spectacle (for example, when the child pulls a string in order to prolong the swinging of a watch, from a distance, when he was in the process of pulling this string in order to swing the hood of his bassinet), or else they are borrowed from schemata which have become so familiar or even automatic (for instance, drawing oneself up, etc.) that no effort is any longer necessary to rediscover them and they apply to everything. In both cases the "procedure" accordingly remains, so to speak, "empty" without a precise connection with the effect sought after. On the contrary, true acts of intelligence involve a combination *sui generis* of the means and of the situation. In effect, they strive in vain to be borrowed from earlier circular reactions, for they are adjusted to the goal by a special accommodation, and it is this adjustment which characterizes the beginning of intelligent action.

In short, compared to the earlier stage ("secondary circular reactions" and "procedures to prolong an interesting spectacle"), the behavior patterns analyzed here present two new characteristics. The first pertains, not to the very nature of the goal, but to the situation in which it is pursued, hence the way in which the subject assigns it to himself. Instead of merely "reproducing" that which he has seen or done, in the situation of the initial act, the child tries to attain the desired result in the midst of difficulties not yet observed or of unforeseen combinations, that is to say, always in a new situation. The second (behavior pattern) pertains to the means employed. These means are henceforth entirely differentiated from the end itself, the child's behavior consequently consisting in a coördination of two independent schemata—the one, final (the schema assigning an end to the action), the other transitional (the schema utilized as means)—and no longer in the application of a single more or less complex schema. It is only after the event that the means and the ends become differentiated in the midst of a "secondary circular reaction." In reality, it is always a question of a single act, of a completely constructed schema, so that the use of the means supplied always is on a par with the same end, or the same kind of ends. When the child generalizes the schema, that is to say, applies it to other objects (pulling the string in order to shake a new doll which is hanging from it, etc.), one cannot say, either, that the familiar means apply to a new end. It is simply the schema in its entirety the child generalizes to a new object, just as when he grasps one object instead of another or sucks his thumb instead of the maternal breast.—With regard to the "procedures to prolong an interesting spectacle" the same applies, in spite of appearances. The child who draws himself up when confronted by anything at all, in order to prolong a movement or a sound, in no way combines two schemata, he merely generalizes a behavior pattern which he found successful. This is why we remarked before that the use of such means is, so to speak, "empty," without precise adaptation to the goal pursued. On the contrary, the "application of familiar schemata to new situations" always presupposes the coördination of two schemata thitherto independent. Hence there exists simultaneously a clear differentiation of means from ends and an exact adjustment of the former to the latter.

In contrast to the earlier forms, intelligent adaptation is always double, since it involves a relationship between at least two acts of assimilation. The choice and the pursuit of goals constitute the first of these adaptations, the adjustment of means to ends involves, besides, a second adaptation henceforth essential to the first. Let us try to analyze the nature of these two phases.

As far as the first is concerned it can be said that the present behavior patterns merely prolong the preceding ones. Primitive intelligent activity has no other function than that of assimilating the universe to the schemata elaborated by the primary and secondary circular reactions, while accommodating these schemata to the reality of things. In other words, elementary intelligence, like all spontaneous activity, is essentially conservative. What the child seeks, in the observations just made, is to grasp or to hold, to shake or strike, in short, exactly that to which his circular reactions have accustomed him. Now we have seen that the secondary circular reaction, which is already almost intentional, is just as conservative and assimilatory, despite appearances, as the primary reaction. Hence the difference between primitive intelligent behavior patterns and the preceding activities does not stem from the nature of the goals pursued: it simply results, as we have seen, from the fact that obstacles arise between intention and realization and necessitate the use of intermediate means.

With regard to the "means" giving rise to this second adaptation which constitutes the distinguishing characteristic of intelligence, it can be said that they are adapted to the "goal" of the action in the same way that the entire act, in its intention, is adapted to the desired object. In other words, the intermediates or obstacles which intervene between the subject and the goal of his acts are themselves assimilated to familiar schemata in the same way that the object of the action is assimilated to the schema of the goal. But these transitional schemata are not chosen for themselves but as a function of the final schema. Consequently, the intermediate objects are simultaneously assimilated to the transitional schemata and to the final schema and this is what insures the coördination between the former and the latter due to a process of reciprocal assimilation.

In order to make clear the meaning of this formulation, let us first remark that the coördination between means and ends is of the same order, in its point of departure, as that of the sensorimotor schemata belonging to the primary circular reactions. When prehension is coördinated with sucking or with vision the phenomenon is explained, as we have seen, by simple reciprocal assimilation. The mouth tries to suck that which the hand grasps, or the hand tries to grasp what the eyes see, etc. This is what gives the illusion of a subordination of means to ends (the child seems "to grasp in order to suck," etc.) when there is simply a fusion of heterogeneous schemata in new global schemata. Now, the coördination of secondary schemata which constitutes the behavior patterns of the present stage is, in its beginnings, nothing other than a reciprocal assimilation of this kind. This is the case in the elementary and transitional schemata which we have assembled in a first group (Obs. 120–121). For example, when Laurent tries to grasp a piece of paper situated too high up and to do this, searches, then pulls a string hanging from the hood, he at first assimilates the paper to a schema of prehension (or to a more complex schema: feeling it, etc.), then, without ceasing to want to apply this first schema to it, he assimilates the same object to a very familiar schema of "pulling the string in order to shake." This second assimilation is, therefore, itself subordinated to the first; that is to say, pulling the strings in order to move the paper, he continues to desire it in the capacity of an "object to grasp" (he must at least have the impression that by shaking the objective he acquires a power over it which puts it more at his disposition.). Due to this double assimilation the schema of "pulling the string" is coördinated with the schema of "grasping" and becomes a transitional schema in relation to a final schema (Obs. 120; the same applies to Obs. 121). Such a reciprocal assimilation can lead either to a symmetrical relation (pulling in order to grasp and grasping in order to pull), or to a relation of simple inclusion (pulling in order to grasp).

But it is only in the elementary situation in which the child acts on an object only (the paper, for example, which is simultaneously for shaking and grasping) that the coördination of the schemata works due to so primitive a reciprocal assimilation. In such cases there is almost a fusion of the schemata present, as is the case in the coördination of the primary schemata, with the sole difference that the double assimilation is not instantaneous but is arranged in a sequence of two separate moments. On the other hand, in the majority of cases, the existence of an obstacle or the necessity for varied intermediates makes the coördination of the schemata less simple. This coördination most certainly continues at that time to operate, by reciprocal assimilation, but with a double complication. In the first place the schemata henceforth simultaneously subsume several objects whose mutual relationships it is a question of establishing. In the second place, and as a result, assimilation between the schemata ceases to work by simple fusion in order to give rise to diversified operations of inclusion or of hierarchical implication, of interference and even of negation, that is to say, to multiple dissociations and regroupings.

It must be recalled that the secondary schemata hitherto examined (the third stage) only comprehend one object at a time (a rattle for shaking, etc.) even when a complex object is involved (string and hood joined together, etc.). Moreover, when two primary schemata are reciprocally assimilated they apply to one and the same object (one person to look at and listen to simultaneously, etc.). Henceforth, on the contrary, the coördination of schemata bears upon two or several separate objects produced together (the objective and the obstacle or the objective and the intermediate, etc.) in such a way that the reciprocal assimilation of the schemata surpasses simple fusion to construct a series of more complicated relationships. In short, the generic character of the schemata is accentuated according as the relations (spatial, causal, etc.) of the objects to each other multiply, the elaboration of the "kinds" or "classes" and that of the relations or quantitative relationships always being on a par.

An example of transition will enable us to understand the thing. It is that of Observation 121 repeated: striking the doll in order to shake the parrot. In this example the child utilizes an intermediate (the doll) to act upon the objective (the parrot).

But the intermediate is still only one sort of substitute for the object. Wishing to grasp her parrot to shake or strike it and not succeeding, Jacqueline at first tries a procedure to draw it to her and pull the string. Hitherto we are still in the situation of Observations 120–121. But she remembers the doll located at the other end of the string, searches for it and applies to it exactly the schema which she wanted to apply to the parrot. She could, thereafter, have forgotten the parrot and only acted upon the doll; that is how she would have behaved at the stage of the pure secondary circular reactions. But she saves herself the trouble of shaking or striking the parrot and only uses the doll as a "means" toward this "end." This entails a putting of the two objects into relationship by assimilation of their schemata. This coördination, it is true, remains very primitive since it merely results from the fact that the intermediate has been assimilated to the objective. It is nevertheless real, since the two objects are distinguished from one another while being subsumed under an identical schema and are, thenceforth, placed in interrelation. In order that the coördination become effective, it will therefore suffice that this relation become spatialized and truly objectified.

This positive progress is achieved with Observations 127–130. How do Jacqueline and Laurent, for instance, come to utilize someone else's hand in order to act upon the object aimed at? On the one hand, the child already knows how to act upon the objective varied schemata for swinging the material, etc.). Besides, he also knows how to act by imitation (see Vol. II, Chap. III, §2) on someone else's hand and thus knows its power by analogy with that of his own hands. In order that he use this hand as a "means" when the final object is inaccessible, it will therefore suffice for him to assimilate their respective schemata to each other and through this very act to put the intermediate into physical relation with the objective. Now this reciprocal assimilation is easy: The hand of someone else being, like the objective itself, a source of activities which one can make last or reappear etc. by analogy with that of one's own hands, it is natural that, not succeeding in moving the objective at a distance, the child seeks to apply to this hand the schemata he expected to apply to the objective (on the one hand, the child has just seen or has earlier seen the hand joined together with the objective and, moreover, the hand is situated between himself and the objective). Hence the child behaves, with respect to the hand and to the objective, as in Observation 121 repeated, with respect to the doll and the parrot. But reciprocal assimilation does not here proceed by simple fusion, as in the case in which two different schemata apply to the same object (Obs. 120–121) or yet as when interconnected objects are almost entirely assimilable to each other (Obs. 121 repeated); there only exists a more remote connection between the activity of someone else's hand and that of the object aimed at (swinging of the material, etc.). Thereafter, the two objects joined together in the same total schema (someone else's hand and the objective) are maintained distinct from each other and the reciprocal assimilation works no longer by fusion but by virtue of an inclusion of one of the schemata in the other.

Now, through the very fact that the schema of the intermediary (the other person's hand) and that of the objective are assimilated without being confused, the total schema resulting from this junction comprehends two separate objects which have to be put in relationship. Here the real novelty of the behavior patterns of this stage appears. The coördination, in a way formal, of the schemata due to their reciprocal assimilation, is accompanied by a physical connection established between the objects themselves; that is to say, by their being put in spatial, temporal and causal relationships. In other words, the fact that the hand of another person and the objective are mentally connected without being confused involves the construction of a real totality by bringing together the intermediate and the final object. This explains why the child does not limit himself to striking and shaking, etc., the hand of another person, but why this schema becomes differentiated, through accommodation, into a propulsive movement destined to bring this intermediate closer to the objective.

This last remark leads us to examine the most complex of the present behavior patterns: that in which the child comes to remove obstacles and differentiates toward this end the schemata of striking, etc., into movements of repulsion. We recall how this behavior pattern arose in Laurent: After having tried for a long time to go over my hand, or a cushion which prevented him from grasping a visible objective, the child finally pushed away these obstacles, at first by striking them, then, little by little, by really removing them. Now, it is apparent that such a behavior pattern could not be explained as simply as the preceding coördinations. The schema of the obstacle could not be assimilated, without adding something, to that of the objective, since far from joining the object-screen to the objective, the child puts the former further away from the latter. But does not such a complete contrast of meaning conceal a true identity, the tendency to remove the obstacle constituting the negative of that which is, as positive, the utilization of intermediates? It is easy to see this. In effect, the capacity of coördinating the schemata involves that of contrasting them or of feeling them to be incompatible. Affirmation presupposes the power of negation; the latter is even often used before the former, affirmation sometimes remaining implicit before being willed. So also can the first intentional coördinations be very negative. They nevertheless presuppose a reciprocal assimilation. When the child who is trying to grasp the objective knocks against the intervening obstacle, this obstacle only acquires the meaning of an "object to be removed" relatively to this objective which it prevents the subject from reaching. Consequently, it is assimilated to the schema of the objective, but with a negative result. Just as a negation only exists as a function of a previous affirmation,[2] so also an exclusion necessarily rests on an earlier assimilation. Being on the road to the objective, the obstacle is assimilated to the schema of the latter (otherwise it would not be an obstacle), but through a negative connection (as in the judgment "this stone is not heavy," the quality "heavy" is connected to the subject "stone," but in order to be excluded from it). The obstacle is therefore conceived as a thing which takes the place of the objective (in this it is assimilated to it) and from which one must detach oneself in order to reach the latter. Moreover, the child begins by turning away from the obstacle

---

[2] "An affirmative proposition conveys a judgment passed on an object: a negative proposition conveys a judgment passed on a judgment," said H. Bergson (*Creative Evolution*, 12th edit., p. 312) after Kant, Lotze, and Sigwart.

(he passes over it or beside it) which is the simplest form of negation. But the attempt does not succeed. The difficulty requires a special behavior pattern. It is then that the coördination of the schema of the obstacle with that of the objective takes place, but a negative coördination. It is a question of assimilating the obstacle to a schema which is suitable to it in the capacity of object and, at the same time, but negatively, to the final goal of the action, hence to the schema of the objective. In Laurent's case the transitional schema chosen was that of striking. Such a schema is suitable to the hand or the intervening cushion, and at the same time it involves the element of repulsion or of negation necessary to the pursuit of the objective. Moreover, and by virtue of this double assimilation, the object-screen is put in spatial relation to the objective, but in equally negative relation: It is to be put further away rather than brought nearer.—In the case, in short, of a screen completely masking the objective, the double assimilation is of the same nature but with this supplementary difficulty that it involves coördinating the schema related to the obstacle with the pursuit of an objective which has ceased to be directly perceived.

§3. ASSIMILATION, ACCOMMODATION AND OR-GANIZATION PECULIAR TO THE MOBILE SCHEMATA. —The conclusion to which we are thus led is that the coördination of means to ends always involves a reciprocal assimilation of the present schemata as well as a correlative putting into relationships of the objects subsumed by these schemata. In the simplest cases this double assimilation is almost equivalent to a fusion and so calls to mind that which accounts for the coördination of the primary schemata. In other cases it can also remain truly reciprocal and give rise in that way to symmetrical series. For example, when the child taps his hoe with a thimble which he has first rubbed against another object, he applies the schema of striking to the shoe because inversely he made use of his feet shortly before in order to strike objects, etc. But in most cases, reciprocity leads to more complex relationships of inclusion, interference, negation, etc.

In order to understand this diversity we should emphasize

a fact to which we have already referred and which will assume great importance in the rest of our analyses: This is the functional analogy of the schemata of this stage (and of the following stages) with concepts, of their assimilations with judgments and of their coördinations with logical operations or reasonings.

From the point of view of *assimilation*, two complementary aspects characterize the schemata of which we have just spoken, when we compare them to the secondary schemata of the third stage from which they nevertheless derive: they are more mobile and consequently more generic. True, the secondary schemata encroaches upon all the characteristics of the "mobile" schemata peculiar to the present stage, but in a form to some degree more condensed (because undifferentiated) and consequently more rigid. This secondary schema is a complete totality of intercoordinated movements and functions every time the child perceives the objective in connection with which the schema was formed, or analogous objectives. For instance, the schema which consists in pulling a string in order to shake a hanging rattle presupposes a very complex coördination of movements and perceptions related to at least two objects (the string and the rattle). From this first point of view, it presages the schemata of the fourth stage which involve, as we have just stated, a putting into relationship of the objects themselves. Furthermore, the schema of "pulling the string," as has been seen, applies sequentially to a series of objects hanging from the hood (and not only to the first rattle) and even to objects presented from a distance, having no connection with the hood. From this second point of view as well, it presages "mobile" schemata which are capable of unlimited generalization. But, if one examines this closely, one notices that certain essential differences are in opposition to the simple secondary schema (that of the third stage), the same schema having become "mobile" during the present stage. At first the relations between objects, relations already utilized by the secondary schema, are given just as they are in the midst of the latter without the child's having elaborated them intentionally, whereas the relations due to the coördination of "mobile" schemata have really been constructed by the subject. Through the very fact that secondary circular reaction consists in simply reproducing a result discovered by chance, the schema which proceeds from its use constitutes a global and indissoluble totality. It applies itself in one block and if it envelops certain relations between separate objects, these relations remain purely phenomenalistic and can only be taken out of their context to give rise to new constructions. Consequently there is no coördination between schemata and the internal coördinations of each schema remain invariable and hence rigid. The considerable progress in this respect made in the fourth stage is that the same schemata are made "mobile." They intercoördinate and consequently dissociate to regroup in a new way, the relations which they involve, each in itself, becoming capable of being extracted from their respective totalities to give rise to varied combinations. Now these various novelties have combined solidarity. In becoming "mobile"—that is to say, fit for new coördinations and syntheses—the secondary schemata become detached from their usual contents to apply themselves to a growing number of objects. From particular schemata with special or peculiar contents they accordingly become generic schemata with multiple contents.

It is in this sense that the coördination of the secondary schemata, and consequently their dissociations and regroupings, give rise to a system of "mobile" schemata whose functioning is comparable to that of the concepts or judgments of verbal or reflective intelligence. In effect, the subordination of means to ends is the equivalent, on the plane of practical intelligence, of the subordination of premises to conclusions, on the plane of logical intelligence. The mutual involvement of schemata, which the former presupposes, is therefore assimilable to that of concepts, which the latter utilizes. But, in order to understand such a comparison, we should consider separately the logic of classes and that of relations, that is to say, the two complementary systems of operations constituting every act of intelligence.

As we have emphasized, the coördination of the schemata which characterizes the behavior patterns of the present stage is always on a par with a putting into relationship of the objects themselves subsumed by these schemata. In other words, the relations which determine a given object are not only relations of appurtenance which permit it to be inserted in one or several schemata, but all the relations which define it from spatial, temporal, causal, etc., points of view. For example, in order to remove a cushion which is an obstacle to grasping the objective, the child does not simply class the cushion in the schema of striking and assimilate, by inclusion, this schema to that of the end of the action, but he must understand that the obstacle is "in front of" the objective, that it must be removed "before" trying to grasp this objective, etc. In short, the coördination of the schemata presupposes the existence of a system of relations between objects and between schemata other than the simple inherent relations. Let us observe that the schemata themselves involve, in order to be formed, these same relations. Therefore a secondary schema is not only a sort of primitive "concept," it is a number of "relations" in the sense which we have just recalled. But it is only from the time when the schemata become "mobile" that the working of "relations" is clearly dissociated from that of "classes." It is after this fourth stage, as we shall see in Volume II, that the constitutive connections of the object and of space, of causality and of time become truly differentiated from the simple, practical and subjective connections bound to the schemata themselves.—Now such a distinction between schemata and relations recalls exactly the difference brought to light by modern logic between "classes" or "concepts" on the one hand, with their inherent connections (appurtenance and inclusion) and "relations," on the other hand, with their original operations of conversion and multiplication. In order to compare the processes of sensorimotor intelligence to those of reflective intelligence, it is fitting to respect such a classification.

First, with regard to classes or kinds, it is apparent that the "mobile schema," despite all the structural differences which separate it from these logical beings, is functionally analogous to them. Like them, the mobile schema always denotes one or several objects, by "appurtenance." Like them, the mobile schemata involve each other due to diversified connections, proceeding from pure "identification" to fitting in or "inclusion," and to intersections or "interferences." So too can the mobile schema function actively due to an assimilatory operation which constitutes the equivalent of a judgment, or be applied passively in the manner of a concept. Moreover, it is self-evident that, to the extent that sequential assimilations condition each other (as in the subordination of means to ends), such totalities are equivalent to elementary reasonings.—These functional analogies of course do not at all imply an identity of structure between such practical schemata and the unities of reflective thought. Two essential differences contrast, from this second point of view, these two extreme states of infantile intelligence. In the first place, the sensorimotor schemata are not "reflective" but are projected into the things themselves; that is to say, the child is not conscious of the operations of his intelligence and considers the results of his own activity as being imposed merely by facts as such. In the second place, and concurrently, the involvements between the schemata are not yet regulated by a system of internal norms: The only verification of which the child is capable is of the type of *success* and not of *truth*.

Concerning the "relations" implied by the coördination of the mobile schemata, their situation is the same in comparison with that of the relations of reflective intelligence. First, a functional analogy: these relations are also capable of being arranged among themselves, of "multiplying," etc. But also a structural difference: as we shall see when studying, in Volume II, the development of the object, of spatial "groups" and causal or temporal series, the first differentiated relations which the sensorimotor intelligence uses are not "objective" but are centered on the self and dominated entirely by the same perspective.

Despite these structural differences, the "relations" of the fourth stage definitely involve, still more than those of the third, the element of quantity inherent in every system of relations. If it is a question of causal relations, the child perceives a proportionality between the intensity of the cause and that of the effect (one could cite here observations analogous to Obs. 106). If, on the contrary, it is a question of spatial, kinematic, or even temporal relations, the child, in order to put the objects into relationship to each other is obliged to distinguish them in order to arrange them, and this double factor of dissociation and of serialization presages the first rudiments of number.

It is easy to furnish a counterproof:

Observation 131.—At 0;9 (4) Laurent imitates the sounds which he knows how to make spontaneously. I say "papa" to him, he replies *papa* or *baba*. When I say "papa-papa" he replies *apapa* or *bababa*. When I say "papapapapapapa" he replies *papapapa*, etc. There exists, consequently, a global evaluation of the number of syllables: The quantity corresponding to 2 is in any case distinguished from 3, 4 or 5, which are experienced as "many."

At 0;10 (14) Laurent repeats *pa* when I say "pa," *papa* for "papa" and *papapa* for a number of 4 or more than 4.

Such are the "mobile schemata" from the point of view of assimilation. It may thus be seen that the three aspects of assimilation which we have emphasized in connection with the primary and secondary schemata (repetition, recognition, and generalization) tend to join together or to combine more and more closely to the extent that the schemata become more supple and more complex. We shall not return to these distinctions except to study, in the following paragraphs, certain particular aspects of recognition and generalization peculiar to these schemata.

On the other hand, it is fitting to emphasize the process of *accommodation* characteristic of this stage because it is above all this mechanism of accommodation which will permit us to distinguish between the "application of familiar means to new situations" and the behavior patterns of the fifth stage and, in particular, the "discovery of new means through active experimentation."

One remembers that during the preceding stage accommodation consists simply in an effort to rediscover the conditions in which the action has discovered an interesting result. Such a form of accommodation, like that of the first two stages, is therefore, so to speak, dominated by assimilation: To the extent that the child tries to reproduce his acts he accommodates the schemata to the object which does not yet interest him in itself. During the next stage, on the contrary, the child will try to discover new properties in the objects. Moreover, and in correlation with these beginnings of experimentation, in order to attain ends which are unreachable by the simple coördination of already acquired schemata, he will elaborate new means. This elaboration presupposes, as we shall see, an accommodation which also controls assimilation, that is to say, directs it as a function of the properties of the objects.

The accommodation characteristic of the fourth stage, whether it is made manifest in the "explorations" which we shall presently describe (§5), or in the "application of familiar schemata to new circumstances," is exactly intermediate between the two types. On the one hand, it is only to the extent that the coordination of schemata works, hence their reciprocal assimilation, that their accommodation to the objects progresses. Therein, the accommodation characteristic of the fourth stage simply prolongs that of the preceding ones. But, on the other hand, such accommodation, even subordinated to the working of assimilation, leads to the discovery of new relations between objects and so presages the accommodation of the fifth stage.

With regard to the first point, it can therefore be said that during this stage accommodation only progresses as a function of the coördination of the schemata. This is obvious in behavior patterns such as pushing back the obstacle, bringing another person's hand closer to the objective, etc. In such cases the child tries neither to reach a new goal relating to the object nor to discover a new procedure. He limits himself to intercoördinating two schemata according to the variations of that of the two which assigns an end to the action, and it is in order to operate this coordination that he is obliged to accommodate the transitional schema to the situation (pushing the object back instead of simply striking it, etc.). But, while doing this, he discovers in the course of the accommodation itself a new relation ("pushing back in order to," etc.) and in that the second point consists; that is to say, the outline of a more advanced accommodation which will develop during the fifth stage.

Hence the accommodation of this stage is more refined than that of the schemata hitherto under study, since the mobile schema applies to relations between external things and no longer only to things in their mere connection with the activity itself. Does this accommodation involve representation? If one understands representation to mean the capacity to confer upon things a meaning before the action which this meaning permits, it is apparent that representation exists. The act of looking under a shawl for a shoe in order to strike it with a piece of wood (Obs. 129) is the prototype of this behavior pattern. But a capacity of this kind, which naturally increases as a function of the intentional nature of the acts, is already observable before this and goes back to the very beginnings of mental life. On the other hand, if one understands representation to mean the capacity to evoke by a sign or a symbolic image an absent object or an action not yet carried out, then nothing yet warrants asserting its existence. In order that he look for his shoe it is not necessary that the child picture it to himself or that he imagine the contact of the wood with the leather. It suffices that a sensorimotor schema lead him to his foot and that this schema be put to work, by virtue of the fact that the collision of the wood with an object is assimilated to the kicking of the foot.

It remains for us to draw a conclusion, clarifying the meaning of mobile schemata from the point of view of *organization*. As we have already emphasized often, organization or internal adaptation characterizes the interior of each schema as well as the interrelations of the schemata. Now the chief originality of this stage in comparison to the preceding stages is that the organization of the schemata among themselves is established for the first time in an explicit way and thereby reveals the internal organization of the schemata considered as totalities.

Moreover, it is good to distinguish, as before, between the totalities in the process of elaboration and the completed totalities. Concerning the former, what has been said in §2 with regard to the subordination of means to ends sufficiently shows the existence of categories to which we have simply alluded hitherto and which henceforth acquire a precise meaning: those of "value" and of "ideal" totality.

As long as the schemata are not intercoördinated but function each for itself, the child's judgments of value, so to speak, are almost entirely confused with his judgments of reality. More precisely, they are one with the activity inherent in each schema. When confronted by rattles, for instance, either the child shakes them and their value becomes thus identified with their property of being shaken, or else he loses interest in them, and their temporary lack of value becomes identified in the same way with the subject's inaction. On the other hand, another person's hand, in the behavior patterns of the present stage, is no longer characterized by one value only, or by the pair "value" and "nonvalue"; it can be considered either as an obstacle, or as a useful intermediate, or else as an end in itself according as to whether it is put into relationship with an objective from which it separates the child, or with an objective upon which it can act or again, is envisaged in itself. It thus assumes a series of different values according to the way in which it is utilized as means in view of different ends. With respect to these ends, it can be said that, to the' extent that they require, in order to be attained, a more complex coördination of the means for use, they are more remote and so determine more "ideal" totalities. Hence the categories of "value" and of "ideal" become much more clearly differentiated during this stage than when the means and ends were enveloped within the same schemata as was the case with respect to the schemata of the third stage not intercoördinated.

Regarding the completed organizations, these are characterized by the two complementary modes of "totality" and "relation" which also are henceforth revealed more clearly than before.

As far as "totality" is concerned, we have already emphasized that every schema of assimilation constitutes a true totality, that is to say, an ensemble of sensorimotor elements mutually dependent or unable to function without each other. It is due to the fact that the schemata present this kind of structure that mental assimilation is possible and any object whatever can be incorporated or serve as aliment to a given schema. Inversely we have seen that the existence of this "total" structure was connected with the act of assimilation, a sensorimotor coalescence only constituting a true totality if it is capable of conversation or repetition due to the action of assimilation. "Total" organization and assimilation are consequently two aspects of the same reality, one internal and the other external. How can we surpass this analysis and grasp the intimate mechanism of this organization? This is precisely what the behavior patterns of this stage make possible by showing us simultaneously how the schemata are organized in relation to each other and in which respects this coördination corresponds to their internal organization.

The important thing that the behavior patterns of the present stage teach us is that the coördination of the schemata is correlative to their differentiation; in other words, that the organization works by complementary regroupings and dissociations. Thus pushing back the obstacle in order to attain the objective presupposes a coördination between the schema of striking and that of grasping, but such a coördination that from the schema of striking is extracted that of "pushing back" which is immanent in it. Now such correlation between external coördination and internal differentiation reveals a fundamental character of organization. That is that every schema, insomuch as it is a totality, is pregnant with a series of schemata virtually contained within it, each organized totality thus being, not composed of totalities of a lower grade, but a possible source of such formations. These virtual totalities are not encased and preformed in the combined totality but result from it precisely to the extent that the combined totalities intercoördinate and thereby become differentiated.

An organized totality consequently never merely constitutes but one unity relating to the grade under consideration. Let it be said in passing, that explains why psychological assimilation or organization are of the same nature as physiological assimilation or organization, their grade alone contrasting them to these latter. Thus every act of intellectual assimilation presupposes a series of lower-grade assimilations protracted to the plane of truly vital assimilation. Moreover, if one remains on the psychological plane, and considers this relation between the coördination or external organization of the schemata and the differentiation revealing their internal organization, one understands why, in the rest of mental development, the individual's every external conquest founded upon a new coördination will reëcho if the acquisition of consciousness functions normally (that is to say, if no obstacle looms to impede it) in a thought about the self or an analysis of the internal mechanism of organization.

That parenthesis aside, the coördination of the schemata characteristic of this stage constitutes a new organization which forms above the schemata a totality actualizing the balance existing between them since the preceding stages. Now, as we see, this external totality only extends the internal totalities considered hitherto. Furthermore, the very fact that this external totality is constructed by virtue of a reciprocal assimilation of the existing schemata brings to light the existence, until now merely anticipated, of a close relationship between the categories of "totality" and "reciprocity." In effect, the fundamental property of every "totality" is that its elements maintain among themselves the relations of reciprocity.

The category of relation (reciprocity) is as fundamental to the human mind as that of totality. If the purpose of this book did not prohibit us from making digressions in the realm of the psychology of intelligence in general, this would be the time to show that the so-called "identification" in which a famous philosophy of science envisages the characteristic process of the "progress of thought" never gives itself an aim of forming relations of identity but rather of forming systems of reciprocal relations. The ultimate fact, in the analysis of intelligence, consequently is not the static affirmation of identity, but the process by which the mind distinguishes between two terms by putting them into relationship and forms this relation while solidifying them. Reciprocity is, accordingly, a dynastic identity of which the act of coördination is on a par with that of differentiation.

Now, considered thus, reciprocity is the fundamental relation which one finds within each totality. When the totality is constructed by coördination of two or more schemata, the relations existing between these schemata are relations of reciprocity, whereas the relations established between the objects subsumed by these schemata themselves constitute reciprocal relations. With regard to the internal structure of the schemata, the same applies: The parts of an organized whole necessarily maintain among themselves relations of reciprocity. We shall examine this more closely in Volume II when studying the objective, spatial or causal structures. Concerning space, in particular, it is obvious that every motor totality tends to form a "group" whose elements are defined precisely by reciprocity.[3]

But, to be sure, true totality and complete reciprocity are only limited cases that every schema and every ensemble of schemata tend to realize to the extent that they actually tend toward a state of equilibrium. It is this difference between the state of fact and the highest state which justifies the distinction between real totalities and ideal totalities which is characteristic of the categories of organization.

§4. THE RECOGNITION OF SIGNS AND THEIR UTI-LIZATION IN PREVISION.—It goes without saying that an operation as complex as that of the coördination of mobile schemata involves a use of recognitory assimilation as well as of reproductive or generalizing assimilation. Moreover, it is useless to study separately the acts of repetition of which the child becomes capable at this stage. On the other hand, it is interesting to try to describe how the recognition of signs which the "application of familiar schemata to new situations" presupposes, surpasses this behavior pattern and can give rise to previsions independent of the action in progress.

It is only natural that prevision should become independent of action at the present stage and so engender a sort of concrete prevision, precisely because the constitution of the mobile schemata and their coördination attest to the power which the child acquires of dissociating the thitherto global totalities and of again combining their elements. But it is still necessary to understand through analysis of the facts how this liberation of meanings works and in which respect the signs peculiar to this stage differ from the various types of signals which have been under study.

---

[3] Thus, from the logical point of view, the difficulty inherent in the concept of identification is removed. Nothing formally distinguishes false from true identification and the experimental proof necessary for this distinction therefore either remains foreign to the mechanism of reason or else bound together with internal identifications whose validity one does not know how to demonstrate. On the other hand, a system of reciprocal relations obtains its security simultaneously from its internal structure and from the facts which it has succeeded in coördinating. Its constitution is a proof of its value since in itself it comprises an element of verification.

We recall that to each of the preceding stages a particular type of signs and meanings corresponds. To the reflex stage corresponds a type of recognitions and of meanings immanent in the use of the reflex. The child recognizes whether he is sucking without an object, whether he is sucking a tegument or is really nursing. The primary circular reactions then engender a second type of signs, the "signals" acquired by insertion of a new perceptive element in the familiar schemata. Whether they are simple or derived from the coördination of heterogeneous schemata, the signals thus form part of the act which they set in motion in the manner of direct perception of the objective. So it is that a heard sound provokes the search for the corresponding image, etc. As we have seen, with the secondary reactions a third type of signs begins which are intermediate between the "signal" and the "sign," that is to say, form the transition between the sign which simply releases the action and that which permits independent prevision of the act. For instance, when a child hears a bed creak and by this sign recognizes the presence of his mother who will be able to feed him (Obs. 108) he limits himself to inserting a new perception in the complex schemata coördinated with sucking and in that respect the sign is still only a "signal" but he is on the way to attributing to his mother an activity independent of himself and, to this extent, the prevision under consideration presages the true "sign."

This decisive progress, which consists in bringing prevision to bear upon events independent of the action itself, is achieved during the fourth stage in correlation with the objectifying of the relations which characterize this stage in general. In other words, a fourth type of sign is now constituted which we shall call the actual "sign," which permits the child to foresee, not only an event connected with his action, but also any event conceived as being independent and connected with the activity of the object.

Observation 132.—At 0;8 (6) Laurent recognizes by a certain noise caused by air that he is nearing the end of his feeding and, instead of insisting on drinking to the last drop, he rejects his bottle. Such a behavior pattern still pertains to the recognition of "signals" since the perception of sound is inserted in the schemata of sucking, but the fact that, despite his hunger, Laurent at once resigns himself and rejects his bottle seems to us to show that he foresees the events as function of the object itself as much as of the action. He knows that the bottle is emptying although a few grams of milk still remain.

At 0;9 (8) likewise, I observe that Laurent constantly follows my whereabouts in the room without either seeing me or hearing my voice. His mother's voice or his sisters' voices in the hall or the neighboring rooms set no reaction in motion, whereas the slightest creak of my table or armchair starts his search or significant sounds of his voice. Hence he knows I am there and notes my presence as well as my changes of location by all these signs. Now this interest is independent of the hour of his meals.

Observation 133.—At 0;9 (15) Jacqueline wails or cries when she sees the person seated next to her get up or move away a little (giving the impression of leaving).

At 0;9 (16) she discovers more complex signs during a meal than previously. She likes the grape juice in a glass but not the soup in a bowl. She watches her mother's activity. When the spoon comes out of the glass she opens her mouth wide, whereas when it comes from the bowl, her mouth remains closed. Her mother then tries to lead her to make a mistake by taking a spoon from the bowl and passing it by the glass before offering it to Jacqueline. But she is not fooled. At 0;9 (18) Jacqueline no longer even needs to look at the spoon. She notes by the sound whether the spoonful comes from the glass or from the bowl and obstinately closes her mouth in the latter case. At 0;10 (26) Jacqueline also refuses her soup. But her mother, before holding out the spoon to her, strikes it against a silver bowl containing stewed fruit. Jacqueline is fooled this time and opens her mouth due to not having watched the move and to having depended on the sound alone.

At 1;1 (10) she has a slight scratch which is disinfected with alcohol. She cries, chiefly from fear. Subsequently, as soon as she again sees the bottle of alcohol she recommences to cry, knowing what is in store for her. Two days later, same reaction, as soon as she sees the bottle and even before it is opened.

Observation 133 repeated.—Lucienne has revealed most of the same reactions. Thus at 0;8 (23) she also closes her mouth to the spoonsful coming from the bowl (of soup) and opens it to those coming from the glass (of fruit juice). At 0;10 (19) she wails as soon as the person with whom she is playing gives the impression of leaving. It is enough to turn oneself away from her, without rising, to worry her!

Observation 134.—At 0;10 (26) Jacqueline has watched for a long time a red balloon attached to the handle of her bassinet and floating toward the ceiling. At a given moment I detach the balloon without her seeing me. Shortly afterward she looks at the handle at the usual place, looks for the balloon and, not finding it, examines the ceiling. At 0;11 (14) she cries when I take a mirror from her hand without her watching this operation. She therefore knows she will not see it any more.

In a general way, from 0;11 Jacqueline cries when one pretends to take an object away from her because she awaits its disappearance. This kind of understanding is related to the development of the behavior patterns of searching for the absent object (see Vol. II, Chap. I).

So it is that from 0;11 (15) Jacqueline cries as soon as her mother puts her hat on. This is not due to fear or anxiety as before but due to the certainty of the departure.

Observation 135.—It is fitting, moreover, to class among the signs of the fourth stage those which the child uses to identify his own features by those which correspond to them on the face of another person.

We shall study these signs in connection with the acquisition of imitation (see "The Genesis of Imitation") and shall see that in this regard they could not be confused with simple "signals."

For example, before 0;10 (7) Laurent has not succeeded in imitating the act of sticking out the tongue. Now he sticks it out spontaneously while accompanying this movement with a sound of saliva. I then imitate him and he in turn imitates me. But the imitation fails when I stick my tongue out in silence. From 0;10 (10), on the contrary, it suffices that I stick out my tongue, even without the accompanying sound, for him to imitate me. The sound of saliva has consequently served as a sign to permit him to identify his tongue by mine.

That is not a question of a "signal" setting the act in motion since the sound alone does not induce the child to stick his tongue out, but rather of a sign enabling the subject to put a group of factors observed in someone else into relationship with the corresponding parts of his own body. The sign again is brought to bear upon events independent of the self.

The principal novelty of these facts compared with those of the preceding levels is that they presuppose a prevision independent of the action in progress. When the child notes the presence of persons independently of his meals, wails on seeing someone rise, turns on hearing a breath, recognizes an alcohol bottle, etc., he performs an operation more difficult than connecting a signal with the schemata relating to the meal (third type), and trying to see the thing he hears or to grasp an object which has grazed his fingers (second type). In these last three behavior patterns the signal has exclusively a practical meaning; that is to say, its only effect is to set in motion the action of a schema of assimilation to which it is connected by a constant and necessary bond. True, this bond presages prevision, particularly when the intermediates between the signal and the act are complex as in the third type, but this prevision remains connected with the immediate action and is not yet dissociated from it. On the contrary, the behavior patterns of the fourth type reveal a more advanced differentiation between prevision and action. Undoubtedly all the intermediates are given between this level and the preceding ones and some of the behavior patterns cited prolong without adding anything to those of the third type and even of the second. Thus the fact of marking by the sound of the spoon or the sight of the receptacle that which the spoon will contain merely constitutes an extension of the schemata of coördination between sight and eating. But, although the signs of the present type are sometimes derived from more or less habitual schemata they can henceforth enter into new behavior patterns in the capacity of components. If Jacqueline, for example, foresees what the content of the spoons will be, this is in order to reject her soup and only accept the fruit juice. And, above all, it is remarkable that henceforth prevision becomes possible in connection with facts rarely or very recently observed, or even in connection with the actions of other people. Thus to foresee the departure of a person when he rises or even turns away is a prevision which is already very much detached from the action in progress; and to manifest aversion for a bottle of alcohol is to utilize a rare or very recently acquired connection.

In short the novelty of these behavior patterns, although difficult to grasp precisely, is made manifest in that prevision becomes objectified and detached from simply circular reaction. Thus it may be seen that these behavior patterns are in close relation with those of Observations 120–130, that is to say, with the application of familiar schemata to new situations. This application of familiar schemata also presupposes prevision, that is to say, the utilization of signs. And, primarily, the relationship between these two groups of facts consists in that in both cases the schemata utilized are "mobile," in other words, subject to multiple combinations. In the case of Observations 120–130, this mobility of the schemata is recognizable by the fact that the familiar schemata, habitually constituting ends in themselves, serve momentarily as means for a new end. In the case of the present observations they are, on the contrary, signs ordinarily embodied in general schemata which are henceforth understood in themselves and utilized separately in order to give rise to an independent prevision. Thus the signs consisting of creaks of the table or of chairs, of the person rising, etc., were acquired, like most of the others, as function of the schemata of the meal. They are henceforth utilized in any circumstance whatever. In both cases, consequently, whether it is a question of the utilization of familiar schemata in the pursuit of a new end or of the utilization of signs in a new independent situation, the schemata become mobile and subject to unlimited combinations. The only difference between the two behavior patterns is that in Observations 120–130 there is seeking and invention of a means, whereas in the present observations there is chiefly comprehension, but, in both cases, the process of assimilation is the same.

Finally let us remark, before proceeding to the new facts, that the term prevision which we have used must not create an illusion or evoke more than concrete expectation. Deduction does not yet exist, because there is doubtless still no "representation." When Jacqueline expects to see a person where a door is opening, or fruit juice in a spoon coming out of a certain receptacle, it is not necessary, in order that there be understanding of these signs and consequently prevision, that she picture these objects to herself in their absence. It is enough that the sign set in motion a certain attitude of expectation and a certain schema of recognition of persons or of food. Thus the sight of obstacles in a cluttered street permits us to steer a bicycle or an automobile with enough prevision to adapt ourselves to the barely outlined movements of another person without our needing to picture them to ourselves in detail. It is during the later stages that true deduction, with representation, will be superposed on these elementary meanings. But we are not yet there and have not even reached the level at which the meaning of sensorial signs is constituted by the "object" itself, with its characteristics of permanence and solidity.

§5. THE EXPLORATION OF NEW OBJECTS AND PHENOMENA AND THE "DERIVED" SECONDARY RE-ACTIONS.—Granted what we have seen of the application of familiar schemata to new situations and of the understanding of signs independently of the action in progress, we can ask what the child will do when confronted by objects or phenomena which are entirely new to him. Such objects could not set in motion behavior patterns analogous to those in Observations 120–130—that is to say, the application of familiar means to a new end—precisely because the child, when confronted by such objects, cannot set himself any definite goal except "understanding" them. Moreover the understanding of signs, while playing a role in this assimilation, would not suffice to account for it. Then what will happen? We are now to encounter a very significant behavior pattern which, more than any other, will make us grasp the importance of assimilation through mobile schemata. The child will try, by virtue of a sort of "generalizing assimilation," to make the new object enter into each of his habitual schemata, one by one. In other words, the child will try to "understand" the nature of the new object, and as comprehension is still confused with sensorimotor or practical assimilation, he will limit himself to applying each of his schemata to the object. But in doing this he will not, as in the third stage, set the schema as goal and the object as means. On the contrary, the schema will be, so to speak, the instrument of comprehension, whereas the object will remain the goal or intention of this comprehension. To put it more simply, the child will apply himself in acts to the operation to which older subjects apply themselves in words: He will define the object by its use.

Here are examples of these behavior patterns:

Observation 136.—At 0;8 (16) Jacqueline grasps an unfamiliar cigarette case which I present to her. At first she examines it very attentively, turns it over, then holds it in both hands while making the sound *apff* (a kind of hiss which she usually makes in the presence of people). After that she rubs it against the wicker of her bassinet (habitual movement of her right hand, Obs. 104), then draws herself up while looking at it (Obs. 115), then swings it above her and finally puts it into her mouth.

A ball of wool: She looks at it, turns it over, feels it, squeezes it, then lets it go, accidentally. I rest the ball on her stomach. Jacqueline draws herself up three or four times while looking at it, then feels its surface again, pulls the string while staring at it, shakes it in all directions and finally again goes *apff*.

A tin box: Jacqueline grasps it, examines it all over, feels it, then goes *apff*. Afterward she shakes it, then hears a sound when striking it. She then strikes indefinitely, then draws herself up while looking at it and striking it. Then she examines it at length from the side while holding it in the air and going *apff*. Afterward she emits some sounds such as *adda, bva*, etc., while brandishing it and turning it in all directions. Finally, she rubs it against the wicker of the bassinet again going *apff*.

At 0;9 (4) she looks for a long time at a straw table mat, then delicately touches the edge, grows bold enough to touch it, then grasps it, holds it in the air while slowly displacing it, shakes it and ends by tapping it with her other hand. This behavior is accompanied by an expression of expectation and then of satisfaction. Jacqueline finally expresses her feelings by going *apff*. Then she rubs the object against the edge of the bassinet, etc.

Observation 137.—At 0;8 (29) Laurent examines at length a notebook which he has just grasped. He transfers it from one hand to the other while turning it in all directions, touches the cover, then one of the corners, then the cover again, and finally the edge. Afterward he shakes himself, shakes his head while looking at it, displaces it more slowly with a wide motion and ends by rubbing it against the side of the bassinet. He then observes that in rubbing against the wicker the notebook does not produce the usual effect (sound? consistency?) and examines the contact most attentively while rubbing more gently.

At 0;9 (6) he examines a series of new objects which I present to him in sequence: a wooden figure of a man with movable feet, a wooden toucan 7 cm. high, a matchbox case, a wooden elephant (10 cm. long) and a beaded purse. I observe four quite constant reactions. (1) In the first place a long visual exploration: Laurent looks at the objects which are at first immobile, then looks at them very rapidly (while transferring them from one hand to the other). He seems to study their various surfaces or perspectives. In particular, he folds the purse in two, unfolds and refolds it in order to study the transformations; as soon as he sees the hinge, he turns the object over in order to see it full face, etc. (2) After the visual exploration a tactile exploration begins: He feels the object, especially the toucan's beak, the little man's feet, and gently passes his fingers over the unevenness of the object (the carved wood of the toucan, the beads of the purse, etc.), he scratches certain places (the case of the box, the smooth wood of the elephant, etc.). (3) He slowly moves the object in space: chiefly movements perpendicular to his glance, but already perhaps desired displacements in depth. (4) Only at last does he try the various familiar schemata, using them each in turn with a sort of prudence, as though studying the effect produced. He shakes them, strikes them, swings them, rubs them against the bassinet, draws himself up, shakes his head, sucks them, etc.

At 0;9 (21) same reactions in the presence of a big red crayon: He touches its point with interest, then turns the crayon around many times, strikes it, rubs it, shakes it, scratches it, etc. At 0;9 (26) the same applies to a bath thermometer: He looks at it, scratches it, shakes himself in front of it, then shakes it, turns it over, feels the handle around which he finally puts his hand, sucks the end of the handle (without wishing to suck, but "in order to see"), takes it out of his mouth, follows the thermometer itself with his left palm, shakes himself again, examines the glass part, touches it and scratches it, looks at the string and feels it, etc.

At 0;9 (30) same reactions in the presence of a new plush cat: He turns it in all directions, touches its head cautiously, touches the ribbon, the feet, discovers a cardboard disc attached to its tail and scratches it with his nail. He ends by striking the cat, swinging it in space; he shakes himself while looking at it, says *papa, baba*, etc.

Before discussing these facts of "exploration of new objects," let us again see how they can give rise to new "secondary circular reactions," but "derived" ones, when the exploration by chance results in the discovery of an unknown phenomenon. As we have already emphasized (see Chap. III, §4, Obs. 119), new secondary reactions are formed at every age (and not only during the third stage), but in the midst of new contexts. This is precisely what happens in the course of the behavior patterns of "exploration." It suffices that an unforeseen result has been fortuitously set in motion for it to give rise to immediate and simple repetition which in turn results in the elaboration of a schema. Here are some examples:

Observation 138.—We have already seen (Obs. 103) how the schemata of striking hanging objects is derived from simpler schemata (grasping, etc.) and has itself given rise to more complex schemata (hitting with one hand an object held in the other, etc.). Now we shall see how, with respect to Laurent, Lucienne, and Jacqueline, at about the same time, this same schema of striking engendered a new schema of "setting swinging in motion" and how this latter schema was discovered in the course of actual "explorations."

At 0;8 (30) Laurent, for the first time, examines a wooden hen from which hangs a ball which actuates the animal's head by its movements. First he sees the hen, touches it, etc., then examines the ball, feels it and, seeing it move, strikes it immediately; he then attentively watches it swing and then studies it for its own sake; he simply sets it in motion, more and more gently. Then his attention is brought to bear on the accompanying movement of the hen and he swings the ball while watching the hen.

Observation 138 repeated.—Lucienne, at 0;8 (10), likewise, examines a new doll which I hang from the hood of her bassinet. She looks at it for a long time, touches it, then feels it by touching its feet, clothes, head, etc. She then ventures to grasp it, which makes the hood sway. She then pulls the doll while watching the effects of this movement. Then she returns to the doll, holds it in one hand while striking it with the other, sucks it and shakes it while holding it above her and finally shakes it by moving its legs.

Afterwards she strikes it without holding it, then grasps the string by which it hangs and gently swings it with the other hand. She then becomes very much interested in this slight swinging movement which is new to her and repeats it indefinitely.

Observation 139.—At 0;8 (9) Jacqueline looks at a hanging necktie which she has never seen. Her hands move around it and touch it very warily. She grasps it and feels its surface. At a certain moment part of the necktie escapes her grasp: visible anxiety, then, when the phenomenon is repeated, satisfaction and, almost immediately after, something which resembles an experience of letting go and recapturing.

That evening, Jacqueline is lying on her back having at her right a rag which is drying on a line. She tries to grasp it, then immediately swings it; then she draws it toward her, lets it go and watches it oscillate. When it stops, she rebegins, evincing great interest in this movement.

At 0;8 (12) Jacqueline at first tries to make another hanging necktie swing. She grasps it very gingerly, lets it go, etc., in a regular and continuous oscillating movement.

At 0;8 (13) Jacqueline watches her mother who is swinging the flounce on the bassinet. As soon as she stops, Jacqueline pushes her hand to make her continue. Then she herself grasps the flounce and imitates the movement.—That evening Jacqueline swings a hanging doll in the same way, with great delicacy.

At 0;8 (26) Jacqueline feels and explores the surface of a lamp shade which then begins to swing. She waits until this movement has almost stopped (after many oscillations) in order to start the object moving again with one blow of her hand. This reaction reappears regularly the days following as soon as she is brought near the lamp in her room. I again observe it at 0;9 (5), etc.

At 0;9 (6) Jacqueline accidentally starts a sudden movement of the lamp shade by striking it from the inside. She then immediately tries to rediscover the result by placing her hand, not with the palm against the material as usual, but with her palm in the air. She gropes in this way, very warily, becomes entangled in the fringe, then is completely successful.

Observation 140.—Here is a second example of "exploration" leading to a "derived secondary circular reaction" and to a new schema, that of "letting go." This second example is particularly instructive since it presages the most important of the "tertiary circular reactions" and thus will permit us to form the transition between the behavior patterns of the present stage and those of the fifth stage.

At 0;10 (2) Laurent examines an empty (white metal) case of shaving soap which he sees for the first time. He begins by turning it in all directions while passing it from one hand to the other as he did with the objects in Observation 137. But the object being slippery and hard to handle, slips from his hand two or three times. Then Laurent, struck by this phenomenon, applies himself to reproducing it a certain number of times. At first I had some difficulty in deciding whether it was indeed an intentional act for Laurent begins each time by holding the case for a moment and turning it over before letting it go. But then it fell more and more frequently and above all systematically as revealed by the following statements concerning the procedures employed by Laurent for relinquishing the objective.

In effect, what interests Laurent at the beginning of this behavior pattern is not the trajectory of the object—that is to say the objective phenomenon of its fall—but the very act of letting go. Sometimes Laurent delicately opens his hand (his palm upturned), and the case rolls along his fingers, sometimes Laurent turns his hand over (vertically) and the case falls backward between the thumb and index finger which are separated, sometimes Laurent simply opens his hand (palm downward) and the object falls.

It is this characteristic of Laurent's behavior pattern which permits us still to class it among the secondary circular reactions and not among the tertiary reactions. The "tertiary" reaction will begin, in effect, at the time when Laurent will study the trajectory of the object and to do this will organize a true "experiment in order to see." He will vary the conditions, relinquish the object in different situations, watch it, try to recapture it, etc. For the time being, on the contrary, he limits himself to repeating the same gestures and is only interested in his own action which certainly constitutes a "secondary" reaction.

Above all, for several days Laurent has only utilized this schema of relinquishing in connection with the same object, the case of shaving soap. At 0;10 (3), for example, that is to say, the next day, he immediately makes use of the case in order to repeat his behavior of the previous day, but he does not let go either of the little box which he manipulates for a long time or of his plush cat, etc. At 0;10 (4) same reaction. At 0;10 (5) he twice lets fall a small bottle (new to him) which fell from his hands fortuitously the first time. It is only at 0;10 (10) that he begins to throw everything to the ground, but then at the same time he becomes interested in the trajectories of the falling objects and so inaugurates his "tertiary circular reactions."

Hence it is fitting to terminate this observation by drawing the conclusion that this secondary circular reaction is apparently "derived" from "exploration" of the case of soap and thus reveals no relationship to the transitional schema of removing or letting fall the object as studied in Observation 125. On the other hand we have seen how the present schema has subsequently been utilized as a "means," in Observation 130.

Behavior patterns of this sort are found exactly between the generalization of secondary schemata in the presence of new objects (Obs. 110–111) and the "tertiary circular reactions," hence between the behavior patterns of the third stage and those of the fifth.

Like the "generalization of secondary schemata" the present behavior patterns consist, in effect, of applying acquired schemata to new objects or phenomena. Just as, at 4 to 6 months, the child strikes, shakes, rubs, etc., the unfamiliar object which is offered to him, so also, at 8 to 10 months, he displaces it, swings it, shakes it, etc. The exploration of which we now speak therefore prolongs without adding anything to the generalization of the schemata to such a degree that all the transitions are exhibited between the two behavior patterns and it is impossible to draw a definite boundary between them. Nevertheless they do not seem to us to be identical because, however delicate the evaluation of such characteristics may be, their orientation is different. At the beginning of the third stage, in effect, the new object does not interest the child at all as a novelty. Its novelty only arrests his curiosity fleetingly and the object immediately serves as aliment to habitual schemata. Interest is consequently not centered on the object as such but on its utilization. On the other hand, when the 8-month-old child examines a cigarette case or a hanging necktie everything transpires as though such objects presented a problem to his mind, as though he were trying to "understand." Not only does he look at such objects for a much longer time than the 4- to 5-month-old child before proceeding to acts, but furthermore, he engages in an ensemble of exploratory movements relating to the object and not to himself. He feels, explores the surface, the edges, turns over and slowly displaces, etc., and the last behavior patterns are very significant of a new attitude. The unfamiliar obviously represents to the child an external reality, to which he must adapt himself and no longer a substance which is pliable at will or a simple aliment for the activity itself. Finally comes the application of habitual schemata to this reality. But in trying out each of his schemata in turn, the child at this stage gives more the impression of making an experiment than of generalizing his behavior patterns: He tries to "understand."

In other words, it is as though the child said to himself when confronted by the new object: "What is this thing? I see it, hear it, grasp it, feel it, turn it over, without recognizing it: what more can I do with it?" And as understanding, at this age, is purely practical or sensorimotor and the only concepts which exist as yet are mobile schemata, the child tries to make the new object enter into each of his schemata in order to see in which respect they suit it. As we have already noted, such behavior patterns constitute the functional equivalent of "definitions through use" so important to a child's verbal intelligence.

Concerning the secondary circular reactions which can "derive" from this exploration, their genesis is easy to understand when a new phenomenon appears unexpectedly. In effect, when the child tries to assimilate a new object to his earlier schemata, two things can happen. Either the object comes up to expectation and so fits the schemata tried out, and then adaptation is acquired. The new doll can indeed be swung, shaken, rubbed, etc., and the child is satisfied. Or else, on the contrary, the object resists and reveals properties hitherto unknown, but then the child behaves as he has always done in a similar case. He tries to rediscover what he has just discovered by chance and merely repeats the movements which led him to this fortuitous discovery. So it is that, when trying to explore the nature of a hanging necktie or a lamp shade, Jacqueline discovers the phenomenon of the spontaneous swinging of these objects. Until then she was only familiar with the swinging of toys hanging from the hood of her bassinet, a swinging prolonged or maintained by her schemata of "striking" or "drawing herself up," etc. (Obs. 103). Now on the contrary, she becomes aware of a swinging which is in a way inherent in the object, hence of a new phenomenon. She immediately studies it and, to do this, applies herself to reproducing it indefinitely. The same is true of Laurent (Obs. 140) when he discovers the possibility of "letting go" of objects.

New behavior patterns of this kind obviously prepare the "tertiary circular reactions" (such as throwing and picking up, causing sliding, rolling, splashing, etc.) which will develop during the fifth stage and will constitute the first real experimentations of which the child is capable. The "tertiary circular reaction" is, in effect, an "experiment in order to see," which no longer consists in simply reproducing an interesting result but in making it vary in the very course of repetition. At this level of development the object definitely becomes independent of the action. It is the source of completely autonomous activities which the child studies from the outside, as he is henceforth oriented toward novelty as such.

But if these actions of "swinging" and "letting go" which we have seen appear in the course of the "explorations" of this stage presage this kind of "experiments in order to see" it would not yet be possible to identify them entirely by the latter. Not only, in effect, does the child always limit himself to "reproducing" what he observes and not to innovating but furthermore, as we shall state primarily in Volume II, the "object" characteristic of this fourth stage remains partly dependent on the action.

At last it may be understood why we class facts of this kind in the same stage as the "application of familiar means to new situations." Like the intelligent behavior patterns under study above (Obs. 120–130), the latter consist essentially in adapting early schemata to current circumstances. In a sense, it is true, such applications protract without adding anything to secondary circular reactions but, contrary to the "procedures to make an interesting spectacle last," the present behavior patterns have as their function not only to make the given result "last" but to adjust to novelty.

Moreover these facts bring to mind the understanding of

signs, which was treated previously. In the course of attempts at assimilation of new objects many signals and signs intervene which guide the child in his choice of schemata to apply. So it is that in Observation 139 the fact that the object is mobile or immobile, hanging or handed to him, orients his search. We can again remark, in this connection, that the fewer schemata the child has at his disposition the less useful is the sign because assimilation is immediate and global; whereas the more the schemata multiply, the more the organization of signs becomes complicated and necessary to action.

But the difference between the present facts and the preceding ones is that the orientation of the assimilatory effort is different. There is an effort to understand and no longer to invent, or even to foresee. In the case of Observations 120–130 the child, from the outset of the act has the intention of applying a given schema to the object, and the problem is to know which intermediate schemata are suitable to serve as means to this end. There is therefore an attempt to invent and comprehension only intervenes to facilitate invention. In the present case, on the contrary, the problem is to know which schemata are suited to the object. Consequently there exists an attempt to comprehend and, to the extent that invention intervenes in the form of the search for schemata, it is simply in order to facilitate comprehension. With regard to the recognition of signs of which we have spoken in connection with Observations 132–135, it constitutes an intermediate behavior pattern in this respect: It is comprehension, since it is immediate assimilation of a datum to a schema, but this comprehension is oriented toward prevision; that is to say, toward the utilization of the same schema with the intention of assimilating coming events and in this sense it is invention.

In a general way, the behavior patterns peculiar to this fourth stage manifest a real unity. Intercoördination of the schemata and their adaptation to the object are their constant characteristics and these two characteristics are complementary. The "application of familiar means to new situations" is determined by the coördination of two groups of schemata of which some serve as ends and the others as means: whence a more accurate adjustment of the latter to the circumstances motivating this union. The "signs" belonging to this stage permit a prevision which begins to become detached from the action itself. Consequently there exist simultaneously the application of familiar schemata to new situations and progress in adaptation to the date of perception. The same applies to the "explorations" of which we have just spoken. Doubtless the last of these behavior patterns does not necessarily presuppose coördinations between separate schemata; it only implies the application of the schemata to new objects. But, like the first behavior patterns, the last one permits a real accommodation of the schema to the object and no longer merely a global application as in the third stage.

CHAPTER V

THE FIFTH STAGE:

The "Tertiary Circular Reaction" and the "Discovery of New Means Through Active Experimentation"

During the third of the stages which we have delineated, the child, by manipulating things, constructed a series of simple schemata due to the "secondary circular reaction," such as "shaking," "rubbing," etc. These schemata, while not yet inter-coördinated, nevertheless comprise, each in itself, an organization of movements and perceptions and, consequently, a commencement of putting objects into interrelations. But this organization, remaining within each schema, does not involve a clear distinction between "means" and "ends" and this putting into relationship, for the same reason, remains entirely practical and does not lead to the elaboration of actual "objects."

In the course of the fourth stage, which immediately precedes this one, the secondary schemata become intercoördinated and so give rise to the complex actions which we have designated "applications of familiar means to new situations." This co-ordination of schemata, which clearly differentiates "means" from "ends" and so characterizes the first acts of intelligence properly so-called, insures a new putting into relationship of objects among themselves and hence marks the beginning of the formation of real "objects." But two circumstances limit the effectiveness of this behavior and at the same time define the difference which separates it from those of the fifth stage. In the first place, in order to become adapted to the new circumstances in which he finds himself—that is to say, in order to remove the obstacle or discover the requisite intermediate—the child at the fourth stage limits himself to intercoördinating familiar schemata, except for differentiating them through progressive accommodation while adjusting them to each other. In the second place, and through that very fact, the relations which the child establishes between things still depend on completed schemata of which only the coördination is new; besides, they do not lead to the elaboration of objects entirely independent of the action, nor of spatial "groups" which are entirely "objective," etc. This is what we shall see, in particular, in Volume II, in studying concepts of the object, of space, of causality and of time which are characteristic of the fourth stage. In short, the fourth stage, in so far as it is defined by the commencement of the coördination of schemata, appears more as a phase of initiation or of gestation than as a period of realization or accomplishment.

The fifth stage, which we now undertake to study, is, on the contrary, primarily the stage of elaboration of the "object." It is characterized, in effect, by the formation of new schemata which are due no longer to a simple reproduction of fortuitous results but to a sort of experimentation or search for novelty as such. Moreover, in correlation with this same tendency, the fifth stage is recognizable by the appearance of a higher type of coördination of schemata: the coördination directed by the search for new "means."

Now both of these behavior patterns protract those of the preceding stages. As far as the "tertiary circular reaction" is concerned, it derives directly, as we shall see, from the secondary reactions and "explorations" to which the latter finally give rise. The only difference is that in the case of "tertiary" reactions the new effect obtained fortuitously is not only reproduced but modified to the end that its nature may be studied. With regard to the "discoveries of new means through active experimentation" they simply crown the coördination of schemata already in use during the fourth stage, but the reciprocal adjustment of the schemata which we have described in the preceding chapter, becomes accommodation for the sake of accommodation, that is to say, a search for new procedures.

But if the behavior patterns of the fifth stage protract those of the fourth and so constitute their natural result, they nevertheless mark decisive progress and the beginning of a really characteristic phase. In effect, for the first time, the child truly adapts himself to unfamiliar situations, not only by utilizing the schemata acquired earlier but also by seeking and finding new means —whence a series of consequences concerning, on the one hand, the functioning of intelligence and, on the other, the essential categories of concrete thought.

Of the first of these points of view, the coördination of schemata henceforth being accompanied by intentional accommodation and differentiated to new circumstances, it can be said that the mechanism of empirical intelligence has been definitely formed. The child is henceforth capable of resolving new problems, even if no acquired schema is directly utilizable for this purpose, and if the solution of these problems has not yet been found by deduction or representation, it is insured in principle in all cases due to the combined working of experimental search and the coördination of schemata.

With regard to the "real categories" of thought, this kind of accommodation to things, combined with the coördination of schemata already acquired during the preceding stage, result in definitely detaching the "object" from the activity itself while inserting it in coherent spatial groups in the same way as in the causal and temporal series which are independent of the self.

§1. THE TERTIARY CIRCULAR REACTION.—The peculiarity of the behavior patterns which we shall now describe is to constitute, for the first time, an effort to grasp novelties in themselves.

To be sure, from the very beginnings of mental life, it can be said that the external environment imposes a constant enlarging of the subject's reactions and that new experience always causes the old framework to crack. That is why acquired habits are sooner or later superposed on reflex schemata and on the former are superposed the schemata of intelligence. And, of course, it can also be said that the subject accepts this necessity with pleasure since the "circular reaction" at all levels is precisely an attempt to conserve novelties and establish them by reproductive assimilation. In the third place, one can maintain in a sense that novelty stems from assimilation itself, since the heterogeneous schemata, not very numerous, which are bestowed at the beginning, tend reciprocally to assimilate each other and so lead to multiple combinations of coördinations, either intersensorial or intelligent.

But, considered from another angle, the same facts show the resistance of mental life to novelty and the momentary victory of conservation over accommodation. So it is that the peculiarity of assimilation is to neglect what is new in things and events in order to reduce them to the state of aliments for old schemata. With regard to circular reaction, if it tends to reproduce the new result fortuitously observed, it is nevertheless necessary to state that it did not seek it but that it imposed itself by appearing by chance and in connection with familiar movements. To such a degree that circular reaction only remains, at first, pure reproductive assimilation and, if it is applied to a new datum, it is, so to speak, because this datum forced the positions by surreptitiously finding its way into the interior of an already elaborated schema. Let us recall that the new external results which characterize secondary circular reaction appear as if sprung from a differentiation of primary schemata, under pressure from the external environment, and that primary circular reaction develops, by differentiation, from the reflex schemata.

Tertiary circular reaction is quite different: if it also arises by way of differentiation, from the secondary circular schemata, this differentiation is no longer imposed by the environment but is, so to speak, accepted and even desired in itself. In effect, not succeeding in assimilating certain objects or situations to the schemata hitherto examined, the child manifests an unexpected behavior pattern: He tries, through a sort of experimentation, to find out in which respect the object or the event is new. In other words, he will not only submit to but even provoke new results instead of being satisfied merely to reproduce them once they have been revealed fortuitously. The child discovers in this way that which has been called in scientific language the "experiment in order to see." But, of course, the new result, though sought after for its own sake, demands to be reproduced and the initial experiment is immediately accompanied by circular reaction. But, there too, a difference contrasts these "tertiary" reactions to the "secondary" reactions. When the child repeats the movements which led him to the interesting result, he no longer repeats them just as they are but gradates and varies them, in such a way as to discover fluctuations in the result. The "experiment in order to see," consequently, from the very beginning, has the tendency to extend to the conquest of the external environment.

These tertiary circular reactions will lead the child to new complete acts of intelligence which we shall call "discovery of new means through active experimentation." The acts of intelligence hitherto under study have only consisted in an application of familiar means (already acquired schemata) to new situations. But what will happen when the familiar means reveal themselves to be inadequate, in other words, when the intermediates between subject and object are not assimilable to the habitual schemata? Something will transpire which is analogous to what we have just said about tertiary circular reaction. The subject will search on the spot for new means and will discover them precisely through tertiary reaction. It cannot be said that he will apply the tertiary schemata to these situations since, by definition, the tertiary circular reaction is vicarious and only exists during the elaboration of new schemata, but he will apply the method of tertiary circular reaction.

The invention of new means through active experimentation, therefore, is to tertiary reaction what the "application of familiar means to new situations" is to secondary reaction: a combination or coördination of schemata in comparison to the simple schemata. To be more precise, we are confronted here by a distinction analogous to that which can be made on the plane of reflective or verbal intelligence between reason and judgment, reason being a combination of judgments of which some serve as means and the others as ends. In effect, a judgment is nothing other, from the functional point of view which is common to reflective intelligence and to sensorimotor intelligence, than the assimilation of a datum to a schema. From this point of view simple circular reactions, whether primary, secondary or tertiary, are judgments. Moreover, the application of familiar means to new situations or the invention of new means constitute, from the same functional point of view, actual reasonings since, as we have already emphasized, the schema used in the capacity of means (it makes little difference whether it is familiar or invented on the spot) is subsumed under the schema characterizing the final end in the same way that judgments are put into a state of mutual implication in the framework of the conclusion. With regard to the comprehension of signs, it constitutes an intermediate term between judgment and reasoning. It is judgment inasmuch as it is immediate assimilation of the sign, and reasoning inasmuch as this assimilation is fraught with prevision, that is to say, with virtual deduction. But this intermediate state also finds its equivalent in verbal thought: Most judgments are implicit reasonings.

Having stated that, let us now try to analyze the tertiary circular reactions which thus constitute what one might call the functional and sensorimotor point of departure of experimental judgments.

Observation 141.—This first example will make us understand the transition between secondary and "tertiary" reactions: that of the well-known behavior pattern by means of which the child explores distant space and constructs his representation of movement, the behavior pattern of letting go or throwing objects in order subsequently to pick them up.

One recalls (Obs. 140) how, at 0;10 (2) Laurent discovered in "exploring" a case of soap, the possibility of throwing this object and letting it fall. Now, what interested him at first was not the objective phenomenon of the fall—that is to say, the object's trajectory—but the very act of letting go. He therefore limited himself, at the beginning, merely to reproducing the result observed fortuitously, which still constitutes a "secondary" reaction, "derived," it is true, but of typical structure.

On the other hand, at 0;10 (10) the reaction changes and becomes "tertiary." That day Laurent manipulates a small piece of bread (without any alimentary interest: he has never eaten any and has no thought of tasting it) and lets it go continually. He even breaks off fragments which he lets drop. Now, in contradistinction to what has happened on the preceding days, he pays no attention to the act of letting go whereas he watches with great interest the body in motion; in particular, he looks at it for a long time when it has fallen, and picks it up when he can.

At 0;10 (11) Laurent is lying on his back but nevertheless resumes his experiments of the day before. He grasps in succession a celluloid swan, a box, etc., stretches out his arm and lets them fall. He distinctly varies the positions of the fall. Sometimes he stretches out his arm vertically, sometimes he holds it obliquely, in front of or behind his eyes, etc. When the object falls in a new position (for example on his pillow), he lets it fall two or three times more on the same place, as though to study the spatial relation; then he modifies the situation. At a certain moment the swan falls near his mouth: now, he does not suck it (even though this object habitually serves this purpose), but drops it three times more while merely making the gesture of opening his mouth.

At 0;10 (12) likewise, Laurent lets go of a series of objects while varying the conditions in order to study their fall. He is seated in an oval basket and lets the object fall over the edge, sometimes to the right, sometimes to the left, in different positions. Each time he tries to recapture it, leaning over and twisting himself around, even when the object falls 40 or 50 cm. away from him. He especially tries to find the object again when it rolls under the edge of the basket and hence cannot be seen.

Observation 142.—At 0;10 (29) Laurent examines a watch chain hanging from his index finger. At first he touches it very lightly simply "exploring" it without grasping it. He then starts it swinging a little and at once continues this, thus rediscovering a "derived secondary reaction" already described in Observation 138 (schema of swinging). But, instead of stopping there, he grasps the chain with his right hand and swings it with his left while trying some new combinations (here the "tertiary reaction" begins); in particular he slides it along the back of his left hand and sees it fall off when it reaches the end. Then he holds the end of the chain (with his right index finger and thumb) and lets it slide slowly between the fingers of his left hand (the chain is now horizontal and no longer oblique as before). He studies it carefully at the moment when the chain falls from his left hand and repeats this ten times. Afterward, still holding the end of the chain in his right hand, he shakes it violently which makes it describe a series of varied trajectories in the air. He then slows these movements in order to see how the chain slides along the quilt when he merely pulls it. Finally he drops it from different heights and so rediscovers the schema acquired in the preceding observation.

From his twelfth month Laurent has repeated this kind of experiments with everything that his hand came upon: my notebook, "plugs," ribbons, etc. He entertains himself either by making them slide or fall or by letting them go in different positions and from different heights in order to study their trajectory. Thus, at 0;11 (20) he holds a "plug"

3 cm. above the ground, then 20 cm., etc., each time observing the fall most attentively.

Observation 143.—Here is another example of an "experiment in order to see," observed with respect to Laurent and pertaining to sound.

At 1;1 (24) Laurent finds himself for the first time in the presence of a piece of furniture of which we shall speak later in connection with the "invention of new means through active experimentation": a tiered table of which each circular tier pivots around a single axis. Laurent takes hold of one of the tiers in order to draw it to him. The tier moves, but turns around instead of being displaced in a straight line as the child was expecting. Laurent then shakes it, knocks it, then yields to a definitely "experimental" reaction in order to study the sound. He strikes it several times in succession, sometimes gently, sometimes hard, and between times hits the surface of his own table. There is no doubt whatever that he is comparing the sounds. Then he strikes the back of his chair and again the wide circular tier. Consequently this is more than "exploration" since there is a comparison of several objects to each other and a serialization of the effects produced.

Afterward he again wants to pull the tier toward him and happens to make it turn. But we shall describe the rest of this behavior in Observation 148 repeated, for it quickly became complicated.

Observation 144.—From 0;11 it seemed to me that, in the same way, Jacqueline intentionally let objects she was holding fall to the ground, to take them up subsequently or limit herself to looking at them. But at first it is difficult to distinguish between chance and intention. At 0;11 (19), on the other hand, the thing is quite clear: During her meal, while she is seated, she moves a wooden horse to the edge of her table until she lets it fall. She watches it. An hour later she is given a postcard. Jacqueline throws it to the ground many times and looks for it. At 0;11 (28) likewise, she systematically pushes a thimble to the edge of the box on which it is placed and watches it fall. But it is necessary to note, in observing such behavior patterns, that the child has not yet perceived the role of gravity. In other words, when he lets go of an object, it is without knowing what is going to happen; and, when he tries to send it to the ground, he believes himself to be obliged to push it down, without confining himself simply to letting it go. Thus, at 1;0 (26), Jacqueline pushed her ball to the ground instead of letting it fall. The same day she tries to get rid of a cushion which eclipses an object. She then simply puts this cushion against the back of the sofa, as though it would stick there, and starts over again indefinitely, not through circular reaction, but to get rid of the object which is annoying her.[1] At 1;1 (28), in the same way, Jacqueline watches me while I let go

[1] A. Szeminska pointed out to me an observation she made on a one-year-and-a-half-old boy. This child tried to draw a large object to himself

of a napkin ring 15 cm. above her table, several times in succession. She then takes it and simply places it on the table; afterward she reveals definite disappointment when she notices that nothing else happens. She then does this five or six times; then, as I repeat the experiment, she systematically places the object at the same place as I did (15 cm. above the table), then, instead of letting it go, from there she places it on the table!

Concerning the schema of throwing to the ground and picking up, it has been conserved a long time while being differentiated little by little. At 1;3 (21) and 1;3 (27) I note that Jacqueline begins to let fall instead of throwing to the ground. In particular she raises her arm by holding her hand backward and so manages to let go of objects from behind. At 1;4 (1) she throws an object under her mother's work table several times in succession and has difficulty in obtaining it again. Same reaction under the tablecloth of the lunch table. Finally there is progressive accommodation in the very manner of picking things up. At 1;5 (7) Jacqueline picks up objects without sitting down and gets up without leaning on anything.

Observation 145.—At 0;11 (20), that is to say, the day after the experiment with the wooden horse (see the foregoing observation), Jacqueline slides a series of objects along her slanting coverlet. This is an experiment and not merely repetition, because she varies the objects and the positions. At 1;0 (2) she rolls a pencil on a table by dropping it just above the surface or by pushing it. The next day she does the same with a ball.

At 1;0 (3) also, she takes her plush dog and places it on a sofa, obviously expecting a movement. As the dog remains motionless, she places it somewhere else. After several vain attempts she pushes it gently, while it is several millimeters above the material, as though it would roll better. Finally she grasps it and places it on a slanting cushion, so that the dog rolls. She then immediately begins all over again. Experimentation certainly exists. But in the last attempt definite prevision cannot be seen. We know (Obs. 144) that still at 1;0 (26), Jacqueline is not able to foresee the effects of gravity.

Same reactions at 1;1 (18) with her rabbit.

At 1;1 (19), likewise, Jacqueline places her red ball on the ground and waits to see it roll. She repeats the attempt five or six times and reveals a lively interest in the object's slightest movement. Then she puts it down and gives it a slight push with her fingers: the ball rolls better. She then repeats the experiment while pushing harder and harder.

---

through the bars of a play pen. Not succeeding, he decided to pull it over the bars. To do so he raised the object to the place where his arm was held back by the horizontal bar, then let go the object to try to catch it on the other side!

At 1;3 (6) having dropped a stick parallel to the framework of her play pen, Jacqueline watches it roll several centimeters on the floor (outside the play pen). As soon as I bring the stick toward her, Jacqueline grasps it and repeats the experiment. She raises it slightly, then lets it fall, so that it may roll. The same happens ten times. Then I place a cloth under the framework to prevent the stick from rolling. Jacqueline lets it fall, then seeing that it remains motionless, passes her hand through the bars and gives it a fillip. She repeats this two or three times then, noticing her failure she gives up, without trying to throw the stick from higher up.

Same attempts at 1;4 (0). During one of these, she happens to let the stick drop from a height and it rolls superbly to the end of the room. Jacqueline is stupefied by this result but, as soon as I return the stick to her, she simply places it gently on the ground 3 or 4 cm. from the pen. She looks at it for a long moment, apparently expecting it to roll by itself.

Observation 146.—At 1;2 (8) Jacqueline holds in her hands an object which is new to her: a round, flat box which she turns all over, shakes, rubs against the bassinet, etc. She lets it go and tries to pick it up. But she only succeeds in touching it with her index finger, without grasping it. She nevertheless makes an attempt and presses on the edge. The box then tilts up and falls again. Jacqueline, very much interested in this fortuitous result, immediately applies herself to studying it.— Hitherto it is only a question of an attempt at assimilation analogous to that of Observations 136 to 137, and of the fortuitous discovery of a new result, but this discovery, instead of giving rise to a simple circular reaction, is at once extended to "experiments in order to see."

In effect, Jacqueline immediately rests the box on the ground and pushes it as far as possible (it is noteworthy that care is taken to push the box far away in order to reproduce the same conditions as in the first attempt, as though this were a necessary condition for obtaining the result). Afterward Jacqueline puts her finger on the box and presses it. But as she places her finger on the center of the box she simply displaces it and makes it slide instead of tilting it up. She amuses herself with this game and keeps it up (resumes it after intervals, etc.) for several minutes. Then, changing the point of contact, she finally again places her finger on the edge of the box, which tilts it up. She repeats this many times, varying the conditions, but keeping track of her discovery: now she only presses on the edge!

A moment later I offer my cigarette case to Jacqueline. She throws it as far as possible and presses it at different points with her index finger to tilt it up. But the problem is above her level and she tires of it.

Observation 147.—In her bath, Jacqueline engages in many experiments with celluloid toys floating on the water. At 1;1 (20) and the days following, for example, not only does she drop her toys from a height to see the water splash or displace them with her hand in order to make them swim, but she pushes them halfway down in order to see them rise to the surface.

At 1;7 (20) she notices the drops of water which fall from the thermometer when she holds it in the air and shakes it. She then tries different combinations to splash from a distance. She brandishes the thermometer and stops suddenly, or makes it catapult.

Between the ages of a year and a year and a half, she amuses herself by filling with water pails, flasks, watering cans, etc., and studying the falling of the water. She also learns to carry the water carefully without spilling it and by holding the basin horizontally.

She entertains herself by filling her sponge with water and pressing it against her chest or above the water; by filling the sponge at the faucet; by running the water from the faucet; by running the water from the faucet along her arm, etc.

The relationship between these tertiary circular reactions and the secondary or even primary reactions is evident: On the one hand, the new result is always discovered by chance since, even in searching for novelty as such, the child does not know how to find it except by groping. Moreover, the "experiment" always begins by repetition. In order to study changes in position, the trajectory of objects thrown or rolled, etc., it is always necessary to return to the same movements, with the intention of varying them little by little. The "experiment in order to see" is therefore surely a circular reaction, of a higher type undoubtedly, but conforming in principle to the preceding reactions.

But the tertiary reaction brings several innovations. At first, even in repeating his movements to seek and find an interesting result, the child varies and gradates them. So it is that, when throwing objects from a distance or rolling them (Obs. 144 and 145), tilting up a box or making it slide (Obs. 146), etc., he drops these objects from increasingly high altitudes, places his finger on a certain part of the box or on another part, etc. Doubtless this is the case since the earlier circular reactions. During the secondary reactions, in particular, the child always gradates his effects. He shakes his bassinet more or less, pulls harder or less hard on the hanging strings, gradates the sound of the rattle he shakes, etc. But, in the latter cases, it is always in the same fixed framework that these variations are made manifest and one has the impression that the child is trying rather to reproduce a certain result while exploring all possible modalities, than to discover a new one. On the contrary, in the present case, the child does not know what will happen and he tries to ferret out new phenomena, which are unfamiliar or which he simply senses. For example, in Observations 141–144, the child constantly repeats the act of letting go, of throwing or rolling; but it is without knowing what will follow and precisely with the intention of finding out. True, in Observations 146 and 147 Jacqueline tries to reproduce an effect already observed (tilting up a box, floating, throwing, pouring water, etc.), but this effect is a theme with variations, and chiefly constitutes a phenomenon to be understood rather than a simple result to be repeated. In the case of the earliest secondary reactions, on the other hand, the child seems to try less to analyze and understand than merely to reproduce.

It is this last nuance which best characterizes tertiary reaction. As we said at the beginning of this chapter, the originality of these behavior patterns is that they constitute a search for novelty. For the child it is no longer a question of applying familiar schemata to the new object but of grasping with the mind this object as it is. In this respect, varying positions, throwing or rolling objects, tilting a box, floating objects, pouring water, etc., are active experiments which, it goes without saying, are still far removed from the verification of a preliminary deduction, as in the scientific experiment, but which already constitute the functional equivalent of the "experiment in order to see." Moreover, by virtue of the very fact that the experiments are accompanied by variations and gradations, they almost presage the right experiment. When Jacqueline discovers the necessity of pressing her box at the edge, and not in the middle, in order to tilt it up (Obs. 146), she reveals a directed and controlled effort. Doubtless, here also secondary reaction outlines all that; when the child must pull a string in order to shake the objects hanging from the hood of his bassinet, he must also discover the correct movement. But it is one thing to select almost automatically the right movements in the course of more or less diffuse groping and it is another thing to search for the condition essential to a certain result.

This search for the new raises the most interesting question which we have to discuss in connection with these behavior patterns. How does it happen, when all the behavior patterns hitherto under study are essentially conservative, that at a certain time the child comes to pursue novelties? The problem is found again, in analogous conditions, in connection with situations in which the child invents new means due to this same process of active experimentation. But let us limit ourselves, for the moment, to this precise question: How to account, through the play of assimilations and accommodations, for the interest in novelties peculiar to the "experiment in order to see"?

In the course of the primitive behavior patterns, in effect, through a paradox which we must subsequently analyze, accommodation and assimilation are simultaneously slightly differentiated and antagonistic. They are relatively undifferentiated in the sense that every attempt at assimilation is at the same time an attempt at accommodation without its yet being possible to distinguish in the child's intellectual activity a particular moment corresponding to what is deduction in reflective thought (assimilation as such) and another moment corresponding to what is experience (accommodation as such). Every schema of assimilation is therefore forthwith a schema of accommodation; primitive assimilation, whether reproductive, generalizing or recognitory, only functions to the extent that it is accommodation growing toward reality. However, although differentiated and, in this sense, closely correlative, assimilation and accommodation are, in another sense, antagonistic at first. In effect, in the beginning the child only accommodates himself to things when he is in some way forced by them, whereas at the outset he tries to assimilate the real, impelled by an invincible and vital tendency. So it is that, during the first stages, he is only interested in the external environment to the extent that objects can serve as aliments to his schemata of assimilation. This is why the child's activity begins by being essentially conservative and only accepts novelties when they are imposed within a schema already constituted (as when, busy grasping the strings hanging from the hood of his bassinet, the child perceives that he thus shakes the hood).

But after the progress of assimilation, things change little by little. In effect, once assimilation has been organized through mobile schemata (we have seen how it protracted, by continuous differentiation, assimilation through simple schemata), the child reveals two important tendencies from the point of view which now occupies us. On the one hand, he becomes increasingly interested in the external result of acts, not only because this result is to be seen, heard, grasped, etc. (hence, because it is to be assimilated by means of "primary" schemata), but also because this result, imposed at first by the external environment, progressively differentiates the "secondary" schemata and thus concentrates on itself the subject's attention. Moreover, the child then tries to make all new objects enter into the schemata already acquired and this constant effort to assimilate leads him to discover the resistance of certain objects and the existence of certain properties irreducible to these schemata. It is then that accommodation assumes an interest in itself and that it becomes differentiated from assimilation, subsequently to become more and more complementary.

Accommodation to novelties acquires interest precisely by reason of the two tendencies which we have just called to mind. To begin with the second one, it is clear that to the extent that the child, seeking to assimilate new objects, will encounter resistance, he will become interested in the unforeseen properties which he will thus discover. This interest in novelty, therefore—however paradoxical this assertion may seem—results from assimilation itself. If the new object or phenomenon had no connection with the schemata of assimilation they would not be of interest and that is why, in fact, they rouse nothing in the child who is too young (even if he already knows how to grasp) except visual or auditory attention. Whereas, to the extent that they are almost assimilable, they rouse an interest and an attempt at accommodation still greater than if they were assimilable immediately. That is why, the more complex the system of the schemata of assimilation, the greater the interest in novelty in general. New events have the more opportunities of animating at least one particular schema according as the ensemble of the schemata formed is large. For instance, interest in changes of perspective and displacements of objects, throwing, rolling, etc., takes root in many secondary circular schemata (shaking, swinging, rubbing, etc.) to which the new schemata are analogous but not at all identical. In this first sense, the progress of assimilation brings with it that of accommodation. Accommodation becomes an end in itself, separate from assimilation but complementary. We have already stated something similar in connection with vision: The more objects the child sees the more new ones he wishes to see. But, in the latter case, accommodation only forms one entity with the generalizing extension of as assimilatory schema, whereas henceforth accommodation exists before every true assimilation, and this accommodation is simply set in motion by earlier assimilations without being directly derived from them.

With regard to interest in the external result of acts, characteristic of the secondary circular reactions, it is also sooner or later a source of accommodation for the sake of accommodation. In effect, as we shall emphasize in connection with the concept of object and of causality, the very progress of assimilatory utilization of material objects results in substantiating them. For example, a hanging object which one can shake, swing, strike and finally drop, becomes little by little an independent center of forces and ceases to be simply an element of a self-enclosed cycle circumscribed by the schema of assimilation. Now at the time when causality thus becomes objectified and the universe becomes stocked with the centers of forces, it is apparent that the child's effort will no longer only consist in making things enter into known schemata but also, in the case of thwarting of the immediate assimilation, in discovering which are the properties of these centers of forces. For example, in Observation 145, it can clearly be seen how the attempts to "cause rolling" engender attitudes of expectation, surprise, and almost of anxiety and great astonishment [as when the stick rolls at 1;4 (0)] which reveals the progressive spontaneity that the child concedes to things. This is not yet the place to speak of people, to whom the child naturally attributes a still greater spontaneity. In short, the objectification of causality is the source of experimentation. Here again, assimilation is protracted in accommodation and the latter becomes differentiated from the initial tendency which gave rise to it.

Thus can be explained how the growing complexity of assimilation brings with it the advent of an interest in novelty as such, that is to say, of an experimentation composed of accommodation henceforth differentiated. But must the assertion be made that this liberated accommodation will remain antagonistic to assimilation or that it will become more and more complementary? In studying the invention of new means through active experimentation we shall see how assimilation and accommodation are reconciled when there is a question of attaining a certain end. In such cases accommodation realizes what assimilation assigns as the goal of the action. But, from now on, when accommodation seems to remain in its pure state under the form of "experiment in order to see" it is possible to discern what close correlation it in fact maintains with assimilation.

The procedure of accommodation, in the case of the experiment in order to see, is that of groping. Now there is a number of distinct types of groping as we shall see when discussing Claparède's theory (see conclusions §4). Regarding the present case, let us limit ourselves to the following remark. Far from constituting pure groping which would furnish the prototype of accommodation without assimilation, the experiment in order to see consists in a sort of cumulative groping in the course of which each new attempt is directed by the preceding ones. So it is that when Jacqueline varies the perspectives of an object, throws or rolls what she holds in her hands, she doubtless experiments blindly at first, but directs increasingly her subsequent attempts; this is particularly apparent when she tilts up the box in Observation 146. Thereafter it can be maintained that, if the ensemble of the behavior pattern is due to a need for accommodation, the successive attempts are assimilated to each other as they occur. In this respect tertiary reaction is certainly a "circular" reaction despite the search for novelty which characterizes it. Thereafter, if there is differentiated accommodation, it immediately evokes assimilation.

In the last analysis, in order to contrast these behavior patterns with the earlier ones, it must simply be said that in the "experiment in order to see" accommodation becomes differentiated from assimilation while directing it at each moment, while in the secondary circular reactions and the behavior patterns which are derived from them, it is the attempt at assimilation which controls and precedes accommodation. Moreover, in the earlier cases, accommodation remains simultaneously undifferentiated from and partly antagonistic to assimilation, whereas henceforth accommodation begins to become complementary to the assimilatory tendency from which it dissociates itself.

Finally, let us recall, in order to avoid ambiguity, that, even while in a sense preceding assimilation, the accommodation peculiar to the "experiments in order to see" is always the accommodation of a schema, and that the act of accommodating an earlier schema of assimilation consists in differentiating it according to the variations of the actual experiment. There is never, in effect, a "pure experiment." Even when he gropes in order to discover something new, the child only perceives and conceives of the real as a function of his assimilatory schemata. Besides, groping when confronted by a new experiment is always only an accommodation—but henceforth one which is desired and sought for its own sake—of these earlier schemata. Varying the perspectives, dropping or throwing, rolling, floating, etc., is, at the point of departure, a simple differentiation of secondary schemata such as displacing, swinging, etc. While preceding and henceforth directing new assimilations, accommodation always prolongs earlier assimilations. We shall see this still more clearly in connection with the following behavior patterns.

§2. THE DISCOVERY OF NEW MEANS BY EXPERIMENTATION. I. THE "SUPPORTS," THE "STRING" AND THE "STICK."—The "discovery of new means through active experimentation" (an abstraction drawn from the speed of development) is to the tertiary circular reactions what the "application of familiar means to new situations" is to secondary circular reaction. The behavior patterns which we shall study thus constitute the highest forms of intellectual activity before the advent of systematic intelligence which implies deduction and representation. Furthermore, contrary to the acts of intelligence described in Observations 120 to 130, those acts which we shall now examine constitute inventions or at least real discoveries, already manifesting the constructive element peculiar to human intelligence. All the more reason, consequently, to examine these facts closely. Moreover, we shall analyze each of them separately, and shall ony group afterward the conclusions obtained.

The first manifestation of inventive intelligence which we observed in our children consisted in bringing distant objects closer by drawing to oneself the supports on which they were placed. We shall call this behavior pattern the "behavior pattern of the support" in contradistinction to that of the string or that of the stick. This kind of a behavior pattern, being at the same time the simplest of those of the fifth stage, will enable us from the outset, like all cases of transition, to understand the difference between the behavior patterns of the fourth stage and those of the present one.

In principle, nothing would prevent the "behavior pattern of the support" from arising during the fourth stage and, in fact, it sometimes appears sporadically during this period in the capacity of a simple coördination of schemata. But, as we shall see, its systematization requires more than such a coördination: It presupposes a special accommodation whose function we shall precisely try to understand. To do this, let us take as our point of departure the episodic situations in which the behavior pattern of the support is made manifest in the fourth stage. In such a case the child, trying to attain a too-distant objective, satisfies an ungratified need by applying the schema of "grasping" to the first object which appears and, when this object happens to be the support of the objective, he thus draws the latter to him. The schema of prehension of the objective is thus momentarily coördinated with the prehension of another object, just as, in Observation 121 repeated, the act of striking a doll attached to a string is coördinated with the schema of striking a parrot attached to the other end, or again, as in Observation 127, the action exerted upon the hand of another person is coördinated with that which the child wishes to apply to the objective itself. But, if such an episodic coördination can give rise to some fortuitous success when the support is particularly mobile, it could not insure the formation of a stable procedure, and this is why. In the examples cited of behavior patterns of the fourth stage, the connections established by the child between the objects in play are always on a par with the coördination of the schemata, given the apparent or real simplicity of these relationships. So it is that, in order to push back an obstacle or utilize someone else's hand as intermediary, etc., the child has no connections to understand except those which are given either in the familiar schemata envisaged separately (the hand of another, for instance, is assimilated to his own), or in the very fact of their coördination (the connection implied in the act of removing the obstacle presupposes nothing more than the comprehension of an incompatibility between the presence of this obstacle and the action which the child wishes to exert on the objective). To put it more simply, the coördination of the schemata peculiar to the fourth stage does not involve any invention or construction of new "means." On the contrary, the relation which exists between an object and its support is a relation unfamiliar to the child at the time that the behavior pattern which we are going to describe makes its appearance.[2] At least the thing took place in this way with our children and that is why we class this behavior pattern in the fifth stage: If the relation "placed upon" had already been known to them (which could doubtless happen with other subjects), the behavior pattern of the support would only have been a matter of coördination of schemata and we would have classed it in the fourth stage. This relation thus being new to the child he will only come to utilize it systematically (in contrast to the fortuitous and episodic successes which have been under study) by understanding it, and he

[2] The relation "placed upon" or relation between an object and its support could not, in effect, be discovered except through "tertiary circular reaction" (see Vol. II, Chap. II, §§3 and 4).

will understand it due only to active experimentation, analogous to that of "tertiary circular reaction." It is precisely in this respect that the behavior pattern which we are about to examine is new and differs from a simple coördination of schemata. But it rests upon that kind of coördination and it is even under the influence of this coördinating activity that the child applies himself to searching for new means by accommodating in the process of coördination to the unknown data of the problem.

In a general way, the "discovery of new means through active experimentation" involves, therefore, not only a coördination of familiar schemata (like the behavior patterns of the fourth stage that the present behavior thus protracts), but also a construction of new relations, obtained by a method similar to that of tertiary circular reaction.

Here are the facts:

Observation 148.—Until 0;10 (16) it can be said that Laurent has not understood the relation "placed upon," hence the relation existing between an object and its support. This is what we shall try to demonstrate at greater length in Volume II (Chap. II, Obs. 103) when studying the concept of space characteristic of the fourth stage.

I. With regard to the "behavior pattern of the support," numerous experiments repeated between 0;7 (29) and 0;10 (16) reveal that Laurent, until the latter date, has remained incapable of utilizing it systematically. At 0;7 (29) he has succeeded, once in four attempts, in drawing a cushion toward him in order to grasp a box placed upon it; at 0;8 (1) he behaves in the same way, as well as at 0;8 (7) etc. But there it is still only a question of a coördination of schemata, analogous to that of the fourth stage. Being unable to grasp the box directly, the child instead takes possession of the first object encountered, while subordinating this act to the persistent desire to attain the objective. The proof that this is the case is the existence of the following reactions: (1) When the support (the cushion, for example) is not within immediate reach of the child's hand (when it is 15 or 20 cm. away), Laurent does not try to reach it in order to draw the objective toward him, but tries to grasp the objective directly, and subsequently grasps the objects situated on this side of the support (for instance he pulls his covers or his sheets). (2) When I hold the objective in the air, 20 cm. above the support, Laurent pulls the latter toward him, as though the object were placed upon it. (3) When the support is placed obliquely, thus being at the child's disposition, not exactly in front of him but a little to the side (20 cm. from his waist), Laurent does nothing to reach it, trying to grasp the objective directly or, failing this, the objects interposed between himself and the objective (the sheets, for example). For more details on these preliminaries, see Volume II, Observation 103.

II. At 0;10 (16) on the other hand, Laurent discovers the true relations between the support and the objective and consequently the possibility of utilizing the first to draw the second to him. Here are the child's reactions:

(1) I place my watch on a big red cushion (of a uniform color and without a fringe) and place the cushion directly in front of the child. Laurent tries to reach the watch directly and not succeeding, he grabs the cushion which he draws toward him as before. But then, instead of letting go of the support at once, as he has hitherto done, in order to try again to grasp the objective, he recommences with obvious interest, to move the cushion while looking at the watch. Everything takes place as though he noticed for the first time the relationship for its own sake and studied it as such. He thus easily succeeds in grasping the watch.

(2) I then immediately attempt the following counterproof. I put two colored cushions in front of the child, of identical form and dimensions. The first is placed as before, directly in front of the child. The second is placed behind, at an angle of 45°, that is to say, so that a corner of the cushion is opposite the child. This corner is placed on the first cushion but I manage to flatten the two cushions at this place, where one is partially superposed on the other, so that the second does not protrude and is not too visible. Finally I place my watch at the other extreme end of the second cushion.

Laurent, as soon as he sees the watch, stretches out his hands, then grasps the first cushion which he pulls toward him by degrees. Then, observing that the watch does not move (he does not stop looking at it), he examines the place where the one cushion is superposed on the other (this is still the case despite the slight displacement of the first one), and he goes straight to the second one. He grasps it by the corner, pulls it toward him over the first cushion, and takes the watch.

The experiment, when repeated, yields the same result the second time.

(3) I now place the two cushions next to each other, the proximal side of the second parallel to the distal side of the first. But I superpose the first on the second on a strip about 20 cm. wide (the watch of course being at the extremity of the second cushion). Laurent immediately pulls the first cushion but, observing that the watch is not displaced, he tries to raise this cushion to reach the second one. At a certain moment he has succeeded in raising up the first cushion, but without removing it, and he holds it against his chest with his left hand while trying to pull the second one with his right hand. He finally succeeds and takes

possession of the watch, thus revealing his perfect comprehension of the role of the support.

(4) Finally I place the second cushion as in (2) but sideways, the proximal corner of the second superposed on one of the distal corners of the first. Laurent does not make a mistake and at once tries to reach the second cushion.

These four reactions combined reveal that the relation between the objective and its support has been acquired.

Observation 148 repeated.—During the weeks that follow, Laurent rediscovers the same schema every time there is a question of drawing an object toward himself, and displaces the support following a rectilinear trajectory. On the other hand, the supports necessitating a rotary movement give rise to a new apprenticeship.

In Observation 143 it has been shown how Laurent, at 1;1 (24) had unsuccessfully tried to pull toward him one of the circular tiers of a table. The tier pivoting around an axis then began to turn slightly, instead of coming nearer. In order to strengthen the child's interest I immediately placed an interesting toy beyond his reach. The "experiment in order to see" was thus transformed into an effort entering the present group of behavior patterns.

At first Laurent looks at the toy without moving but never tries to reach it directly. Then he grasps the tier of the table and tries to draw it toward him in a straight line. The tier again turns by chance (a few degrees only). Laurent lets it go again, then recommences, and so on a certain number of times. That is only a series of attempts without being linked to each other which the child apparently considers failures. But he suddenly seems to perceive that the desired object comes closer. He again grasps the tier, lets it go and grasps it again until he has attained success. But the child's behavior does not yet give the impression that he has understood the role of rotation; he simply repeats a movement which was once efficacious, without turning the tier intentionally.

At 1;2 (6) Laurent is again confronted by the tier of the table and looks at a pebble which I place at the opposite extremity. He immediately tries to pull the tier toward him in a straight line, but only succeeds in making it turn on itself a few degrees. He then grasps it in the same way a certain number of times until he is able to reach the pebble. However one does not always have the impression that the child is turning the tier intentionally.

At 1;2 (7) on the other hand, Laurent only tries to pull the table once; he then definitely pivots the tier. From 1;2 (10) he tries at the outset to move the tier circularly in order to get hold of the objects out of reach. The schema appropriate to the situation accordingly is definitely acquired.

Observation 149.—As early as 0;9 (3), Jacqueline discovers by chance the possibility of bringing a toy to herself by pulling the coverlet on which it is placed. She is seated on this coverlet and holds out her hand to grasp her celluloid duck. After several failures she grasps the coverlet abruptly, which shakes the duck; seeing that she immediately grasps the coverlet again and pulls it until she can attain the objective directly.— Two interpretations are possible. Either she perceives the duck and the coverlet as a solidified whole (like a single object or a complex of connected objects) or else she simply satisfies her need to grasp the duck by grasping no matter what and so discovering by chance the possible role of the coverlet.

Until 0;11 Jacqueline has not again revealed analogous behavior. At 0;11 (7), on the other hand, she is lying on her stomach on another coverlet and again tries to grasp her duck. In the course of the movements she makes to catch the object she accidentally moves the coverlet which shakes the duck. She immediately understands the connection and pulls the coverlet until she is able to grasp the duck.

During the weeks that follow Jacqueline frequently utilizes the schema thus acquired but too rapidly to enable me to analyze her behavior. At 1;0 (19) on the other hand, I seat her on a shawl and place a series of objects a meter away from her. Each time she tries to reach them directly and each time she subsequently grasps the shawl in order to draw the toy toward herself. The behavior pattern has consequently become systematic; but it seems that it does not yet involve conscious foresight of the relationships since Jacqueline only utilizes this schema after having attempted direct prehension of the object.

Observation 150.—In the case of Lucienne, the same behavior pattern appeared at 0;10 (27). Seated on her bed Lucienne tried to grasp a distant toy when, having by chance moved the folded sheet she saw the object sway slightly. She at once grasped the sheet, noticed the object shake again and pulled the whole thing toward her. But as this reaction was too rapid to be properly analyzed, I devise the following:

At 1;0 (5) Lucienne is seated on her folding chair and in front of her a small tier A erected on the tier B of the table attached to the chair. The tier A only covers part of tier B. I spread a handkerchief on tier B in such a way that the frontal edge of the handkerchief is under tier A and cannot be grasped directly. Then I place a small bottle on the handkerchief. Lucienne then grasps the handkerchief at once, without any hesitation, and draws the bottle to her. The same occurs five or six times whether I place the bottle or my watch on the handkerchief. But the reaction again being so rapid, it is not even possible to know whether Lucienne has tried to grasp the object or whether the handkerchief itself attracted her. I repeat the experiment, but in the following way:

I place a handkerchief in the same way as before but instead of putting the object upon it I place it next to it, about 5 cm. away from the left edge of the handkerchief, also on tier B. Lucienne at once pulls the handkerchief, then tries to reach the bottle. Not succeeding, she then searches for the handkerchief, holds it for one or two seconds and then rejects it. Same reactions to my watch during a second attempt but she rejects the handkerchief still more quickly after having sought it.

I now increase the distance between the object and the handkerchief. I place the bottle 10–15 cm. to the side of the handkerchief. Lucienne then limits herself to trying to reach the object directly and no longer bothers with the handkerchief. When I bring the object nearer she looks alternately at the bottle and the handkerchief and finally, when I place the bottle on the handkerchief, she at once grasps the latter. It therefore seems that she has grasped its signification.—I repeat the experiment, again gradating the distances from 15 cm. to direct contact: same reactions.

This time I place my watch 15–20 cm. away from the handkerchief: Lucienne tries to grasp it directly. Then I stretch the chain between the watch and the handkerchief, leaving the watch at a distance of 15 cm. and putting the end of the chain on the handkerchief: Lucienne, who at first did not notice what I was doing, begins by trying to reach the handkerchief, then perceives the chain and then pulls the handkerchief![3] This last behavior pattern well shows that the prehension of the handkerchief is not a mechanical act.

Observation 150 repeated.—The same day, seeing a green bottle which is inaccessible but placed on a cover which is within reach, she at once pulls the cover in order to grasp the bottle (see Obs. 157).

Observation 151.—At 1;0 (16) Lucienne is seated before a big square cushion C, placed on the ground. Beyond cushion C is a second identical cushion D, so that Lucienne has two cushions facing her. I place my watch on D, the farthest from the child. Lucienne looks at the watch but does not try to grasp it directly. She takes cushion C and removes it at once, then pulls cushion D toward her and takes the watch.

At 1;1 (4) Lucienne is seated on an adult's bed in front of a cleaning rag placed on the sheet. As soon as I put my eyeglasses on the rag, Lucienne pulls it. When I place my glasses beyond the rag, she removes it at once and pulls the sheet toward her.

Observation 152.—At 1;0 (5), that is to say, right after the attempts described in Observation 150, Lucienne is confronted with a solid support and no longer a soft one (such as coverlets, shawls, or handkerchiefs. On tier B of her table I place a box with upturned edges (the cover of a large box, turned upside down), in such a way that the

---

[3] It is necessary to know that since 1;0 (3) Lucienne knows how to use the chain to draw the watch to her.

frontal side of the box is wedged under tier A and I place on the box, as far away as possible, the bottle or the watch which were used with the handkerchief (Obs. 150). I was thus able to observe seven sequential reactions:

(1) Lucienne at first tries to grasp the box, but she goes about it as though the handkerchief were still involved. She tries to pinch it between two fingers, in the center, and tries this for a moment without being able to grasp it. Then, with a rapid and unhesitating movement she pushes it at a point on its right edge (apparently Lucienne, unable to grasp it at the center, tried to roll it up or unstick it or simply to displace it slightly, and that is why she pushed it to the edge). She then notes the sliding of the box and makes it pivot without trying to lift it; as the box revolves, she succeeds in grasping the bottle.

(2) This time I place the watch at the extremity of the box. Lucienne again tries to grasp the box in the middle. Being unsuccessful, she gives up more quickly than in (1) and displaces the box by pushing it on the right edge.

(3) She no longer tries to grasp it at the center and immediately makes the support pivot.

(4) I place a new doll on the box in order to revive her interest: Lucienne again tries at first to make the box pivot. But not having brought it sufficiently near to her, she cannot grasp the object. She then returns to the right edge and pushes it more.

(5) Same play, with corrections at the center.

(6) She tries, doubtless for the sake of greater speed, to raise the box right away by grasping it in the same place as before, but by pulling it toward her instead of sliding it. Failing in this (the box is held by tier A), she gives up and resumes the pivoting.

(7) Same reactions, but Lucienne resumes the pivoting more promptly.

At 1;0 (11), that is to say, six days later, I repeat the same experiment with another box without edges (a simple box and no longer a cover). I also wedge this under tier A, and place different objects on the farthest extremity from Lucienne. She then manifests three sequential reactions:

In the first place, she tries to pinch the box in the center, as though it were a piece of material.

In the second place, she tries to lift the box by the right edge and so to draw it directly to her. This second attempt lasts several minutes because she always thinks she is near success.

In the third place, she finally returns to sliding. By gently pushing the right edge of the box, she makes it slide over tier B with the part wedged under tier A as center of the pivoting, and so succeeds in grasping the objects. In the subsequent attempts she adopts this last method right away.

The first examples show us at once in what the behavior pattern which we call "discovery of new means through active experimentation" consists. The whole situation is exactly the same as with respect to Observations 120 to 130, that is to say, the "application of familiar means to new circumstances": The child tries to attain a goal but obstacles (distance, etc.) prevent him. The situation is therefore "new" and the problem is to discover appropriate means. But,' reversely from the behavior patterns mentioned (Obs. 120–130), no familiar method presents itself to the child any more. It is therefore a question of innovating. It is then that a behavior pattern intervenes which is analogous to that of the tertiary circular reactions, that is to say, an "experiment in order to see": the child gropes. The only difference is that, now, the groping is oriented as a function of the goal itself, that is to say, of the problem presented (of the need anterior to the act) instead of taking place simply "in order to see."

In the particular case, and without yet wishing to discuss the ensemble of the general problems raised by these observations, it is apparent that the groping leading to the discovery of new means presupposes an accommodation of familiar schemata to the present experiment. The accommodation as such is groping, but only the earlier schemata give meaning to what this groping discovers. When, for instance, Jacqueline, unable to catch her duck, grasps the coverlet instead and sees the duck shake, she would not understand this phenomenon at all if she were not accustomed to seeing objects move when a string is pulled (secondary schemata). But, knowing that intermediates can make it possible to act upon objects which cannot be directly grasped, she at once perceives a connection between the coverlet and the duck: impelled by the need to grasp the latter, she then haphazardly pulls the support and success ensues. In such a behavior pattern, then, there exists on the one hand a groping directed by the schema of the goal (to grasp the duck) and on the other hand an ensemble of significations attributed to intermediate events as a function of the earlier schemata and as a function of this very goal.

So also, when Lucienne tries to grasp an object on a box (Obs. 152) and discovers the possibility of making the box pivot, it is certainly due to groping that the child comes to push the box by its edge, but the groping is double directed. It is directed at first by the schema assigning an end to the action. Wanting to draw to herself the object placed on the box and treating this like the handkerchief to which she is accustomed, Lucienne tries to grasp the box. Not succeeding immediately, she gropes, that is to say, tries to accommodate the schema to the present situation. It is then that she goes so far as to touch the edge of the box. In the second place, the groping is directed by the earlier schemata which give a meaning to the events arising by chance and again as a function of the goal of the action. Having touched the edge of the box, Lucienne sees it move and at once assimilates it to an object which can be displaced; she then pushes it in order to grasp the desired object.

Such is the nature of groping: As in the case of the tertiary circular reactions, it is an accommodation of earlier schemata which become differentiated as a function of the present experiment. But, in the particular case, accommodation, instead of being an end in itself, is only a means at the service of the pursuit of the goal.

Furthermore, groping, in which this accommodation consists, is cumulative, that is to say, each successive attempt constitutes a schema of assimilation with regard to the following attempts. When Lucienne discovered that it was necessary to push the box in order to draw the object to her, this means is rediscovered more rapidly each time in the course of the subsequent attempts. In this there is apprenticeship. Accommodation is therefore directed not only from the exterior (by earlier schemata), but also from within (due to this apprenticeship): It is therefore dually united to assimilation.

A second example of "discovery of new means through active experimentation" is the "behavior pattern of the string," which was so well studied by Karl Bühler: drawing an object to oneself by using its extension string, chain), etc.[4]

4 Ch. Bühler and H. Hetzer (Kleinkindertests, in *Testing Children's Development from Birth to School Age,* translated by H. Beaumont, London, G. Allen & Unwin, 1935) believe this behavior pattern appears during the eleventh and twelfth months.

Observation 153.—It has been shown, in Observations 121 and 121 repeated, how Jacqueline made use of the strings hanging from the hood of her bassinet in order to pull desired objects to her. But it is not yet possible to compare these efforts to the behavior pattern which consists in pulling an object by means of a string. In the latter case the string is, in effect, considered as being the extension of the object, whereas in the first case the object is simply assimilated to the objects which can be swung by means of a string.

The true behavior pattern of the string began in Jacqueline's case at 0;11 (7). She was playing with a brush when, before her eyes, I attached this object to a string. Afterward I placed the bruᶜʰ at the foot of the armchair on which Jacqueline was seated, so that she was no longer able to see it (but the child could follow all my movements) and I left the end of the string on the arm of the chair. As soon as my preparations were finished, Jacqueline leaned toward the brush while stretching forth her hands. But not observing anything other than the string, she grasps it and pulls. The end of the brush then appears; Jacqueline at once drops the string in order to try to grasp the object directly. Of course the brush falls again, Jacqueline bends to look for it, rediscovers the string, pulls it again and lets it go once more when she perceives the desired object. The same series of operations ensues three or four times; each series ends in failure because Jacqueline lets go of the string as soon as she perceives the brush. However, when Jacqueline pulls the string she definitely looks in the direction of the brush and so expects to see it.

It is accurate to add that the child is still unaware of the role of gravity (see Obs. 144) and so, when he lets go of the string to grasp the brush he acts as though both were on a horizontal plane. The only real accommodation to the situation has been this: At a certain moment Jacqueline pulled the string with one hand when she perceived a very obvious knot not far from the brush (10–15 cm. away). The fraction of string between the knot and the brush appeared to her to constitute the extension of the brush. In effect, while she was still trying to pull the end of the string with her right hand, she tried to catch the knot with her left hand. As soon as the knot was grasped it served to pull the brush.

During the subsequent series of efforts the behavior pattern seems to have been acquired. I detach the brush and replace it, before Jacqueline's eyes, with a parrot; then I place this at the foot of the armchair and leave the other end of the string next to the child. Jacqueline grasps the string and, hearing the sound of the rattle inside the parrot, immediately pulls while looking beforehand at the place where the latter must appear. When she sees the toy she tries to grasp it with one hand while still pulling the string with the other. During the subsequent attempts, same reactions and same success.

Third series: I replace the parrot with a book. Jacqueline pulls the string while staring at the place where the object will appear. As soon as she sees it she manages to grasp it. Same reactions with a clothespin and a safety pin.

Observation 154.—At 1;0 (7) Jacqueline is seated in her bassinet whose handle is supported by a table facing the child. I show Jacqueline her swan whose neck has a string attached to it, then I put the swan on a table while leaving the string in the bassinet. Jacqueline grasps it immediately and pulls it while looking at the swan. But as the string is long she does not stretch it out but is limited to waving it. Each shake of the string makes the swan move but it comes no nearer.

After many attempts of the same kind I move the swan farther away which results in stretching the string. Jacqueline still shakes it, without really pulling it. The swan falls; Jacqueline holds onto the string, pulls it, but as the swan does not come at once, she resumes shaking the string.

New attempt: Jacqueline shakes harder and harder which results in making the swan move forward a little. But she tires of this and gives up.

At 1;0 (8), the next day, I resume the experiment. At first Jacqueline shakes the string, then pulls it. When the swan is near enough she tries to reach it directly with her hand. When she does not succeed she gives up instead of resuming pulling. The following days, same reactions, but it seems that she shakes the string less each time and pulls it more.

Finally, at 1;0 (19) Jacqueline draws the object to her correctly by pulling the string but she never does it without shaking it beforehand as though that were necessary. Only ten days later does she pull it right away.

Observation 155.—At 1;0 (26) in Jacqueline's presence I place my watch on the floor, beyond her field of prehension. I put the chain in a straight line in Jacqueline's direction but place a cushion on the part which is nearest the child. Jacqueline at first tries to grasp the watch directly. Not succeeding, she looks at the chain. She notes that the latter is under the cushion. Then Jacqueline removes the latter at one stroke and pulls the chain while looking at the watch. The movement is adapted and quick. As soon as the watch is within reach, Jacqueline lets go of the chain in order to grasp the object directly. There is, consequently, no interest in the chain itself; it is the watch that is wanted.

Same reaction several times in succession in a variety of conditions.

In the same way, Lucienne, at 1;0 (3) and the days following, looks at the watch as soon as she perceives the chain around her mother's neck. When she finds a necklace she confines herself to grasping it, whereas sight of the chain always sets in motion search for the watch and the action of pulling.

Observation 156.—In a single day Laurent acquired the "behavior pattern of the string" but he only succeeded in this through "active experimentation" and not through immediate comprehension or mental construction.

It is noteworthy that until 0;11 despite his earlier utilizations of hanging strings I was not able to cause Laurent to reveal the existence of any tendency to make use of extensions of the objective in the capacity of intermediates or of "strings." Thus at 0;8 (1) after having played with my detached watch chain he does not have the idea of using it to draw to him the watch he wants once the chain is again attached. He stretches out his hand toward the watch only and neglects the chain which I place between him and the watch. Various analogous attempts either with the same chain or with strings attached to several objects yielded nothing until 0;10.

On the other hand, at 0;11 (16) Laurent manifests the following behavior pattern: He is seated on a dark rug. I show him a red object (a shoehorn) hanging from a string, then I place this objective about a meter from him while making the string describe a winding trajectory culminating next to the child. But Laurent, instead of using the string to attain the objective, confines himself to stretching out his hands toward it. I displace the string several times to draw Laurent's attention to it but each time avoid stretching it out in a straight line between the child and the objective. Each time Laurent looks at the string but without utilizing it, again trying to grasp the object directly.

Then I stretch the string in a straight line but making it end next to Laurent and not yet in front of him. He nevertheless reacts as before; that is to say, he still does not pay attention to the string and tries to reach the objective directly (it must be said that I displace the latter slightly, at each new attempt, in such a way as to revive the child's interest).

Finally I give the string once more a sinuous shape but this time making it end in front of Laurent. Laurent, after trying twice to grasp the objective directly, takes possession of the string. He does not try to stretch it but confines himself to looking at it while shaking it slightly. He therefore took it simply for its own sake because of having been unable to reach the shoehorn he wanted; he does not yet understand at all the relations which exist between the two. But, in shaking the string he perceives that the shoehorn moves. He shakes the string more and more vigorously while attentively observing the movements of the shoehorn.

This last behavior pattern still does not differ in any way from the secondary circular reactions such as those in Observations 94–104:

pulling a string in order to shake the bassinet hood, etc., when the child has just discovered by chance the effect thus produced. But, having discovered the possibility of acting upon the shoehorn by means of the string, Laurent returns to his initial desire, which is to attain the object. Instead of shaking the shoehorn in every direction, he then seems to pull the string intentionally and thus gradually brings the objective nearer to him. Once he has grasped it, I repeat the experiment several times in succession. Every time Laurent at first grasps the string, shakes it a moment and then pulls it more or less systematically.

But this last behavior pattern does not, it seems to us, yet constitute an authentic example of "behavior pattern of the string." In effect, while already attaining his ends, Laurent still believes himself to be obliged, before pulling the string, to shake it for a moment, and he contrives all the transitions between the act of shaking and that of pulling. In other words, he utilizes an already acquired schema toward a new end. The action thus carried out therefore still remains at the level of the actions of the fourth stage, that is to say, the stage of the coördination of schemata. At 0;6 (1) Laurent has already revealed a very similar behavior pattern (Obs. 120).

How does the child transcend this stage of simple coördination of schemata to arrive at the discovery of the role of the string? During subsequent attempts, I make the string describe an increasingly winding trajectory so that Laurent, in shaking one end of it, does not at first succeed in moving the shoehorn. He nevertheless still tries, once or twice, to shake the string. But each time he applies himself more promptly to pulling it. It is difficult to describe in detail, without the aid of a film, how the movement of traction is learned. But, in the main, one can say that there was groping by progressive correction; the child eliminates from his earlier schemata the movements consisting of shaking and develops those which result in pulling. Very rapidly, despite the complications I introduce into the experiment, Laurent succeeds in finding the best procedure. He pulls the string with each hand alternately and so attains the objective with only a few movements.

Observation 156 repeated.—An hour later I put Laurent on a sofa and place the same red shoehorn on a chair, facing him. The string to which this objective is attached hangs from the chair onto the floor, then goes up the sofa next to the child. He looks at the objective for a moment, then his eyes follow the string, he grasps it and pulls it first with one hand, then with the other. When the shoehorn disappears from his visual field he nevertheless continues his maneuver until he has been completely successful.

I then present several objects to him (books, toys, etc.) but out of reach and attached to ribbons, cords, etc. (different from the string hitherto involved). Moreover, I vary the trajectories of these intermediates in such a way as to avoid any visual suggestion. Laurent succeeds, however, in all these attempts with almost no groping; the "schema of the string" has therefore been acquired.

The following days I regulate the thing with several new objects. Laurent immediately uses both hands to draw them to him by means of the cords to which they are attached. At first he looks at the objective, then seeks the proper intermediate.

Let us resume, in connection with this "behavior pattern of the string," the discussion of "supports." The child's behavior, which once more consists in finding a procedure to draw distant objects to him is constituted here also by a groping accommodation doubly directed by the schemata of assimilation. It is important to determine exactly the role of this accommodation and that of assimilation. It is the problem of the relations between experience and intellectual activity of which we shall find a particular aspect once more.

Accommodation is necessarily the adjustment of earlier, already constituted schemata to new circumstances. It is in this sense, at first, that it is directed by assimilation. It is directed by the schema assigning an end to the present action as well as by certain schemata serving here as means and which accommodation will differentiate. Confronted by a brush attached to a string, for example, Jacqueline wishes to grasp this brush and, to do so, utilizes once more the schema of objects hanging from the hood and from which hangs a string. We recall, in effect, that she has already made use of these strings to grasp objects attached to them (Obs. 121 repeated). Hence she pulls the string in order to attain the brush. But, in acting thus, Jacqueline still only considers the string as being a magic-phenomenalistic procedure and not at all an extension of the object [see Obs. 153, at 0;11 (7)].

In effect, when she sees the brush appear, she forgets about the string, tries to grasp the object directly and fails. It is then that actual accommodation and groping begin. The experiment shows the child that his earlier schema is not adequate and Jacqueline finds herself obliged to find the true relations joining the string to the object attached. The same applies exactly to Observation 154: Jacqueline shakes the string as though a string hanging from the hood were involved, then, observing her failure, she must accommodate herself to the new situation.

How does this accommodation work? Through tertiary circular reaction. In Observation 153, Jacqueline tries new combinations; at first she grasps the string at a visible knot and so succeeds in catching the brush, or else she pulls the string more and more until she is able to attain the parrot and hand it over. In Observation 154 she shakes the string less and less and stretches it more and more, etc. Hence there is experimentation and utilization of this experimentation. But how can this dual capacity be explained?

As far as accommodation in the capacity of experimental contact with the given reality is concerned, there is nothing to explain if not that in searching, the child hits upon facts. This happens by chance and the facts obtrude to the extent that they refute the expectation due to earlier schemata. All that we have said regarding interest in novelty in connection with tertiary circular reaction easily applies here. Lying in wait for the new experience, the child encounters it to the extent that he no longer tries to force reality to enter into his earlier schemata.

With regard to what is, on the other hand, utilization of the experience, groping accommodation must once again be directed by assimilation, but in a second sense. This time it is directed by the schemata capable of supplying a meaning to the events arising by chance, these schemata being themselves subordinated to the schema which assigns an end to the ensemble of the action. The events which arise in the course of the experiment could not be apprehended by the subject's consciousness except as a function of the earlier schemata of assimilation. For example, when Jacqueline discovers that by pulling and stretching the string she draws to her the object attached to it, she necessarily assimilates this fact, however new to her, to familiar schemata. She "understands" that the string is a "means for bringing," that is to say, she classes it among the other "means for bringing" such as the "supports," etc. The vicissitudes of searching, therefore, only acquire meaning as functions of the schema of the goal pursued and of the schemata which were earlier in relationship with this precise goal.

In short, accommodation is directed by two kinds of assimilation: by the "initial" schemata (the schema of the end and those of the means) which it is precisely a question of adjusting to the new situation, and by the schemata evoked on the way (let us call them "auxiliary" schemata) which give meaning to the products of experience or accommodation, and that again as function of the goal of the action. But then, do these products of accommodation present no new aspect to the child's eyes? In other words, by dint of being interpreted, does the new experiment seem from the outset as though it were already familiar? There is of course nothing to this, precisely since accommodation upsets and differentiates all the schemata which direct it, as we have noted in connection with tertiary circular reaction.

How should this acquisition be regarded? Here apprenticeship intervenes, that is to say, the cumulative element of groping. While being directed or oriented by the earlier schemata of assimilation, accommodation (hence experience) makes them flexible, differentiates them and so precedes, this time directing a new attempt at assimilation. This assimilation, interior or immanent in successive acts of accommodation, is the apprenticeship: Each attempt constitutes a mold for the next one, hence the embryo of an assimilatory schema. So it is that after having learned to pull the string by stretching it, Jacqueline pulls it better and better. The three series of Observation 153 and the successive series of attempts described in Observation 154 demonstrate this progress very well.

Now it is not a play upon words again to speak of assimilation to characterize this progress immanent in accommodation. Apprenticeship is nothing else but a circular reaction proceeding by reproductive, recognitory and generalizing assimilations. As we have seen at the beginning of this chapter, it is only because the complexity of the schemata of assimilation henceforth permits intentional searching for novelty for its own sake, that circular reaction is "tertiary," that is to say, oriented toward accommodation as such.

In short, one understands how extremely complicated is that which associational empiricism considered a primary factor: the contact with experience. The contact, that is to say, the accommodation, is always inserted between two (or even three) series of assimilatory schemata which frame it: the schemata (initial or auxiliary) which give direction to accommodation and those which register its results by thus letting themselves be directed by it.

Let us note, finally, that once the new schema is acquired, that is to say, once the apprenticeship is finished, this schema is applied from the outset to analogous situations. Thus it is that in Observation 155 the "behavior pattern of the string" is without any difficulty applied to the watch chain. Thus at each acquisition we fall back on the application of "familiar means to new situations" according to a rhythm which will extend to the beginning of systematic intelligence (Chap. VI).

A third "discovery of new means through active experimentation" will permit us to make this analysis still more precise. This is the "behavior pattern of the stick." The string is not an instrument; it is the extension of the object. On the contrary, the "stick" is an instrument. How is the command of this first tool acquired? Possibly this occurs by a sudden mental construction when the child only discovers the stick late, at the level of systematic intelligence (see Chap. VI, §1). Or else it might occur by means of groping and active experimentation. Lucienne and Jacqueline have furnished us with the example of the latter procedure, Lucienne by acting in an entirely spontaneous way, Jacqueline aided by imitation. We shall emphasize here the case of Lucienne, that of Jacqueline merely serving as supplementary means of analysis:[5]

Observation 157.—At 1;0 (5) Lucienne already possesses the "behavior pattern of the support," as has been seen in Observations 150 and 152. I try to determine, the same day, if she is capable of that of the stick. One will see that she is not.

The child is playing with a very elongated cover which can fulfill a stick's function; with it she hits the tiers of her table, the arms of her chair, etc. Then I place before her, out of reach, a small green bottle for which she immediately has a strong desire. She tries to grasp it with outstretched hands, struggles vigorously, wails, but does not have the idea of using the cover as a stick. I then place the cover between

5 According to Ch. Bühler and H. Hetzer (*op. cit.*, p. 63) the behavior pattern of the stick normally appears during the second half of the second year.

her and the bottle: same lack of comprehension. Then I place the bottle at the end of the cover: Lucienne pulls the cover to her and grasps the bottle as we have observed in Observation 150 repeated. Then I again put the bottle out of reach, but this time I place the cover next to the object and at the child's disposal; nevertheless it does not occur to Lucienne to use it as a stick.

At 1;2 (7), on the other hand, Lucienne happens to make a notable discovery: While playing at hitting a pail with a stick she is holding (all this without preliminary goals) she sees the pail move at each blow and then tries to displace the object. She strikes it more or less obliquely to augment the movement and does this many times; but she does not utilize this finding to bring the pail nearer to her nor to move it in a certain direction.

Observation 158.—At 1;4 (0) Lucienne is seated opposite a sofa on which is placed a small aluminum flask. Next to it lies the same stick as before with which she amused herself of recent weeks, using it to hit objects and the floor, but without progress since 1;2 (7). At first, she tries to grasp the flask directly, with her right hand. Not succeeding, she takes the stick. This behavior constitutes an important novelty: The stick is no longer only utilized when it is already in hand, it is sought for its own sake. Moreover, having grasped it by the middle and observing, after trying it out, that it is not long enough, Lucienne switches it to her other hand, then takes it again in her right hand, this time by the end. But the rest of the observation shows that the stick is not yet grasped with the purpose of pushing the flask; Lucienne merely hits the object and this does not authorize us to envisage that as prevision of its falling. The flask, however, falls and Lucienne picks it up. It is clear that the desire to attain the flask aroused the schema of striking by means of a stick, but one cannot therefore see in this behavior pattern a procedure already adapted to the particulars of the situation.

A moment later, on the other hand, I place the flask on the floor, 50 cm. away from Lucienne. She begins by wanting to grasp it directly, then she takes the stick and hits it. The flask moves a little. Then Lucienne, most attentively, pushes it from left to right, by means of the stick. The flask is thus brought nearer. Lucienne again tries to grasp it directly, then takes the stick again, pushes it once more, this time from right to left, always bringing the object towards her. Delighted, she grasps it, and succeeds in all the subsequent attempts.

Observation 159.—It has been seen before (Obs. 139) how Jacqueline, at around 8 months, made objects swing by "derived circular reaction." In her case this behavior fortuitously prepared the behavior pattern of the stick. At 1;0 (13) Jacqueline holds an elongated rattle when she perceives the tail of a leather donkey which hangs in front of her. She immediately tries to make it swing. But, having the rattle in her hand, it is not her hand but the rattle which she directs toward the donkey. She thus shakes its tail and repeats the experiment many times. One cannot yet speak of the behavior pattern of the stick in this connection. The rattle has not been grasped in order to act upon the object but was used by chance in the capacity of a chance extension of the hand. As this behavior did not recur during the following days, I tried to reconstruct an analogous situation, making use of imitation, not in order to study the latter but in order better to analyze the mechanism of the acquisition. At 1;0 (28) Jacqueline tries to attain a cork placed before her at eye level but out of reach. In her right hand she holds a stick but does not use it and tries to grasp the cork directly with her left hand. I then take the stick and make the cork fall and Jacqueline at once grasps it. Then I put the cork back in place and return the stick. Jacqueline, who has watched me most attentively, at once repeats my movement with precision. She directs the stick toward the cork and makes it fall.

At this point of the experiment two explanatory hypotheses present themselves to us and it is in order to decide between them that we forced things by causing the factor of imitation to intervene: either when imitation set in motion a sort of already prepared "structure," the child would henceforth apply the latter without any groping, or else when imitation limited itself to setting an example, the child would subsequently grope to rediscover it, in the way in which Lucienne groped when confronted only by objects. The rest of the observation shows that this second solution is the right one.

I put the cork on the edge of the bassinet. The stick is placed next to the child. Jacqueline stretches her arms toward the cork, groans with disappointment and ends almost by crying, but always without thinking of grasping the stick. I show it to her, raising it and resting it in front of her, before her eyes, but she does not take it and continues to try to grasp the cork directly.

New attempt: I offer her the stick; she grasps it and immediately directs it toward the cork which she causes to fall and grasps. The fact that she has the stick in her hand makes her reproduce, by circular reaction, the movement imitated before, but the capacity to perform this movement does not suffice to enable the child to rediscover it and utilize it when he does not hold the stick and he sees it lying before him.

During the three following attempts the same result ensues. Jacqueline continues to wish to attain the cork directly and only uses the stick when I offer it to her. I then interrupt the experiment for a moment.

On resuming it she reveals progress. Jacqueline again tries to grasp the object, she still does not look for the stick which is, however, in front of her within reach and in her visual field, but when I point to it with my finger, she grasps and uses it. Same reaction five times in succession.

A final series: She still tries to reach the cork with her hand (although the cork remains in the same place) but, after a moment's wailing, seeks the stick by herself, in order to use it immediately.

It is noteworthy that, during these attempts, Jacqueline has revealed a sustained interest, that she constantly wailed or even cried in the event of failure (when her hand did not attain the cork) and that each time her expression changed and her lamentations ceased when she understood the role of the stick; in the beginning, when I put it in her hand, then when I pointed to it with my finger and finally when she recalled its use by looking at it. Thus it may be seen that the dynamic schema outlined by the initial imitation only incorporated optical factors little by little, that is to say, it was slow to confer a signification to the visual spectacle of the stick.

Observation 160.—The next day, at 1;0 (29) I present the same cork to Jacqueline, at the same place and putting the stick in front of her, without hesitation she grasps the latter and directs it toward the cork. But she observes while doing this that the stick is too short (she grasped it three quarters of the way down). She transfers it to her other hand by grasping its end. Still without hesitation, she holds it out toward the cork and grasps it and it falls within reach.

After playing with the cork for a moment, I take it back from her and again place it out of reach of her hands. Jacqueline at once looks for it on the floor (she is seated), but, instead of grasping the stick which she sees, she takes her picture book (made of cloth) and directs it toward the cork. The book folds and does not reach the goal. Jacqueline wails but perseveres in about ten attempts. Afterward she puts it down, tries with her hand alone, then with the stick (grasping it so that it is too short); she rejects it and takes a rubber banana. As this is still too short, she removes it after several fruitless attempts and returns to the stick. She finally succeeds.

It may therefore be seen that the behavior pattern of the stick has been acquired and immediately generalized even with respect to flexible objects.

Observation 161.—At 1;1 (0) Jacqueline tries to attain a plush cat located on the wood of her bassinet outside her field of prehension. She gives up after a series of fruitless attempts and without thinking of the stick. I then put my finger 20 cm. above the latter. She perceives the stick, grasps it at once and makes the cat fall. At 1;1 (28) she is seated on the floor and tries to reach the same cat, this time placed on the floor. She touches it with her stick but without trying to make the cat slide to her, as though the act of touching it sufficed to draw it to her.

Finally, at 1;3 (12) she discovers the possibility of making objects slide on the floor by means of the stick and so drawing them to her; in order to catch a doll lying on the ground out of reach, she begins by striking it with the stick, then, noticing its slight displacement, she pushes it until she is able to attain it with her right hand.

These observations make it possible, it would seem, to progress a step further in the analysis of accommodation. But first let us emphasize what they have in common with the preceding ones.

The behavior pattern of the stick, like the behavior patterns of the support and of the string, arises by differentiation of earlier schemata. The desire to strike or swing objects fortuitously reveals to the child the power of the stick when by chance the latter extends the action of the hand. Observation 157 and the beginning of Observation 159 thus show us what makes ready the behavior pattern of the stick. Thereafter, when the child aims to reach an object situated outside his field of prehension, it is natural that his desire should arouse the schemata in question (due to the mechanism of the coördination of schemata, existing from the fourth stage); the beginning of Observation 158 shows us this. At its point of departure, accommodation is therefore directed by the schema of the goal (to grasp the distant object) in the same way as by the schemata coördinated with it (striking, etc.) and serving as "means." But it is a question of accommodating these schemata to the present situation. It is not enough to strike an object with a stick in order to draw it to oneself and it is necessary to discover how to give an object an appropriate movement. It is then that accommodation begins.

Let us again note that this accommodation, as in the case of the supports and of the string, is conditioned by a series of earlier schemata which give a signification to the successive discoveries. So it is that the child, as soon as he sees the object being displaced a little under the influence of the stick's blows, understands the possibility of utilizing these displacements with the view of drawing the object in question to him. This comprehension is not only due to the "initial" schemata which are at the root of the subject's searching (schema of grasping and that of striking) and of which the present accommodation constitutes a differentiation, but it is also due to the "auxiliary" schemata which join themselves to the former. It is doubtless because he already knows how to displace objects by means of the supports and the string that the child understands the signification of little displacements due to blows of the stick.

But how does this accommodation work, that is to say, this differentiates for that purpose (striking); this conjunction conmulative process will give rise to a new assimilation? Here the observations relating to the stick enable us to transcend the conclusions obtained by analyzing the behavior pattern of the support and that of the string. We have seen, in connection with the string, that the acquisition of novelties, that is to say, apprenticeship, consisted in a tertiary circular reaction itself operating through reproductive, recognitory and generalizing assimilations. Accommodation to old schemata thus gives rise to new schemata capable, as such, of assimilation. But how is that possible? The observation of the behavior pattern of the stick will now show us.

Three solutions are conceivable. Either the differentiation of the old schemata, which accordingly constitutes accommodation (in the particular case, the transformation of the schema of "striking" into a new schema of "displacing with the stick") consists in a sort of dislocation of this schema; that is to say, there would be simple, undirected groping, entailing by chance variations on the general theme of the schema. In this first solution, attainment of the end would have to be conceived as being a selection after the event of chance variations. The second solution would consist, on the contrary, of assuming an immediate reorganization of the schemata: the schema of "striking with a stick" coördinated with that of "grasping" or "bringing to oneself" would, at a given moment, suddenly give rise to the system of "bringing to oneself with a stick." This sudden crystallization would therefore be comparable to those reorganizations of the ensemble of the field of perception which Gestalt psychology makes the essence of intellectual invention. In the third place one could posit an intermediate solution which would not at all consist of a mixture of the two others or a compromise but which would introduce a factor of directed activity. The schema serving as means (striking, swinging, etc.) would become differentiated as a function of the final schema (bringing to oneself) and consequently would be directed by it, but this conjunction of two schemata instead of giving rise to a sudden reorganization would simply engender a series of cumulative efforts, that is to say, a progressive accommodation whose every term would be assimilated to the preceding terms while being oriented by the ensemble of the conjunction. The originality of this third solution, in relation to the second one, would therefore be that the new schema would not be structured at the outset but would remain in a state of structuring activity until the time when it would have assimilated to itself the ensemble of the situation.

These three solutions having been separately delineated, it is clear that the third is the only one which conforms to Observations 157–161, as well as to the preceding ones. The first solution must be withdrawn because in such cases the child's groping never consists in a series of acts performed by chance. On the one hand, accommodation is enclosed in the schema of the goal (to bring to oneself) and that which serves as means which it differentiates for that purpose (striking); this conjunction consequently reduces chance to small proportions. On the other hand, each attempt conditions the attempts that follow and depends on the preceding ones. Doubtless chance can sometimes play a role in discovery. So it is that in Observation 157, Lucienne perceives that by hitting a pail she displaces it. But this discovery which characterizes a pure tertiary circular reaction (but which we class here because it could just as well occur in the course of seeking to bring things to oneself) is immediately assimilated and at once conditions the subsequent attempts. Chance, therefore, in the accommodation peculiar to sensorimotor intelligence, plays the same role as in scientific discovery. It is only useful to the genius and its revelations remain meaningless to the unskilled. In other words, it presupposes a directed search and is incapable of orienting it by itself.

The second solution is more satisfactory. But it encounters the difficulty that, in our observations, accommodation is not immediate. What is essential appears as being not the structure in which this accommodation results, but the structuring activity which makes possible its culmination. In this respect Observation 159 is very instructive. By presenting Jacqueline with an already structured example to imitate with regard to the behavior pattern of the stick I must have, it would seem, evoked in the child's mind an immediate comprehension of the use of that instrument. Jacqueline imitates me unhesitatingly, with interest and precision, giving the impression that she would now be able to repeat the same behavior pattern indefinitely. Now the rest of the observation shows that the schema aroused by imitation remains simply in the state of tendency or dynamism and does not give rise at the outset to a reorganization of perception. During the attempts immediately following the imitation, the sight of the stick does not suffice to set in motion its utilization and Jacqueline must already hold it in her hands in order to rediscover its signification which she can then do without any difficulty. Subsequently, on the other hand, visual elements are incorporated into this dynamic schema, very slowly and progressively. First I must point to the stick with my finger in order that the stick be used, then the sight of it alone suffices to produce this result.

We can conclude from such observations that accommodation characteristic of the discovery of new means operates due not to a sudden reorganization but due to a series of cumulative attempts being assimilated to each other and thus entailing the formation of a schema which assimilates to itself the ensemble of the situation (including, little by little, visual elements). It may thus be seen how, as we glimpsed in connection with the "supports" and the "string," accommodation is directed not only from the outside by the coördination of the final schema (the schema assigning an end to the action) and of the initial schemata serving as means, schemata that accommodation differentiates, not only by the auxiliary schemata which give meaning to the discoveries made by this accommodation, but that it is also and primarily directed by an assimilation immanent in accommodation and resulting from it just as circular reaction results from the novelties which give rise to it.

It is noteworthy that, as in connection with the "string" and the "supports," the new schema, as soon as it has been acquired, is applied by generalization to analogous situations, the behavior pattern thus entering the group which we have called "applications" of familiar means to new situations. So it is that, in Observation 160, Jacqueline, knowing how to use a stick without hesitation, also uses a book and a banana as instruments.

§3. THE DISCOVERY OF NEW MEANS THROUGH ACTIVE EXPERIMENTATION. II. OTHER EXAMPLES.— The analysis we have just attempted to make concerning the accommodation characteristic of the discovery of new means can now be extended by the study of more complex behavior patterns. We shall first try to find out how the child goes about drawing objects to him through the bars of his pen. This kind of an experiment is such as to permit us to examine the relations between the dynamic schemata and visual perception or representation.

Observation 162.—At 1;3 (12) Jacqueline is seated in her playpen, that is to say, in a square enclosure whose four sides are formed by vertical bars connected at base and summit by a horizontal bar. The bars are 6 cm. apart. I place outside the pen, parallel to the side where Jacqueline is, a stick 20 cm. long which takes up the distance of about 3 spaces between the bars. We shall call these three spaces *a*, *b* and *c*, space *b* corresponding to the middle part of the stick and spaces *a* and *c* to the end parts. The problem is to transfer this stick from outside to inside the pen.

1. Jacqueline begins by grasping the stick through space *b*, she raises it along the bars but holds it horizontally and parallel to the frame so that the harder she pulls the less it moves. She then extends her other hand through *c*, but holds the stick horizontally and does not succeed in making it come through. She finally lets go of the object which I put back in its initial position.

2. Jacqueline at once begins over again, by again grasping the stick at *c*. But, in raising it, she tilts it up a little, by chance, and so makes it slightly oblique. She immediately takes advantage of what she perceives and, passing her hand through *c*, she tilts the stick until it is sufficiently vertical to pass through. She then brings it into the pen through *b*.—Why did she tilt it up? Was it through foresight or did she simply extend the movement which was due to chance so as to see what would happen? The rest of these attempts rather substantiate this second interpretation.

3–4. This time Jacqueline grasps the stick through space *c*, that is to say, at one of its ends (doubtless because she tilted it up at *c* during the preceding attempt). She draws it horizontally against the bars but encountering resistance from them she quickly makes it vertical and pulls it through without difficulty. The speed of this adaptation is due to the fact that the stick was grasped by one of its ends; the subsequent attempts show that nothing systematic yet exists.

5. Jacqueline again grasps the stick by the middle, at *b*. She raises it, puts it horizontally against the bars, as in 1. She pulls and seems very surprised by her failure. It is only after a while that she tilts it up (this time, it appears, intentionally) and succeeds in bringing it in.

6–10. Same reactions. At each new attempt, she begins by trying to make it penetrate horizontally, parallel to the frame. It is only after this preliminary failure that she tilts up the stick, still quite slowly.

11. This time Jacqueline turns the stick more rapidly because she grasped it at *c*.

12–15. She again grasps it at *b* and recommences to try to bring it through horizontally, as in 5–10. Then she tilts it up, more slowly than in 11, and succeeds.

16. She continues to take it at *b* and to try to pull it through horizontally but, this time she does not persist and tilts it up immediately.

17. For the first time Jacqueline tilts the stick before it touched the bars and no longer tries to bring it in horizontally. However, she grasped it at the middle (at *b*).

18–19. She again begins by trying to bring it through horizontally but it seems that this was due to automatism and she tilts it up immediately afterwards.

20 et seq. She finally turns it systematically before it touches the bars (see 17).

Observation 163.—At 1;3 (13) we resume the same experiment with Jacqueline, but by complicating it in the following way: the stick henceforth used is too long to pass through horizontally. The bars of the pen are 50 cm. high (with a space of 46 cm. between the lower bar and the upper one) and the stick given to the child is 55 cm. long. We shall call the middle of the stick *A*, and *B* and *C* the two points situated at one third and two thirds of the distance between the middle and the end. The stick is again placed on the ground parallel to the side of the frame which Jacqueline is seated facing. Ten attempts were enough to enable her to solve the problem:

1. Jacqueline grasps the stick at *B*. She raises it horizontally and thus pulls it against the bars. She pulls it against the bars with all her strength and then displaces it unsystematically, raises it and all at once brings it through by chance without having understood how she did it.

2. This time she grasps the stick at *A*, puts it horizontally against the bars and pulls as hard as she can. She then tilts it up systematically

but the stick, touching the ground at its lower end, remains oblique. She again pulls very hard, then gives up.

3-4. She still begins by pulling horizontally, then raises it, pulls again and finally tilts it in such a way as to bring it through correctly. Both times she grasped it at *B*.

5. Jacqueline grasps the stick at C, pulls it horizontally, then raises it. But she tilts it up so that it is higher than the frame at the top and remains caught at the bottom. She then shakes it and ends by bringing it through accidentally.

6. Same beginnings. The stick is held at the top by the edge of the frame and at the bottom by Jacqueline's dress which is pressed against the lower edge of the pen. Jacqueline then watches both ends of the stick attentively, then raises it gently to disengage it from her dress. She then brings it in slowly by the bottom part and then pulls until she has been completely successful.

7. First she grasps the stick at *A*, applies it horizontally and pulls. Then she grasps it with the other hand at *C* (still holding it firmly at *A*, tight against the bars) and brings it through by raising it first and then pulling it by the lower part, as before (in 6).

8. Jacqueline succeeds at once this time, almost without pulling the stick against the bars. She grasps it, tilts it up and brings it through by the lower end.

9. She grasps it with the wrong hand (too high to be able to pull it through by the lower part). She immediately switches to the other hand and succeeds at once.

10. Immediate success, without groping and without first touching the bars: she barely grazes them when bringing the stick through.

At 1;3 (15) Jacqueline fails at the first attempt and again pulls horizontally but, during this second attempt, she rediscovers the combined two acts of tilting up the stick and bringing it in by the lower part. At 1;4 (0) after an interruption of several days, she relapses into her former mistakes, then succeeds.

Observation 164.—The following facts will help us to clarify the powers and limitations of visual perception. At 1;3 (13) Jacqueline tries to bring in a case for eyeglasses: she succeeds at once. However, she grasped it but turned it to the vertical position before it touched the bars. Same success subsequently with a stick of sealing wax.

Then I place a book on its edge outside the frame (the spine of the book upward and parallel to the frame). She grasps it and pulls the whole width of it against the bars. Afterward she pulls it with the spine of the book placed horizontally against the bars, then, thirdly, she tilts up the book and brings it through vertically, spine first, without any difficulty.

A half hour later Jacqueline begins again by pulling the whole width of the book against the bars in order to bring it inside in this .

way, and she again pulls with all her strength. Afterward, she places
it on the floor on its edge, parallel to the frame, then she grasps it
with her other hand by the spine, raises it up vertically before it
touches the bars and brings it through.

In the course of a final experiment she tilts it up right away before another attempt and brings it in unhesitatingly.

At 1;4 (21), on the other hand, she tried to take out of her pen
cylindrical, wooden, Russian dolls, too wide to push through the
bars. She does not understand her failure and pushes them anyway.
She does not succeed in inventing the procedure which would consist
in sliding them along the bars in order to bring them over the top.

Observation 165.—At 1;3 (14) Jacqueline received a cardboard rooster
by means of which I try the following experiment. I place it lying on
the ground, outside the frame but introducing the head and tail of the
cock in the direction of the child. In other words, the head passes
through a space between two bars, the tail passes through the next
space and the rooster's back is held back by the bar separating these
two spaces. If the child wishes to pull the rooster to him he must first
push it away, then tilt it up and finally bring it through head or tail
first.

During this first experiment Jacqueline confines herself to merely
pulling the rooster by the head or by the tail but without previously
pushing it away or tilting it up; she consequently fails completely.

At 1;3 (16), on the other hand, I simplify things a little by putting the rooster back a little; it still faces a bar but, instead of being
in contact with it, it is 5 cm. behind it. Here is the series of attempts:

1. Jacqueline pulls the rooster toward her and it gets caught in
the bars. She pulls hard for a while, then switches hands. While she is
doing this, the rooster happens to fall quite far away so that when
picking it up again, she tilts it to a vertical position without difficulty.
She then sees it in profile and has only to turn it full face to bring it
through. These acts of raising the recumbent animal, then of bringing it in full face only constitute, of course, the application of discoveries made in connection with the stick (Obs. 162 and 163) and primarily in connection with the book (Obs. 164), that is to say, the discoveries made the preceding days.

2. In grasping the rooster Jacqueline pushes it back slightly and
so again succeeds in tilting it up without difficulty. She does this systematically and without hesitation.

3. The rooster gets caught this time. Jacqueline nevertheless pulls
it without thinking of pushing it back. After vain attempts she changes
hands and begins over again. Then she takes it in her right hand and
pulls it with renewed strength. At last she tries to tilt it up, but still
without pushing it back. She then gives up and lets it go.

4–6. The rooster again gets caught at each attempt. Jacqueline recommences to pull with each hand alternately. But each time the rooster finally falls sufficiently far away to enable her to tilt it up without difficulty. She therefore knows how to tilt the object up but still does not know how to push it away for this purpose; it is only chance that allows her to do it.

7. The rooster remains caught for a long time. She pulls it with both hands. It falls but she gets it caught while trying to tilt it up; she does not understand and pulls harder. At last it falls far enough away to permit her to tilt it up and pull it in without difficulty.

8. This time the rooster, caught at first, falls six times a short distance away and each time it would have sufficed to pull it back even a little bit to tilt it up. However, she got it caught at each new attempt and resumed pulling without understanding.

9–10. Same reactions. She fatigues and we pause.

The afternoon of the same day, around 1 o'clock, we resume the experiment: complete failure.

That evening, around 6 o'clock, new attempts which this time are successful. Here is the series of attempts:

1. Failure: she pulls, switches hands, and gives up.

2. She succeeds by chance in tilting it up before it touches the bars and doubtless before it becomes caught. It goes through without difficulty.

3. It becomes caught and she pulls it for a moment, then lets it drop, perhaps intentionally, after which she tilts it up before it touches the bars.

4–9. Same beginning, but this time it is certain that she lets it fall intentionally and sooner after the beginning of the attempts. Then she tilts it up very well, taking care to do so ahead of time (before pulling) and at last she pulls it to her. The game amuses her to such an extent that as soon as the rooster is inside the frame, she puts it outside by herself in order to begin all over again.

10. I now wedge it ahead of time as at the beginning of our experiment [at 1;3 (14)]. Jacqueline then pulls at first and is surprised by her failure; she still does not know how to push the object back beforehand. On the other hand, when she observes the failure, she knows how to drop the rooster intentionally. It then falls 3 cm. away from the bars, she tilts it up and brings it in without difficulty.

11–12. This time, a noteworthy novelty: The rooster gets caught, she pulls it for a moment, then, without letting it fall, she places it on the floor (while holding it by its head) tilts it up and pulls it to her. She has not definitely pushed it away but by placing it on the floor she had sufficient leeway to enable her to tilt it up without difficulty.

13. She pulls, then lets it fall again (intentionally), as in 4–10. Then she tilts it up and brings it in.

14. Jacqueline pulls, then once more tilts the rooster up, on the floor, without letting it fall or letting it go (as in 11–12).

15–16. She again lets it fall but then returns it very carefully, while watching its tail which was in danger of catching in the bars.

17. This time, Jacqueline definitely pushes the rooster back before pulling it and tilts it up without letting it go.

18. Same reaction, but in addition, she takes the rooster outside the bars by herself, as soon as she has brought it in, in order to repeat the experiment because she is so delighted at her last discovery. This play goes on until satiety.

Observation 166.—At 1;3 (17) the day after the preceding series, I resume the experiment of pulling the rooster through the bars. It is worthwhile to describe in a new observation the results of these repeated attempts after the discovery of the correct procedure, for they are of a kind to clarify the relations of visual representation with the dynamic schema.

Here is the series of these new attempts:

1. Jacqueline pulls the rooster to her, as if the bar located between the head and the tail were not going to catch the animal's back. She pulls as she did the first day, perseveringly and recommencing with vigor after short rests. Then the rooster falls by chance and she is then able to tilt it up without difficulty and to pull it to her.

2. Same reaction, but she lets it go quickly, perhaps intentionally, and tilts it up on the ground.

3. She begins again by pulling, then, without letting it go, lowers it to the ground, pushes it back intentionally, tilts it up and brings it in.

4. Same reaction, very definite, but she pushes it back by making it slide along the floor and turns it so much that it catches on the other side.

5–7. She pushes it back almost immediately, but commences each time by pulling it directly.

It may thus be seen how much more rapid is the discovery of the correct procedure than it was the day before but one observes that, nevertheless, progress always takes place through motor assimilation and not through representation. A quarter of an hour later, I resume the experiment and observe the ten following attempts:

1–4. Jacqueline first pulls the rooster, then pushes it back soon after, and tilts it up without letting it go.

5–6. She pushes it back, this time, right away. She even pushes it back the second time 15 cm. along the floor, without letting it go, and once it is tilted up, brings it in victoriously.

7. She begins again by pulling first, then pushes it back and tilts it up.

8–10. Correct procedure as in 5–6.

At 1;3 (21), that is to say, four days later, Jacqueline again pulls the rooster directly twice and then pushes it back at the third attempt. At 1;3 (27) same sequence. At 1;4 (0), she pushes it back beforehand at the second attempt but simply from habit because, at the fifth attempt, when the rooster gets caught by chance, she pulls it again with all her strength without knowing how to correct it. Then at the sixth attempt, she again pushes it back beforehand. At 1;4 (20) I make the same observation. But it suffices to show her a new rooster to make her succeed in bringing it in right away and push it away and tilt up ahead of time both the old and the new rooster.

This new series of facts warrants our resuming the discussion of the mechanism of accommodation. As we have seen in connection with the "stick," there are three possible solutions for interpreting such facts; chance and selection, the hypothesis of "structures," and that of a structuring assimilatory activity which is not structured from the outset.

The first of these solutions seems at first very likely. These observations, still more than those pertaining to the stick (see Obs. 159 during which Jacqueline learns little by little to utilize an imitated example) seem to speak in favor of a sort of training, the incorrect procedures being gradually replaced by correct methods. But, on examining things closely, one sees that this is only apparent and that the gradual victory of the correct procedures is not at all due to an automatic selection: It is simply a question of progressive comprehension analogous to that which we observe in ourselves when we only grasp little by little the factors of a problem and only after much groping arrive at clear and unified vision. In such cases, we begin by anticipating, in a way, the right solution. In other words, an accommodation of familiar schemata to the new situation permits us to differentiate them in a relatively adequate schema but the latter remains in the state of intention or of simply structuring outline; that is to say, it orients searching without yet being sufficiently strong to eliminate false solutions, it coördinates the progress of groping without itself being structured, and finally it utilizes fortunate chance circumstances without being yet able to do without

their coöperation (but it is never derived from them). The same
is true of our Observations 162 to 166. The child tries to bring
the object to him (there is the schema assigning an end to the
action and thus directing the groping), and quickly understands,
when he fails, that certain displacements of the object become
necessary (there are the schemata serving as means which accommodation will differentiate). With regard to the origin of
these latter schemata, it is to be sought in the tertiary circular
reactions relating to changes of position (Obs. 141–142 and 144–
145) and primarily in the many experiments which the child
makes each day in order to grasp a cumbersome object, to tilt it
up, to dissociate it from those in which it is inserted, etc. (see
Obs. 146). This outline of a solution, obtained by directed differentiation of earlier schemata, then gives rise to a series of attempts in the course of which chance certainly intervenes unceasingly, but which are not dominated by chance. If, thereafter,
the false solution continually reappears (drawing the object directly to oneself), that simply means that the outline of the correct solution is too weak to counterbalance the influence of a
procedure having the force of habit and the allurement of apparent evidence; that does not mean at all that the correct solution is obtained by purely automatic training founded upon
chance and selection. The correct solution, once glimpsed, grows
progressively stronger, not in the manner of a phenomenon that
statistically outweighs another as function of a selection taking
place in time, but in the manner of a cumulative experience or
comprehension. For example, in Observation 165, the first ten
attempts reveal no progress because the solution (pushing the
object back in order to tilt it up) has not been glimpsed; but as
soon as it has been (beginning of the second series) it becomes
consolidated (attempts 3–10), then becomes explicit (attempts 11–
14), and finally is definitively established (attempts 17–18). This
development is therefore not that of a series of blind gropings
in the course of which propitious acts become fixed due to confirmation; it is that of a directed apprenticeship, analogous to
the example of a student trying to solve the same problem in
arithmetic twenty times, knowing the final result but without

having understood the connection, which he guessed at, between the different operations to be performed.

These remarks make us realize at the same time the differences existing between the cumulative assimilation presupposed by such accommodations and the ready-made "structures" of Gestalt psychology. Again referring to Observation 165, there are three operations to perform: pushing back the rooster, tilting it up, and bringing it in full face. Jacqueline knows how to perform the two latter ones due to her recent acquisitions (Obs. 162–164). It only remains for her to discover the necessity for the first in order to intercoördinate the other two. Now she anticipates this solution as soon as she lets the rooster fall and thereafter acquires the possibility of tilting it up without difficulty. The schema thus outlined (beginning of the second series) becomes consolidated, explicit and finally established, as we have just recalled. How can this development be explained? It cannot be a question of an immediate structurization precisely because, in the course of attempts 1 to 16, there is no correct solution but simply progress towards a solution. All that remains is to assert the existence of a cumulative assimilation, analogous to that of the tertiary circular reactions and according to which the new motor schema, outlined by accommodation, like every assimilatory schema, is developed by repetition, recognition and generalization. Once again we find a structuring assimilation and not at the outset a structured coördination. It is by functioning that a schema structures itself and not before functioning. It is true that, in order to function, that is to say, in order to assimilate the real situation, a schema has need of at least a *minimum* of structure; but this structure is nothing independently of the act of assimilation and so only becomes crystallized in the course of this act.—Regarding Observations 162–164, the same is true: The solution outlined at the beginning becomes consolidated and explicit through reproductive, generalizing and recognitory assimilation.

In connection with this dynamism it remains to speak of the respective roles of visual representation and simple motor assimilation. How does it happen that, in the course of Observations 165 and 166, Jacqueline tries again and again to bring a rooster through the bars when she sees that one of these bars holds it back systematically and when she has already discovered the correct solution beforehand and several times in succession? How does it happen (Obs. 162 and 163) that she even tries to bring in a long stick held back by 2, 3 or 4 bars at once, as though the stick were going to cut the bars or cross them as a wire cuts butter? Or why (Obs. 164) does she persist in trying to bring through the space between two bars a doll which is wider than this space? Is it because visual perception only plays a secondary role in such behavior patterns and that they are purely a matter of motor searching; or because this perception is different and does not take account of the solidity of objects? In fact, it seems to us that both solutions amount to the same thing. Everything occurs as though, to the child, the bars constituted pure images without depth or solidity (pictures and not substances) and as though these images could be traversed through and through without difficulty. But why is this so? Precisely because a sensorimotor elaboration has not yet conferred upon them the qualities of resistance and substantiality which they lack. Here again it is difficult to speak with the Gestalt psychologists of a sudden reorganization of the perceptual field independently of structuring assimilatory activity: It is the action that fashions the field of perception and not the reverse.

In short, the theory of pure groping makes of the discovery of new procedures a simple accommodation, thus neglecting the formal coördination belonging to assimilation: hence this theory is analogous to an empiricism ascribing invention to experience alone and neglecting the activity of the mind. The theory of "structures," on the contrary, emphasizes the existence of formal coördinations but neglects accommodation, in this being comparable to an apriority which disdains experience. For us, accommodation is necessarily on a par with a cumulative assimilation, structuring and not structured from the outset. The schema of assimilation thus reconciles the necessary role of experience, that is to say, of accommodation, with the no less necessary role of formal coördination.

Before concluding, let us cite a certain number of mixed observations in which the discovery of new means through active experimentation simultaneously raises all the problems discussed hitherto:

Observation 167.—At 1;3 (12) Jacqueline throws a plush dog outside the bars of her playpen and she tries to catch it. Not succeeding, she then pushes the pen itself in the right direction! By holding onto the frame with one hand while with the other she tried to grasp the dog, she observed that the frame was mobile. She had accordingly, without wishing to do so, moved it away from the dog. She at once tried to correct this movement and thus saw the pen approach its objective. These two fortuitous discoveries then led her to utilize movements of the playpen and to push it at first experimentally, then systematically. There was a moment's groping, but it was short.

At 1;3 (16), on the other hand, Jacqueline right away pushes her playpen in the direction of the objects to be picked up.

Observation 168.—This last observation during which the child displaces himself in order to attain the objective, leads us to the situation in which the subject is obliged to withdraw part or all of his own body in order not to interfere with the movements of the object. For instance, at 1;6 (15) Jacqueline is standing on a rag (50 x 30 cm.) which she is trying to pick up. She pulls, is surprised at the resistance, but it does not occur to her to move. Finally, she gives up.

At 1;7 (0), on the contrary, she is standing on a handkerchief and, after having pulled it, she moves her feet until it is free. At the second attempt, she moves away beforehand, but at the third, she continues to pull a long time before taking away the foot that was impeding her.

Observation 169.—Here is a behavior pattern intermediate between the preceding ones and those that consist in utilizing the relationships of contents and container. At 1;3 (14) Jacqueline tries to open a jewel case (3 x 5 cm.). With one hand she holds it and without knowing it tightens the cover on the box, and with the other hand she tries to raise this cover, of course without succeeding! However, by dint of transferring the object from one hand to the other without the possibility of noting all the vicissitudes, she finally draws back her right hand (which holds the case) as much as possible while she pulls at the lid with the other. But there is not yet any systematic procedure.

At 1;3 (15) on the other hand, after two attempts during which Jacqueline recommences trying to hold the cover with one hand while she tries to displace it with the other, she places the box on the ground and opens it without difficulty. This act of placing it on the ground was not the result of invention, properly so called. She simply removed her right hand and, unable simultaneously to hold the box and open it with her left hand, she placed it on the ground.

That evening, she tries to open a pipe case (same kind of fastening:

two valves applied against each other). She tries indefinitely to open it with one hand while holding it closed with the other. But then the case happens to fall and opens: Jacqueline opens it and then closes it several times in succession on the ground and with one hand. Then she takes it up again in one hand and recommences to try to open it with the other: complete failure. She then rests it on the ground, this time intentionally, and opens it without difficulty.

After a new attempt with both hands, she rests it again on the floor and only tries this way.

At 1;3 (16) same reaction. On the one hand, Jacqueline well knows how to open the case when she rests it on the ground. She searches for the slit with one finger and raises one of the valves without touching the other. When her finger again covers both, she lowers it very attentively until she feels the slit and then opens the case easily. But, on the other hand, when she holds the case in both hands, she is incapable of proceeding. While trying to raise a valve, she holds it firmly with the other hand. In the latter case, she rests the case on the table and succeeds in opening it by means of one hand only. Finally, she only attempts this second procedure and gives up all efforts with both hands.

Observation 170.—Here is an analogous observation concerning Lucienne. At 1;1 (23) Lucienne puts (by chance?) a cake in the form of a ring or a torus in a circular wooden box. She immediately tries to take it out. But she puts her thumb against the outside of the box while pulling the cake with her index and other fingers so that the very palm of her hand prevents the object from coming out. She finally attains her goal after extensive efforts. She then at once begins over again and so on twenty times in succession through an apparent need of assimilation. From time to time she does it by simple empirical groping, by shaking the box or turning it upside down (not deliberately), but, on the whole, there is definite progress. Little by little she manages to hold the box in one hand while she pulls the cake with the other without obstructing the cake with her thumb.

There exists in this case, besides cumulative assimilation, a process of progressive dissociation. The child detaches three objects from one another: box, cake and hand. At first she does not see that the hand is an obstacle as well as an instrument. Then, due to her directed gropings, she understands the exact interrelations of the objects and succeeds in solving the problem she herself raised.

Observation 171.—These last behavior patterns lead us to the acts relating to the connection between container and contents. Here is the simplest of those we have observed:

At 1;3 (28) Jacqueline receives a toy consisting of hollow blocks which fit into each other and which we separate before her eyes and scatter about. The problem is to know how she will learn to put the little blocks into the large ones.

1. Jacqueline begins by manipulating eight blocks of different sizes by trying to put the little ones in the big ones and the big ones into the little ones, varying the combinations (see particulars in Vol. II, Chap. II).

Toward the end of these first gropings she seems more rapidly than before to abandon the project of putting a large block into a small one.

She finally grasps a large block with one hand, a small one with the other and looks for the opening of the former in order to place the second one systematically in it; hence the experiment is accompanied at this time by a sort of reflection or mental concentration.

2. At 1;3 (29), the following day, I again give the blocks to Jacqueline who is in her playpen. She begins by trying to make a block which is too big come through the bars. After having given up, she puts a small block into a big one and shakes the latter in order to make a block which is too big come through the bars. After having given up, she puts a small block into a big one and shakes the latter in order to make a noise. She is not interested in anything else so I take the game away from her.

3. At 1;4 (0) she tries at first to put one block into another which is slightly larger. Then she recommences trying to place a large one in a small one but corrects herself very quickly.

4. From 1;4 (5) Jacqueline's attempts lead to satisfying results on the whole. She no longer tries to put large blocks inside small ones, she takes account of the position of the angles and succeeds in extricating the enclosed blocks by sliding them out with her index finger. These three behavior patterns have consequently been acquired due to directed gropings and the progressive correction of the initial schemata.

Observation 172.—Here is a slightly more complex example. At 1;1 (3) I present Lucienne with a wooden pail (10 cm. in diameter) to which she is accustomed and place my watch chain next to it. At first Lucienne tries to put the chain into the pail, being accustomed to putting different objects into it. She grasps the middle of the chain between thumb and index finger and places it on the edge of the pail. But of course the greater part of the chain remains outside the pail. Lucienne at once grasps the outside end in order to make it all go inside, but she grasps it so high up, as though the part already inside were not joined to the other, that the whole chain comes out and she has to begin all over again. This recurs many times because Lucienne, through lack of assimilation, each time puts the chain into the pail but always goes about it in the same way. However, little by little she manages to make her movements gentler and to pick up the hanging end of the chain without jostling the other. At last she succeeds once in making the whole chain enter the pail.

At 1;3 (13) she tries to solve the same problem by herself, but with a necklace and a watering can. First she puts the end of the necklace inside, then the rest of it by degrees without making the already introduced part fall out. She thus succeeds, after several failures, in making the whole necklace go inside the can twice.

Observation 173.—These last experiments now lead us to the analysis of a proof which has shown itself to be particularly fruitful: making a watch chain enter a narrow opening. This experiment, which in Lucienne's case took place after the preceding ones, yielded quite different results than with Jacqueline, results which were new both with respect to the chain and pail and to the necklace and watering can. Lucienne solved this problem by an act of true invention which we shall study in the course of Observation 179. With regard to Jacqueline, on the other hand, the behavior pattern was revealed to be exactly analogous to that of Lucienne in the preceding observation.

At 1;7 (25) Jacqueline holds a rectangular box, deep and narrow, whose opening measures 34 x 16 mm. (for this purpose I use the cover of a match box which is three quarters open), and she tries to put my watch chain into it (45 cm. long). During the first fifteen attempts, she goes about it in the following way: First she puts one end of the chain into the box (2 to 4 cm.), then she grasps the chain about 5 cm. from this end and thus puts a second segment into the box. She then gets ready to do the same with a third segment when the chain, no longer supported by the child's hand, slides out of the box and falls noisily. Jacqueline recommences at once and fourteen times in succession sees the chain come out as soon as it is put in. It is true that, around the tenth attempt, Jacqueline has tired of it and was about to give up; but I placed the chain in the box (without the child's seeing how) and then she regained hope by noting that such a result was not impossible.

At the sixteenth attempt, a new phenomenon: Jacqueline having grasped the chain nearer the middle, the chain no longer lengthened as before at the time when the child raises it but takes the form of two entwined cords. Jacqueline then understands the advantage she can take of this new presentation and tries to make the two ends enter the box together (more precisely, one immediately after the other, the second following shortly after the first). She no longer lets the chain go after putting one of the ends into the box, as was the case in attempts 1–15, but tries to put all of it in. But, as always occurs when a child of this age manipulates flexible objects, Jacqueline considers the chain as being rigid and lets go the whole of it when both extremities have been put in the box. The chain then comes out again somewhat, but Jacqueline gently reintroduces the part that hangs (the middle part).

Attempt 17: Jacqueline distinctly tries to repeat the preceding movement. At first she does not grasp the chain at one end but pulls it together somewhat and grasps the middle part (without of course trying to find the actual middle). She again succeeds in putting both ends in together.

Attempt 18: resumes the initial procedure and fails.

Attempt 19: rediscovers the procedure of attempts 16 and 17.

Attempt 20: same reaction, but this time Jacqueline encounters some difficulty in putting the second end in. Not succeeding, she recommences trying to put in a single end first. But as the chain slides out, she resumes the procedure of attempts 16, 17 and 19.

Attempts 21–22: same hesitations, with ultimate success.

Observation 173 repeated.—An hour later I again present the box and chain to Jacqueline. Four interesting attempts ensue.

1. Jacqueline grasps the chain with both hands, probably by chance. Then she examines with curiosity the shape thus obtained: the chain being grasped simultaneously at about one third and two thirds of its length, these two ends hang parallel, about 15 20 cm. away, while the middle part is horizontal. But then Jacqueline, instead of putting both ends inside simultaneously by bringing them near each other, confines herself to putting one of them in the box with great delicacy, and lets the whole of the chain go as though this end would draw the rest after it: the chain collapsed.

2. She now grasps the chain toward the middle and tries to put both ends in at once. This is the procedure discovered during the preceding series and it succeeds again this time.

3. This time she begins by grasping the chain not far from one of its ends but she corrects this movement before letting it all go. Seeing that only a small part of the chain entered the box, she intentionally displaces her hand toward the middle of the chain in such a way as to acquire a better grip and to put both ends inside at the same time. But, experiencing some difficulty in this operation (the chain spreads out and becomes too wide) she corrects herself a second time and simultaneously invents a new procedure.

4. Seeing both parts of the chain separate, Jacqueline rolls the chain up and puts it into the box very easily.

This last procedure, which is the simplest, is only discovered after the stage constituted by attempts 16–22 of the preceding series, by attempt 1 of the present series and finally by correction of the beginning of attempt 3. Instead of inventing all at once the procedure of "rolling up," as Lucienne will do, Jacqueline forms it progressively by combined assimilation and accommodation.

At 1;8 (2) Jacqueline rediscovers the procedure of rolling up at the very beginning, then returns to the system of the chain hanging by a middle part. This last method is alone utilized at 1;9 (21) after failure due to a regression of the initial incorrect procedure.

Observation 174.—These kinds of apprenticeship can be further compli-cated by requiring the child to correct the position, not only of the object to be put in, but also of the container. So it is that at 1;1 (23) Lucienne sees me put a ring into half of a case for eyeglasses. She looks at the object inside the case, shakes the case and lets the ring fall out. She then tries immediately to replace it but the apprenticeship is ac-complished on two occasions.

During a first phase, Lucienne tries four sequential maneuvers, all unsuccessful. (1) She first' presses her three fingers holding the ring against the opening of the case and drops the ring. The ring falls to the side because her fingers prevent it from entering. (2) She presses the ring against the closed end of the case and lets it go. (3) She holds the case upside down and puts the ring into the opening but without tilting it up. The ring falls out at the first movement of the case. (4) She places the ring on the floor and presses both ends of the case against it, alternately, as though the ring would enter it by itself.

During a second phase, on the contrary, Lucienne learns to cor-rect her attempts. First, she no longer places the case on the ring as though the latter would enter by itself. Then when she presses the ring against the wrong end of the case, she does not let it go but turns the case over in order to slide it into the opening. She holds the case al-most vertically and, when it is too slanting, she straightens it before letting the ring go. Finally, she learns only to drop it inside the case by first sliding it to the end of her fingers instead of letting it fall when the fingers still obstruct an opening of the case.

At 1;1 (24) after having disengaged the ring from her thumb around which it fell by chance, Lucienne sees me put it around a stick. She then tries to draw it toward her without putting it along the wood. Then she shakes the stick and the ring falls. In order to put it around the stick again, she simply presses it at a certain place and lets it go. Same reaction six times in succession. Then she tries to put it on at the end, but lets it drop. That afternoon she succeeds twice in putting it on the stick but she merely presses it several times against the stick. The fol-lowing days both reactions subsist without excluding each other, but the attempts to put it on the stick prevail increasingly above the others.

§4. THE DISCOVERY OF NEW MEANS THROUGH ACTIVE EXPERIMENTATION. III. CONCLUSIONS.—

These last facts having thus completed the preceding ones, let us try to draw from all our data a conclusion relating to the present type of behavior patterns, beginning by trying to place them in the general picture of intelligence.

The behavior patterns peculiar to sensorimotor intelligence

can be divided into two big groups. First there are those whose goal is in some way imposed by the external environment. Such are the circular relations, secondary or tertiary, which consist in merely repeating or varying an interesting result obtained by chance. Such, too, are the facts of the comprehension of signs or of exploration in which an external factor obtrudes without having been chosen and requires assimilation by the subject. These different behavior patterns certainly constitute intelligent behavior since it is always a question of adjusting means to ends, and whether these ends consist in repeating, understanding, or foreseeing is of little importance. But they are intelligent in different degrees. It can be said, on the whole, that an act is the more intelligent the greater the number of schemata it subsumes and the more difficulties the latter present in intercoördinating. Thereafter, the operation requiring the least intelligence is that of secondary circular reaction: merely rediscovering the means that made it possible to obtain an interesting result. Concerning comprehension, prevision and exploration, they are the more "intelligent" the more complex they become, and they can reach a high degree of complexity. But as these behavior patterns are in a way directed from the outside by the facts which come to the child's attention, they do not give rise to actual inventions, that is to say, to the most complex systematizations of which sensorimotor intelligence is capable at its beginnings. Moreover, the first comprehensions, previsions and explorations simply consist in making an object or an event enter into one or more sequential schemata, intelligent search consisting not in coördinating the schemata, but in appropriately choosing between them.

A second group of intelligent behavior patterns is constituted by those whose purpose is, on the contrary, due to the subject's spontaneous intention. It goes without saying that this distinction is relative, since intention is always occasioned by encountering an external fact. But this fact does not here impose itself in the capacity of an external motor of thought; it is simply an opportunity for various projects and it is these projects which impose themselves on it. It goes without saying, thereafter, that obstacles arise between the intention and its realization and that a more or less large number of means must be put to work to remove these difficulties. It is the subordination of means to end that constitutes the intelligent act. In such behavior patterns the principal schema which, by assimilating the data, gives a purpose to the action, and the secondary schemata which constitute the means and become coördinated with the former; a certain number of auxiliary schemata can intervene besides as the search goes on; the final schema is thus called upon to systematize the ensemble of these terms in a new unit. If behavior patterns such as secondary or tertiary circular reaction, the comprehension of signs or exploration constitute the sensorimotor equivalent of judgment, the more complex behavior patterns of which we now speak constitute reasonings. As we have already seen, the subordination of means to ends is, in effect, comparable to the subordination of premises to the conclusion. This situation explains why the behavior patterns of the first group enter ceaselessly in the capacity of elements into those of the second group. This distinction must not, however, be considered as being too absolute; just as judgment is virtual reasoning, so also there exist all intermediates between the two groups until the time when comprehension even becomes an end in itself and gives rise to the same complex and deductive steps as invention itself.

Regardless of this last point, this second group of intelligent behavior patterns admits of three distinct types: the "application of familiar means to new situations," the "discovery of new means through active experimentation," and the "invention of new means through mental combination." In order to understand the nature of the behavior patterns of the present type it is necessary to analyze them in relation to the two others: discovery through experimentation is essentially a transition between simple application of the familiar to the new and invention properly so called.

Two characteristics common to these varied behavior patterns should be noted here in order simultaneously to grasp the continuity and relative contrast of the three types under consideration. These are experimentation through directed groping, the source of acquisition, and the application of familiar schemata, source of systematization. In a word, it can be said that the first type is defined by the primacy of application, the second by the primacy of groping, and the third by the unification of these two characteristics. But groping is not foreign to any of the three terms of the series, as we shall see, and application remains essential to the second one, although dominated by groping.

The relationship between the three types of behavior patterns therefore consists in that the subject finds himself confronted by a situation new to him and, in order to arrive at his ends, he must discover suitable means not immediately given. The simplest solution in such a case, it goes without saying, consists in searching in the stores of already acquired schemata for some known procedure which might solve the problem. It is this step which constitutes the first type of behavior patterns: the "application of familiar means to new circumstances." It goes without saying that application predominates in such a behavior pattern. But groping is not excluded from it since it is a question of adapting old schemata to the new situation and this adaptation presupposes, on the one hand, a search for the right schema and an elimination of the useless schemata and, on the other hand, an adjustment of this suitable schema. Consequently, either in the course of this search or of this adjustment, the subject will be seen to hesitate and correct himself, in short, behave in a way which presages the second type. Moreover all the intermediates exist between them: Observation 122 thus furnishes us with an example of evident groping. But as long as this groping simply results in rediscovering a familiar procedure and adjusting it without transforming it, we remain confronted by a behavior pattern of the first type. The behavior patterns of the second type begin in exactly the same way; but, after having tried an initial means (which was discovered by the child due to the assimilatory process belonging to the "application of familiar means to new situations"), the subject finds himself obliged to differentiate it. It is in the course of this operation that groping accommodation intervenes, as we have seen in connection with the "supports," the "string," and the "stick": from the time when the familiar means does not suffice to solve the problem, it is necessary to grope. This groping begins by attempts at simple adjustment, then, gradually as the child's experiments go on this adjustment is transformed so that out of the differentiation of the initial schemata come new schemata, thus implying a real discovery. But such a behavior pattern which is increasingly distinguished from the simple "application of the familiar to the new" nevertheless conserves one of its essential characteristics. As we have remarked in connection with each of the examples analyzed, it is by constant application of earlier schemata to the present situation that groping is deserted and the events arising during this searching are interpreted. In short, if there is a difference between types I and II, there is nevertheless complete continuity.

Analogous comments apply, as we shall see, to the relations which connect types II and III. Groping, which has primacy in type II, does not disappear in the "invention of new means through mental combination" but is internalized and proceeds by means of representations instead of depending exclusively on external and immediate activity. In other words, effective experimentation becomes "mental experience." On the other hand, the application of earlier schemata which is not absent from behavior patterns of type II (effective groping) again assumes, in invention through mental combination, the importance it had in behavior patterns of type I (application of the familiar to the new). Invention thus synthesizes searching and deduction by merely protracting the two preceding types of behavior patterns.

These remarks enable us to understand the relations between assimilation and accommodation in empirical groping. As we have seen, it is only at the level of tertiary circular reactions that assimilation and accommodation begin to become truly differentiated. At the time of acquisition of the first habits through primary circular reaction, the two terms remain relatively undifferentiated. Every attempt at assimilation is simultaneously an attempt at accommodation. With the advent of secondary circular reaction a new fact appears: interest in the external results of acts. This interest surely marks progress toward differentiation, since the external result of acts, by differentiating the primitive schemata, thus compels them to incessant accommodation. But, as we have noted, this accommodation is still imposed and not yet sought after for its own sake. The interesting act which the child tried to conserve through assimilation arises *ex abrupto* and, if it interests the subject, it is inasmuch as it is connected, by continuity or contrast, with the already existing schemata. On the contrary, with the advent of tertiary circular reaction, accommodation becomes an end in itself which certainly protracts the earlier assimilations (the subject only accommodates already formed schemata), but which precedes new assimilations and so intentionally differentiates the schemata from which it sprang. It is then that experience begins to be formed and is distinguished from simple utilization of the real with a view to fueling the internal functioning. Henceforth there exists interest in the new as such. But will this differentiated accommodation be antagonistic or complementary to assimilation? Study of empirical groping in the search for and discovery of new means furnishes in this respect an exact answer. Accommodation to experience and deductive assimilation henceforth alternate in a movement whose rhythm can vary but whose cyclical character attests to an increasingly close correlation between the two terms. It is, in effect, under the pressure of necessity (hence of the principal assimilatory schema) and of the schemata tried out in the capacity of initial means, that groping accommodation goes in quest of new means and results in the formation of new schemata capable of being coördinated with the old ones. The "discovery of new means through active experimentation" thus marks the beginning of a union of experience and assimilatory activity, a union which "invention through mental combination" will consecrate by raising it to the rank of interdependence.

However, we must not exaggerate. At the level of empirical groping, this union, however remarkable it may be with reference to the preceding behavior patterns, remains in a state of promise or outline, compared to its future developments. Primitive accommodation to experience and complementary assimilation of the datum which characterize empirical groping present the common aspect of being immediate and hence limited. "Experience" as practiced by sensorimotor groping, is immediate in the sense that it considers things as they appear to be instead of correcting them and elaborating them mentally. Assimilation, on the other hand, only bears upon direct perception, and not yet on representation. These two characteristics constitute one and the same phenomenon, only envisaged from two different points of view.

As far as representation is concerned, we have already dealt with it in connection with the experiment of objects to be brought through the bars of the playpen. Observations 167–174 wholly confirm these conclusions: At the level of groping, representation does not precede action and does not even directly result from it. On the contrary, everything occurs as though the object seen were conceived as being identical to that which it appears to be in immediate perception. So it is that, in Observation 173, Jacqueline, in order to put a long chain into a small box, confines herself to putting one end of this inside, without rolling up the whole chain or foreseeing the object's flexibility and fall. Despite the first fruitless efforts she recommences indefinitely and sensorimotor groping alone corrects her vision of things. So also in Observation 174 Lucienne, in order to put a ring in a case or around a stick confines herself to placing the ring under the case or against the stick. Now it is again experience, and not representation, which permits her to transcend this initial level. In accounting for such facts one is in the habit of saying that "optical contact" prevails over the subject's every other preoccupation. But it is necessary to understand that, if the visual seems thus to predominate, this does not speak in favor of the primacy of representation. On the contrary, it shows that the subject's optics remains immediate and does not yet give rise to the mental constructions transforming the object as it appears to be into the object as it is. Furthermore, this transformation is effected as a function of the motor schemata in the very course of the experimental groping; therefore it could not be directed by representations precisely because it consists in preparing their elaboration. In short it can be said that, at the level of empirical groping, representation does not yet intervene and that progressive comprehension is assured by a purely sensorimotor assimilation.

With regard to accommodation, that is tantamount to saying that the subject's experience remains immediate and consequently victim of the most naïve phenomenalism. That is demonstrated not only by the primacy of the "optical contact" as we have just interpreted it, but also by Observations 168–170. Two correlative conditions are necessary to replace the universe such as it is: the constitution of permanent objects (inserted in coherent groups of displacements and maintaining among themselves clear causal relations) and the elimination of illusions due to the particular point of view (by insertion of this point of view in an objective system of laws of perspective). These two processes are interdependent: In order to constitute "objects" in a system of spatial and causal relations, one must place oneself among these objects and, in order thus to come out of one's own perspective one must elaborate a system of spatial, causal, and objective relations. Now Observations 168–170 show us, in the most naïve and concrete form, how immediate experience does not consist in relating oneself to the object and how the constitution of the object first consists in detaching it from oneself. Jacqueline and Lucienne do not at first succeed in picking up rags, opening boxes or removing contents from the container because unknowingly they create an obstacle to their own efforts and because the most difficult obstacle to perceive in everything is oneself! It can readily be seen how such facts again reveal the primacy of action over representation and consequently the immediate character of the subject's experiences as well as his assimilatory activity.

On the other hand if, during this fifth stage, representation is not yet freed from perception, the system of signs due to the growing mobility of the schemata effects new progress toward prevision. We recall that from the time when the secondary schemata begins to be coördinated (fourth stage), this mobility allows the signals to become detached from the activity itself in order to constitute a prevision relating to the objects themselves. This capacity for prevision still develops during the fifth stage and, without resulting in actual representation, it gives rise to practical anticipations based upon generalization of earlier experiences.

Here are some examples:

Observation 175.—At 1;2 (30) Jacqueline is standing in a room which is not hers and examines the green wallpaper. Then she touches it gently and at once looks at her fingertips. This is evidently the generalization of schemata due to the following secondary or tertiary circular reactions: touching food (jams, etc.) and looking at her fingers, or dipping her fingertips in soap lather while being washed and examining them afterward.

Another example. At 1;1 (23) Jacqueline, finding an orange peel, turns it upside down on the table to make it rock. She therefore immediately foresees the signification of this object.

At 1;3 (12) she is standing in her playpen and I place a clown, which she recently received, on the top of the frame, in different places in sequence. Jacqueline advances laboriously along the frame but, when she arrives in front of the clown, she grasps it very cautiously and delicately, knowing that it will fall at the slightest shake. She behaved in this way ever since the first attempt.

One observes that, in each of these three cases, Jacqueline foresees certain properties of the object which are independent of its action with respect to herself. The green wallpaper is conceived as though it ought to leave colored traces, the orange peel as being able to rock itself once it is placed in a suitable position and the clown as falling down at the first touch. These previsions, like those of the fourth stage, reveal an objectification of the signals into signs relating to the external processes themselves. In other words, the signification of perceived objects is not only that they are to be grasped, shaken, swung, rubbed, etc., but that they are the cause of phenomena external to the action itself. But, on the other hand, these signs are not limited, like those in Observations 132–135, to basing prevision on sequences already observed in the same form. It would seem that there exists, in the three cases of Observation 175, a generalization from analogous experiences and a generalization with present groping. In short, such signs add to the characteristics of those which are based on simple mobile schemata the advantage of the "experiment in order to see" or of the directed groping belonging to the present stage.

Before proceeding to the study of inventions through mental combinations and representations, it is fitting again to remember that the directed groping of active experimentation is essentially vicarious. As soon as this process results in the formation of new schemata, the latter can function either in invention through mental combination as we shall see, or in the capacity of familiar means which apply to new circumstances. In the second case we refer to the situations studied in Chapter IV: that is quite natural and amounts to saying that "familiar means" can have been acquired just as well through active experimentation as through secondary circular reaction.

In a general way, the fact should be emphasized that the behavior patterns characteristic of the different stages do not succeed each other in a linear way (those of a given stage disappearing at the time when those of the following one take form) but in the manner of the layers of a pyramid (upright or upside down), the new behavior patterns simply being added to the old ones to complete, correct or combine with them. In this connection we can cite certain behavior patterns in the course of which the schemata in process of formation due to the process of tertiary circular reaction are applied to new circumstances, not through "active experimentation" nor even through "application of familiar means to new situations," but simply in the manner of the "procedures to make an interesting spectacle last" (studied in Chapter III, §4). Here is an example:

Observation 176.—At 1;6 (8) Jacqueline is seated on an adult's bed having in front of her a big slanting quilt. I place a little wooden lamb on the peak of this mountain and, striking the lower part of the quilt, I made the animal descend several centimeters at each shake. Jacqueline at once profits from this observation and brings the animal back to her each time I put it again on the summit of the quilt.

I then place the lamb on a table, 1 m. away from the bed, at the same height but separated by a corridor 50 cm. wide which Jacqueline notices; nevertheless she strikes the quilt as before while watching the lamb. I remove the latter after a moment and then put it back on the same table; Jacqueline recommences hitting the quilt.

A quarter of an hour later I begin the experiment over again with a celluloid fish. Jacqueline makes it fall by hitting the quilt and, when I place the fish on the table, she continues to hit the quilt. On the other hand, when I place the fish (or the lamb) on a window sill, further away and higher up, she abandons all efforts.

At 1;6 (12) Jacqueline spontaneously engages in behavior of the same kind but without any possible suggestion from the preceding experiment. She happens to shake a chair whose back touches the open window. She thus indirectly makes the window move and then recommences intentionally to shake the chair while watching the window. Then she walks in the room without seeming to think about the thing any more. But, knocking another chair 1.50 m. away, she immediately shakes it in the same way and looks at the window. She continues for a while in spite of failure while attentively watching the window.

At 1;6 (20) Jacqueline brings down a watch chain from the top of a quilt by hitting the latter. I then place the chain on a chair, 50 cm. from the bed. She strikes the quilt three times while watching the chain but without conviction and as though "to see if" that can yield something.

Thus it may be seen how directed groping as well as the application to the experiment of schemata due to tertiary circular reaction can, in situations of which the child does not understand the particulars, be extended in "applications of familiar means to new situations" and even in "procedures to make an interesting spectacle last" reminiscent of the behavior patterns of the fourth and third stages.

In conclusion, the behavior patterns characteristic of the fifth stage constitute a homogeneous totality: The "tertiary circular reaction" marks the beginning of experimental behavior, whereas the "discovery of new means through active experimentation" utilizes the method thus found by the child for the solution of new problems. As we shall see in Volume II, moreover, this more advanced adaptation of intelligence to the real is accompanied by a structurization of the external environment into permanent objects and coherent spatial relations as well as by a correlative objectification and spatialization of causality and time.

CHAPTER VI

THE SIXTH STAGE:

The Invention of New Means Through Mental Combinations

The ensemble of intelligent behavior patterns studied hitherto—secondary circular reaction, application of familiar means to new situations, tertiary circular reaction and discovery of new means through active experimentation—characterizes a single, big period. To be sure, there is progress from one type to another behavior pattern and so one can consider the three main groups which we have delineated in the preceding chapters as forming three sequential stages (it being understood that the advent of each new stage does not abolish in any way the behavior patterns of the preceding stages and that new behavior patterns are simply superposed on the old ones). But the facts remain so complicated and their sequence can be so rapid that it would be dangerous to separate these stages too much. On the other hand, with the behavior patterns, which we are now going to describe, begins a new period which everyone will concur in considering as appearing tardily, much later than the preceding behavior patterns. We can therefore speak of a sixth stage which does not mean that the behavior patterns hitherto under study will disappear, but merely that they will henceforth be completed by behavior patterns of a new type: invention through deduction or mental combination.

This new type of behavior patterns characterizes systematic intelligence. Now it is the latter which, according to Claparède, is governed by awareness of relationships and no longer by empirical groping. It operates, according to Köhler, by sudden structurizations of the perceptual field or, according to Rignano, is based on purely mental experience. In short, all writers, whether associationists like Rignano, believers in "structures" like Köhler or, like Claparède, believers in a more or less directed groping, agree that there exists an essential moment in the development of intelligence: the moment when the awareness of relationships is sufficiently advanced to permit a reasoned prevision, that is to say, an invention operating by simple mental combination.

We are consequently confronted by the most delicate problem which any theory of intelligence has to treat: that of the power of invention. Hitherto the different forms of intellectual activity which we have had to describe have not presented particular difficulties of interpretation. Either they consisted in apprenticeships during which the role of experience is evident, discovery consequently surpassing true invention, or else they consisted in simple applications of the familiar to the new. In both cases, thereafter, the mechanism of adaptation is easy to explain and the play of assimilations and of primitive accommodations suffices to explain all the combinations. On the other hand, as soon as real invention arises the process of thought baffles analysis and seems to escape determinism. Will the schemata to which the preceding facts have accustomed us fail in the task, or will the new facts which we are about to describe appear once more to be prepared by all the functional mechanism of earlier activities?

Let us observe at the outset, in this connection, but without wishing to find an explanation ahead of time, that real invention arises as a function of a sort of rhythm conditioned by the ensemble of the preceding behavior patterns. This rhythm determines the sequence of acquisitions and applications. With secondary circular reaction we are in the midst of acquisition: New schemata are constructed through reproductive assimilation and accommodation combined. With the application of familiar means to new situations, these same schemata give rise to some original applications (through generalizing assimilation) without actual acquisition being involved. With tertiary circular reaction and the discovery of new means through apprenticeship, we are once again in a period of apprenticeship but, in this case, the very complexity of acquisition involves a constant intervention of all that has been acquired earlier. With invention through mental combination we can at last speak of a new process of application, for all invention presupposes a mental combination of already elaborated schemata, but an application on a par with acquisition since there is invention and consequently there are original combinations. Given this rhythm, invention is therefore comparable to the "application of familiar means to new situations" since, like the latter, it operates by deduction; but this deduction, being creative, also partakes of the processes of acquisition hitherto under study and, oddly enough, of the discovery of new means through active experimentation.

§1. THE FACTS.—First, here is a series of observations beginning with those most reminiscent of the discoveries due to directed groping. It happens that the same problem, such as that of the stick to be brought through the bars, can give rise to solutions through real invention as well as to solutions involving simple experimental groping. Analysis of such cases will enable us to see right away both the originality of the new behavior patterns and their relationship to the preceding ones. This relative contrast of solutions can be observed either in passing from one child to another or in the same child several months later.

Observation 177.—In order to explain the difference between the present and preceding behavior patterns it can be instructive to examine the way in which Laurent all at once discovered the use of the stick after not having known how to utilize that instrument for several months.

In contradistinction to Jacqueline and Lucienne whom we know were subjected to numerous experiments during which they had opportunity to "learn" to use the stick, Laurent only manipulated it at long intervals until the time when he knew how to use it spontaneously. It is therefore worth while, in order to characterize that moment, briefly to retrace the ensemble of Laurent's earlier behavior patterns relating to the stick.

As early as 0;4 (20), that is to say, at the beginning of the third stage, Laurent is confronted by a short stick which he assimilates to some object. He shakes it, rubs it against the wicker of his bassinet, draws himself up, etc. In a general way he makes it the equivalent of the paper knife in Observation 104. But, at 0;4 (21), when Laurent is holding the stick, he happens to strike a hanging toy and immediately continues. But during the next hours Laurent no longer tries to reproduce this result even when I put the stick back into his hand.—This first situation, then, is not an example of the "behavior pattern of the stick." Laurent confined himself to momentarily inserting a new element in an already constructed schema (the schema of striking). But the fortuitous intervention of the latter gave rise to no immediate comprehension or even experimentation. The following days I give him the stick again and try to make him associate it to the activity of the various schemata. But Laurent does not react then or in the following weeks. The "behavior pattern of the stick," that is to say, the utilization of the stick in the capacity of intermediate or instrument, does not seem able to be acquired during the stage of the secondary circular reactions, even when chance has favored the momentary insertion of the stick in an already existing schema.

In the course of the fourth stage, characterized by the coördination of the schemata, the use of the stick makes no progress. However, during this stage, the child comes to use the hand of another person as an intermediate to act upon distant objects, thus succeeding in spatializing causality and preparing the way for experimental behavior. But when, at 0;8 or even 0;9 I give Laurent the stick, he only uses it to strike around him and not yet to displace or bring to him the objects he hits.

At 1;0 (0)—that is to say, well into the fifth stage (it is during this stage that Jacqueline and Lucienne succeeded in discovering the utilization of the stick)—Laurent manipulates a long wooden ruler for a long time, but only arrives at the three following reactions. In the first place, he turns the stick over systematically while transferring it from one hand to the other. Then he strikes the floor, his shoes and various objects with it. In the third place, he displaces it by pushing it gently over the floor with his index finger. Several times I place, at a certain distance from the child, some attractive objective to see whether Laurent, already holding the stick, will know how to use it. But each time Laurent tries to attain the object with his free hand without having the idea of using the stick. Other times I place the stick on the floor, between the objective and the child, in order thus to provoke a visual suggestion. But the child does not react to that either.—There does not yet exist, therefore, any trace of the "behavior pattern of the stick."

At 1;0 (5), on the other hand, Laurent is playing with a little child's cane which he handles for the first time. He is visibly surprised at the interdependence he observes between the two ends of this object. He displaces the cane in all directions, letting the free end drag along the floor, and studies the coming and going of this end as function of the movements he makes with the other end. In short, he begins to conceive of the stick as a rigid entity. But this discovery does not lead him to that of the instrumental signification of the stick. In effect, having by chance struck a tin box with the cane, he again strikes it but without the idea either of making it advance in that way or of bringing it to him.—I replace the box with various more tempting objectives: the child's reaction remains the same.

At 1;2 (25) I give him back the stick because of his recent progress. He has just learned to put objects on top of one another, to put them into a cup and turn it upside down, etc.: the relationships which belong to the level of the behavior pattern of the stick (see Vol. II). He grasps the stick and immediately strikes the floor with it, then strikes various objects (boxes, etc.) placed on the floor. He displaces them gently but it does not occur to him to utilize this result systematically. At a given moment his stick gets caught in a rag and drags it for a few moments in the course of its movements. But when I put various desirable objectives 50 cm. or 1 m. away from Laurent he does not utilize the virtual instrument he holds.—It is apparent that, if I had repeated such experiments at this period, Laurent, like his sisters, would have discovered the use of the stick through directed groping and apprenticeship. But I broke off the attempt and only resumed it during the sixth stage.

At 1;4 (5) Laurent is seated before a table and I place a bread crust in front of him, out of reach. Also, to the right of the child I place a stick about 25 cm. long. At first Laurent tries to grasp the bread without paying attention to the instrument, and then he gives up. I then put the stick between him and the bread; it does not touch the objective but nevertheless carries with it an undeniable visual suggestion. Laurent again looks at the bread, without moving, looks very briefly at the stick, then suddenly grasps it and directs it toward the bread. But he grasped it toward the middle and not at one of its ends so that it is too short to attain the objective. Laurent then puts it down and resumes stretching out his hand toward the bread. Then, without spending much time on this movement, he takes up the stick again, this time at one of its ends (chance or intention?), and draws the bread to him. He begins by simply touching it, as though contact of the stick with the objective were sufficient to set the latter in motion, but after one or two seconds at most he pushes the crust with real intention. He displaces it gently to the right, then draws it to him without difficulty. Two successive attempts yield the same result.

An hour later I place a toy in front of Laurent (out of his reach) and a new stick next to him. He does not even try to catch the objective with his hand; he immediately grasps the stick and draws the toy to him.

Thus it may be seen how Laurent has discovered the use of the stick almost without any groping when, during the preceding stages, he

handled it without understanding its usefulness. This reaction is therefore distinctly different from that of his sisters.

Observation 178.—We recall Jacqueline's gropings at 1;3 (12) when
confronted by a stick to be brought through the bars of her playpen
(Obs. 162). Now it happens that the same problem presented to Lucienne at 1;1 (18) gives rise to an almost immediate solution in which
invention surpasses groping. Lucienne is seated in front of the bars
and I place against them, horizontally and parallel to the bars (half
way up them) the stick of Observation 162. Lucienne grasps it at the
middle and merely pulls it. Noticing her failure, she withdraws the
stick, tilts it up and brings it through easily.

I then place the stick on the floor. Instead of raising it to pull it
directly, she grasps it by the middle, tilts it up beforehand and presses
it. Or else she grasps it by one end and brings it in easily.

I start all over again with a longer stick (30 cm. long). Either she
grasps it by the middle and tilts it up before pulling it, or else she
brings it in by pulling on one end.

Same experiment with a stick 50 cm. long. The procedure is obviously the same but, when the stick gets caught, she pulls it away briefly,
then lets it go with a groan and begins over again in a better way.

The next day, at 1;1 (19), same experiments. Lucienne begins by
merely pulling (once), then tilts up the stick and so rediscovers the
procedures of the day before. At 1;2 (7) I resume the observation. This
time Lucienne tilts up the stick before it touches the bars.

It may thus be seen how these attempts are reminiscent of Jacqueline's, taking place through groping and apprenticeship. Lucienne
begins by merely pulling the stick and repeats this once the next day.
But, in contrast to her sister's prolonged efforts, Lucienne at once
profits from her failure and uses a procedure which she invents right
away through simple representation.

Observation 179.—The example of the watch chain to be put into an
aperture 16 x 34 mm. is more complex. Here again we remember Jacqueline's gropings (Obs. 173 and 173 repeated). But Lucienne has
solved the problem by sudden invention:

At 1;4 (0) without ever having contemplated this spectacle, Lucienne looks at the box which I bring nearer and return without her
having seen the contents. The chain spreads out on the floor and she
immediately tries to put it back into the box. She begins by simply
putting one end of the chain into the box and trying to make the rest
follow progressively. This procedure which was first tried by Jacqueline,
Lucienne finds successful the first time (the end put into the box stays
there fortuitously), but fails completely at the second and third attempts.

At the fourth attempt, Lucienne starts as before but pauses, and
after a short interval, herself places the chain on a flat surface nearby

(the experiment takes place on a shawl), rolls it up in a ball intentionally, takes the ball between three fingers and puts the whole thing in the box.

The fifth attempt begins by a very short resumption of the first procedure. But Lucienne corrects herself at once and returns to the correct method.

Sixth attempt: immediate success.

Thus one sees the difference between the behavior patterns of Jacqueline and of Lucienne. What was, in the former, the product of a long apprenticeship, was suddenly invented by the latter. Such a difference is surely a question of the level. So it is that at 2;6 (25) Jacqueline, with whom I repeat the experiment, solves the problem unhesitatingly. By grasping the chain in both hands she puts it in with her left hand while holding the remaining part in her right, to prevent it from falling. In the event that it gets caught, she corrects the movement.

Observation 180.—Another mental invention, derived from a mental combination and not only from a sensorimotor apprenticeship was that which permitted Lucienne to rediscover an object inside a matchbox. At 1;4 (0), that is to say, right after the preceding experiment, I play at hiding the chain in the same box used in Observation 179. I begin by opening the box as wide as possible and putting the chain into its cover (where Lucienne herself put it, but deeper). Lucienne, who has already practiced filling and emptying her pail and various receptacles, then grasps the box and turns it over without hesitation. No invention is involved of course (it is the simple application of a schema, acquired through groping) but knowledge of this behavior pattern of Lucienne is useful for understanding what follows.

Then I put the chain inside an empty matchbox (where the matches belong), then close the box leaving an opening of 10 mm. Lucienne begins by turning the whole thing over, then tries to grasp the chain through the opening. Not succeeding, she simply puts her index finger into the slit and so succeeds in getting out a small fragment of the chain; she then pulls it until she has completely solved the problem.

Here begins the experiment which we want to emphasize. I put the chain back into the box and reduce the opening to 3 mm. It is understood that Lucienne is not aware of the functioning of the opening and closing of the matchbox and has not seen me prepare the experiment. She only possesses the two preceding schemata: turning the box over in order to empty it of its contents, and sliding her finger into the slit to make the chain come out. It is of course this last procedure that she tries first: she puts her finger inside and gropes to reach the chain, but fails completely. A pause follows during which Lucienne manifests a very curious reaction bearing witness not only to the fact that she tries to think out the situation and to represent to herself through mental combination the operations to be performed, but also to the role played by imitation in the genesis of representations. Lucienne mimics the widening of the slit.

She looks at the slit with great attention; then, several times in succession, she opens and shuts her mouth, at first slightly, then wider and wider! Apparently Lucienne understands the existence of a cavity subjacent to the slit and wishes to enlarge that cavity. The attempt at representation which she thus furnishes is expressed plastically, that is to say, due to inability to think out the situation in words or clear visual images she uses a simple motor indication as "signifier" or symbol. Now, as the motor reaction which presents itself for filling this role is none other than imitation, that is to say, representation by acts, which, doubtless earlier than any mental image, makes it possible not only to divide into parts the spectacles seen but also to evoke and reproduce them at will. Lucienne, by opening her mouth thus expresses, or even reflects her desire to enlarge the opening of the box. This schema of imitation, with which she is familiar, constitutes for her the means of thinking out the situation. There is doubtless added to it an element of magic-phenomenalistic causality or efficacy. Just as she often uses imitation to act upon persons and make them reproduce their interesting movements, so also it is probable that the act of opening her mouth in front of the slit to be enlarged implies some underlying idea of efficacy.

Soon after this phase of plastic reflection, Lucienne unhesitatingly puts her finger in the slit and, instead of trying as before to reach the chain, she pulls so as to enlarge the opening. She succeeds and grasps the chain.

During the following attempts (the slit always being 3 mm. wide), the same procedure is immediately rediscovered. On the other hand, Lucienne is incapable of opening the box when it is completely closed. She gropes, throws the box on the floor, etc., but fails.

Observation 181.—At 1;6 (23) for the first time Lucienne plays with a doll carriage whose handle comes to the height of her face. She rolls it over the carpet by pushing it. When she comes against a wall, she pulls, walking backward. But as this position is not convenient for her, she pauses and without hesitation, goes to the other side to push the carriage again. She therefore found the procedure in one attempt, apparently through analogy to other situations but without training, apprenticeship, or chance.

In the same kind of inventions, that is to say, in the realm of kinematic representations, the following fact should be cited. At 1;10 (27) Lucienne tries to kneel before a stool but, by leaning against it, pushes it further away. She then raises herself up, takes it and places it against a sofa. When it is firmly set there she leans against it and kneels without difficulty.

Observation 181 repeated.—In the same way Jacqueline, at 1;8 (9) arrives at a closed door—with a blade of grass in each hand. She stretches out her right hand toward the knob but sees that she cannot turn it without letting go of the grass. She puts the grass on the floor, opens the door, picks up the grass again and enters. But when she wants to leave the room things become complicated. She puts the grass on the floor and grasps the doorknob. But then she perceives that in pulling the door toward her she will simultaneously chase away the grass which she placed between the door and the threshold. She therefore picks it up in order to put it outside the door's zone of movement.

This ensemble of operations, which in no way comprises remarkable invention, is nevertheless very characteristic of the intelligent acts founded upon representation or the awareness of relationships.

Observation 182.—At 1;8 (30) Jacqueline has an ivory plate in front of her, pierced by holes of 1–2 mm. in diameter and watches me put the point of a pencil in one of the holes. The pencil remains stuck vertically there and Jacqueline laughs. She grasps the pencil and repeats the operation. Then I hold out another pencil to her but with the unsharpened end directed toward the plate. Jacqueline grasps it but does not turn it over and tries to introduce this end (the pencil is 5 mm. in diameter) into each of the three holes in succession. She keeps this up for quite a while even returning to the smallest holes. On this occasion we make three kinds of observations:

1. When I return the first pencil to Jacqueline she puts it in the hole correctly at once. When I hand it to her upside down, she turns it over even before making an attempt, thus revealing that she is very capable of understanding the conditions for putting it in. On the other hand, when I hold out the second pencil correctly directed (the point down) she also puts it in by the point. But if I offer it to her upside down she does not turn it over and recommences wishing to put it in by the unsharpened end. This behavior pattern remained absolutely constant during thirty attempts, that is to say, Jacqueline never turned the second pencil over whereas she always directed the first one correctly. Everything happens as though the first attempts had given rise to a sensorimotor schema which persisted in acting during the whole series: the two pencils were accordingly conceived as being in contrast to each other, the first being that which one puts into the hole easily and the second that which resists. However, the pencils are of course identical from the point of view of the facility with which they can be put in the hole; the first is merely shorter than the second and is green and the second is brown (both have hard, black lead).

2. Several times Jacqueline, seeing the second pencil will not go in, tries to put it in the same hole as the first one. Hence, not only does she try to put it in by the unsharpened end but also she wants to put it into a hole which is already filled by the other pencil. She

resumed this strange procedure several times despite total failure. This observation shows very well how, in a child of this age, representation of things is still ignorant of the most elementary mechanical and physical laws and so makes it possible to understand why Jacqueline so obstinately tries to put in the second pencil by the wrong end. Ignorant of the fact that two objects cannot occupy the same small opening, there is no reason for her not to try to put an object 5 mm. in diameter in a 1–2 mm. hole.

3. At about the thirtieth attempt, Jacqueline suddenly changes methods. She turns the second pencil over as she does the first and no longer tries a single time to put it in by the wrong end. If the series of these new attempts is compared with the first series, one has the impression of a sudden understanding, as of an idea which arises and which, when it has suddenly appeared, definitively imposes itself. In other words, the second pencil has suddenly been assimilated to the first. The primitive schema (connecting the two pencils by contrast) has dissociated itself and the pencil which one did not turn over has been assimilated to the particular schema of the pencil that one had to turn over. This kind of a process is consequently again capable of making us understand the mechanism of invention.

The respect in which these behavior patterns are original in relation to the preceding ones may thus be seen. The child finds himself in a situation which is new to him, that is to say, the objects arising between his intentions and the arrival at an end demand unforeseen and particular adaptation. It is therefore necessary to find adequate means. Now these means cannot be brought back to the procedures acquired earlier in other circumstances (as in the "application of familiar means to new circumstances"); it is therefore necessary to innovate. If these behavior patterns are compared to all the preceding ones, they resemble most the "discovery of new means through active experimentation." Their functional context is exactly the same. But, contrary to the latter, the present behavior patterns do not appear to operate by groping or apprenticeship, but by sudden invention; that is to say, that instead of being controlled at each of the stages and *a posteriori* by the facts themselves, the searching is controlled *a priori* by mental combination. Before trying them, the child foresees which maneuvers will fail and which will succeed. The control of the experiment therefore bears upon the whole of this deduction and no longer, as before, upon the details of each particular step. Moreover, the procedure conceived as being capable of succeeding is in itself new, that is to say, it results from an original mental combination and not from a combination of movements actually executed at each stage of the operation.

§2. INVENTION AND REPRESENTATION.—The two essential questions raised by such behavior patterns in relation to the preceding ones are those of *invention* and *representation*. Henceforth there exists invention and no longer only discovery; there is, moreover, representation and no longer only sensorimotor groping. These two aspects of systematic intelligence are interdependent. To invent is to combine mental, that is to say, representative, schemata and, in order to become mental the sensorimotor schemata must be capable of intercombining in every way, that is to say, of being able to give rise to true inventions.

How can this transition from directed gropings to invention, and from motor schema to representative schema be explained? Let us begin by reëstablishing the continuity between the extremes in order subsequently to account for the differentiations.

It must be understood, with regard to the first point of view, that the contrast between directed groping and actual *invention* is primarily due to a difference in speed. The structuring activity of assimilation only operates step by step in the course of experimental groping, so that it is not immediately visible, and one is tempted to attribute the discoveries which result from it solely to fortuitous contact with external facts. In invention, on the contrary, it is so rapid that the structurization seems sudden. The structuring assimilatory activity thus once again passes unnoticed at first glance and one is tempted to consider the "structures" as organizing themselves. Thereafter the contrast between the empiricism of simple groping and the intelligence of deductive invention seems to be complete. But if one thinks about the role of intellectual activity peculiar to combined assimilation and accommodation, one perceives that this activity is neither absent from empirical groping nor useless to the structuring of representations. On the contrary, it constitutes the real motor of both, and the primary difference between the two situations stems from the speed at which the motor goes, a speed slowed down in the first case by the obstacles on the road and accelerated in the second case by the training acquired.

But this continuous increase of speed entails a differentiation in the very procedure of the functioning. At first cut up and visible from the outside, it becomes regularized and seems to be internalized by becoming rapid. In this respect, the difference between empirical groping and invention is comparable to that which separates induction from deduction. The empiricists have tried to reduce the second to the first, thus making induction the only genuine reasoning. Induction being, according to them, only a passive recording of the results of experience, deduction then became a sort of internal replica of this experience, a "mental experience" as Mach and Rignano put it. In contrast to this thesis is that of a certain logicism according to which induction and deduction have nothing in common, the former consisting, according to the empiricists, in a catalogue of statements, and the second in purely formal combinations. At last came the sound logistic analysis which showed the relationship as well as the contrast between these two complementary processes. Both consist in constructions of relationships, induction, thus involving deduction and resting upon its constructive activity. But in the first, construction is ceaselessly controlled from without and so can appeal to those extralogical procedures of anticipation which appeared to the empiricists to constitute the essence of thought, whereas in the second, construction is regulated from within, solely by the play of operations. So also, empirical groping already presupposes the mechanism of invention. As we have seen, there is no pure accommodation, but accommodation is always directed by a play of schemata whose reorganization, if it were spontaneous, would become identified with the constructive deduction of the present behavior patterns. But as this reorganization peculiar to accommodation is unable, when the problem transcends the subject's level, to dispense with a continuous external control, it always works through cumulative assimilation; that is to say, the structuring activity keeps a slow pace and only intercombines the sequential data of assimilation. In the present case, on the contrary, in which the question raised is addressed to a mind sufficiently furnished with already constructed schemata so that the reorganization of these schemata operates spontaneously, the structuring activity no longer needs always to depend on the actual data of perception and, in the interpretation of these data, can make a complex system of simply evoked schemata converge. Invention is nothing other than this rapid reorganization and representation amounts to this evocation, both thus extending the mechanisms at work in the ensemble of the preceding behavior patterns.

From this point of view let us again take up Observations 177–182, comparing them to the mechanism of empirical gropings. As before, the point of departure of these behavior patterns consists in the impetus given by the schema assigning an end to the action; for instance, in Observation 180, sight of the chain in the matchbox sets in motion the schema of grasping. This schema of the goal immediately arouses a certain number of schemata which the child will utilize as initial means and which he must accommodate, that is to say, differentiate according to the variations of the new situation. In Observation 180, Lucienne tries to turn the box over or to slide her finger into the slit in order to extract the chain. But in utilizing these schemata the child perceives at the same time the difficulties of the present situation. In other words, there occurs here, as in the course of empirical groping, an encounter with the unforeseen fact which creates an obstacle (the slit is too narrow to admit the finger). Now in both cases, this encounter entails a new intervention of earlier schemata. It is due to the latter that these unforeseen facts acquire meaning. The only difference is that, henceforth, such encounters with the obstacle no longer take place in the course of discovery (since the latter is no longer groping and consists in sudden invention) but beforehand, at the moment when the first procedures tried out as hypotheses fail, and when the problem is clarified by virtue of that very failure. In Observation 180, these auxiliary schemata which attribute a meaning to the facts are those that permit the child to understand what the slit is that he sees before him (= sign of a subjacent opening) and how it is troublesome (because it is too narrow). The child often opens and closes boxes, wants to put his hand through very small openings, etc. Those are the schemata which confer a meaning on the present situation and which at the same time direct the search. They intervene, therefore, as secondary means and hence are subordinated to the initial procedure. It is then that invention comes in, in the form of sudden accommodation of the ensemble of those schemata to the present situation. How does this accommodation work?

It consists, as always, in differentiating the preceding schemata according to the variations of the present situation, but this differentiation, instead of operating through actual groping and cumulative assimilation, results from a spontaneous assimilation, hence more rapid and operating by means of simply representative attempts. In other words, instead of exploring the slit with his finger and groping until he has discovered the procedure which consists in drawing to him the inner side (of the box) in order to enlarge the opening; the child is satisfied to look at the opening, except for experimenting no longer on it directly, but on its symbolic substitutes. Lucienne opens and closes her mouth while examining the slit of the box, proving that she is in the act of assimilating it and of mentally trying out the enlargement of the slit; moreover, the analogy thus established by assimilation between the slit perceived and other openings simply evoked leads her to foresee that pressure put on the edge of the opening will widen it. Once the schemata have thus been spontaneously accommodated on the plane of simple mental assimilation, Lucienne proceeds to act and succeeds right away.

An interpretation of this sort applies to each of our observations. In Observation 179, for example, if Lucienne rolls the chain up into a ball to put it into the box after having noted the failure of the direct method, it is because the schemata acquired in putting the chain into a pail or a necklace into a watering can (Obs. 172) or again in squeezing materials, putting her pillow or handkerchief in her mouth, etc., afford her sufficient assimilation of the new situation. Instead of groping she mentally combines the operations to be performed. But this mental experience does not consist in mnemonic evocation of already manufactured images; it is an essentially constructive process the representation of which is only a symbolic adjuvant, since genuine invention exists and it never perceived a reality identical to the one it is in the process of elaborating. In Observations 180 and 180 repeated there also exists spontaneous functioning of the schemata of displacement, by analogy, to be sure, with the experiments the child was able to make in reality, but this analogy entails imagination of new combinations. Finally, in Observation 182, we see how an initial schema can be differentiated, without progressive groping, through sudden dissociation and assimilation.[1]

But how can we account for the mechanism of this spon-

[1] In order better to understand the mechanism of this assimilation which has become deductive while remaining on the plane of sensorimotor operations, let us again analyze a case of elementary practical invention observed in an adult and consequently capable of correct introspection. While driving an old automobile I am bothered by oil on the steering wheel which makes it slippery. Lacking time to stop, I take out my handkerchief and dry the spots. When putting it in my pocket I observe that it is too greasy and look for a place to put it without soiling anything. I put it between my seat and the one next to me, as deeply as possible in the crevice. An hour later the rain forces me to close the windshield but the resulting heat makes me try to open it a little. The screws being worn out, I cannot succeed; it only stays wide open or completely shut. I try to hold the windshield slightly open with my left hand, but my fatigue makes me think that some object could replace my hand. I look around me, but nothing is in evidence. While looking at the windshield I have the impression that the object could be put, not at the bottom of the windshield (one pushed it at the bottom to open it), but by wedging it in the angle formed by the right edge of the windshield and the vertical upright of the body of the car. I have the vague feeling of an analogy between the solution to be found and a problem already solved before. The solution then becomes clarified. My tendency to put an object into the corner of the windshield meets a sort of motor memory of having just a few minutes before placed something into a crevice. I try to remember what it was, but no definite representation comes to mind. Then suddenly, without having time to imagine anything, I understand the solution and find myself already in the act of searching with my hand for the hidden handkerchief. Therefore the latter schema directed my search and directed me toward the lateral corner of the windshield when my last idea was a different one.

This trite observation demonstrates very well how a sensorimotor search can arouse schemata previously acquired and make them function independently of internal language and clear representation. The tendency to introduce an object into a slit, in this example, is modeled exactly on a schema remaining in an almost purely motor state, and the conjunction thus produced suffices to insure discovery of a solution. One therefore understands how a sensorimotor deduction is possible in the small child through simple practical evocation of the schemata and independently of a well-defined system of representations.

taneous reorganization of schemata? Take, for example, the construction of the schema of "rolling into a ball" in Observation 179, or that of "widening the slit" in Observation 180; does this construction consist in a sudden structurization of representations or of the perceptual field, or is it the result of assimilatory activities prior to invention? As we have just recalled, a certain number of already acquired schemata direct the search at the moment of invention without, however, any one of them containing in itself the correct solution. For example, before rolling the chain up into a ball to put it in the narrow opening, Lucienne has already: (1) squeezed the material, (2) put the chain in a wide opening, and (3) compared large objects to inadequate openings (as when she tried to bring objects through the bars of her playpen). In Observation 180 she also possesses the earlier schemata we have already emphasized. The question raised is therefore to find out how these schemata will intercoördinate in order to give rise to invention: Is it by a structuring independent of their genesis or due to the very activity which engendered them and which is now pursued without any longer depending on the external circumstances in which it began? One might as well ask whether ideas organize themselves in the course of theoretical invention or whether they are organized as a function of implicit judgments and of the potential intelligent activity they represent. We do not doubt that the second of these two theses is in both cases (in sensorimotor intelligence as well as in reflective thought) much the most satisfying to the mind, the first only consisting in a manner of speaking which veils the dynamism of the facts with static language.

But how is this reorganization of schemata to be conceived if it must fulfill the dual condition of extending their assimilatory activity and of liberating itself from the external circumstances in which this activity began? It is due to the process of reciprocal assimilation but in so far as it is henceforth extended on a plane independent of the immediate action.

Here we rediscover a remark already made in connection with the "application of familiar means to new circumstances"; it is that, in the act of practical intelligence, means are subordinated to ends through a coördination analogous to that of the heterogeneous schemata in the case of intersensorial coördinations (hearing and sight, etc.), hence through reciprocal assimilation of the schemata. In other words, each schema tends to extend the assimilatory activity that gave rise to it (just as every idea tends to extend the judgments from which it derived), and consequently applies to the ensemble of the situations which lend themselves to it. Thereafter, when there is a watch chain to be put into a narrow opening, the schemata presenting some analogy to the situation and so capable of assimilating the data will enter into activity by themselves. We have constantly met with examples illustrating this process. But, until the present time, the activity thus set in motion has always given rise to real actions, that is to say, to immediate applications ("application of familiar means to new circumstances") or to empirical gropings. The novelty of the case of invention consists, on the contrary, in that henceforth the schemata entering into action remain in a state of latent activity and combine with each other before (and not after) their external and material application. This is why invention seems to come from the void. The act which suddenly arises results from a previous reciprocal assimilation instead of manifesting its vicissitudes before everyone. The best example of this process is in footnote 1 of this chapter. Introspection enabled us to observe clearly how the schema of the handkerchief wedged down into a slit assimilated progressively and mentally the schema of the object to be slid into the opening of the windshield and vice versa, this reciprocal assimilation bringing with it the invention of the correct solution. With respect to Lucienne, Observation 180 also shows this explanation to be well founded. The gesture of opening and closing the mouth in the presence of the opening to be widened indicates sufficiently clearly how the internal reorganization of the schemata works through assimilation. G. Tarde's[2] well-known formula illustrates this mechanism: Invention, Tarde said, results from the interference of independent currents of action. The process of this interference could only be, in our language, that of reciprocal assimilation.

In short, invention through sensorimotor deduction is

2 G. Tarde, *Les lois sociales,* Paris, Alcan.

nothing other than a spontaneous reorganization of earlier schemata which are accommodated by themselves to the new situation, through reciprocal assimilation. Until the present time, that is to say, including empirical groping, the earlier schemata only functioned due to real use, that is to say, by actual application to a concretely perceived datum. So it is that in Observation 165 Jacqueline must really see that the rooster is stopped by the bars of the playpen and she must really have noted the possibility of tilting it up when it fell backward by chance, in order that she might acquire the idea of pushing it back systematically before tilting it up and bringing it in between the bars. The earlier schemata thus intervene to give a meaning to these events, but they only intervene when a concretely perceived datum (the rooster's fall, etc.) excites and makes them function. On the contrary, in preventive deduction, the schemata function internally by themselves, without requiring a series of external acts to aliment them continually from without. It is also necessary, of course, that a problem be raised by the facts themselves and that this problem set up, in the capacity of hypothesis, the use of a sensorimotor schema serving as initial means (otherwise we would no longer be in the realm of practical intelligence and would already reach the plane of reflective intelligence). But, once the goal has been set and the difficulties encountered by the use of initial means have been perceived, the schemata of the goal, those of the initial means and the auxiliary schemata (evoked by awareness of the difficulties) organize themselves into a new totality, without there being need of external groping to support their activity.

It is therefore inaccurate to speak, as does the empiric theory of "mental experience," of a simple internalization of earlier actual experiences; what has been internalized is solely the knowledge acquired due to these experiences. But actual or external experience involves from the outset, as does simply mental deduction, an internal assimilatory activity which forms schemata, and it is this activity, internal from the very beginning, which henceforth functions by itself without having any further need of external alimentation. Let us keep the term "mental experience" to designate these primitive deductions. But this is on condition that we remember that all experience, including empirical groping, presupposes a previous organization of assimilatory schemata and that contact with the facts is nothing, at any level, outside of accommodation to these schemata. The baby who mentally combines the operations to be performed in order to widen the slit of the matchbox is in the same situation as the older child who no longer needs to count apples with his fingers in order to establish that "2 + 2 are 4" and who confines himself to combining the numbers. But the latter "mental experience" would be incomprehensible if, ever since the numeration of concrete objects, an abstract activity did not assimilate the realities not provided by themselves with numerical properties. Mental experience is therefore an assimilation functioning by itself and thus becomes partly formal, in contrast to the initial material assimilation. So also, Lucienne's deduction pertaining to the matchbox results from a spontaneous functioning of her assimilatory schemata when they succeed in intercombining without any immediate perceptive content and only now operating through evocations. Deduction thus appears at its beginnings as the direct extension of earlier mechanisms of assimilation and accommodation, but on a plane which begins to become differentiated from direct perception and action.

Thereafter can one state, as does the theory at the opposite extreme, that invention is due to an immediate structuring of the perceptual field independently of any apprenticeship and of earlier actions? The foregoing observations do not seem to favor so radical a thesis any more than the thesis of "mental experience" of the pure empiricists. The defect of the empirical thesis is that it does not explain the creative element of invention. By making all deduction the internal repetition of external gropings, it ends by negating the existence of a constructive activity, remaining internal (at all levels) and which alone accounts for the progressive purification of reasoning. But the theory of "structures," by emphasizing the originality of invention too much, leads to the same result and, in order to account for novelties without invoking the activity belonging to combined assimilation and accommodation, finds itself obliged to attribute them to a structural preformation. While empirical associationism considered all constructive deduction as being the internal replica of external experiences already completely organized, according to the theory of structures it is an outward projection of internal forms also completely prepared in advance (because they are connected with the nervous system, with the *a priori* laws of perception, etc.). But analysis of the assimilatory activity leads us to doubt this. If the schemata of assimilation seem to us, in the case of Observations 177–182, to reorganize themselves spontaneously when confronted by the problem raised by the external environment, that does not mean at all that these schemata, however global and totalizing they may be, are identical to "structures" imposing themselves independently of any intellectual construction. The assimilatory schema is not, in effect, an entity separable from assimilatory and accommodating activity. It is only formed by functioning and it only functions in experience. The essential is, therefore, not the schema in so far as it is a structure, but the structuring activity which gives rise to the schemata. Thereafter if, at a given moment, the schemata reorganize themselves until they bring about inventions through mental combination, it is simply because the assimilatory activity, trained by many months of application to the concrete data of perception, finally functions by itself by only using representative symbols. That does not mean at all, let us repeat, that this purification is a simple internalization of earlier experiences: Gestalt psychology has happily emphasized this point by showing that the reorganization peculiar to invention creates the new. But that means that the reorganization is not produced by itself, as though the schemata were endowed with a structure independently of the assimilatory activity which gave rise to them; the reorganization that characterizes invention simply extends this activity. So it is that, in observing our children (Obs. 177–182) and doubtless every time the history of the subjects examined is known in detail, it is possible to discover which old schemata intervened in the course of invention. Invention is no less creative, for all this, but it also presupposes a genetic process which functioned long before it.

What is now the role of *representation* in these first ꜱ nsorimotor deductions? At first it seems vital: due to representation, reciprocal assimilation can remain internal instead of giving rise, from the outset, to empirical gropings. It is therefore due to representation that "mental experience" succeeds actual experimentation and that assimilatory activity can be pursued and purified on a new plane, separate from that of immediate perception or action properly so called. That explains how Köhler, in his research concerning animal intelligence, was led to place all emphasis on the reorganization of the field of perception, as though it were that reorganization which brought intellectual invention after it, and not the reverse.[3] Representation is, in effect, a novelty essential to the formation of the behavior patterns of the present stage; it differentiates these behavior patterns from those of earlier stages. As we have seen, the most complex behavior patterns of the preceding stages, including the "discovery of new means through active experimentation," can dispense with representations, if one defines the latter as the evocation of absent objects. The motor anticipation peculiar to the mobile schemata of assimilation suffices to insure the comprehension of signs and the coördination of means and ends, without need for perception to substitute for representation. Rolling a chain up into a ball to put it in a narrow opening (when the subject never had occasion to roll anything up in such circumstances), combining in advance the positions of a stick before bringing it through bars (when the experiment is new to the child, widening a slit in advance in order to pull a hidden object out of it (when the child comes to grips with such a problem for the first time), all that presupposes that the subject represents the data offered to his sight otherwise than he perceives them directly. In his mind he corrects the thing he looks at; that is to say, he evokes positions, displacements or perhaps even objects without actually contemplating them in his visual field.

But if representation accordingly constitutes an essential acquisition, characteristic of this stage, we should not, however, exaggerate its scope. Representation is surely necessary for in-

3 This role attributed to visual representation is not essential to Gestalt explanations, as revealed by the applications made by K. Lewin on the theory of form on the activity itself.

vention, but it would be erroneous to consider it the only cause. Furthermore, it can be maintained, with at least as much veri- similitude, that representation results from invention. The dy- namic process belonging to the latter precedes the organization of images, since invention arises from spontaneous functioning of the schemata of assimilation. The truth seems to be that be- tween invention and representation there is interaction and not simply a connection. What can be the nature of this interaction?

Things are clarified as soon as, with the theory of signs, one makes of the visual imagery peculiar to representation, a simple symbolism serving as "signifier," and of the dynamic process pe- culiar to invention the signification itself, in other words, the signified. Representation would thus serve as symbol to inven- tive activity which takes away nothing from its utility, since the symbol is necessary for deduction, but which relieves it of the burden of the too-difficult role it is sometimes made to play of being the motor of invention itself.

Here it is necessary to distinguish between two cases. The first is that in which the child merely evokes a movement or an operation already performed previously. For instance, when Lu- cienne perceives that her stick does not enter through the bars and that she tilts it up before trying to bring it through (Obs. 178), it is very possible that, in combining the new movements required by the operation, she visually evokes the movements of the stick previously performed (either just before or during other experiments). In that case representation plays the role of sim- ple visual memory and one might think that invention consists in merely intercombining these image memories. Unfortunately this simple hypothesis, which is all on which the associationist theory of mental experience rests, encounters serious obstacles. Observation does not seem to show at all that during the first year of life the visual image extends action so easily. The ob- servations described in connection with the "invention of new means through active experimentation" (Obs. 148–174) would be unexplainable if visual imagery formed itself by itself as a function of perception. How can it be explained, for example, that in Observation 165 Jacqueline had so much difficulty in profiting from her experiences (impossibility of bringing the rooster through the bars) if an adequate visual representation allowed her to record what she sees? It seems, on the contrary, in such a case as though the apprenticeship were of a motor kind and the image did not yet extend the movement. Thereafter it would seem difficult to interpret invention through mental combination as a simple reorganization of the perceptual field. That reorganization results from the organization of the movements themselves and does not precede it. If images intervene it is therefore in the capacity of symbols accompanying the motor process and permitting the schemata to depend on them to function by themselves, independently of immediate perception. Images are not in this case elements but simply the tools of nascent thought.[4]

With regard to finding out why the image does not intervene at the level of empirical groping and seems necessary for invention through mental combination, that can be explained in accordance with the same hypothesis. The image being a symbol, it does not merely extend movement and perception joined together, and that is why it does not intervene in empirical groping. On the other hand, as soon as the schemata begin to function spontaneously, that is to say, outside of immediate groping and so to combine mentally, by that very fact they confer meaning on the traces left by perception,[5] and thenceforth raise them to the rank of symbols by relation to themselves. The image so constituted therefore becomes the signifier of which the signified is none other than the sensorimotor schema itself.

This leads us to the second case: when representation accompanies invention or mental combination, it happens that the

4 See the excellent article by I. Meyerson, on Sur les images, in Dumas, Nouveau Traité de Psychologie, vol. II.

5 Perhaps it will be said that these traces constitute images by themselves and that thus the image precedes invention. But, as we shall see ("The genesis of imitation"), perception is only extended in a representative image, that is to say only leaves a durable trace to the extent that it is revealed in imitation and that imitation itself is internalized. Now this internalization of imitation (of things as of persons) only occurs during the sixth stage at the time of the conquest of the mechanism of imitation under the influence of the liberation of schemata in connection with the immediate action. There is an ensemble of united intellectual processes and not at all a simple seriation going from sensation to the image as classic associationism believed.

child does not simply evoke the operations already performed but combines or compares the various images in his imagination. A good example is furnished by Observation 180, in which Lucienne opens her mouth while looking at a slit to be widened and so reveals the representative combinations she is in the process of realizing. But in such a case, the image is *a fortiori* a symbol. To utilize the imagined movements of the mouth in order to think out the operations to perform on an opening given in perception is surely to make the image into a simple "signifier" whose signification is to be sought in the motor operation itself.

In short, the fact that invention is accompanied by representation does not speak in favor either of the associationist theory of mental experience or even of the thesis of a spontaneous reorganization of the perceptual field, the thesis maintained by certain famous works derived from the Gestalt theory. All representation admits of two groups of elements which correspond to words or symbols, on the one hand, and to the concepts themselves, on the other, with regard to theoretical representation: Those are the signs and significations. Now the image is to be classed in the first group, whereas the second group is formed by the schemata themselves whose activity engenders invention. This shows that if invention presupposes representation, the converse is true, because the system of signs could not be elaborated independently of that of significations.

The manner of this advent of the image still remains to be clarified, inasmuch as it is derived from the activity of the schemata. But this is not the place to discuss it, for an important question must first be taken up: the problem of imitation. If it is true that the image does not, from the outset, accompany the movement, an intermediate term must be able to explain the transition from the motor to the representative and the image must in some way be acted before being thought. This intermediate is none other than imitation. Observation 180, in which Lucienne imitates the opening contemplated and imitates it with movements of the mouth—that is to say, with an organ not directly perceived by sight—is an excellent example of this transition. Let us postpone the problem until we can give the history of the motor schemata from the particular point of view of imitation.

Let us limit ourselves to concluding that the intervention of "representations" in the mechanisms of the present stage implies that of a sixth and last type of "signifiers," that of *symbolic images*. One recalls that, during the fourth stage, the "signals" thitherto connected with the child's very movements begin to break away from the immediate action in the form of "signs," permitting prevision of events independent of the activity itself (Obs. 132–135). In the course of the fifth stage, the character of these "signs" is again accentuated; that is to say, they allow the child to foresee the properties of the objects themselves, thus adapting to the mechanism of the "tertiary circular reactions" (Obs. 175). Now, the development of signs in the dual sense of accommodation to the things themselves and of detachment with respect to the immediate action reaches its conclusion during the sixth stage when the schemata become capable of functioning alone through purely mental combination. On the one hand, due to the progress of accommodation (which, as we shall state later on, is perforce extended in imitation), the signs are modeled increasingly upon the characteristics of things and so tend to form "images." On the other hand, due to the progressive detachment of the signs with respect to the immediate action for the benefit of mental combination, these images are liberated from direct perception and become "symbolic."

One observes this dual movement in the facts of imitation and of play. Imitation characteristic of the sixth stage becomes representative as much because the child begins to imitate new movements by means of parts of his body invisible to him (imitation relating to head movements, etc., which leads to a representation of his own face), as because of the "deferred imitations" which presage symbolism (imitating absent persons, etc.). On the other hand, play, during the same period, becomes symbolic inasmuch as it begins to involve the "as if."

Now, from the point of view of meanings and of intelligence in general, the development of representations is not only predicated on the "invention of new means through mental combination" but on a series of other behavior patterns bearing witness to the existence of representative images necessary for the evocation of absent objects. Here is one example:

Observation 183.—At 1;6 (8) Jacqueline plays with a fish, a swan and a frog which she puts in a box, takes them out again, puts them back in, etc. At a given moment, she lost the frog. She places the swan and the fish in the box and then obviously looks for the frog. She lifts everything within reach (a big cover, a rug, etc.) and (long after beginning to search) begins to say *inine, inine* (= "*grenouille* = "frog"). It is not the word which set the search in motion, but the opposite. There was therefore evocation of an absent object without any directly perceived stimulus. Sight of the box in which are found only two objects out of three provoked representation of the frog, and whether this representation preceded or accompanied the act is of little importance.

Thus may be seen the unity of the behavior patterns of the sixth stage: Mental combination of schemata with possibility of deduction surpassing actual experimentation, invention, representative evocation by image symbols, so many characteristics marking the completion of sensorimotor intelligence and making it henceforth capable of entering the framework of language to be transformed, with the aid of the social group, into reflective intelligence.

CONCLUSIONS

"Sensorimotor" or "Practical" Intelligence and the Theories of Intelligence

There exists a sensorimotor or practical intelligence whose functioning extends that of the mechanisms of a lower level: circular reactions, reflexes and, still more profoundly, the morphogenetic activity of the organism itself. That is, it seems to us, the main conclusion of this study. It is now fitting to clarify the scope of such an interpretation by trying to supply a view of the whole of this elementary form of intelligence.

First, let us recall the picture of the possible explanations of the different psychobiological processes, in order to be able to insert our description. There are at least five different ways of conceiving the operation of intelligence and they correspond to the conceptions which we have already enumerated with regard to the genesis of acquired associations and of habits (Chap. II, §5) and of biological structures themselves (Introduction, §3).

In the first place, one can attribute intellectual progress to the pressure of the external environment whose characteristics (conceived as being constituted independently of the subject's activity) would impress themselves little by little on the child's mind. Such an explanation, a principle of Lamarckism when applied to hereditary structures, leads to setting up habit as a primary act and to considering mechanically acquired associations as being the source of intelligence. It is, in effect, difficult to conceive of links between environment and intelligence other than those of atomistic association when, like the empiricists, one neglects intellectual activity for the benefit of the constraint of things. The theories which regard the environment as a totality or a collection of totalities are obliged to admit that it is intelligence or perception which endows it with this quality (even if the latter corresponds to data independent of ourselves, which then implies a preëstablished harmony between the "structures" of the object and those of the subject). One does not see how, in the empirical hypothesis, the environment, were it regarded as constituting a totality in itself, could impose itself on the mind if not by successive fragments, that is to say, again by association. The primacy accorded to the environment therefore brings with it the *associationist* hypothesis.

In the second place, one can explain intelligence by intelligence itself, that is to say, presuppose the existence of an activity structured since its beginnings by merely applying itself to increasingly rich and complex contents. Accordingly an "organic intelligence" would exist as early as the physiological plane and would be extended into sensorimotor intelligence and, in the end, into truly reflective intelligence. This kind of an interpretation is of course on a par with vitalism in biology. With regard to associations and habits, as we have already seen, it considers them derived from intelligence at its different levels and not as primary facts. We shall call this second solution *intellectualistic*.

In the third place one can, in accordance with the *a priori* conceptions, consider the progress of intelligence as being due not only to a faculty given in a completed state but to the manifestation of a series of structures which are imposed from within on perception and intelligence in proportion to the needs aroused by contact with the environment. The structures would thus express the very contexture of the organism and its hereditary characteristics, which would nullify any reconciliation between intelligence and the associations or habits acquired under the influence of the environment.

In the fourth place, intelligence can be conceived as consisting in series of attempts or gropings, inspired by needs and the implications that result from them but selected by the external environment (as in biology the mutations are endogenous but their adaptation is due to a selection after the event). This pragmatic interpretation of intelligence would be intermediate between the empiricism of the first solution and the apriority of the third. From the point of view of the relationship between intelligence and association based on habit it results, like the latter, in contrasting these two types of behavior, but less radically, since acquired association plays an essential role in groping.

Finally, in the fifth place, one can conceive of intelligence as the development of an assimilatory activity whose functional laws are laid down as early as organic life and whose successive structures serving it as organs are elaborated by interaction between itself and the external environment. Such a solution differs from the first in that it does not place the accent on experience alone but on the subject's activity making this experience possible. It therefore allies itself principally with the three other solutions. It is distinguished from the second one in that it does not consider intelligence as being ready made and given from the very beginning: Intelligence elaborates itself and only its functional laws are involved in organic organization and assimilation. To the static apriority of the third solution it presents in contrast the idea of a structuring activity, without preformed structures, which engenders the organs of intelligence in proportion to the functioning in contact with experience. Finally, it differs from the fourth solution in that it limits the role of chance in groping in behalf of the idea of directed searching, this direction being explained by the continuity of the assimilatory activity, of the reflex organization and of the elaboration of the most elementary habits to that of the most complex structures of deductive intelligence. But this continuity does not amount to reducing the higher to the lower nor to effecting the inverse reduction; it consists in a gradual construction of organs obeying the same functional laws.

To justify the fifth interpretation, let us first examine the four others possible, limiting ourselves to discussing them in the light of our results.

§ 1. ASSOCIATIONIST EMPIRICISM.—It seems impossible to deny that environmental pressure plays an essential role in the development of intelligence and we cannot follow Gestalt psychology in its effort to explain invention independently of acquired experience (§3). That is why empiricism is destined to arise perpetually from its ashes and to play its useful role of antagonist of *a priori* interpretations. But the whole problem is to find out how the environment exerts its action and how the subject records the data of experience. It is on this point that the facts demand departure from associationism.

It is permissible to invoke, in favor of empiricism, everything that in the sequence of our stages manifests an influence of the history of the behavior patterns on their present state. The importance of the environment is only evident in an historical unfolding, when additional experiences put the individual series sufficiently in opposition to each other to make it possible to determine the role of external factors. On the contrary, the actual pressure of things on the mind, in an act of comprehension or of invention, for example, can always be interpreted as a function of internal qualities of perception or intellection. Now the role of the history lived by the subject, that is to say, the action of past experiences on present experiences, has seemed to us to be considerable in the course of the successive stages we have studied.

As early as the first stage one notices how the use of a reflex mechanism influences its maturation. What does this mean if not that, from the beginning, environment exerts its action. The use or nonuse of an hereditary arrangement of parts depends principally on external circumstances. During the second stage the importance of experience merely increases. On the one hand, conditioned reflexes, acquired associations and habits whose advent characterizes this period, consist in connections imposed by the external environment. Whatever explanation one adopts with regard to the capacity for establishing such connections (hence relatively to their formal mechanism), it is beyond doubt that their content is empirical. On the other hand, we have observed that certain maturations ordinarily considered as depending solely on internal factors, are in reality controlled, at least partially, by the environment. So it is that coördination between vision and prehension occurs at dates which vary between 0;3 and 0;6 according to the experience acquired by the subject (Obs. 84–93).

The behavior pattern whose apparition characterizes the third stage is, it will be recalled, the secondary circular reaction. Now, here again, no matter what interpretation one may give to the capacity of reproducing interesting results obtained by chance, there is no doubt that the connections acquired by virtue of such behavior patterns are due to empirical comparisons. Secondary circular reactions thus merely extend the primary reactions (to which the first habits are due). Whether acting upon things or his own body, the subject only discovers real connections through continuous exercise whose power of repetition presupposes as substance the data of experience as such.

With the advent of the coördination of schemata belonging to the fourth stage, the child's activity no longer only consists in repeating or conserving but also in combining and uniting. One might then expect the role of experience to diminish to the advantage of *a priori* structurizations. That is not the case. First of all, the schemata always being abridgments of experience, their reciprocal assimilations or combinations, however refined they may be, only express an experimental reality, past or future. Next, if these coördinations of schemata presuppose, as do the circular reactions and the reflexes, an activity peculiar to the subject, they only operate as function of the action, its successes or its failures. The role of experience, far from diminishing from the third to the fourth stage, only increases in importance. During the fifth stage, the utilization of experience spreads still more, since this period is characterized by the "tertiary circular reaction" or "experiment in order to see," and the coördination of schemata extends henceforth into "discoveries of new means through active experimentation."

Lastly, the sixth stage adds one more behavior pattern to the preceding ones: the invention of new means through deduction or mental combination. As with regard to the fourth stage, one can ask oneself if experience is not thereafter held in check by the work of the mind and if new connections, of *a priori* origin, will not henceforth double the experimental relationships. This is not the case, at least with respect to the content of the relations elaborated by the subject. Even in invention itself, which apparently precedes experience, the latter plays its role as "mental experience." Moreover invention, however free it may be, joins experience and, in the last analysis, subjects it to its findings. This subjection can, it is true, sometimes assume the aspect of immediate and complete harmony, whence the illusion of a structure endogenous in its very content and joining the real through preëstablished harmony. But, in the majority of cases observed by us (in contrast to the facts of the first type cited by W. Köhler) the harmony is only progressive and does not at all exclude a series of indispensable corrections.

In short, at every level, experience is necessary to the development of intelligence. That is the fundamental fact on which the empirical hypotheses are based and which they have the merit of calling to attention. On this question our analyses of the origin of the child's intelligence confirm that point of view. But there is more in empiricism than just an affirmation of the role of experience: Empiricism is primarily a certain conception of experience and its action. On the one hand, it tends to consider experience as imposing itself without the subject's having to organize it, that is to say, as impressing itself directly on the organism without activity of the subject being necessary to constitute it. On the other hand, and as a result, empiricism regards experience as existing by itself and either owing its value to a system of external ready-made "things" and of given relations between those things (metaphysical empiricism), or consisting in a system of self-sufficient habits and associations (phenomenalism). This dual belief in the existence of an experience in itself and in its direct pressure on the subject's mind explains, in the last analysis, why empiricism is necessarily associationist. Every method of recording experience other than association in its different forms (conditioned reflex, "associative transfer," association of images, etc.) presupposes an intellectual activity partaking of the construction of the external reality perceived by the subject.

To be sure, empiricism thus presented is nowadays only a limited doctrine. But certain famous theories of intelligence are still very close to it. For example, when M. Spearman describes his three steps of intellectual progress, the "intuition of experience" (immediate apprehension of the data), the "eduction of relations," and the "eduction of correlatives," he uses language very different from that of associationism and which seems to indicate the existence of a *sui generis* activity of the mind. But what comprises it, in the particular case? Immediate intuition of experience does not surpass passive awareness of immediate data. Concerning the "eduction" of relations or correlatives, it is only the reading of an already completely formed reality and one which does not clarify the particulars of the mechanism. M. N. Isaacs, subtly continuing the ideas of Spearman, has, it is true, recently tried to analyze this process.[1] The important thing in experience would be "expectation," that is to say, anticipation resulting from earlier observations and destined to be confirmed or belied by present events. When prevision is invalidated by the facts, the subject would yield himself to new anticipations (would form new hypotheses) and finally, in case of failure, would return to himself to modify his method. But, either the schemata thus serving "expectation" and the control of its results only consist in a mnemonic residue of past experiences, and we fall back into an associationism whose sole progress is to be motor and no longer only contemplative, or else they involve intellectual organization properly so called (an active elaboration of the schemata of anticipation due to an assimilatory or constructive mechanism) and we depart from empiricism since, in this case, experience is structured by the subject himself.

Now if we admit the necessity for experience, at all levels, and if, in particular, we can follow Isaacs in all that he affirms (if not in everything that he negates), the facts analyzed in this volume seem to prohibit us from interpreting this experience in the empiricist fashion, that is to say, as a direct contact between things and the mind.

The first reason may seem paradoxical but, if it is carefully weighed, it carries all the others with it. It is that the importance of experience augments rather than diminishes in the course of the six stages we have singled out. The child's mind advances to the conquest of things as if the progress of experience presup-

[1] In S. Isaacs, *The Intellectual Growth in Young Children*, London, Routledge, 1930.

posed an intelligent activity which organizes the latter instead
of resulting from it. In other words, contact with things is less
direct at the beginning than at the end of the evolution envisaged. Furthermore, it never is direct, but only tends toward becoming so. This is what we have established by showing that experience is only an "accommodation," however exact it may become. Now, it is the essence of empiricism, on the contrary, to
put the "thing" or, lacking it, the "immediate datum," that is
to say, always the receptive attitude of the mind, at the point
of departure of all intellectual evolution, the progress of intelligence simply consisting in constructing abridgments of reactions
or increasingly "deferred" reactions, destined to dispense with
direct contact to find it only at long intervals.

Let us recall how things occur in the course of our six stages
from the point of view of this progressive accommodation with
the external environment. During the first stage there exists, of
course, no direct contact with experience, since activity is simply
reflex. Accommodation to things is therefore confused with reflex use. During the second stage, new associations are formed
and so the pressure of experience begins. But these associations
are limited, at the beginning, to interconnecting two or more
movements of the body or else a reaction of the subject to an
external signal. That is certainly an acquisition due to experience. But this "experience" does not yet put the mind in the
presence of the "things" themselves; it places it exactly half-
way between the external environment and the body itself.
Hence accommodation remains undissociated from the activity
of repetition, the latter bearing simply on the results acquired
fortuitously instead of being due to the development of reflex
activity. In the third stage, the acquired associations constitute
relations between the things themselves and no longer only between different body movements. But these relations still remain
dependent on the action, that is to say, the subject still does not
experiment; his accommodation to things remains a simple attempt at repetition, the results reproduced just being more complex than in the preceding stage. In the fourth stage, experience
comes still closer to the "object," the coördinations between schemata permitting the child to establish real relations between

things (in contrast to practical, purely phenomenalistic relation-ships). But it is only in the fifth stage that accommodation is definitively liberated and gives rise to true experience which still develops in the course of the sixth stage.

The mind, then, proceeds from pure phenomenalism whose presentations remain half-way between the body and the external environment, to active experimentation which alone penetrates inside things. What does this mean, if not that the child does not undergo simple external pressure from the environment but tries, on the contrary, to adapt himself to it? Experience, accord-ingly, is not reception but progressive action and construction: This is the fundamental fact.

Now this first reason for correcting the empirical interpreta-tion entails a second one. If the "object" is not imposed at the beginning of mental evolution but is proposed as highest goal, would this not be because it cannot be conceived independently of an activity of the subject? Examination of the facts seems to us to admit of a decisive answer: "Accommodation" by which we have defined contact with experience is always indissociable from "assimilation" of the data to the activity of the subject himself. Let us choose something which we, as observers, shall consider as an "object" independent of ourselves—which doubtless means that we assimilate it to the mental structures of our adult mind —and let us try to find out how the child progressively adapts himself to it.

During the first two stages, external reality can have only one meaning: Things are only aliments for reflex use (sucking, etc.) or mechanisms in process of being acquired (following with the glance, etc.). If, then, the subject adapts himself empirically to the qualities of the objective, it is only a question of accom-modating to it the innate or acquired schemata to which he was assimilated from the outset. Acquisition of schemata of the sec-ond type necessitates assimilation. It is by trying to assimilate the objective to an earlier schema that the child accommodates the latter to the former (thus going back to the reflex schemata), and it is by repeating (through "reproductive assimilation") the movement which is successful that the subject performs this op-eration and constitutes the new schema. Experience cannot therefore be, even at the beginning, a simple contact between the subject and a reality independent of himself, since accommodation is inseparable from an act of assimilation which assigns to the objective a meaning relating to the activity itself.

During the third stage it may seem that experience is freed from assimilation. For example, when the child discovers that the movements of his hand in grasping a cord set in motion those of the bassinet hood, it seems that such a phenomenon, whose sudden appearance was not anticipated, constitutes the prototype of pure experience. Nevertheless this spectacle gives rise, in the child, to an immediate attempt at reproduction, that is to say, to an assimilatory reaction, accommodation simply intervening in order to rediscover the movements which led to the desired result. Now this repetition would be unexplainable if, as soon as it was produced, the fortuitous phenomenon had not been assimilated, in one of its aspects, to an earlier schemata, of which it is a differentiation. So it is that, from their earliest manifestations, the movements of the bassinet hood are perceived, not only as things to see, to hear, etc. (primary schemata), but as extensions of the action of the hand (pulling the cord, etc.) or of the whole body (shaking oneself, etc.). Moreover, as soon as these first secondary reactions, through their assimilatory activity, result in the formation of new schemata, the latter assimilate in their turn all the new empirical events which will differentiate them. The first secondary schemata, consequently, derive from the primary schemata by a continuous assimilatory process and engender all the later secondary schemata by differentiation. Never is accommodation free from any assimilation.

In the course of the fourth stage, the coördination of schemata results in attempts which are confirmed or nullified by experience alone. But that coördination being itself the result of a reciprocal assimilation, the accommodation of schemata is consequently again inseparable from their assimilation. In the course of the fifth stage, on the other hand, accommodation tends to free itself in order to give rise to essentially experimental behavior patterns. But with regard to these "tertiary" reactions, two circumstances suffice to demonstrate that they always presuppose assimilation. On the one hand, the tertiary schemata derive through differentiation from the secondary schemata. It is during the use of the latter that the new fact arises which provokes experimentation. Concerning the latter, it too consists in a circular reaction, that is to say, in active searching, and not in pure reception. However advanced the accommodations to which it gives rise may be, it always has assimilation itself as motor and is limited to differentiating circular reactions in the direction of conquest of the new. On the other hand, the behavior patterns of "discovery of new means through active experimentation" consist in coördinations analogous to those of the fourth stage, but with, in addition, an adjustment to the data of experience due precisely to the method of the tertiary reactions. Hence this means that such behavior patterns are doubly dependent on assimilation. In the course of the sixth stage the same is true *a fortiori*, since the "mental experiences" which then appear attest to the assimilatory power of the schemata which thus intercombine internally.

In conclusion, not only does experience become more active and comprehensive as intelligence matures, but also the "things" on which it proceeds can never be conceived independently of the subject's activity. This second statement reinforces the first and indicates that, if experience is necessary to intellectual development, it cannot be interpreted as being self-sufficient as the empirical theories would have it. It is true that the more active experience is, the more the reality on which it bears becomes independent of the self and consequently "objective." We shall demonstrate this in Volume II in studying how the object is dissociated in proportion to intellectual progress. But, far from substantiating empiricism, this phenomenon seems to us, on the contrary, the better able to characterize the true nature of experience. It is, in effect, to the extent that the subject is active that experience is objectified. Objectivity does not therefore mean independence in relation to the assimilatory activity of intelligence, but simply dissociation from the self and from egocentric subjectivity. The objectivity of experience is an achievement of accommodation and assimilation combined, that is to say, of the intellectual activity of the subject, and not a primary datum imposed on him from without. The role of assimilation is consequently far from diminishing in importance in the course of the evolution of sensorimotor intelligence, by virtue of the fact that accommodation is progressively differentiated. On the contrary, to the extent that accommodation is established as centrifugal activity of the schemata, assimilation fills its role of coördination and unification with growing vigor. The ever-increasing complementary character of these two functions allows us to conclude that experience, far from freeing itself from intellectual activity, only progresses inasmuch as it is organized and animated by intelligence itself.

A third reason is added to the first two reasons to prevent us from accepting the "empirical" explanation of intelligence: It is that contact between the mind and things does not consist, at any level, in perceptions of simple data or in associations of such unities, but always consists in apprehensions of more or less "structured" complexes. That is clear during the first stage, since the elementary perceptions which can accompany reflex use necessarily extend its mechanism. They are therefore organized from the outset. With regard to the second stage, we have tried to establish that the first elementary habits and associations are never made manifest as connections constituted later between isolated terms, but that they result from behavior patterns which have been complex and structured ever since their point of departure. An habitual association is only formed to the extent that the subject pursues a determined end and consequently attributes to the presenting data a meaning relating to this exact end. That results from the already mentioned fact that accommodation to things always depends on an assimilation of these things to schemata already structured (the formation of a new schema always consists in a differentiation of the preceding schemata). It goes without saying that the connections which are established in the later stages (from the third to the sixth), are still less simple, since they derive from secondary and tertiary reactions and from the various reciprocal interassimilations of schemata. Thereafter they can lay claim still less to the quality of pure associations. They are always formed in the midst of totalities which are already organized or are in process of reorganization.

Now, as we have already said, one does not very well see how empiricism could stop being associationist. To say, as does Hume, that spatial and temporal perceptions are from the outset "compound impressions" and to say that the order of the sequence of sounds, in a musical phrase, constitutes a directly perceived "form" is to abandon, on these points, the empirical explanation. To the extent that experience appears to perception as organized from the outset, this is either because perception is itself structured in a corresponding way, or else because it imposes its own structure on the matter perceived. In both cases, contact with experience presupposes an organizing or structuring activity, as experience does not impress itself just as it is on the subject's mind. It is only in the hypothesis of isolated mnemonic traces and of associations due to mechanical repetition (to the repetition of external circumstances) that one understands that there can be pure reception. Every hypothesis surpasses empiricism and attributes to the subject a power of adaptation with all that such a concept allows.

In short, if experience appears to be one of the conditions necessary to the development of intelligence, study of the first stages of that development invalidates the empirical conception of experience.

§2. VITALISTIC INTELLECTUALISM.—If intelligence is not a sum of traces laid down by the environment nor of associations imposed by the pressure of things, the simplest solution consists in making it a force of organization or a faculty inherent in the human mind and even in all animal life of whatever sort.

It is useless to recall here how such an hypothesis, abandoned during the first phases of experimental psychology, reappears today under the influence of preoccupations which are at the same time biological (neovitalism) and philosophical (the revival of Aristotelianism and of Thomism). We are not interested here in the various historical or contemporary forms of intellectualism, but only in the grounds for such an interpretation to the extent that it is applicable to our results. Now it is undeniable that the hypothesis has its merits and that the very reasons which militate in favor of vitalism in biology are of a kind favoring intellectualism in the psychology of intelligence.

These reasons are at least two in number. The first stems from the difficulty of accounting for intelligence, once it has been achieved, by anything other than its own organization considered as a self-sufficient totality. Intelligence in action is, in effect, irreducible to everything that is not itself and, moreover, it appears as a total system of which one cannot conceive one part without bringing in all of it. From that to making intelligence a power *sui generis* just as vitalism makes the organism the expression of a special force) is only a step. Now, in speaking, as we have done, of an "organization" of schemata and of their spontaneous "adaptation" to the environment, we have constantly skirted this kind of explanation of totalities by themselves in which the vitalistic and spiritualistic interpretation consists. We resist it inasmuch as we call neither organization nor assimilation forces, but only functions; we yield, on the other hand, as soon as we substantiate those functions; that is to say, as soon as we conceive them as being mechanisms with a completed and permanent structure.

Whence the arguments of the second group which are genetic in kind. Granted that intelligence constitutes a self-explanatory mechanism, the organization which characterizes it is immanent in the most primitive stages. Intelligence thus germinates in life itself, either because the "organic intelligence" which is at work on the physiological plane potentially contains the highest realizations of abstract intelligence, or because it progressively rouses them by conducing toward them as a necessary end. Now let us not try to conceal the fact that, despite the difference in vocabulary, our interpretations also lead to establishing behavior which is between the vital and the intellectual and, to this extent, they can make use of vitalistic inspiration. We have always emphasized the profound unity of the phenomena of organization and adaptation on the morphological reflex plane of systematic intelligence itself. Intellectual adaptation to the external environment and the internal organization it involves thus extend the mechanisms which one can follow from the beginnings of the elementary vital reactions. The creation of intelligent structures is related to the elaboration of forms which characterizes life as a whole. In a general way, it is difficult not to make the relationships between knowledge and reality the ideal balance to which all biological evolution leads because they alone completely blend assimilation and accommodation thitherto more or less mutually antagonistic. Nothing, therefore, would be easier than to translate our conclusions into vitalistic language, to appeal to the hierarchy of vegetative, sensitive and rational souls to express the functional continuity of development and to oppose in principle life and unorganized matter in order metaphysically to justify the activity of the intelligent subject.

But if vitalism has the merit, unceasingly renewed, of underlining the difficulties or above all the gaps in the positive solutions, it is only too clear that its own explanations reveal the disadvantages of their simplicity and their realism; that is to say, they are always threatened by the progress of biological analysis as well as by that of the reflection of intelligence on itself. Now our ambition being precisely to make the dual light of the biological explanation and the critique of knowledge converge on the development of reason, it would be paradoxical if that union were to result in a reinforcement of the vitalistic thesis. In reality, three essential divergences distinguish the description we have adopted from the system we are now examining: The first pertains to the realism of intelligence as a faculty, the second to that of organization as a vital force, and the third to the realism of adaptive knowledge.

In the first place, it is of the essence of vitalistic intellectualism to consider intelligence a faculty, that is to say, a mechanism complete in its structure and its operation. Now, an essential distinction obtrudes in this connection. If epistemological analysis, whether it is simply reflexive or bears upon scientific knowledge, results in considering intellection an irreducible act, in the latter case it is only a question of knowledge itself, inasmuch as it is obedient to the ideal norms of truth and translates itself in thought in the form of different states of consciousness *sui generis*. But from this intimate experience of intellection nothing can be drawn concerning factual conditions, that is to say, psychological and biological ones, of the intellectual mechanism: proof that, without speaking of metaphysical theories of knowledge, harmony is far from being realized, in the scientific field, between the various logical-mathematical analyses of rational truth, between the multiple theories of the psychology of intelligence, nor *a fortiori* between these two groups of research. Now, intellectualism claims to draw from the fact of intellection the conclusion that there exists a psychic faculty which is easy to know, which would be intelligence itself. It is therefore not intellection as such that this doctrine posits as irreducible, it is a certain reification of that act in the form of a given mechanism in the completely formed state.

Now, it is from this point on that we can no longer follow. From the fact that the living being achieves knowledge and that the child is one day destined to master science, we certainly believe the conclusion must be drawn that there is a continuum between life and intelligence. Furthermore we infer, from the fact that the most complex operations of logical thought seem prepared from the time of the elementary sensorimotor reactions, that this continuum can be already observed in the transition from the reflex to the first acquired adaptations and from the latter to the simplest manifestations of practical intelligence. But the entire question remains of finding out what is permanent in the course of this evolution and what remains characteristic of each level under consideration.

The solution to which our observations lead is that only the functions of the intellect (in contradistinction to the structures) are common to the different stages and consequently serve as connecting link between the life of the organism and that of the intelligence. So it is that at every level the subject assimilates the environment, that is to say, incorporates it to the schemata while maintaining the latter through this use and by means of a constant generalization. At every level accommodation is hence simultaneously accommodation of the organism to objects and assimilation of objects to the organism's activity. At each level this adaptation is accompanied by a search for coherence which unifies the diversity of experience by intercoördinating the schemata. In short, there exists an operation common to all stages of sensorimotor development and of which the operation of logical intelligence seems to be the extension (the formal mechanism of concepts and relationships extending the organization of the schemata and adaptation to experience following accommodation to the environment). Moreover, this sensorimotor operation in turn extends that of the organism, the working of schemata being functionally comparable to that of the organs, whose "form" results from an interaction of the environment and the organism.

But it is apparent that one could not draw from this permanence of functioning the proof of the existence of an identity of structures. The fact that the working of reflexes, of circular reactions, mobile schemata, etc., is identical to that of the logical operations does not prove at all that concepts are sensorimotor schemata nor that the latter are reflex schemata. It is therefore necessary, beside the functions, to make allowance for the structures and admit that the most varied organs can correspond to the same function. The psychological problem of intelligence is just that of the formation of those structures or organs and the solution of this problem is in no way prejudiced by the fact that one acknowledges a permanence of the functioning. This permanence does not at all presuppose the existence of a ready-made "faculty" transcending genetic causality.

Could one not, however, raise the objection that a permanence of functions necessarily implies the idea of a constant mechanism, of a "function" conserving itself, in short, whether one likes it or not, of a "faculty" of invariant structure? So it is that, in current psychological parlance, the word "function" is sometimes used as a synonym for "faculty," and under cover of this terminology is hidden a virtual collection of entities. Memory, attention, intelligence, will, etc., are thus too often called "functions" in a sense which hardly has anything "functional" in it any longer and which tends to become structural or pseudo-anatomical (as though one said "the circulation" no longer thinking of the function but only of the assemblage of organs involved). That being the case, have we the right to concede the existence of a permanent intellectual function without recognizing the existence of an intelligence faculty? Here the comparisons with biology seem decisive. There are functions whose absolute invariability is accompanied by considerable structural variations from one group to the other (nutrition, for instance). It can even be said that the most important and general functions by means of which one can try to define life (organization, assimilation in the wide sense of the word, etc.) do not correspond to any particular organ but have as their structural instrument the whole organism. The permanency of these functions is on a par with a still greater variability of the organ. Consequently, to assert that a permanent intellectual function exists is in no way to prejudge the existence of an invariable structural mechanism. Perhaps it exists, just as a circulatory system is necessary to the circulation. But perhaps also intelligence is confused with the whole of behavior[2] or with one of its general aspects without there being need of isolating it in the form of a particular organ endowed with powers and conservation. Moreover, if it characterizes the behavior as a whole, it is not therefore necessary to call it a faculty or the emanation of a substantial soul, for the same reasons.

Biological realism to which the vitalistic interpretation refers is exactly parallel to intellectualistic realism which we have rejected; just as the permanency of intellectual functions may seem to imply the existence of an intelligence faculty, so also the fact of vital organization leads improperly to the hypothesis of a "force" of organization. The vitalistic solution is the same in both cases. From the function one proceeds to the structural interpretation and thus one "realizes" the functional totality in the form of a single and simple cause. Now, with respect to this second point too, we are unable to follow vitalism. From the fact that the organization of the living being implies a power of adaptation which leads to intelligence itself, it does not follow at all that these various functions are unexplainable and irreducible. But the problems of organization and of adaptation (including that of assimilation) surpass psychology and presuppose a biological interpretation of the whole.

These first two expressions of vitalistic realism lead to a realism of adaptation itself, in relation to which the contrast

[2] H. Piéron, *Psychologie Expérimentale*, Paris, 1927, pp. 204–208.

between the results of our studies and the system of interpretation we are now examining seems to us still more marked. Inasmuch as it considers life as irreducible to matter, and intelligence as a faculty inherent in life, vitalism conceives knowledge as an adaptation *sui generis* of that faculty to an object given independently of the subject. In other words, this adaptation, while remaining mysterious because of these very contrasts, is reduced in fact to what common sense has always envisaged as being of the essence of knowledge: a simple copy of things. Intelligence, we are told, tends to conform to the object and possess it due to a sort of mental identification; it "becomes the object" in thought. Thus vitalism always joins empiricism on the field of knowledge as such with this faint difference that, from our present point of view, intelligence subordinates itself to the thing instead of being subordinated to it from without. There is voluntary imitation and not simple reception.

But that epistemological realism, it seems to us, clashes with the fundamental fact we have emphasized in the course of our analyses. That is, that adaptation—intellectual and biological, hence adaptation of intelligence to "things" as well as of the organism to its "environment"—always consists in a balance between accommodation and assimilation. In other words, knowledge could not be a copy, since it is always a putting into relationship of object and subject, an incorporation of the object to the schemata which are due to activity itself and which simply accommodate themselves to it while making it comprehensible to the subject. To put it still differently, the object only exists, with regard to knowledge, in its relations with the subject and, if the mind always advances more toward the conquest of things, this is because it organizes experience more and more actively, instead of mimicking, from without, a ready-made reality. The object is not a "known quantity" but the result of a construction.

Now this interaction of intelligent activity and experience finds its counterpart, on the biological plane, in a necessary interaction between the organism and the environment. To the extent that one refuses to explain life, as does vitalism, by a force *sui generis* of organization, one is obliged to consider living beings simultaneously as being conditioned by the physicochemical universe and as resisting it by assimilating it. Consequently there is interdependence between the organism and the entire universe, on the one hand, objectively, because the former results from the latter while completing and transforming it, on the other hand, subjectively, because the adaptation of the mind to experience presupposes an activity which enters as a component into the play of objective relationships.

In short, the biological interpretation of intellectual processes based upon the analysis of assimilation does not result at all in the epistemological realism of vitalistic intellectualism. Even by making knowledge a singular case of organic adaptation one ends, on the contrary, with the conclusion that true reality is neither an organism isolated in its entelechy, nor an external environment capable of subsisting if one abstracts life and thought from it. Concrete reality is the ensemble of the mutual relationships of the environment and the organism, that is to say, the system of interactions which unify them. Once those relationships have been posited, one can try to elucidate them either by the biological method starting with a ready-made environment to try to explain the organism and its properties, or by the psychological method, starting with mental development to try to find out how environment is constituted for the intelligence. Now, if adaptation does consist, as we have asserted, in a balance between accommodation of the schemata to things and the assimilation of things to the schemata, it is self-evident that these two methods are complementary: but provided one no longer believes in ready-made intelligence or a vital force independent of the environment.

§3. APRIORITY AND THE PSYCHOLOGY OF FORM. —If intellectual development results neither from constraint exerted by the external environment nor from the progressive affirmation of a ready-made faculty for knowing that environment, perhaps it should be conceived as being the gradual explanation of a series of preformed structures in the psychophysiological constitution of the subject himself.

Such a solution obtrudes in the history of philosophical theories of knowledge when, disappointed by both English em-

piricism and classical intellectualism (and above all by the Wolff-
ian theory of the rational faculty), Kantianism resorts to the *a
priori* hypothesis to explain the possibility of science. In biology,
moreover, apriority arose when the difficulties related to the
problem of heredity of acquired characteristics led it to reject
Lamarckian empiricism. Some people tried to return to vitalism,
whereas others tried to account for evolution and adaptation by
the hypothesis of the preformation of genes. Finally, in the
psychological field, a solution of the same kind took the place of
associationist empiricism and intellectual vitalism. It consists in
explaining every invention of intelligence by a renewed and
endogenous structuring of the perceptual field or of the system of
concepts and relationships. The structures which thus succeed
each other always constitute totalities; that is to say, they cannot
be reduced to associations or combinations or empirical origin.
Moreover, the Gestalt theory to which we allude, appeals to no
faculty or vital force or organization. As these "forms" spring
neither from the things themselves nor from a formative faculty,
they are conceived as having their root in the nervous system or,
in a general way, in the preformed structure of the organism. In
this regard we can consider such a solution *"a priori."* Doubtless,
in most cases, the Gestalt psychologists do not clarify the origin
of the structures and confine themselves to saying that they are
necessarily imposed on the subject in a given situation. This
doctrine is reminiscent of a sort of Platonism of perception. But,
as Gestalt psychology always returns to the psycho-physiological
constitution of the subject himself when it is a question of explaining this necessity for forms, such an interpretation certainly
consists in a biological apriority or a variety of preformation.

Now, the theory of form, far from confining itself to the
enunciation of general principles, has furnished a series of fundamental works for understanding the mechanism of intelligence:
those of Wertheimer on the psychological nature of the syllogism,
of Köhler on intelligence and invention, of K. Lewin on the
"field" theory, etc. These studies all result in explaining by
structures of the field of conception or perception what we attribute to assimilation. It is therefore essential to compare closely
this system of explanation with that which we have used and

even, in order the better to conclude this comparison, to interpret our results in terms of "Gestalt." On at least two essential points we agree with the "theory of form."

In the first place, it is quite true that every intelligent solution and even every behavior pattern in which the comprehension of a given situation intervenes (however wide the meaning attributed to the word "comprehension") appear as totalities and not as associations or syntheses of isolated elements. In this respect the "schema" whose existence we have always acknowledged can be compared to a "form" or "Gestalt." The system, composed of determined and completed movements and perceptions, reveals the dual character of being structured (hence of itself structuring the field of perception or comprehension) and of constituting itself from the outset inasmuch as it is a totality without resulting from an association or synthesis between elements separated earlier. Without speaking of the reflex schemata which are the more totalized and structured since they were already assembled at birth, one can observe these characteristics as early as the first nonhereditary schemata, due to the primary circular reactions. The simplest habits, as well as the so-called acquired "associations" do not result from true associations, that is to say, interuniting the terms given as such, but also result from connections implying a structured totality from the outset. Only the global signification of the act (the place of assimilation which connects the result to the need to be satisfied) insures, in effect, the existence of relations which, from the outside may seem to be "associations." The "secondary schemata," moreover, also always constitute systems of the whole analogous to "Gestalts." It is only to the extent that a child tries to reconstruct a spectacle which he has just witnessed or created that he connects one movement with another. Perceptions and movements are hence only associated if their significations are already related to each other and if this system of mutual relations itself implies a meaning of the whole given in the initial perception. With regard to the coordinations between schemata characteristic of the fourth stage, one could not consider them associations either. Not only do the coördinations work by reciprocal assimilation—that is to say, due to a process which stems more from global reorganization

than from simple association—but also this reorganization results at once in the formation of a new schema revealing all the
characteristics of a new and original totality. With the "experiments in order to see" and the acts of intelligence which flow
from them (fifth stage) we are surely outside the realm of pure
"Gestalt." But the theory of form has never claimed to suppress
the existence of groping searching; it has only tried to remove it
from the realm of actually intelligent behavior patterns in order
to consider it a substitute for structuring and place it in the
intermediate periods between two structures. At the sixth stage
we again find, on the contrary, authentic "structures." The invention of new means through mental combination manifests all the
characteristics of these rapid or even instantaneous regroupings
by means of which Köhler has described the true act of intelligence.

Taken as a whole, except with regard to groping—whose role
is really constant but is revealed particularly during the first
experimental behavior patterns (fifth stage)—the schemata whose
existence we have recognized manifest the essence of the characteristics of a structured totality by means of which the theory of
form opposed the "Gestalts" to classic associations.

A second point of convergence between the two systems of
interpretations is the rejection of every faculty or special force
of organization. W. Köhler emphasizes the fact that his criticism
of associationism frequently rejoins analogous objections already
formulated by vitalism. But, he adds, with reason, one cannot
deduce from this agreement that the "forms" are to be interpreted as the product of a special energy of organization; Vitalism too quickly reaches the conclusion that totalities exist
from the hypothesis of a vital principle of unification. We therefore sympathize completely with the effort of Gestalt psychology
to find the roots of intellectual structures in the biological processes conceived as systems of relationships and not as the expression of substantial forces.

Having thus defined these common traits, we find ourselves
more free to show how the hypothesis of assimilation tries to
surpass the theory of forms and not to contradict it, and how the
"schema" is a "Gestalt" made dynamic and not a concept destined

to react against the progress of the Gestalt movement. To resume our comparison between the theory of form and epistemological apriority, the "Gestalt" manifests the same advantages over association as were formerly made manifest by Kantian apriority over classical empiricism, but only to arrive at parallel difficulties: having conquered static realism without, apriority finds it again within the mind and runs the risk, in the last analysis, of ending in a restored empiricism. In effect, the theory of form, like former epistemological apriority, wanted to defend the internal activity of perception and intelligence against the mechanism of external associations. It has therefore located the principle of organization in ourselves and not outside us, and, the better to shelter it from empirical experience, it rooted it in the preformed structure of our nervous system and our psycho-physiological organism. But, by trying thus to guarantee the internal activity of organization against the immixtures of the external environment, it finally withdrew it from our personal power. It consequently enclosed it in a static formalism conceived as pre-existing or as being elaborated outside of our deliberate intention. This formalism certainly marks great progress over associationism because it predicates the existence of syntheses or totalities instead of remaining atomistic, but it is precarious progress. To the extent that "forms," like the categories of yore, antecede our intentional activity, they revert to the rank of inert mechanisms. That is why, in the theory of form, intelligence ends by disappearing to the advantage of perception, and the latter, conceived as being determined by ready-made internal structures —that is to say, consequently as preformed from within—ends by becoming more and more confused with "empirical" perception, conceived as preformed from without: In both cases, in effect, the activity disappears to the advantage of the elaborated whole.

Our critique of the theory of form must therefore consist in retaining all that is positive which it opposes to associationism—that is to say, all the activity it discovers in the mind—but in rejecting everything in it which is only restored empiricism— that is to say, its static apriority. In short, to criticize Gestalt psychology is not to reject it but to make it more mobile and consequently to replace its apriority with a genetic relativity.

The analysis of a primary divergence will permit us to define these positions from the outset. A "Gestalt" has no history because it does not account for earlier experience, whereas a schema embodies the past and so always consists in an active organization of the experience lived. Now this point is fundamental: the analysis of three children, almost all of whose reactions were observed, from birth to the acquisition of speech, has convinced us of the impossibility of detaching any behavior pattern whatever from the historical context of which it is a part, whereas the hypothesis of "form" makes the history useless and the Gestalt psychologists deny the influence of acquired experience on the solution of new problems.[3]

So it is, to begin at the end, that we have never, even during the sixth stage, observed "intelligent" reorganizations, even unforeseen and sudden ones, unless the invention or mental combination which determined them was prepared, however little, by earlier experience. With regard to the theory of form, on the contrary, an invention (like that of the ladder of boxes made by Köhler's chimpanzees) consists in a new structuring of the perceptual field, which nothing in the subject's past can explain: whence the hypothesis according to which this structure would come solely from a certain degree of maturation of the nervous system or the organs of perception so that nothing from without, that is, no present or past experience, would cause its formation (present experience is confined to starting or necessitating structuring, but without explaining it). True, some of our observations of the sixth stage seem at first to corroborate this outlook. Thus if Jacqueline and Laurent gradually discovered the use of the stick due to empirical groping, Laurent, whom we let go much longer without putting him in the same situation, understood at once the signification of that instrument. Everything occurs as though a structure not yet mature in the case of the two former were imposed ready-made on Laurent's perception. So also Lucienne immediately found the solution to the problem of the watch chain, whereas Jacqueline groped laboriously. But before

---

[3] See Claparède, La Genèse de l'hypothèse, *Archives de Psychol.*, XXIV, the summary (pp. 53–58) of the works of K. Duncker and N. R. F. Maier, intended to demonstrate the uselessness of acquired experience.

concluding that there is radical novelty in such mental combinations, and consequently before having recourse, in order to explain them, to the emergence of endogenous structures having no root in the individual's past experience, it is necessary to make two remarks. The first is that, in default of external groping one cannot exclude the possibility of a "mental experience" which would occupy the moments of reflection immediately preceding the act itself. The most sudden inventions which we can introspect always reveal at least a beginning of search or internal groping outside of which ideas and perceptions cannot regroup themselves all alone. It goes without saying and we have emphasized that this "mental experience" is not simply the passive extension of states lived through earlier and that it consists, like actual experience, in real action. But the fact remains that, even without visible groping from the outside, the subject's thought can always yield internally to experimental combinations, however rapid. Sudden reorganization can therefore be conceived as an extreme case of mental combination. Now, and this second remark is essential, these mental experiences, even if the known quantities of the problem are entirely new, can always apply to the present situation earlier schemata utilized in more or less analogous cases, whether these schemata merely apply to some aspect of this situation or simply inspire the method to be followed in order to solve the problem. Thus, if Lucienne never rolled up a watch chain in order to put it in a small opening, she was able to execute similar movements when rolling up pieces of material, cords, etc. So also Laurent, without ever having utilized the stick, is able to apply to the new situation the schemata drawn from the use of other intermediates ("supports," strings, etc.). Between simple prehension and the idea that one solid can cause displacement of another is found a series of imperceptible transitions.

The idea is therefore conceived that the sudden inventions characteristic of the sixth stage are in reality the product of a long evolution of schemata and not only of an internal maturation of perceptive structures (the existence of the latter factor having of course to be reserved). This is revealed by the existence of a fifth stage, characterized by experimental groping and situated between the fourth (coördination of schemata) and the sixth (mental combinations). If, with respect to the theory of form, groping search constitutes an activity in the margin of the maturation of structures and without influence on what maturation, we, on the other hand, believe we have established that the sudden invention of new structures, which characterizes the sixth stage, only appears after a phase of experimentation or of "tertiary circular reaction." What does this mean if not that the practice of actual experience is necessary in order to acquire the practice of mental experience and that invention does not arise entirely preformed despite appearances?

Furthermore, the entire sequence of stages, from the first to the two last, is there to attest to the reality of the evolution of schemata and consequently to the role of experience and of history. A complete continuity exists between the behavior patterns characteristic of the different stages. The primary circular reactions thus prolong the activity of the reflex schemata by systematically extending their sphere of application. The secondary circular reactions, moreover, derive from the primary reactions to the extent that every discovery historically entails a series of others. Thus coördination between vision and prehension induces the child to grasp the objects which hang from the hood of his bassinet and the manipulation of these objects leads him to act upon the hood itself, etc. Thereafter, once the secondary schemata have been formed as function of the historical development of the circular reactions, a coördination of schemata is established during the fourth stage, which itself results from earlier activities. The act of pushing back the obstacle, for example, coördinates the cycles of prehension with the schemata such as striking, etc., and it has seemed to us impossible to explain the advent of such coördinations without knowing the subject's past, in each particular case. Concerning the discovery of new means through active experimentation (fifth stage), it constitutes a coördination of schemata extending that of the preceding stage, with only this difference that the coördination no longer occurs in an immediate way but necessitates a more or less laborious readjustment, that is to say, an experimental groping. Now this groping is itself prepared by the exploratory behavior patterns inherent in assimilation by mobile schemata.

In short, the new behavior patterns whose appearance marks each stage are always revealed as developing those of the preceding stages. But two interpretations can be given of this same fact. One could see in it, first of all, the expression of a purely internal maturation, such as that the formal structure of perceptions and of acts of intelligence develops by itself without use as a function of experience or transmission of the contents from one stage to another. One can, on the contrary, conceive of this transformation as being due to an historical evolution such as that the use of the schemata is necessary to their structuring and that the result of their activity is thus transmitted from one period to the other. Now this second interpretation alone seems reconcilable with the particulars of the individual facts. In comparing the progress of intelligence in three children, day after day, one sees how each new behavior pattern is formed by differentiation and adaptation of the preceding ones. One can follow the particular history of each schema through the successive stages of development, as the formation of structures cannot be dissociated from the historical development of experience.

The schema is therefore a Gestalt which has a history. But how does it happen that the theory of form came to dispute this role of past experience? From the fact that one refuses to consider the schemata of behavior as being the simple product of external pressures (like a sum of passive associations) it clearly does not necessarily follow that their structure is imposed by virtue of preëstablished laws, independent of their history. It is enough to acknowledge an interaction of form and content, the structures thus being transformed gradually as they adapt themselves to increasingly varied conditions. For what subtle reasons do writers as informed as the Gestalt psychologists reject an interaction which seems so obvious?

A second divergence should be noted here: A "schema" is applied to the diversity of the external environment and hence is generalized as a function of the contents it subsumes, whereas a "Gestalt" is not generalized and even is "applied" less than it is imposed in an immediate way and internally to the situation perceived. The schema, as it appeared to us, constitutes a sort of sensorimotor concept or, more broadly, the motor equivalent of a system of relations and classes. The history and development of a schema therefore consist primarily in its generalization, through application to increasingly varied circumstances. Now a "Gestalt" manifests itself quite differently. Take two objects, for example an objective and its "support" at first perceived without interrelationships, then suddenly "structured"; and let us say that the subject, after having "understood" the connection which links them, subsequently understands a series of analogous relations. In order to explain this, the theory of form does not maintain either that the "Gestalt" which intervenes here is generalized, or even that it is "applied" successively to various objects. If perception, at first not structured, suddenly acquires a "form," this is because at any degree of maturation whatever it is impossible for the subject to see things differently, given the ensemble of the situation. The "form" thus constitutes a sort of ideal necessity or immanent law which is imposed on perception, and when the Gestalt psychologists describe the thing from the phenomenological point of view, they speak of this form as Platonists speak of an "idea" or logicians of a "subsistent" being: The Gestalt is simply established by virtue of its "pregnance." When the same writers speak as physiologists, they add that this internal value is related to the subject's nervous constitution. In both cases it is always a question of an immediate necessity which can be renewed at the time of each perception but which does not require the existence of a generalizing schematism. This is what the Gestalt psychologists again express by invoking the *Einsicht* or the total comprehension which arises according to the variations of the goal pursued and by specifically stating, as does Duncker,[4] that "reasoning is a battle which creates its own weapons." If we say that the theory of form constitutes a sort of apriority, this is simply because, according to this doctrine, structuring results from an intrinsic necessity and not at all from experience, and is thus connected with the conditions of the subject himself; the criterion of the *"a priori"* has always been necessity as such. The "Gestalten" do not therefore consist in mobile frames successively

4 Quoted by Claparède (above-mentioned article), p. 53.

applied to various contents: structuring is simply a predetermined process, that is to say, obtruding necessarily, sooner or later, and thereafter this process can repeat itself every time the situation demands, but without involving the activity of schemata supplied with a history and capable of generalization.

How does genetic observation determine the choice between necessary preformation and generalizing activity? It is apparent that, to the extent that one attributes a history to the structures, one is obliged to admit an element of generalization, that is to say, one is led to detach the structures from structured situations to make active schemata of them which are due to a structuring assimilation. As nearly as the use of hereditary reflexes, one has the impression that the subject searches for aliments for his activity and that thus the latter is generalizing: so it is that the baby sucks, looks, listens in a growing number of given situations. But if, during this first period, just as during that of the primary circular reactions, it is difficult to dissociate active generalization from simple structuring, the contrast becomes striking from the third stage on, that is to say, with the advent of the secondary circular reactions. From the moment when the child truly acts upon the external world each of his conquests gives rise, not only to immediate repetition, but also to a generalization which is henceforth very obvious. Thus after having grasped a cord hanging from his bassinet hood and having by chance discovered the results of this traction, the child applies this behavior to all hanging objects. Now it is very hard not to interpret the thing as a generalization since the child is not satisfied to shake the hood in a different way but will go so far as to use the same means to make interesting spectacles last, whatever the distance which separates him from them may be. This perpetual extension which we have noted of the secondary schemata into "procedures to make interesting spectacles last" is the best proof of their generalizing power. Concerning the fourth stage, it is characterized by a greater mobility of schemata than before, that is to say, by new progress in generalization. In effect, not only is the coördination of certain schemata due to their reciprocal assimilation, that is to say, to a generalizing process, but in addition the power of generalization belonging to the mobile schemata is confirmed by certain special behavior patterns which we have called "exploration of new objects." These behavior patterns, which extend the generalizing assimilations of the third stage, consist in applying to new objects all the familiar schemata in succession, so as to "understand" these objects. It seems evident, in such a case, that the effort to generalize obtains over all preformed structures, since there is a laborious adjustment of the familiar to the unfamiliar and since this search presupposes a series of choices. So also, during the fifth stage, the series of gropings which lead the child to discovery of the use of supports, of strings and of sticks is directed by the ensemble of the earlier schemata which give meaning to the present search. This application of the known to the unknown also presupposes constant generalization. Finally, we have considered generalization as being indispensable to the mental combinations of the sixth stage.

If one follows, then, the development of schemata, stage after stage, either in general or taken each individually, one proves that this history is one of continuous generalization. Not only is all structuring capable of reproducing itself when confronted by events which caused its appearance, but also it is applied to new objects which differentiate it in case of need. This correlative generalization and differentiation reveal, it seems to us, that a "form" is not a rigid entity to which perception leads as though under the influence of predetermination, but a plastic organization, just as frames adapt themselves to their contents and so depend partially on them. This means that "forms," far from existing before their activity, are rather comparable to concepts or systems of relationships whose gradual elaboration works when they are generalized. Observation forces us, therefore, to detach them from pure perception and raise them to the rank of intellectual schemata. Only a schema, in effect, is capable of real activity, that is to say, of generalization and differentiation combined.

This leads us to examine a third difficulty in the theory of structure. To the extent that the "forms" do not have a history or a generalizing power, the very activity of intelligence is preterit to the advantage of a more or less automatic mechanism. The "Gestalten" do not have any activity in themselves. They arise at the time of the reorganization of the perceptual fields and are imposed as such without resulting from any dynamism anterior to themselves; or, if they are accompanied by an internal maturation, the latter is itself directed by preformed structures which it therefore does not explain.

Now, it is there that the facts envisaged in their historical continuity prevent us all the more from accepting unreservedly the theory of form, whatever the static analogy which can exist between the "Gestalt" and the schemata may be. In effect, the schemata have always seemed to us to be not antonomous entities but the products of a continuous activity which is immanent in them and of which they constitute the sequential moments of crystallization. As this activity is not external to them, it therefore does not constitute the expression of a "faculty," and we have already seen why. It only forms one whole with the schemata themselves, as the judgment's activity is made manifest in the formation of concepts; but, just as the concepts become dissociated from the continuous chain of the judgments which gave rise to them, so also the schemata detach themselves little by little from the organizing activity which engendered them and with which they became confused at the time of their formation. More precisely, the schemata, once formed, serve as instruments for the activity which engendered them, just as the concepts, once they have been derived from the judicatory act, are the point of departure of new judgments.

What, then, is this organizing activity, if it is not external but immanent in the schemata, without however consisting in a simple maturation? As we have constantly repeated, the organization of schemata is only the internal aspect of their adaptation which is simultaneously accommodation and assimilation. The primary fact is therefore the assimilatory activity itself without which no accommodation is possible, and it is the combined action of assimilation and accommodation which accounts for the existence of the schemata and consequently of their organization.

In effect, however high one may raise the advent of the first psychological "behavior pattern," they are revealed in the form of mechanisms leading to the satisfaction of a need. That means that the behavior patterns are from the outset the function of the general organization of the living body. Every living being constitutes a totality which tends to conserve itself and consequently to assimilate to itself the external elements it needs. From the biological point of view, assimilation and organization are on a par, without its being possible to consider organized forms as being anterior to assimilatory activity or the contrary. Need, the satisfaction of which is insured by the reflexes subordinated to the whole of the organism, is thus to be considered as the expression of an assimilatory tendency simultaneously dependent on the organization and fit to conserve it. But, from the subjective point of view, this same need, however complex the reflex organization of which it is the expression may be, appears, in its primitive form, as a global tendency simple to satisfy, that is to say, as barely differentiated from states of consciousness proceeding from desire to satisfaction and from satisfaction to the desire to conserve or recommence. From the psychological point of view, the assimilatory activity, which is immediately extended in the form of reproductive assimilation, is consequently the primary fact. Now this activity, precisely to the extent that it leads to repetition, engenders an elementary schema—the schema being formed by active reproduction—then, due to this nascent organization, becomes capable of generalizing and recognitory assimilations. Moreover, the schemata thus constituted accommodate themselves to external reality to the extent that they try to assimilate it and so become progressively differentiated. Thus, on the psychological as well as on the biological plane, the schematism of the organization is inseparable from an assimilatory and accommodating activity, whose functioning alone explains the development of successive structures.

It can now be understood how the fact of considering the "forms" as having no history and of conceiving their continuous reorganizations as independent of active generalization amounts sooner or later to neglecting the activity of the intelligence itself. To the extent that the schemata are regarded as subtended by an activity at once assimilatory and accommodating, only then do they appear as being capable of explaining the later progress of systematic intelligence in which conceptual structures and logical relationships are superposed on simple sensorimotor mechanisms. To the extent, on the contrary, that static "form" excels activity, even if this "form" is endowed with an undefined power of maturation and of reorganization, one does not understand why intelligence is necessary and is dissociated from simple perception. Here we probably touch on the essential point of divergence: In the theory of form, the ideal is to explain intelligence by perception, whereas for us perception itself must be interpreted in terms of intelligence.

There is undoubtedly a continuity of mechanism between perception and intelligence. All perception appeared to us to be the elaboration or the application of a schema, that is to say, a more or less rapid organization of sensorial data as function of an ensemble of acts and movements, explicit or simply outlined. Moreover, intelligence, which in its elementary forms involves an element of search and groping, ends, in the course of the sixth stage, in sudden reorganizations consisting in extreme cases, in almost immediate "perceptions" of the correct solution. Hence it is accurate to emphasize, with the theory of form, the analogy of perception and of practical intelligence. But this identification can have two meanings. According to the first, perceptions are self-sufficient, and search only constitutes a sort of accident or interlude revealing the absence of organized perception. According to the second, on the contrary, all perception is the product of an activity whose most discursive or groping forms are only the clarification. Now, it is in this way that things are always presented to us: All perception is an accommodation (with or without regrouping) of schemata which have required, for their construction, systematic work of assimilation and organization; and intelligence is only the progressive complication of this same work, when immediate perception of the solution is not possible. The reciprocating motion between direct perception and searching does not warrant considering them as essentially opposites; only differences of speed and complexity separate perception from comprehension or even from invention.

These remarks lead us to examine a fourth objection to the theory of form. How is it possible to explain the mechanism of the reorganizations essential to the act of intelligence, and more precisely, to account for the discovery of "good forms" in contradistinction to those which are less good? When it is only a question of static perception (for example, perceiving a figure formed by scattered points on a white sheet of paper) and of a high mental level, one often finds that such a form is more satisfactory than that which immediately succeeds it. Thus, after having perceived the points as constituting a series of juxtaposed triangles one suddenly perceives a polygon. Thereafter one has the impression that forms succeed one another according to a "law of pregnance," the good forms, which end by prevailing, being those which fulfill certain *a priori* conditions of simplicity, cohesion and completion (those which are "closed," etc.). Thence the supposition that the act of comprehension consists in reorganizing the perceptual field by replacing the inadequate forms with more satisfactory ones and that in general the progress of intelligence is due to an internal maturation directed toward the best forms. But, in our hypothesis, the perceptions of completed structure constitute the coming to a head of complex elaborations, in which experience and intellectual activity intervene and cannot therefore be chosen as representative in the problem of the discovery of "good" forms. As soon as one goes beyond the particular case of static perceptions to analyze how the perceptions are structured once they are placed in intelligent activity in which they bathe as in their natural environment, one observes that the "good forms" do not arise all by themselves, but always as a function of previous searching which, far from being lost in simple maturation or use, constitutes real searching, that is to say, involving experimentation and control.

Groping, let us repeat, appears in the theory of form as an extraintelligent activity, destined to replace by the empiricism of fortuitous discoveries the reorganizations too difficult to accomplish systematically. If we have often recognized the existence of disordered gropings, corresponding in part to this conception and proceeding from the fact that the problem involved was too far above the subject's level, we have constantly emphasized, on the other hand, the existence of another type of groping which is directed and manifests this activity whose completed structures constitute the result. This second groping would therefore be the very expression of the reorganization in progress and of the dynamism of which the schemata are the static product.

In effect, if at all stages, the schemata seemed to us to emanate from assimilatory activity, the latter was always revealed as a functional exercise before resulting in the various structures. As early as the first stage it is apparent that a certain use is necessary to make the reflex mechanisms function normally, this use of course allowing an element of groping. During the second and third stages, the primary and secondary reactions result from a reproductive assimilation, whose gropings are therefore necessary to the formation of the schemata. The same is true of the coordinations belonging to the fourth stage. With regard to the behavior patterns of the fifth stage, they reveal still better than the preceding ones the connection that exists between groping and the organization of the schemata. Far from manifesting itself as a passive recording of fortuitous events, the search characteristic of this type of behavior is directed simultaneously by the schemata assigning a purpose to the action, by those which serve by turns as means and by those which attribute a meaning to the vicissitudes of experience. In other words, groping of the second type is primarily gradual accommodation of the schemata to the conditions of reality and to the exigencies of coördination. Whether it is external as during the fifth stage or becomes internal at the same time as the behavior patterns of the sixth stage, it thus presupposes a permanent process of active correction or control.

Now this question of control of schemata is fundamental. By very reason of its hypothesis of pregnance (or theory of best shape), the theory of form has been led to neglect almost entirely the role of correction. The good forms, it is true, are supposed to eliminate those that are less good, not only to the extent that the latter are not very satisfactory in themselves, but also to the extent that they are inadequate to the whole of the given situation. But the process of reorganization, although set in motion by a sort of global control, remains, in its intimate mechanism, independent of this very control. On the contrary, every reorganization of the schemata has always seemed to us to constitute a correction of earlier schemata, through progressive differentiation, and every organization in the process of becoming has manifested itself to us as a balance between the assimilatory tendency and the exigencies of accommodation, hence as controlled use.

Thus as early as the first stage, reflex use is corrected by its very effects; it is reinforced or inhibited according to circumstances. During the second and third stages, the formation of the circular reactions presupposes a development of this control; in order to rediscover the interesting results obtained by chance, one must correct the searching according to its success or its failures. The coördination of the schemata, characteristic of the fourth stage, also only works by being sanctioned by its results. From the fifth stage on, the control operations become differentiated still more; the child no longer limits himself to suffering an automatic sanction from facts, he tries to foresee, by a beginning experimentation, the object's reactions and so submits his search for novelty to a sort of active control. Finally, during the sixth stage, the control is internalized in the form of mental correction of the schemata and their combinations. It can therefore be said that control exists from the very beginning and becomes more and more established in the course of the stages of sensorimotor development. To be sure, it always remains empirical, in the sense that it is always the success or failure of the action which constitutes the sole criterion, the search for truth as such only beginning with reflective intelligence. But control suffices to insure an increasingly active correction of the schemata and so to explain how the good forms take the place of the less satisfactory ones through a gradual accommodation of the structures to experience and to each other.

We have hitherto taken up four main divergences between the hypothesis of forms and that of schemata. A fifth difference results, it would seem, from the four preceding ones and even sums them up in a certain way. In a word, it can be said that the "forms" exist by themselves whereas the schemata are only systems of relationships whose developments always remain interdependent.

The various extensions of the theory have adequately demonstrated that the "Gestalten" are conceived as existing by themselves. To the writers who have confined themselves to the analysis of the psychological fact of perception or intellection, the forms are, it is true, simply given in the same capacity as any relationships whatever and the very concept of "form" thus involves no realism. But, to the extent that one refuses to try to explain the genesis of these forms, they tend to become entities of which perception or intellection partake (in the Platonic way). Then one passed from this phenomenological "subsistence" to the hypothesis of their *a priori* character. One is thus tempted to account for their necessity by the innate psychobiological structure of the organism, which makes them definitely anterior to experience. Finally there comes a third step: the "forms" become the condition for all possible experience. This is how, on the plane of scientific thought, Köhler has described "physical forms" as though they conditioned the phenomena of the external world and imposed themselves on the electromagnetic, chemical or physiological systems.

Now, if the foregoing reservations are taken into account, nothing warrants our believing in the existence of "structures" in themselves. As far as their external existence is concerned, in the first place, it is self-evident that, to the extent that phenomena are structurable in conformity to the framework of our mind, it can be explained by an assimilation of the real to the forms of intelligence as well as by the realistic hypothesis. With regard to the forms of intelligence they cannot be considered, either, as "subsisting" by themselves, inasmuch as they have a history and reveal an activity. In so far as they are mobile, the forms are therefore only good or bad relatively to each other and to the data to be systematized. Relativity, here as always, must temper a constantly renascent realism.

Undoubtedly such relativity presupposes the existence of some invariants. But the latter are functional and not structural. Thus a "form" is the better the more it satisfies the dual exigency of organization and adaptation of thought, organization consisting in an interdependence of given elements and adaptation consisting in a balance between assimilation and accommodation. But if this dual postulate excludes chaotic forms, the coherence it claims can no doubt be attained by means of an infinity of diverse structures. Thus the principle of contradiction does not teach us whether two concepts contradict each other, and that two propositions can appear to be mutually compatible for a long time and subsequently be disclosed to be contradictory (the reverse also being possible).

§4. THE THEORY OF GROPING.—According to a famous hypothesis due to Jennings and taken up by Thorndike, an active method of adaptation to new circumstances exists—the method of groping: on the one hand, a succession of "trials" admitting, in principle, of "errors" as well as of fortuitous success, on the other hand a progressive selection operating after the event according to the success or failure of these same trials. The theory of "trials and errors" thus combines the *a priori* idea, according to which the solutions emanate from the subject's activity and the empirical idea according to which adoption of the right solution is definitely due to the pressure of the external environment. But, instead of acknowledging, as we shall do (§5), an indissoluble relation between subject and object, the hypothesis of trials and errors makes distinction between two terms: the production of trials which are due to the subject since they are fortuitous in relation to the object, and their selection, due to the object alone. Apriority and empiricism are here juxtaposed, in a way, and not outstripped. Such is the dual inspiration of the pragmatic system in epistemology and the mutational system in biology. Intellectual or vital activity remains independent in origin from the external environment, but the value of its products is determined by their success in the midst of the same environment.

In his well-known theory of intelligence[5] Claparède takes up Jennings' hypothesis, but by generalizing and inserting it in a concerted conception of adaptational acts. Intelligence, according to Claparède, constitutes a mental adaptation to new circumstances or, more precisely, "the capacity to resolve new problems by thought." Hence every complete act of intelligence presupposes three periods: the question (which orients searching), the hypothesis (or actual searching), and control. Moreover, intelli-

[5] Claparède, La Psychologie de l'intelligence, *Scientia,* XI (1917), pp. 353–367.

gence would not be derived from the adaptations of a lower order, the reflex or hereditary adaptation and the habitual association or adaptation acquired in circumstances which repeat themselves, but it would arise at the time of the insufficiencies of the reflex and of habit. What happens when the novelty of the situation overflows the framework of instinct or of acquired associations? The subject does not remain passive but, on the contrary, manifests the behavior pattern emphasized by Jennings: He gropes and abandons himself to a series of "trials and errors." That is, according to Claparède, the origin of intelligence. Before the "systematic intelligence" characterized by the internalization of the processes of search is elaborated, intelligence is revealed in an empirical form which prepares the higher forms and constitutes their practical or sensorimotor equivalent. Thus to the "question" corresponds the need aroused by the new situation in which the subject finds himself. To the "hypothesis" groping corresponds, the series of trials and errors being nothing but the successive suppositions assumed by action before being assumed by thought. Finally, to the "control" corresponds the selection of trials which results from the pressure of things before the awareness of relations enables thought to control itself by mental experience. Empirical intelligence would consequently be explained by groping and it would be the progressive internalization and systematization of these processes which would subsequently account for intelligence properly so called.

The generality of the phenomenon of groping in all the stages we have outlined can be cited in favor of such a solution. In the first place, the "correction" of schemata by progressive accommodations, which we have just emphasized in connection with the "Gestalt," constitutes a primary example of this groping. Now it is stated, on the one hand, that groping is internalized during the sixth stage in the form of a sort of experimental reflection or mental experience (as when Lucienne, in Observation 180, opens her mouth in front of the opening which must be enlarged in order to reach the contents of the match box), and, on the other hand, that before this internalization, the same groping is revealed externally during all the fifth stage during which it constitutes the basis for the "tertiary circular reactions" and the "discovery of new means through active experimentation." Then it is easy to observe that this groping, which is so evident in the fifth stage, is itself prepared by a series of analogous processes discoverable as early as the first stage. Ever since reflex accommodation we have noted the groping of the newborn child seeking the nipple. Since the acquisition of the first habits, moreover, one finds the importance progressively augmenting with the formation of the secondary schemata and the later coordination of those schemata. In short, the history of groping is nothing but that of accommodation with its successive complications and, in this respect, it seems as though much truth must be ascribed to the theory which identifies intelligence with searching which proceeds by active groping.

But there are two ways of interpreting groping. Either one asserts that groping activity is directed, from the outset, by a comprehension related to the external situation and then groping is never pure, the role of chance becomes secondary, and this solution is identified with that of assimilation (groping being reduced to a progressive accommodation of the assimilatory schemata); or else one states that there exists a pure groping, that is to say, taking place by chance and with selection, after the event, of favorable steps. Now, it is in this second sense that groping was at first interpreted and it is this second interpretation that we are unable to accept.

It is true that certain facts seem to substantiate Jennings. It happens that groping really does develop by chance, that the right solutions are fortuitously discovered and become fixed by simple repetition before the subject has been able to understand their mechanism. Thus the child sometimes prematurely discovers the solutions which transcend his level of understanding, this discovery being only due to happy fortuitous circumstances and not to a directed search (proof of which is that the acquisitions are often lost and later give rise to an intelligent rediscovery). But that is because, as we have already said, two kinds of groping exist, or rather, two extreme terms between which a whole series of intermediates extends. The one emerges when a problem, while being at the subject's level, does not give rise to an immediate solution, but to a directed search; the other appears when the problem transcends the intellectual level or the subject's knowledge and then the search operates by chance. It is only to the second of these two situations that Jennings' schema applies, whereas the other interpretation applies to the first case. The whole question, therefore, is to ascertain which relationship unites these two kinds of groping: Are they independent or does the one derive from the other and which?

Now, in order to resolve this question, nothing is more instructive than to examine the evolution of Claparède's doctrine which, from 1917 to 1933, has been thoroughly examined and, influenced by excellently analyzed facts relating to the "genesis of the hypothesis,"[6] has resulted in an exact delimitation of the role of groping.

From the very beginning of his studies, Claparède has distinguished between the two kinds of groping which we have just reviewed:

> I had then established two kinds or degrees of groping: *non-systematic* groping, which is purely fortuitous and the "trials" at which would be selected, chosen mechanically, as by a sieve, by external circumstances; and *systematic* groping, guided and controlled by thought, especially by the awareness of relationships. Nonsystematic groping would characterize what I call "empirical intelligence"; the other belongs to intelligence properly so called.[7]

But, between the study of 1917 and that of 1933, a reversal of meaning is observable with regard to the relationships of these two kinds of gropings. In 1917 nonsystematic groping was considered the primitive act of intelligence which is supposed to explain the development of systematic groping, through the progressive contact with experience to which it gives rise and the awareness of relationships which springs from it: "The act of intelligence consists essentially in groping which derives from the groping manifested by animals of the lowest order when they find themselves in a new situation."[8] On the contrary, in the study made in 1933, three innovations in reality result in reversing the

[6] Claparède, La Genèse de l'hypothèse, *Arch. de Psychol.*, XXIV, 1933, pp. 1–155.
[7] *Ibid.*, p. 149.
[8] *Ibid.*, p. 149.

order of that filiation: (1) The two kinds of groping are no longer conceived "as two entirely separate types, but as the two extremities of a chain which comprises all the intermediates";[9] (2) Nonsystematic groping itself is already relatively directed:

> No groping is altogether incoherent because its function always is to attain some end, to satisfy some need, it is always oriented in some direction. . . . In the lower forms of thought, this direction is still very vague, very general. But the higher the mental level of the seeker becomes, the more the awareness of relationships is strengthened and, consequently, the more specific becomes the direction in which the search for the problem's solution must take place. . . . Thus every new groping tightens a little the circle within which the next gropings will occur. . . . Groping, *at first guided by the awareness of relationships—relationships between certain acts to be performed and a certain end to be attained*[10]—is consequently the agent which permits the discovery of new relationships.[11]

(3) Finally, and most important, not only does nonsystematic groping presuppose, as has just been shown, awareness of certain relationships which direct it from the outset, but furthermore those elementary relationships themselves stem from a fundamental mechanism of adjustment to experience which Claparède wisely emphasizes in his 1933 article, and which like the logicians he calls "implication": "Implication is a process indispensable to our needs in adjusting. *Without it we would not know how to profit from experience.*"[12] Hence implication is a primitive phenomenon which does not result from repetition, as does association, but on the contrary, from the outset introduces a necessary link between the terms which are implied. Thus implication is rooted in organic life: "The organism seems to us, as early as its most reflex manifestations, to be a machine for implication."[13] It is also the source of the conditioned reflexes and the circular reactions. Moreover, from its inception it directs even nonsystematic groping. "To imply is to expect, and that is

9 *Ibid.*, p. 149.
10 Our italics.
11 *Ibid.*, pp. 149–150.
12 *Ibid.*, p. 104 (italicized in the text).
13 *Ibid.*, p. 106.

to aim toward what one expects,"[14] to the extent that the expectation is not disappointed, groping is useless, but to the extent that it is disappointed, groping, oriented by expectation, is directed toward the goal by the implications which connect it with the need experienced.

Having said this, we should now like to show why the hypothesis of a pure groping should not be retained and how the corrections made by Claparède in his last interpretation not only completely square with what we have observed regarding the origins of intelligence in children but also seem to us to involve the theory of schemata and assimilation in general.

The hypothesis of pure groping conceived as being the point of departure of intelligence cannot be justified because, either this nonsystematic groping appears in the margin of directed groping and often even after it, or else it precedes directed groping, but then it is either without influence on the latter or else it is itself relatively directed and consequently already systematic.

In a general way, let us recall first of all that the difference between nonsystematic and directed groping is simply a matter of proportion and that the situations in which these two types of behavior are made manifest only differ from one another in degree and not in quality. Systematic groping is, in effect, characterized by the fact that the successive trials condition each other with cumulative effect, that, in the second place, they are illuminated by earlier schemata conferring a meaning on the fortuitous discoveries and, last, they are directed by the schemata assigning a purpose to the action and by those serving as initial means and whose groping attempts constitute the differentiations or gradual accommodations (see Obs. 148–174). Systematic groping is therefore triply or quadruply directed, according to whether the end and the initial means form a whole or are separate. On the contrary, in nonsystematic groping like that of Thorndike's cats, the successive trials are relatively independent of each other and are not directed by experience acquired earlier. In this sense groping is fortuitous and the discovery of the solution is due to chance. But, from the time when the gropings, even nonsystematic, are always oriented by the need experienced,

14 *Ibid.*, p. 102.

hence by the schema assigning a purpose to the action (Thorndike himself recognizes that the selection is made among the attempts due to annoyance at failure)—it is apparent that earlier experience plays a role in spite of everything and that the system of schemata already elaborated is not unconnected with the subject's seemingly most disorganized behavior. The successive gropings are only relatively independent of each other and the results to which they lead, while largely fortuitous, only acquire meaning from hidden but active schemata which illuminate them. The difference between nonsystematic gropings and directed search is therefore only of degree and not of kind.

That being true, it is evident that very often, far from preceding the directed search, nonsystematic groping only appears in the margin of this search, or after it, and that, when it precedes it in appearance it is either already oriented by it or without influence on it. In effect, the relationship between the two extreme types of behavior is determined by the situations in which they are made manifest. There is directed groping whenever the problem is sufficiently adapted to the intellectual level and knowledge of the subject for the latter to seek the solution by means of an adjustment of his habitual schemata, whereas there is groping when the problem is too far above the subject's level and when a simple readjustment of the schemata does not suffice to solve it. Groping, consequently, is the more directed when the situation approximates the first kind, and the less systematic when it approaches the second.

There are two possible cases with regard to the sequence of the two kinds of groping. Concerning the first, the subject only adopts the method of pure groping by "trials and errors" after having exhausted the resources of directed searching. This mode of sequence is observable even in the adult. When an automobile breaks down, the intellectual, who is not a mechanic, begins by trying to utilize various bits of knowledge pertaining to the carburetor, the spark plugs, the ignition, etc. That constitutes a search directed by earlier schemata, hence a systematic groping. Then, having achieved nothing, he tries everything haphazardly, touches parts of whose function he is ignorant and thus succeeds in repairing his motor by a purely chance maneuver: this is nonsystematic groping. In such a case, it is clear that pure groping extends the directed search. It is the fact of having tried an increasing number of solutions that induces the subject to generalize that behavior and it is to the extent that he understands the data of the problem less and less that he goes from directed groping to nonsystematic groping. In this first case, groping is the most slack form, so to speak, of intellectual searching, and not the point of departure of the act of intelligence.

But there is a second case: that in which the problem is absolutely new to the subject and in which nonsystematic groping seems to appear before directed searching. For example, an animal seeking food can get involved by chance in a series of successive ways without being capable of perceiving the relationships, or a child, in order to attain an object half hidden by various obstacles, can manage to extricate it without understanding the relation "situated under or behind." But then, one of two things: either the role of chance is considerable in the successful trial and the nonsystematic gropings thus crowned with success remain unconnected with intelligence and do not engender by themselves and as such later directed searches, or else nonsystematic groping is already sufficiently directed so that one may attribute success to that direction and then it is this beginning system which explains the later systematic searching. In the example of the child who wants to grasp a half-hidden object, it is possible, clearly, that the subject may achieve his ends without knowing how; but in this case, the nonsystematic groping which led to this fortuitous result does not at all pave the way for the directed searching which will later enable the child to discover the relations "placed upon," "situated below," etc. Nonsystematic groping is, then, only a sporadic behavior pattern appearing in the margin of intelligence and prolonging the attitude of groping search common to all stages (reflex use, circular reaction, etc.). It is only the extreme limit of accommodation, when the latter is more controlled by assimilation. On the contrary, it is possible that the search for the half-hidden object, while not yet involving more than knowledge of the relation "situated below" and thus permitting a great deal of haphazard groping, may nevertheless be directed by certain general schemata, such as those of pushing back the obstacle, of utilizing a mobile object to bring a distant objective to oneself (in the case of the toys hanging from the bassinet hood, etc.). In this case, nonsystematic groping certainly paves the way for later directed searching (which will permit the child really to understand the relation "situated below"); but this groping is already itself directed although in a vague and general way. The difference between these two possibilities is easily discerned by the fact that, in the first, the child's fortuitous discovery is not followed by any lasting utilization, whereas in the second, it gives rise to various uses (to circular reactions or acts of reproductive assimilation with gradual accommodation) and to a more or less continuous progress.

Thus it may be seen that, even when nonsystematic groping seems to appear before the directed search, it does not explain the latter but is already explained by it, since from the very beginning it allows a *minimum* of direction. Without rejecting the idea of groping, we do not consider it adequate, in itself alone, to explain the mechanism of intelligence. Now, this is precisely what Claparède, in his most recent study, has pointed out with great wisdom. Led to reject the hypothesis of pure groping, he has come to acknowledge that, if needs and awareness of an end to be attained orient even the most elementary gropings, that is because an elementary implication of the acts and interests constitutes the primary datum presupposed by the groping itself. We should now like to show how this implication necessarily comprises assimilation and the system of schemata.

As far as reflective intelligence is concerned, it is self-evident that implication presupposes a system of concepts and consequently the assimilatory activity of judgment. To say that A implies B (for example that the fact of being "right angle" implies that a triangle satisfies Pythagoras' theorem), is to affirm that one is in possession of a certain concept C (for example that of the "right angle triangle"), in which A and B are united by logical necessity or by definition. The implication is thus the result of the judgments which have engendered the concepts C, A and B, and the necessity of the implication results from previous assimilation operated by those judgments.

The same is true of sensorimotor intelligence, including its preparatory phases constituted by the acquisition of the first habitual associations (second stage). Claparède, who rightly considers implication to be the condition of experience ("without it, we could not profit from experience"), shows in some very suggestive pages that the conditioned reflex is a phenomenon of implication. In effect, he says, "B is implied in A when, A being given, the subject behaves toward it as he would behave toward B." "If the dog sees a pink-colored A presented at first with the meal B, this will provoke the salivary and gastric reaction set in motion by meal B. The dog reacts to A as if B were contained, were implied in A." "If there were simple association and not implication, the color pink would simply evoke in the dog's memory the recollection of the meal but without being followed by any reaction signifying that the color pink *is taken for* the meal, *functions like* the meal."[15] But how can it be explained why, according to this excellent description, the color "is taken for" the meal? Claparède emphasizes the fact that the necessity for such connections appears from the beginning: "Far from its being the repetition of a pair of elements which creates between them a link of implication, the implication already arises at the first meeting of the two elements of this pair. And experience only intervenes to break this rapport of implication where it is not legitimate." And again: "The necessity for a connection tends, accordingly, to appear at the very beginning. If the necessity did not exist at the very beginning, one does not see when it will ever appear, for habit is not necessity."[16] But the problem is only extended. How is it possible to explain this necessity which appears at the first meeting of two terms thitherto foreign to each other so that they immediately appear to the subject as implying each other?

In the same way Mr. Claparède interprets the classic analogy of perception and reasoning in the light of implication: "If the operation which constitutes perception is identical to that which forms the backbone of reasoning, *it is because this operation is an implication*. If we notice the sweet flavor in the col-

15 *Ibid.*, pp. 105–106.
16 *Ibid.*, p. 105.

ored spot which the orange forms to our eye, this is not solely by virtue of association but due to implication. It is because this sweet flavor is *implied* in the other characteristics of the orange. . . ."[17] But, here again, how can it be explained why the given qualities in the sensation immediately assume a deeper signification and invoke an ensemble of other qualities necessarily interconnected?

The only possible answer is that schemata exist (that is to say, the organized totalities whose internal elements are mutually implied) as well as a constitutive operation of these schemata and of their implications, which is *assimilation*. In effect, without this formative operation of implications which is the sensorimotor equivalent of judgment, anything at all would imply anything at all, at the mercy of the fortuitous comparisons of perception. Implication would be governed by William James' "law of coalescence" according to which the data perceived simultaneously form a totality as long as they have not been dissociated by experience. "The law of coalescence," Claparède also says, engenders implication on the plane of action and syncretism on the plane of representation."[18] But then one can ask oneself if the idea of implication still keeps its value and if the necessity of which the implying relationships admit is not illusory. Claparède's interpretation is much more profound when he connects implication with his "law of reproduction of the similar" and when he adds: "Implication is rooted in the being's motor strata. It might be said that life implies implication."[19] But then a connecting link between the motor organization and the implication is lacking, and this connecting link is assimilation. But, in effect, assimilation explains how the organism tends simultaneously to reproduce the actions which have been profitable to it (reproductive assimilation)—which suffices to constitute schemata, not only due to the repetition of external conditions, but also and primarily due to an active reproduction of earlier behavior patterns as function of those conditions—and to incorporate, in the schemata thus formed, data capable of

17 *Ibid.*, p. 107.
18 *Ibid.*, p. 105.
19 *Ibid.*, pp. 104–105.

serving them as aliments (generalizing assimilation). But, consequently, assimilation explains how active reproduction engenders implication. On the one hand, in effect, in order to reproduce the interesting behavior patterns, the subject constantly assimilates to the schemata of these behavior patterns the familiar objects already utilized in similar circumstances, that is to say, he confers a signification upon them; in other words, he inserts them in a system of implications. So it is that the doll hanging from the bassinet hood implies to the baby the quality of being pulled or struck, shaken, etc., because every time he perceives it, it is assimilated to the schemata of pulling, etc. Moreover, the new objects are themselves assimilated, due to their apparent characteristics or their situation, to familiar schemata, whence new networks of significations and implications. Thus in Observation 136 the cigarette case examined by Jacqueline is successfully sucked, rubbed, shaken, etc. Reproductive (and recognitory) assimilation, on the one hand, and generalizing assimilation, on the other, are hence the source of the implication which could not be explained without them, and these implications, far from resulting from simple "coalescences," are from the outset directed and organized by the system of schemata.

In the conditioned reflex, to resume Claparède's examples, the pink A is implied in the meal A because, according to the author's terms, that color "is taken for" the meal. What does this mean, if not that the color is assimilated to the meal itself, or that it receives a signification as a function of this schema? Here as everywhere, the implication results from a previous assimilation. So also, in perception, the orange's sweet flavor is implied in the color perceived at first, because this color is immediately assimilated to a familiar schema. In short, without assimilation, this implying "necessity" which Claparède places "at the source" and which he rightly distinguishes from habit due to passive repetition (which is quite different from active reproduction), remains unexplainable and implication remains without organic basis. Inasmuch as implication is really rooted in the organism, which seems to us indisputable, this is because all sensorimotor activity develops by functioning (reproductive assimilation) and through generalizing assimilation utilizes the ob-

jects capable of serving it as aliments. Thereafter every external
datum is perceived as function of the sensorimotor schemata and
it is this incessant assimilation which confers on all things meanings permitting implications of every degree. Through that very
fact it can be understood why all groping is always directed, however little: Groping proceeds necessarily by accommodation of
earlier schemata and the latter become assimilated or tend to assimilate to themselves the objects on which the former operates.

So it is that, corrected by Claparède's remarks concerning the
controlling role of need or the issue and concerning the priority
of implication in relation to "trials and errors," the theory of
groping joins that of assimilation and the schemata.

§5. THE THEORY OF ASSIMILATION.—Two conclu-
sions seem to us to derive from the foregoing discussions. The
first is that intelligence constitutes an organizing activity whose
functioning extends that of the biological organization, while
surpassing it due to the elaboration of new structures. The second is that, if the sequential structures due to intellectual activity differ among themselves qualitatively, they always obey the
same functional laws. In this respect, sensorimotor intelligence
can be compared to reflective or rational intelligence and this
comparison clarifies the analysis of the two extreme terms.

Now, whatever the explanatory hypotheses between which
the main biological theories oscillate, everyone acknowledges a
certain number of elementary truths which are those of which
we speak here: that the living body presents an organized structure, that is to say, constitutes a system of interdependent relationships; that it works to conserve its definite structure and, to
do this, incorporates in it the chemical and energetic aliments
taken from the environment; that, consequently, it always reacts
to the actions of the environment according to the variations of
that particular structure and in the last analysis tends to impose
on the whole universe a form of equilibrium dependent on that
organization. In effect, contrary to unorganized beings which are
also in equilibrium with the universe but which do not assimilate
the environment to themselves, it can be said that the living
being assimilates to himself the whole universe, at the same time

that he accommodates himself to it, since all the movements of every kind which characterize his actions and reactions with respect to things are regulated in a cycle delineated by his own organization as well as by the nature of the external objects. It is therefore permissible to conceive assimilation in a general sense as being the incorporation of any external reality whatever to one part or another of the cycle of organization. In other words, everything that answers a need of the organism is material for assimilation, the need even being the expression of assimilatory activity as such; with regard to the pressures exerted by the environment without their answering any need, they cannot give rise to assimilation as long as the organism is not adapted to them but, as adaptation consists precisely in transforming constraints into needs, everything, in the last analysis, can lend itself to being assimilated. The functions of relationship, independently even from psychic life which proceeds from them, are thus doubly the sources of assimilation: On the one hand, they help the general assimilation of the organism, since their use is essential to life; but, on the other hand, each of their manifestations presupposes a particular assimilation since this use or exercise is always related to a series of external conditions which are peculiar to them.

Such is the context of previous organization in which psychological life originates. Now, and this is our whole hypothesis, it seems that the development of intelligence extends that kind of mechanism instead of being inconsistent with it. In the first place, as early as the reflex behavior patterns and the acquired behavior patterns grafted on them, one sees appear processes of incorporation of things to the subject's schemata. This search for the functional aliment necessary to the development of behavior and this exercise stimulating growth constitute the most elementary forms of psychological assimilation. In effect, this assimilation of things to the schemata's activity, although not yet experienced by the subject as an awareness of objects and though consequently not yet giving rise to objective judgments, nevertheless constitutes the first operations which, subsequently, will result in judgments properly so called: operations of reproduction, recognition and generalization. Those are the operations which, already involved in reflex assimilation, engender the first acquired behavior patterns, consequently the first nonhereditary schemata, the schema resulting from the very act of reproductive and generalizing assimilation. Thus every realm of sensorimotor reflex organization is the scene of particular assimilations extending, on the functional plane, physicochemical assimilation. In the second place, these behavior patterns, inasmuch as they are grafted on hereditary tendencies, from the very beginning find themselves inserted in the general framework of the individual organization; that is to say, before any acquisition of consciousness, they enter into the functional totality which the organism constitutes. Thus they contribute immediately to insuring and maintaining that equilibrium between the universe and the body itself, an equilibrium which consists in an assimilation of the universe to the organism as much as in an accommodation of the latter to the former. From the psychological point of view, that means that the acquired schemata form, from the outset, not only a sum of organized elements, but also a global organization, a system of interdependent operations, at first virtually due to their biological roots, then actually due to the mechanism of the reciprocal assimilation of the presenting schemata.

In short, at its point of departure, intellectual organization merely extends biological organization. It does not only consist —as accepted by a reflexology entirely impregnated with empirical associationism—in an ensemble of responses mechanically determined by external stimuli and in a correlative ensemble of conductions connecting the new stimuli with old responses. On the contrary, it constitutes a real activity, based upon an appropriate structure and assimilating to the latter a growing number of external objects.

Now, just as sensorimotor assimilation of things to the subject's schemata extends biological assimilation of the environment to the organism, so also it presages the intellectual assimilation of objects to the mind, such as is proven to exist in the most evolved forms of rational thought. In effect, reason simultaneously manifests a formal organization of the ideas it utilizes and an adaptation of those ideas to reality—an organization and adaptation which are inseparable. Now, the adaptation of reason to experience presupposes an incorporation of objects to the subject's organization as well as an accommodation of the latter to external circumstances. Translated into rational terminology, it can therefore be said that organization is formal coherence, accommodation is "experience" and assimilation the act of judgment inasmuch as it unites experimental contents to logical form.

Now these comparisons, which we have often emphasized, between the biological plane, the sensorimotor plane and the rational plane, make it possible to understand how assimilation, from the functional point of view, constitutes the primary fact whence analysis must proceed regardless of the real interdependence of the mechanisms. On each of the three planes, in effect, accommodation is only possible as function of assimilation, since the very formation of the schemata called upon to accommodate themselves is due to the assimilatory process. Concerning the relationships between the organization of those schemata and assimilation, one can say that the latter represents the dynamic process of which the former is the static expression.

On the biological plane one could, it is true, raise the objection that every assimilatory operation presupposes a previous organization. But what is an organized structure, if not a cycle of operations of which each one is necessary to the existence of the others? Assimilation is hence the very functioning of the system of which organization is the structural aspect.

On the rational plane, this primacy of assimilation is expressed by the primacy of judgment. To judge is not necessarily to identify, as has sometimes been said, but it is to assimilate; that is to say, to incorporate a new datum in an earlier schema, in an already elaborated schema of implications. Hence rational assimilation always presupposes a previous organization. But whence comes that organization? From assimilation itself, for every concept and every relationship demands a judgment in order to be formed. If the interdependence of judgments and concepts thus demonstrates that of assimilation and organization, at the same time it emphasizes the nature of that interdependence. Assimilatory judgment is the active element of the process of which the organizing concept is the result.

Finally, on the sensorimotor plane which is that of elementary intellectual life, we have always emphasized the assimilatory mechanism which gives rise to the schemata and to their organization. Psychological assimilation in its simplest form is nothing other than the tendency of every behavior pattern or of every psychic state to conserve itself and, toward this end, to take its functional alimentation from the external environment. It is this reproductive assimilation that constitutes the schemata, the latter acquiring their existence as soon as a behavior pattern, however small its complexity, gives rise to an attempt at spontaneous repetition and thus becomes schematized. Now, this reproduction which, by itself and to the extent that it is not encased in an earlier schematism does not involve any organization, necessarily leads to the formation of an organized whole. In effect, the successive repetitions due to reproductive assimilation at first bring with them an extension of assimilation in the form of recognitory and generalizing operations. To the extent that the new objective resembles the old one, there is recognition and, to the extent that it differs from it, there is generalization of the schema and accommodation. The very repetition of the operation hence entails the formation of an organized totality, the organization resulting merely from the continuous application of an assimilatory schema to a given diversity.

In short, in every realm, assimilatory activity appears simultaneously as the resultant and the source of organization; that is to say, from the psychological point of view which is necessarily functional and dynamic, it constitutes a veritable primary act. Now, if we have shown, stage after stage, how the progress of the assimilatory mechanism engenders the various intellectual operations, it remains to be explained, more synthetically, how the initial act of assimilation takes into account the essential characteristics of intelligence, or the combined workings of mental construction leading to deduction and to actual or representative experience.

The principal problem to be resolved for an interpretation based upon assimilation as well as for every theory of intelligence entailing the biological activity of the subject himself is, it seems to us, the following: If the same process of assimilation of the universe to the organism occurs from the physiological to the rational plane, how is it possible to explain why the subject comes to understand external reality sufficiently to be "objective" and to place himself in it? Physiological assimilation is, in effect, entirely centered on the organism. It is an incorporation of the environment to the living body, and the centripetal character of this process is so advanced that the incorporated elements lose their specific nature to be transformed into substances identical to those of the body itself. Rational assimilation, on the contrary, as revealed in judgment, does not at all destroy the object incorporated in the subject since, by manifesting the latter's activity, it subordinates it to the reality of the former. The antagonism of these two extreme terms is such that one would refuse to attribute them to the same mechanism if sensorimotor assimilation did not bridge the gap between them. At its source, in effect, sensorimotor assimilation is as egocentric as physiological assimilation, since it only uses the object to aliment the functioning of the subject's operations, whereas at its end the same assimilatory impetus succeeds in inserting the real in frameworks exactly adapted to its objective characteristics, so that the frameworks are ready to be transported to the plane of language in the form of concepts and logical relationships. How can this transition from egocentric incorporation to objective adaptation be explained, a transition without which the comparison of biological assimilation with intellectual assimilation would only be a play on words?

An easy solution would consist in attributing this evolution to the progress of accommodation alone. One recalls that accommodation, at first reduced to a simple global adjustment, gives rise, at the time of the coördination of the secondary schemata and above all of the tertiary circular reactions, to directed gropings and increasingly accurate experimental behavior patterns. Would it not suffice, then, to explain the transition from distorted assimilation to objective assimilation, to invoke the concomitant factor of accommodation?

It is undoubtedly the progress of accommodation which marks the increasing objectivity of the schemata of assimilation. But to be satisfied with such an explanation would be tantamount either to answering the question by the question itself, or else to saying that the assimilation of things to the subject loses in importance in proportion as intelligence develops. In reality, at each step assimilation conserves the same essential role and the true problem, which is to find out how the progress of accommodation is possible, can only be resolved by having recourse once again to analysis of the assimilatory mechanism.

In effect, why is the accommodation of the schemata to the external environment, which becomes so accurate in the course of development, not given at the outset? Why does the evolution of sensorimotor intelligence appear as a progressive extraversion instead of the elementary operations being turned toward the external environment from the very beginning? In reality this gradual externalization, which seems at first to be the essential characteristic of the sequence of our six stages, only constitutes but one of the two aspects of that evolution. The second movement, exactly complementary and necessary to the explanation of the first, is none other than the process of growing coördination marking the progress of assimilation as such. Whereas the initial schemata are only interconnected due to their reflex and organic substructure, the more evolved schemata, at first primary, then secondary and tertiary, become organized little by little into coherent systems due to a process of mutual assimilation which we have often emphasized and which we have compared to the increasing implication of concepts and relationships. Now, not only is this progress of assimilation correlative to that of accommodation, but also it makes possible the gradual objectification of intelligence itself.

In effect, it is the nature of a schema of assimilation to apply itself to everything and to conquer the whole universe of perception. But by being thus generalized it is necessary for it to become differentiated. This differentiation does not only result from the diversity of the objects to which the schema must accommodate itself. Such an explanation would lead us back to the solution already rejected which is too simple because nothing forces the child to take into consideration the multiplicity of reality so long as his assimilation is distorted, that is to say, so long as he utilizes objects as simple functional aliments. The differentiation of schemata works to the extent that objects are assimilated by several schemata at once and that their diversity thus becomes sufficiently worthy of interest to be imposed on accommodation (for example, visual images are differentiated by prehension, sucking, hearing, etc.). Undoubtedly, even without being coördinated with other schemata, each of them gives rise to spontaneous differentiations, but they remain of small importance and it is the infinite variety of combinations possible among schemata which is the big factor in differentiation. This explains how the progress of accommodation is correlative to that of assimilation: It is to the extent that the coördination of schemata leads the subject to interest himself in the diversity of reality that accommodation differentiates the schemata, and not by virtue of an immediate inclination toward accommodation.

Now this coördination and differentiation of schemata suffice to account for the growing objectification of assimilation without need to break the unity of this process to explain the transition from the egocentric incorporation at the beginnings to judgment properly so called. For example, let us compare the attitude of the baby toward an object he swings or a body he throws to the ground to that which is presupposed by the judgments "this is a hanging object" or "bodies fall." These judgments are certainly more "objective" than the active corresponding attitudes in the sense that the latter are confined to assimilating perceived data to a practical activity of the subject, whereas the formulated propositions insert them, no longer into a single, elementary schema, but into a complex pattern of schemata and relationships. The definitions of the hanging object or the fall of bodies presuppose an elaboration of things in hierarchical classes joined by multiple relationships, the schemata and relationships comprising, from far or near, all the subjects present and past experience. But, apart from this difference in complexity, hence in differentiation and coördination of schemata (without, of course, speaking of their symbolic translation to the plane of language and the regrouping that this verbal construction and socialization presuppose), these judgments do nothing other than incorporate perceived qualities into a system of schemata definitively resting upon the subject's action. There would be no difficulty in showing that the hierarchical classes and relationships implied by these judgments in the last analysis apply to the sensorimotor schemata subjacent to any active elaboration. Thus the qualities of position, form, movement, etc., perceived in the hanging object or the falling bodies are in themselves neither more nor less objective than the more global qualities enabling the baby to recognize the object to be swung or the object to be thrown. It is coördination itself; that is to say, the multiple assimilation constructing an increasing number of relationships between the compounds "action X object" which explains the objectification. This is what we shall see in detail in Volume II, when studying the construction of the object and the objectification of space, of causality and time during the first two years of childhood.

Hence it is one and the same process of assimilation which leads the subject who is in process of incorporating the universe in himself to structure that universe according to the variations of its own organization and finally to place his activity among the things themselves. But if this gradual reversal of the meaning of assimilation is not due to experience alone, the role of accommodation to experience is no less necessary to it, and it is fitting to recall it now. The current theories tend either to overestimate the role of experience, as does neoassociationist empiricism, or to underestimate it, as does the psychology of form. In reality, as we have just seen, accommodation of the schemata to experience develops to the very extent of the progress of assimilation. In other words, the relationships between the subject and his environment consist in a radical interaction, so that awareness begins neither by the awareness of objects nor awareness of the activity itself, but by an undifferentiated state and from this state proceed two complementary movements, the one of incorporation of things to the subject, the other of accommodation to the things themselves.

But in what does the subject's share consist and how to discern the object's influence? In the beginning the distinction remains illusory: the object as functional aliment and the activity itself are radically confused. On the other hand, inasmuch as accommodation is differentiated from assimilation, one can say that the subject's role is essentially established in the elaboration of forms whereas it is up to experience to provide them with a content. But, as we have already observed, form cannot be dissociated from matter. The structures are not preformed within the subject but are constructed gradually as needs and situations occur. Consequently they depend partly on experience. Inversely, experience alone does not account for the differentiation of schemata since through their very coördinations the schemata are capable of multiplications. Assimilation is therefore not reduced to a simple identification, but is the construction of structures at the same time as the incorporation of things to these structures. In short, the dualism of subject and object is brought back to a simple progressive differentiation between a centripetal pole and a centrifugal pole in the midst of the constant interactions of organism and environment. Also, experience is never simply passive receptiveness: it is active accommodation, correlative to assimilation.

This interaction of accommodation to experience and of organizing assimilation makes it possible, it would seem, to supply an answer to the crucial question of every theory of intelligence: How can the union of the fecundity of intellectual construction with its progressive rigor be explained? It must not be forgotten that if, in the order of the sciences, psychology stems from the biological disciplines, it is nevertheless on the former that the formidable task devolves of explaining the principles of mathematics—for, given the interdependence of subject and object, the sciences themselves constitute a circle and, if the physicochemical sciences which furnish biology with their principles are based on the mathematical sciences, the latter, in turn, stem from the activity of the subject and are based on psychology and, consequently, on biology. So it is that geometers resort to psychological data in order to explain the formation of space and of solid objects and that we shall see, in Volume II, how the laws of sensorimotor intelligence account for the beginning of "groups of displacements" and for the permanence of the object. It is therefore necessary, in every theory of intelligence, to think of the generality of problems that it raises, which was understood by

Wertheimer, for example, when he tried to apply Gestalt theory
to the question of the syllogism.

As far as the fecundity of reasoning is concerned, one can
conceive of the act of intellectual construction in a great number
of ways varying from the discovery of a ready-made external
reality (empiricism) to the making explicit of a preformed internal structure (theory of form). But, in the first case, if the work
of intelligence leads to indefinitely fruitful results, since the mind
is called upon to discover little by little a universe which is already completely structured and constructed, this work does not
admit of any internal principle of construction and consequently
of any principle of deductive rigor. In the second case, on the
contrary, it is from the subject as such that intellectual progress
stems, but if the internal maturation of the structures is capable
of explaining their progressive coherence, this is at the expense of
fecundity, because what reason have we to think that forms, however numerous they may be, sprung only from the subject's
structure without his experience playing any part, will suffice to
embrace reality *in toto*? Now, inasmuch as one acknowledges the
necessary interdependence of accommodation to experience and
of assimilation to activity itself, fecundity becomes correlative to
coherence. In effect, all the intermediates are then made manifest
between simple empirical discovery which results from the purely
fortuitous insertion of a new datum in a schema, and the internal
combination of schemata resulting in mental combination. In
the most empirical discovery (like that which results from the
tertiary circular reactions), an element of assimilation already
intervenes which, in the case of active repetition and of the intellectual need for conservation, presages the judgment of identity, just as in the most refined internal combination (such as
mathematical constructions) a factor again intervenes to which
thought must accommodate itself. Consequently, there is naturally no antithesis between discovery and invention (no more
than between induction and deduction), both simultaneously
revealing activity of the mind and contact with reality.

Thereafter will it be said that the assimilatory organization
does not show any fecundity in itself and is limited to work of
identification, novelty always resulting from assimilated external

reality? But the interaction of subject and object is precisely such, given the interdependence of assimilation and accommodation, that it is impossible to conceive of one of the terms without the other. In other words, intelligence is the construction of relationships and not only identification. The elaboration of schemata involves a logic of relationships as well as a logic of classes. Consequently, intellectual organization is fecund in itself, since the relationships engender each other, and this fecundity is one with the richness of reality, since relationships cannot be conceived independently of the terms which connect them, any more than the reverse.

With regard to the rigor or the coherence thus obtained, it is in direct proportion to the fecundity, to the extent that the coordination of schemata equals their differentiation. Now, as it is precisely this growing coördination which permits accommodation to the diversity of reality, and as the coördination is obtained not only by identifying fusion but also by any system whatever of reciprocal relationships, there is certainly a correlation between the unity of the system of schemata and its richness. In effect, the rigor of the operations does not necessarily result from identification, but from their reciprocity in general. The reciprocal assimilation which accounts for the coördination of the schemata is therefore the point of departure of this reversibility of operations which, at all levels, appears as the criterion of rigor and coherence.

In short, the problem of invention, which in many respects constitutes the central problem of intelligence, does not, in the hypothesis of the schemata, require any special solution because the organization which assimilatory activity reveals is essentially construction and so is, in fact, invention, from the outset. That is why the sixth stage, or the stage of invention through mental combination, seemed to us the crowning of the five preceding ones and not the beginning of a new period. As early as the empirical intelligence of the fourth and fifth stages and even as early as the construction of primary and secondary schemata, this power of construction is in bud and is revealed in each operation.

In conclusion, assimilation and accommodation, at first antagonistic to the extent that the first remains egocentric and the second is simply imposed by the external environment, complete each other to the extent they are differentiated, the coördination of the schemata of assimilation favoring the progress of accommodation and vice versa. So it is that, from the sensorimotor plane on, intelligence presupposes an increasingly close union of which the exactitude and the fecundity of reason will one day be the dual product.